Network Storage

Network Storage
Tools and Technologies for
Storing Your Company's Data

James O'Reilly

AMSTERDAM • BOSTON • HEIDELBERG • LONDON
NEW YORK • OXFORD • PARIS • SAN DIEGO
SAN FRANCISCO • SINGAPORE • SYDNEY • TOKYO

Morgan Kaufmann is an imprint of Elsevier

Morgan Kaufmann is an imprint of Elsevier
50 Hampshire Street, 5th Floor, Cambridge, MA 02139, United States

Notices
Knowledge and best practice in this field are constantly changing. As new research and experience broaden our understanding, changes in research methods, professional practices, or medical treatment may become necessary.

Practitioners and researchers must always rely on their own experience and knowledge in evaluating and using any information, methods, compounds, or experiments described herein. In using such information or methods they should be mindful of their own safety and the safety of others, including parties for whom they have a professional responsibility.

To the fullest extent of the law, neither the Publisher nor the authors, contributors, or editors, assume any liability for any injury and/or damage to persons or property as a matter of products liability, negligence or otherwise, or from any use or operation of any methods, products, instructions, or ideas contained in the material herein.

Library of Congress Cataloging-in-Publication Data
A catalog record for this book is available from the Library of Congress

British Library Cataloguing-in-Publication Data
A catalogue record for this book is available from the British Library

ISBN: 978-0-12-803863-5

For information on all Morgan Kaufmann publications
visit our website at https://www.elsevier.com/

Working together
to grow libraries in
developing countries

www.elsevier.com • www.bookaid.org

Publisher: Joe Hayton
Acquisition Editor: Brian Romer
Editorial Project Manager: Amy Invernizzi
Production Project Manager: Mohana Natarajan
Designer: Victoria Pearson

Typeset by TNQ Books and Journals

Contents

Acknowledgment

In my own journey through the magic world of storage, I have been lucky to have the support of some great mentors. I would like to recognize four in particular who had a major impact on my carrier, my knowledge base, and my achievements.

In my first job at International Computers in Stevenage in the United Kingdom, Jim Gross allowed me the freedom to run some big projects, saved me from imploding, and thoroughly grounded me in the how-to of doing good designs.

When I moved on to Burroughs, Arnie Spielberg gave me a lot of sage advice, while Mark Lutvak acted as my marketing guru, and was instrumental in getting me to move to the US. Arnie, incidentally, was Steven Spielberg's dad and I still remember the day that he came up to me and said, "My boy Steven, he's decided to go into the movie business. I'm worried for him…the business is full of gonifs. Still, I've got to stand back and let him try!".

Ray Valle proved to be a good friend while I was at Memorex and beyond. When I went on to NCR, Dan Pigott, the GM, allowed me a great deal of room to innovate, all the while protecting me from the intense politics of the company. Dan later hired me again to run the PC Division of Memorex-Telex.

There have been many others over the years. The NCR team in Wichita, Kansas, was a joy to work with. They learned to enjoy innovation and not fear the challenges. I would go so far as to say they were the best engineering team in the IT industry at the time, though of course I might not be totally objective.

I would like to thank my editors at Elsevier, without whom this book would never have seen the light. Brian Romer approached me to write a book on the subject and guided me through the early stages while selling Elsevier on the idea. Amy Invernizzi picked up the herding task to get me to complete close to schedule, and she mentored me throughout the writing process. They are both great people to work with and made a daunting task somehow manageable.

Obviously, I have missed a lot of names. Many people have worked with me over the years and most I remember with respect and fondness. Their willingnesses to help projects move forward quickly and to put in more-than-the-required effort have allowed some great team successes and I will always remain grateful.

Finally, I would like to thank my wife Angela for uncomplaining support over these many years. We have moved house as I changed jobs and made new sets of friends too many times to count. Through it all, she has supported me, put up with my ranting and periods of intense concentration on the job, laughed at my silliness and listened to my ideas. She also knows when to feed me tea and her glorious homemade mince pies! Without her, I don't think I could have done this.

Introduction

The world of storage is beginning to undergo a massive evolution. The next few years will bring changes to the technology, market, and vendor base like nothing we have ever seen. The changes will be as profound and far-reaching as the migration from mainframes to UNIX and then to Linux in their impact on the IT industry.

Many pillars of our industry are about to be toppled. We are seeing consolidation already, as with Dell and EMC, and acquisitions too are changing the face of the industry. The advent of new technologies such as SSD and the ascendancy of Ethernet as a storage network have doomed the traditional RAID array and forced very rapid changes across array vendors.

At the same time, alternatives to network-attached storage such as object storage have taken the role of scaled-out storage away from the likes of NetApp, forced into workforce shrinkage and massive catch-up efforts, while open-source software is eroding their market.

The largest immediate change factor, though, has been the advent of cloud computing. With unparalleled economics, the public cloud is absorbing secondary storage functions such as backup and archiving almost in their entirety. For the first time, the cry that "Tape is dead!" looks to be coming true. As a result, the whole backup segment of the IT industry has turned upside down and new vendors now own the market leadership.

In all of this churning, most IT folk struggle to find a consistent and trustable direction. This book addresses that issue. It is not intended to explain how to set up a LUN, or the cabling of a storage array. There are plenty of other sources for that level of information. This book is intended to be a guide in the what and why of storage and storage networking, rather than the how to.

CEOs and CFOs will get an understanding of the forces in play and the direction to choose, while CIOs and senior IT staff will be able to figure out what pieces of the puzzle make sense for their need and why. In this sense, the work is a strategic, rather than tactical, guidebook to storage over the next decade.

The first section of the book is an overview of the industry. This is followed by a look at where we have been and what technologies we have used traditionally for connecting up storage, segueing into why we needed to change. Then we look at the new technologies in the storage space, followed by a visit to the cloud.

The next chapters look at some topics that need a great deal of evolution still. Data integrity and security still leave much to be desired, for instance. Finally, we look at the 5-year and 10-year horizons in technology and see the vast changes in storage still to come.

This is a broad vista and with limited space available it has been difficult to fully expound on some of the issues. For this I apologize. Even so, there is enough on any topic to engender strategic thinking, and the right queries to ask Google.

I have endeavored to make this a readable and occasionally humorous book. All of us struggle with writing that is verbose and dry and I would hate you to put down this book on those grounds. I hope I succeeded!

Why Storage Matters

In the big picture of information technology (IT), why is storage demanding so much more attention than in the past? In part, the change of emphasis in IT is a result of ending some three decades of functional stagnation in the storage industry. While we saw interfaces change and drive capacities grow nicely, the fundamentals of drive technology were stuck in a rut.

The speed of hard drives barely changed over that 30-year period. Innovations in caching and seek optimization netted perhaps a 2× performance gain, measured in IO operations per second (IOPS). This occurred over a period where CPU horsepower, following Moore's law, improved by roughly 1 million times (Fig. 1.1).

We compensated for the unchanging performance by increasing the number of drives, using RAID (redundant array of inexpensive disks) to stripe data for better access speeds. The ultimate irony was reached in the late 1990s when the CTO of a large database company recommended using hundreds of 9-GB drives, with only the outside 2 GB active, to keep up with the system. At the prices the storage industry giants charged for those drives, this made for a very expensive storage farm!

In the last few years, we've come a long way towards remediating the performance problem. Solid-state drives (SSD) have changed IO patterns forever. Instead of a maximum of 300 IOPS for a hard drive, we are seeing numbers ranging from 40,000 to 400,000 IOPS per SSD, and some extreme performance drives are achieving 1+ million random IOPS [1].

The result is radical. Data can really be available when a program needs it, rather than after seconds of latency. The implications of this continue to ripple through the industry. The storage industry itself is going through a profound change in structure, of a level that can fairly be called a "storage revolution," but the implications impact all of the elements of a datacenter and reach deeply into how applications are written. Moreover, new classes of IT workload are a direct result of the speed impact of SSD. Big Data analytics would be impossible with low-speed hard drive arrays, for example, and the Internet of Things implicitly requires the storage to have SSD performance levels.

Since SSD first hit the market in 2007, the hard disk drive (HDD) vendors have hidden behind a screen of price competitiveness. SSDs cost more per gigabyte than HDD, though the gap has closed every year since the introduction of SSDs into the market. They were helped in their story by decades of comparing drives essentially on their cost per gigabyte—one thing you learn in storage is that industry opinion is quite conservative—rather than comparing say 300 of those (really slow) 9-GB drives with one SSD on an IOPS basis.

Network Storage. http://dx.doi.org/10.1016/B978-0-12-803863-5.00001-7

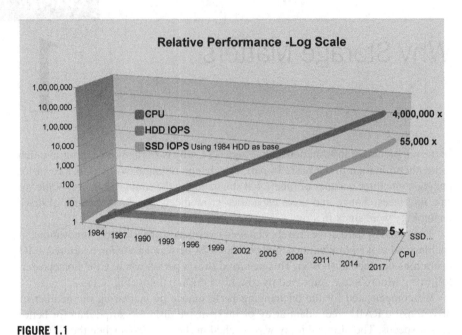

FIGURE 1.1

Relative performance of CPUs compared with hard drives over three decades. *HDD*, hard disk drive.

Today, SSD prices from distributors are lower than enterprise HDD, taking much of the steam out of the price per capacity argument. In fact, it looks like we'll achieve parity on price per gigabyte [2] even with commodity bulk drives in the 2017 time-frame. At that point, only the most conservative users will continue with HDD array buys, and effectively HDDs will be obsolete and being phased out.

I phrased that last sentence carefully. HDDs will take a while to fade away, but it won't be like magnetic tape, still going 25 years after its predicted demise. There are too many factors against HDDs, beyond the performance question. SSDs use much less power than HDDs and require less cooling air to operate safely. It looks like SSDs will be smaller too, with 15 TB 2.5 inch SSDs already competing with 3.5 inch 10 TB HDDs, and that appeals to anyone trying to avoid building more datacenter space. We are also seeing better reliability curves for SSDs, which don't appear to suffer from the short life cycles that occasionally plague batches of HDDs.

The most profound changes, however, are occurring in the rest of the IT arena. We have appliances replacing arrays, with fewer drives but much higher IOPS ratings. These are more compact and are Ethernet-based instead of the traditional fiber channel (FC). This has spurred tremendous growth in Ethernet speeds. The old model of 10× improvement every 10 years went out the window a couple of years back, and we now have 10 GbE challenged by 25 GbE and 40 GbE solutions. Clearly Ethernet is winning the race against the fiber channel SAN (storage area network), and with all the signs that FCoE (Fiber-Channel-over-Ethernet) has lost the war [3] with other Ethernet protocols, we are effectively at the end of the SAN era.

That's a profound statement in its own right, since it means that the primary storage architecture used in most datacenters is obsolescent, at best [4]. This has major implications for datacenter roadmaps and buying decisions. It also, by implication, means that the large traditional SAN vendors will have to scramble to new markets and products to keep their revenues up.

In a somewhat different incarnation, all-flash arrays (AFA), the same memory technology used in SSD is being deployed with extreme performance in the millions of IOPS range. This has triggered a rethink of the tiering of storage products in the datacenter.

We are moving from very expensive "Enterprise" HDD primary arrays (holding hot, active data) and expensive "Nearline" secondary arrays (holding colder data) to lower capacity and much faster AFA as primary storage and cheap commodity hard drive boxes for cold storage. This is a result of new approaches to data integrity, such as erasure coding, but primarily to the huge performance gain in the AFA.

The new tiering is often applied to existing SANs, giving them an extra boost in life. Placing one or two AFAs inline between the HDD arrays and the servers gives the needed speed boosts, and those obsolescent arrays can be used as secondary storage. This is a cheaper upgrade than new hybrid arrays with some SSDs.

Other datacenter hardware and networking are impacted by all of this too. Servers can do more in less time and that means fewer servers. Networks need to be architected to give more throughput to the storage farms, as well as getting more data bandwidth to hungry servers. Add in virtualization, and especially the cloud, and the need for automated orchestration extends across into the storage farm, propelling us inexorably towards software-defined storage.

Applications are impacted too. Code written with slow disks in mind won't hold up against SSD. Think of it like the difference between a Ferrari and a go-kart! That extra speed, low latencies, and new protocols and tiering all profoundly affect the way apps should be written to get best advantage from the new storage world.

Examples abound. Larry Ellison at Oracle was (rightly) proud enough to boast at Oracle World in 2014 that in-memory databases, with clustered solutions that distributed storage and caching, had achieved a 100× performance boost [5] over the traditional systems approach to analytics.

Even operating systems are being changed drastically. The new NVMe protocol is designed to reduce the software overhead associated with very high IOPS rates, so that the CPUs can actually do much more productive work.

Another major force in storage today is the growth of so-called "Big Data" [6]. This is typically data from numerous sources and as a result lacks a common structure, hence the other name "unstructured data." This data is profoundly important to the future both of storage and IT. We can expect to see unstructured data outgrow current structured data by somewhere between 10 and 50 times over the next decade, fueled in part by the sensor explosion of the Internet of Things.

Unstructured data is pushing the industry towards highly scalable storage appliances and away from the traditional RAID arrays. Together with open-sourced storage software [7], these new boxes use commodity hardware and drives so as a result they are very inexpensive compared with traditional RAID arrays.

New management approaches are changing the way storage is presented. Object storage is facilitating huge scale. In many ways, this has made the cloud feasible, as the scale of AWS S3 storage [8] testifies. Big Data also brings innovative approaches to file systems, with the Hadoop File System a leading player.

The cloud is perhaps the most revolutionary aspect of computing today. The idea of off-loading computing platforms to a third party has really caught on. In the process it has sucked a major part of the platform business away from traditional vendors and placed it in the hands of low-cost manufacturers in Taiwan and the PRC.

The economics of cloud storage bring substantial savings for many tasks, especially backup and disaster recovery archiving. One result of this may be that tape will finally die! Across the board, these economics are raising questions about our current practices in storage, such as the price differential between commodity storage units and the traditional arrays.

The low-cost vendors are now strong enough to enter the commercial US and EU markets [9] with branded products, which will create a good deal of churn as aggressively priced high-quality units take on the expensive traditional vendors. We are already seeing the effects of that in mergers such as the one Dell and EMC [10] just completed.

Cloud architectures are finding their way into every large datacenter, while small datacenters are closing down and moving totally to the cloud. It isn't clear that, in a decade or so, we'll have private computing independent from public clouds. My guess is that we will, but just the fact that the question is being asked points up the impact the cloud approach is having on the future of IT.

The bottom line is that the storage revolution is impacting everything that you do in the datacenter. We are beyond the point where change is optional. The message of this book is as follows:

In storage, change is long overdue!

The Storage Revolution brings the largest increment in performance in computer history!

Join the revolution or be left in the past!

REFERENCES
[1] SSDs achieving 1+ million random IOPS. http://hothardware.com/news/seagate-debuts-10gbps-nvme-ssd.
[2] SDD achieving parity on price per gigabyte with hard drives. http://www.networkcomputing.com/storage/storage-market-out-old-new/355694318.
[3] Fibre channel losing the war with Ethernet. http://www.theregister.co.uk/2015/05/26/fcoe_is_dead_for_real_bro/.

[4] Primary storage architecture obsolescent, at best. http://www.channelregister.co.uk/2015/02/23/fibre_channel_trios_confinement/.

[5] Oracle's 100x performance boost. http://www.oracle.com/us/corporate/pressrelease/database-in-memory-061014.

[6] Big Data definition. http://www.gartner.com/it-glossary/big-data/.

[7] Open-sourced storage software. http://www.tomsitpro.com/articles/open-source-cloud-computing-software,2-754-5.html.

[8] Scale of AWS S3 storage. http://www.information-age.com/technology/cloud-and-virtualisation/123460903/how-success-aws-turning-s3-enterprise-storage-%E2%80%98must-have.

[9] Low cost vendors are now strong enough to enter the commercial US and EU markets. http://searchdatacenter.techtarget.com/tip/Is-it-better-to-build-or-buy-data-center-hardware.

[10] Dell and EMC. http://www.forbes.com/sites/greatspeculations/2016/02/25/dell-emc-merger-gets-ftc-approval-remains-on-track-to-close/#261b0c186743

CHAPTER

Storage From 30,000 Feet

2

WHAT IS COMPUTER STORAGE?

It's a broad swathe of technologies, ranging from the dynamic random access memory (DRAM) and read-only memories (ROMs) in smart units to the drive-based storage that keeps a permanent record of data. This book focuses on *Networked Storage*, a segment of the business making the data shareable between many computers and protecting that data from hardware and software failures. Storage is often shown as a pyramid, with the top-most memory being the smallest in size as a result of price per gigabyte, broadening out to cloud archive storage (and, traditionally, magnetic tape) (Fig. 2.1).

It would be nice to say that each tier of the pyramid is clear and distinct from its neighbors, but that is no longer true. The layers sometimes overlap, as technologies serve multiple use cases. An example is the Nonvolatile dual in-line memory module (DIMM) (NVDIMM), where DRAM is made to look like an solid-state drive (SSD), though connected on a very fast memory bus. There are even nuances within these overlaps. There is a version of NVDIMM that operates as a DIMM, but backs up all its data on power off and restores it when the system reboots. These all have an impact on network storage and must be considered in any full description of that segment of storage.

The boundaries between storage and servers are becoming confused as well. Hyperconverged systems [1] use COTS servers for storage, and allow functions to spread from storage to servers and vice versa. These are evolving, too. *Software-defined Storage* (SDS) is an environment where almost all the data services associated with storage are distributed across the virtualized server farm rather than being in the storage array or appliance.

A segment of the market is also pushing the idea of virtual SANs (vSANs) and sharing server storage across networks. This is a crossover between direct-attached storage (DAS) and true networked storage. The subtle but important difference between the two is that vSAN servers have a persistent state, which means that specific data integrity and availability mechanisms are needed to protect against a server failure.

A recent phenomenon, the cloud, is impacting all forms of compute and storage. In one sense, with public/private hybrid clouds [2] being so popular, cloud storage is a networked storage tier, although it is evolving somewhat differently to standard commercial storage products. The public cloud mega-providers' evolution tends to lead the rest of IT, and so deservers a chapter of its own later in this book (see Ch. 10).

Network Storage. http://dx.doi.org/10.1016/B978-0-12-803863-5.00002-9

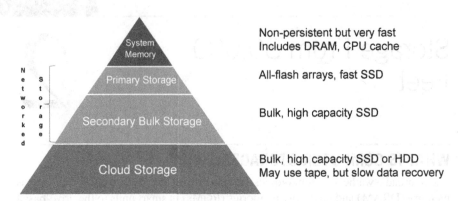

System Memory — Non-persistent but very fast
Includes DRAM, CPU cache

Primary Storage — All-flash arrays, fast SSD

Secondary Bulk Storage — Bulk, high capacity SSD

Cloud Storage — Bulk, high capacity SSD or HDD
May use tape, but slow data recovery

Networked Storage

FIGURE 2.1

The storage pyramid.

Going a little further, SDS [3] is a concept where the compute associated with storage is distributed over virtual server instances. This allows real-time agile response to load, creating configuration elastic that opens up new ways to build a server cloud, but it does make mincemeat of the pyramid picture!

STORAGE TODAY
THE LARGE CORPORATION

The predominant storage solution used by an IT operation will depend on size and budget. At the high end of the market, all of the critical data, and much of the rest of the corporate database, will reside in one or more large SANS. Typically, data is duplicated between multiple datacenters to protect against power failures, etc. and these datacenters are geographically dispersed to protect against natural disasters.

These SANs are complex and expensive beasts. They have expensive top-grade arrays from companies like HDS [4] and EMC [5], and use RAID configurations internally for data integrity. There are multiple SAN setups in any one datacenter, isolating datasets by usage and by degree of corporate importance.

SAN storage is also tiered vertically [6], with the fastest primary tier holding the most active data and a secondary tier with slower cheaper drives acting as bulk storage for cooler data. Many datacenters have a third tier for archived data, and also use a disk/tape-based backup and archiving scheme that involves moving data offsite and keeping multiple static copies for extended periods. Many of this class of users have filer storage as well as the SANs, especially if PC desktops are common.

Large enterprises have extensive local IT staffs, who look at new technologies in a sandbox, as well as running day-to-day operations. In many cases, object stores are just moving from the sandbox to mainstream usage, likely as archiving and backup storage or perhaps as Big Data repositories.

Sold-state products such as All-Flash Arrays [7] have had rapid introductions via the sandbox process and are widely deployed, even though they are a relatively new product class. This reflects the strong feature and performance benefit they bring to existing SAN operations and their ease of installation. This is a real success story given that the large corporate SAN admin teams are the most conservative players in IT.

Corporate goals for critical data storage are very demanding. The expectation is that data is never lost and that downtime is very minimal. RAID made this a possibility, and when Joe Tucci apologized for EMC losing their first bit of client data ever a few years back, most comments were about how the loss of any data had been avoided for so long!

Even so, RAID is at the limit of capability dealing with today's huge capacity drives, and alternatives are necessary. The answer for most enterprise users is to move to a new tiring scheme with fast flash of SSD in the primary tier and inexpensive bulk drives in the secondary tier.

MID-SIZED OPERATIONS

With small IT staffs and budgets, smaller shops tend to avoid the most expensive SAN gear and buy either smaller storage arrays from more competitive providers or else migrate to Ethernet-based storage. Here, the market splits between filer solutions and iSCSI arrays, with the latter forming a SAN configuration but based on Ethernet.

Filers have a lower operating cost and are easier to use, while iSCSI SANSs need much less training than Fiber-Channel solutions. For critical data, vendors such as HP and Dell are often suppliers of the iSCSI solutions, while NetApp has a large portion of the fully-integrated filer market.

When it comes to less critical data, such as PC desktop user shares, the story is mixed. Many IT shops buy inexpensive servers, kit them with say four drives and add free software from their favorite Linux distribution to create a filer. These are not well-featured compared with NetApp, but are sufficient for the use cases they are intended for.

DIY iSCSI solutions are also an option for those IT organizations with a good comfort zone in storage server configuration. Open-e [8] is a leader in iSCSI stacks, for example, and installation is relatively simple.

THE SMALL BUSINESS

IT in small businesses is a vanishing genre. The cloud is absorbing most of this segment [9], though it still has a way to go. With multi-site disaster-proof storage, low cost compute-on-demand, and template operations in place for retailers and other business segments, the cloud is a compelling story, especially with prices lowered by a massive price war.

Cloud connectivity comes in several forms however. At one end of the spectrum, the local IT operation is a tablet or PC acting as a browser to a cloud app and storage.

At the other end, there is a cloud gateway connecting the local network of users to data in the cloud that presents as a filer to the users.

These gateways provide caching for cloud data, and buffer up the slow WAN connections most US and EU users have. Usually kitted with a mirrored pair of hard drives, these will give way to SSD-based units that run considerably faster relatively quickly.

STORAGE IN 3 YEARS

With storage changing so rapidly, this cozy picture of today's storage is very challenged. Many of us remember the UNIX revolution [10] followed by the ascendency of Linux [11], and we can expect many of the same sorts of things to happen. The difference is that the story for the new technologies is much more compelling than Linux ever was. This means we are seeing a rapid transition from "mainframe" storage to mainly open and agile solutions.

The catalyst is solid-state storage [12]. This technology is already cheaper than so-called "enterprise" hard drives [13], and that technology is obsolete, leaving the surviving HDD class as commodity bulk storage. That class is itself under threat from SSD that today achieve parity on capacity, and by 2017 should price level with commodity hard disk drives [14]. Obsoleting the disk drive and using SSD is roughly equivalent to replacing a golf-cart fleet with Ferraris – lots of horsepower, but occasionally a bit difficult to control!

We can make an educated guess as to what storage will typically look like in 2018. First, we will still be in transition, both technically, and in implementation. New ideas will just be entering mainstream deployment, while any market, and especially one as conservative as storage, will have pioneers, early adopters, the field and finally some conservative laggards.

Second, the major traditional vendors will be reacting to the threat to their rice bowls. FUD will fly (an old IBM expression I'm fond of because I see it used so often during business transitions like this. FUD stands for "Fear, Uncertainty and Doubt [15].)" There'll be a spate of acquisitions as the large guys use their war chests to buy IP and take out potential competitors. We may see some mergers of giants [16], aiming to achieve overwhelming mass in the market.

All of this aside, the economic sands of the storage industry are shifting. Recognizing that commodity drives are just that, the average price per primary storage terabyte is going to drop from the $2000 range (and with some vendors much more!) to a $100–200 range very quickly. Chinese ODMs [17] are already shipping huge volumes of storage product to Google, AWs and Azure etc., so their entry into the mainstream US market, which is already occurring in large enterprises, will move vendors from the "mainframe model of 'very high markups with a standard 30% discount' to the PC model of 'low markups on commodity-priced drives'."

The platform hardware associated with storage is now almost exclusively COTS-based, and will see the same pricing model changes as drives. It seems likely that drives and some portion of the chassis will be bought from distribution, while the rest of the gear will come from ODMs like SuperMicro [18] and Quanta [19]. It's worth noting that SuperMicro took over the third position in worldwide server shipments in 2015.

Key trends in storage technology will be the expansion of all-flash arrays sales, object-based universal storage and, emerging strongly, SDS. The last is a storage answer to server virtualization, using virtual machines to host the storage data services and allowing the hardware to truly commoditize.

One result of SDS will be an explosion of new software-only startups targeting the storage space. These will deliver innovation, coupled with intense competition and will tend to erode traditional vendor loyalties. The entrenched large vendors will react by acquisition, but the market will see price point drop way down on the software side, while hardware will near "mail-order" prices. That's good news for an IT industry facing huge storage growth over at least the next decade.

Coupled with SDS will be a general move to Ethernet as the interface of choice for storage. This will be "next-generation" Ethernet, with 25 Gbps and 100 gigabits per second (Gbps) single links and a quad option for backbones that delivers 400 gigabits over fiber connections. Ethernet will have a much higher proportion of remote direct memory access (RDMA)-type link than today, especially for storage needs.

The intense investment in Ethernet, coupled with RDMA capability, does not bode well for Fiber-Channel (FC). With no remaining use cases where it is a winner, behind in raw transfer rates and price points and with a small supplier base, FC is going to fade away. The FC vendors recognize this and are investing in sophisticated RDMA-based Ethernet components.

THE DISTANT FUTURE: 2019 AND BEYOND

Further out on the horizon, we can expect compression, encryption, and other data services to move to much higher levels of performance, as specialized acceleration hardware is merged with the SDS approach. This will change the raw capacity needs for a datacenter, perhaps by as much as a factor of 8, and will also impact network load, since compressed files use a lot less bandwidth.

Flash will be the new disk, replacing hard drives in all applications. There will still be a tail of obsolete storage systems needing magnetic drives, but the demand reduction will make industry pundits scramble for projections. The decline in relative value of the hard-drive gear could be rapid enough to destroy any residual value in the used equipment market.

Economics will determine if the smaller modular appliance with say eight drives is a better fit than jumbo boxes of SSD with the many controllers they require to handle bandwidth. The smaller box tends to favor startups, at least for a while, as it is more akin to the storage-on-demand model of the cloud as well as a generally lower cost per terabyte.

In this line of thinking, the storage farm will be a stack of small "Lego" bricks, possibly from more than one vendor, and all with low-level, but standard interfaces.

Quite likely, new gear will support Ethernet only, with RDMA as a flavor. FC will be heading for the last roundup.

SSDs will have capacities in the 20 to 30 Terabyte [20] range by 2019, and will continue to grow. This amount of storage in a single drive will stress existing interfaces, pushing us inexorably toward *peripheral component interconnect express* (PCIe) for local drives, using the nonvolatile memory express (NVMe) protocol.

It's very possibly the "hot" trend in 2019 will be using Ethernet interfaces rather than SAS or SATA for all networked drives, allowing low-cost data farms with direct drive access as a way to reduce infrastructure overhead and latency. These will be object stores in their own right and will be part of a major effort that will have tuned Ceph and other object-storage software to achieve block-IO levels of operation. This approach is classed as "asymmetric pooling," and fits the SDS model well.

The alternatives for an Ethernet protocol, namely Kinetic [21] and NVMe-over-fabric will have duked it out by this point. NVMe will service the appliance model, while Kinetic, or a similar protocol, will handle the asymmetric pooling model where drives transfer data directly to servers. It is possible NVMe will take the whole pot in a few years, though.

Ethernet will be solidly entrenched as the interface of choice for networked storage, as the unifying value of an all-Ethernet shop becomes de rigeur for *Software-Defined Infrastructure*. Appliances with 50-GbE or 100-GbE links will be common and talk of 200 GbE [22] will turn into reality, as will compression technology to further boost effective bandwidth. With direct-connected disk drives each delivering as much as 5 GBPS of streamed data, it's clear that network topologies are likely to change considerably. It's also clear that telcos will need to accelerate their fiber rollouts [23] to keep up with the workload.

The one great uncertainty is where server-based initiatives like vSAN will land. Lauded as a way to get rid of the storage farm completely, the idea will either be founder on the rocks of economics, or prove to be a slow solution compared with alternatives. Time will tell if this is a jaundiced assessment, however. We could be surprised and find all that hype for hyperconverged systems hid a gem of an idea.

The cloud will be handling pretty well all backup and archiving [24] by this point. Tape will likely, finally, be dead [25] (but beware of the linear tape-open (LTO) zombie!). By 2019, heavily compressed, very inexpensive SSD will be the preferred archiving device, although this use case might be a home for all those obsolete hard drive arrays in some shops. If so, HDD boxes will run in a massive array of idle drives (MAID) [26] format, with drives powered down most of the time.

Will there be serious challenges to the ascendency of flash by 2020? We'll be on the cusp of seeing at least one competitor viably reaching market. Most likely, this will be either ReRAM or PCM storage, but neither is definitively a winner yet, although Intel and Micron in late 2015 jointly announced 3D X-Point memory [27] as a NAND killer. Even if they get through their remaining technical issues, there will be challenges in reaching the same densities and price points as flash, which still has much room for further evolution. It will take an advantage such as near-DRAM latency to make these attractive enough to erode flash quickly.

There are a couple of interesting longshots that might be a hit in a five-year horizon. Anything based on graphene [28] looks interesting. Low-power, high densities, and the intrinsic ability to be stacked are all in favor of this type of technology, but graphene is still very new as a material and we still uncover fundamental physics as we go.

We will be seeing innovative packaging alternatives by the end of the decade. The *hybrid memory cube* (HMC) [29] architecture is firmly directed at opening up DRAM memory performance by increased parallelism coupled with a very low power profile. With products starting to appear in 2015 and mainstream support from AMD, NVidia and, more tentatively, Intel, HMC is going to impact systems architectures quickly.

The hybrid nature of the concept will show up when flash or PCM is part of a module. This will make for a much closer bond for what may be a sizable amount of persistent memory, which will further speed up databases and analytics. This will have a ripple effect into networked storage, especially if the HMC memory is networked to the rest of the cluster. Bandwidth demand will increase, and the methods of delivering data may need to move even beyond NVMe to limit overhead and excess latency.

Potentially, this involves local (DAS) drives with both PCIe and 25-GbE RDMA Ethernet ports. These will talk to the host through the lowest overhead (PCIe) connection while networking directly to the rest of the cluster via RDMA.

REFERENCES

[1] Hyper-converged Systems Description. http://www.webopedia.com/TERM/H/hyper-converged-infrastructure.html.

[2] Hybrid Clouds. http://www.cio.com/article/3022834/cloud-computing/hybrid-clouds-are-hot-sdns-and-devops-coming-on-strong.html.

[3] Software-Defined Storage. http://www.networkcomputing.com/storage/what-software-defined-storage-really/447097217.

[4] HDS Company Website. http://www.hds.com/.

[5] EMC Company Website. http://www.emc.com/.

[6] SAN Storage Tiered Vertically. http://www.ibm.com/support/knowledgecenter/SSQRB8/com.ibm.spectrum.si.doc/tpch_saas_r_volume_optimization_process.html.

[7] All-Flash Arrays. http://www.solidfire.com/lp/gmq-2015?utm_source=google&utm_medium=cpc&utm_content=gmq2015&utm_campaign=All-Flash-Array-NA&mcf=PPC&mcdf=Google+AdWords&mcl=PPC&mcdl=Google+AdWords&_bt=93484570485&_bk=all%20flash%20arrays&_bm=e&gclid=CjwKEAjwuPi3BRC-lk8TyyMLloxgSJAAC0XsjMUcaQ2nX8WkgVzWtIWCNndq16tVg2BPlX7oALdX0h-BoCLPPw_wcB.

[8] Open-e Company Website. http://www.open-e.com/solutions/recommendations/solutions-iscsi/iscsi-storage/.

[9] The Cloud is Absorbing Most of the SMB Segment. https://services.amazon.com/content/sell-on-amazon.htm/ref=footer_soa?ld=AZFSSOA-dT1.

[10] The UNIX Revolution. http://www.computerworld.com/article/2524456/linux/unix-turns-40–the-past–present-and-future-of-a-revolutionary-os.html.

[11] The Ascendency of Linux. http://linux.about.com/cs/linux101/a/linux.htm.

[12] Solid-State Storage. http://www.wired.com/2015/08/flash-storage/.

[13] SSD Storage is Already Cheaper Than So-Called "Enterprise" Hard Drives. http://www.networkcomputing.com/storage/ssd-pricing-vs-hdd-costs/851436865.

[14] SSD Price Level with Commodity Hard Disk Drives. http://www.storagenewsletter.com/rubriques/market-reportsresearch/capacity-ssds-cheaper-than-capacity-hdds-in-2016-wikibon/.

[15] Fear, Uncertainty and Doubt. http://whatis.techtarget.com/definition/FUD-Fear-Uncertainty-and-Doubt.

[16] Mergers of Giants. http://searchstorage.techtarget.com/news/4500269496/Data-storage-vendors-in-the-hot-seat-in-2016-outlook.

[17] Chinese ODMs. http://www.theregister.co.uk/2016/03/09/global_server_market_in_q4/.

[18] SuperMicro Company Website. http://www.supermicro.com/.

[19] Quanta Company Website. http://www.qct.io/.

[20] SSDs Will Have Capacities in the 20 to 30 Terabyte Range. http://www.networkcomputing.com/storage/ssds-bigger-better-faster-and-cheaper/280376343.

[21] Seagate Kinetic Ethernet Drives. http://www.theregister.co.uk/2016/03/17/seagate_has_seen_the_light/.

[22] Talk of 200 GbE. http://www.hpcwire.com/2016/03/22/mellanox-reveals-200-gbps-path/.

[23] Need to Accelerate Fiber Roll-Outs. http://www.fiercetelecom.com/story/cincinnati-bells-fiber-depth-clear-fioptics-footprint-80-ftth-enabled-analy/2016-03-18.

[24] All Backup and Archiving in Cloud. http://searchstorage.techtarget.com/feature/Storage-purchase-plans-move-to-cloud-with-rising-budgets.

[25] Tape Will Likely, Finally, Be Dead. http://www.networkcomputing.com/storage/tape-storage-really-dead/1521473970.

[26] MAID (Massive Array of Idle Drives). http://www.computerweekly.com/feature/Benefits-and-limitations-of-MAID-storage-A-step-toward-a-green-data-centre.

[27] 3D X-Point Memory. http://www.zdnet.com/article/how-intels-3d-xpoint-will-change-servers-and-storage/.

[28] Graphene. http://www.bostoncommons.net/what-are-graphene-transistors/.

[29] Hybrid Memory Cube. http://news.softpedia.com/news/micron-unveils-third-generation-hybrid-memory-cube-in-2016-491406.shtml.

Network Infrastructure Today

3

Today's network infrastructure is the legacy of almost 30 years of relative stagnation in storage architectures. The technologies deployed are thus very mature, well tested, and capable of achieving high standards of data integrity and sophistication.

Each section will look at what the technology is, how it is used, and its inherent upsides and downsides. Most of these technologies have accreted some "urban myths" as they've evolved, and these will be validated or busted. Finally, each section has a review of the future.

STORAGE AREA NETWORKS IN TRANSITION

The *Storage Area Network* (SAN) [1] has been the mainstay of enterprise storage for the best part of three decades, starting as lowly *Redundant Arrays of Inexpensive Disks* (RAID) arrays [2] directly connected via *Fiber-Channel* (FC) or *Small Computer System Interface* (SCSI) to host systems in the late 1980s and growing to petabyte size clusters of arrays beginning with the arrival of FC switches in the mid-90s.

New interfaces entered the SAN space after 2000. These include Ethernet-based *FC over Ethernet* (FCoE) [3], which can connect via a router in a relatively seamless manner to existing FC SANs, and *internet SCSI* (iSCSI), and which is a somewhat simpler and less constrained protocol. iSCSI [4] has become dominant among these Ethernet block-IO storage interfaces.

HOW SANS WORK

A typical SAN (see Fig. 3.1) today will consist of a set of FC switches [5]. Switches are either relatively simple boxes with a low port count, or directors, which are large switches with high port counts and redundancy features built in.

Attached to these will be host systems, which use a Host-Bus Adapter [6] to connect to FC that provides one to four links; and storage array units.

Storage arrays come in several flavors. SAN arrays are either boxes of roughly 60 drives with a pair of redundant controllers built in or "head-nodes with the two controllers, connected via SAS or FC to a set of JBODs (Just a Bunch of Drives [7]) each of which holds 48 to 80 drives. Both types of structure are built into RETMA computer racks, with switches at the top of the rack (See Fig 3.2).

Network Storage. http://dx.doi.org/10.1016/B978-0-12-803863-5.00003-0

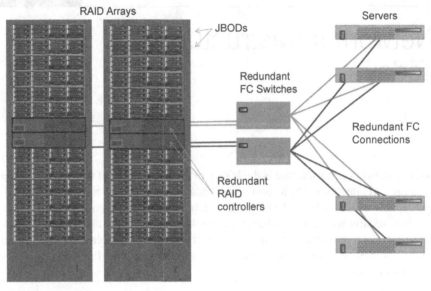

FIGURE 3.1

A Typical SAN configuration.

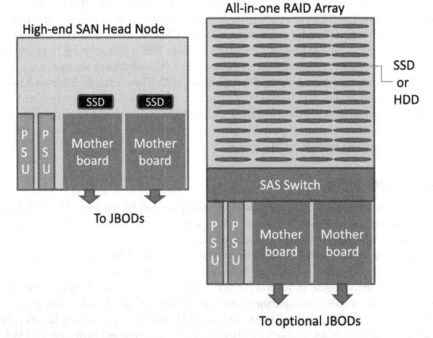

FIGURE 3.2

San array construction.

Controllers are usually designed so that drives can be accessed redundantly through either one of the pair. The objective is to avoid a single point of failure. Often hosts are able to connect to either controller, with redundant switches and dual ports on the HBA (or even two separate HBAs). These paths may both be active, or the set up can have one active and the other passive, in stand-by mode.

Some designs even went to the extent of having two ports on each drive [8] for access redundancy. This has always seemed like an urban myth issue, since the amount of electronics that is port dependent is minute, given that the interface on the drives is buried in a single ASIC in both a single or dual interface case. Marketers used dual-porting as a differentiator for enterprise drives compared with generally available (and cheap) consumer drives, but its contribution to data availability is negligible.

The array boxes (or the JBODs) can hold SAS drives, which typically spin at 10,000 rpm, or SATA drives spinning at 7200 or 5400 rpm. Figs. 3.3 and 3.4 show typical RAID storage units.

Typically the SATA drives hold much more capacity, with 10 Terabyte (TB) HDD and 15 TB SSD capacities available at the time of going to press. Drives are held in caddies [9] that are easily removable allowing failed drives to be replaced and, in theory, the ability to migrate data from a failed box to one that is working.

FC is capable of long distance connections, such as across a large campus, depending on the type of optical fiber used. There is even a copper option for close-in usage. Proliferation of HBAs is avoided by having active cables, with the fiber optic drivers and receivers built in, so that different optical cables plug into the same host adapter.

With FCoE, the FC protocol achieved the capability for long-haul connections. In theory, intercity connections are possible. To change from FC to FCoE, a router is used. FCoE uses *Converged Ethernet*, which adds port buffers in the switch to reduce retry rates and impose sequential delivery. This increases installation price.

FIGURE 3.3

Typical large RAID array.

FIGURE 3.4

Arrays today.

ISCSI (INTERNET SMALL COMPUTER SYSTEM INTERFACE) SANS

High SAN prices opened up an opportunity, beginning around 2001, for an alternative SAN architecture based on an Ethernet-based storage protocol, iSCSI. Able to provide similar functionality to FC SANs, iSCSI proved attractive to the higher end of the market as the *Block-IO* alternative to FC. As you can see from the name, iSCSI shares the same SCSI protocol origins as FC, so that iSCSI vendors were able to establish credibility quickly.

Incidentally, the "Small Computer" part of the name is misleading, stemming from some inter-vendor politics (and humor) at ANSI back in the 1980s. Both iSCSI and SCSI can and do connect large configurations together. Recently, solutions for linking iSCSI systems into FC SANs have been developed, including EMC's ViPR [10] and Brocade routers.

From the start, iSCSI has taken advantage of COTS hardware such as Intel XEON motherboards for controllers. This approach has allowed iSCSI vendors to keep close to the leading edge of technology in a lot of areas, while reducing cost over the proprietary packaging and electronics of typical FC boxes.

Unlike FC, iSCSI doesn't require dedicated cabling. It can share any Ethernet network. This is especially important for mid-sized companies, who avoid both the extra switch gear, specialized wiring, and the admin costs associated with a different protocol. Security and performance issues may support having a separate link for storage only, although typically in large configurations, providing on the one hand a private storage network not accessible to the Internet, and on the other, avoiding contention with other traffic for storage transfers.

The tech recession of 2008–2010 delayed the move to 10 GbE, placing iSCSI systems at a performance disadvantage against four and then 8-Gbps FC. Now that 10 GbE is ubiquitous and cheap, iSCSI is the performance leader, though 16-G FC is in a horserace to market in 2016 against 25 GbE. FC fans will note that 16G is available, but pricy and still in the early adopter phase as of writing, while 25 GbE is just about to enter the market, so FC has a slight edge in schedule. When 25 GbE hits its stride, it should be cheaper and quite a bit faster than the FC and the market dynamics will change in iSCSI's favor. Future speed improvements favor the Ethernet approach on both schedule and cost grounds and we can expect Ethernet to stride ahead of FC over time.

iSCSI, with Ethernet connectivity, can support disaster recovery via the WAN as well as the other use cases for the SAN. This approach likely will be superseded by cloud-based disaster recovery (DR) archiving and backup in the next few years, with 40 GbE and 100 GbE available in 2016 and 200 GbE announced.

The vendor base for iSCSI originally consisted of a bunch of startup companies, notably EqualLogic and Isilon. These were acquired by large storage and systems-vendors in the 2003–2006 timeframe. Most of the product lines still continue to be shipped with the original brand names, suggesting some strategic dissonance with the parent company, and there are still some overlaps in product lines within companies.

iSCSI software stacks are available that can easily be ported to a COTS server. The leader in this area is Open-e [11], a very creative Polish company. This do-it-yourself approach runs into strong competition from filers. Code like this may well underlie the huge configurations of block-IO storage in the cloud, but CSPs are notoriously tight-lipped on the issue of cloud internals.

iSCSI usually uses the motherboard-provided Ethernet ports in a server, but several companies provide accelerators for both iSCSI and TCP-IP as plug-in port cards. Many large storage arrays support an ISCSI target solution as an alternative to either an FC SAN or a filer interface. "Universal" storage software solutions such as Ceph serve block-IO via iSCSI.

SAN USE CASES

SANs support block-IO [12], an extension of the disk storage access mechanisms of the 1970s and 1980s. Individual blocks of data can be written, read, appended, or deleted from a file, and at its simplest, the SAN drive looks like a local hard disk drive.

Looking under the covers, a typical SAN has a large amount of storage. Vendors provide management tools that allow *Logical Units* (LUNs) [13] to be set up by selecting space on a set of drives, then defining the RAID level that controls that space. LUNs are normally contained within a single array box, since parity generation across boxes would be very slow. RAID 1 LUNS are also constrained to a single box, since the mirror is generated in the RAID controller in the array. LUNS are mounted onto host systems, whether Windows or Linux, or any other major operating system.

Mechanisms exist for multiple systems to access the same shared LUN, and for multipathing to any given LUN. FC switches permit large configurations to be built, with flexibility to connect or reconnect LUNs as needed.

With that as background, the versatility of the SAN is obvious. The resulting use cases are very broad, and cover all of the primary storage uses in IT. SANs are deployed by very large enterprises, government operations, and mid-sized companies.

Primary vendors for SAN gear are EMC [14], with the largest market share, HPE [15], HDS [16], Fujitsu [17], IBM [18], and Dell [19]. Several smaller vendors are notable as niche players. These include DDN [20] and Dot Hill [21].

SANs are not the best choice when data sharing is involved. This is currently the province of the filer or the object store, because with a SAN implementation management of the file system resides in the host server and it is complex and even risky to allow multiple servers change access to alter the file map tables. Any multi-host access mechanism needs a complicated locking scheme, which would have to handle scale-out configurations.

UPSIDES OF SANS

SANS are well characterized and predictable today, although the additions of *all-flash arrays* and SSD/HDD hybrid arrays with FC connectivity are upsetting long-established practices. Many companies have invested in management software, training, and governance processes that are resistant to change, for the simple reason that they work well.

Until recently, it was a brave engineer who claimed that a filer or other storage solution out-performed [22] an FC SAN. FC itself had kept up on speeds and feeds by using a performance doubling every 3 or 4 years or so to refresh the technology. In contrast, the Ethernet faction had a "10× every 10 years" approach, leaving FC with a performance edge. That changed abruptly in 2012. FC development now lags Ethernet by at least a couple of years, and the pace of evolution of Ethernet is more like "2+× every 3 years".

With SANS having the same API as internal disk, applications design is simplified, giving the block-IO approach an edge in the market, since rewriting isn't required.

SANs also have demonstrable reliability. EMC used to boast of never having lost a bit of data, which resonated well with corporate IT. EMC admitted to a small data loss, but given the installed base, even that did nothing to tarnish their reputation. This has set a standard for all other storage to measure against.

DOWNSIDES OF SANS

We've talked about the technical issues RAID has with SSD and large drives, and it's that very reliance on RAID that is undermining SAN's place in the storage world. The amount of data needing to be stored is growing rapidly and SANs just can't handle the scaling of installation size and complexity that involves.

SANs have always required a separate admin team with deep training in the particular SAN gear installed. The corollary of having these teams is that administration of the SAN is typically heavily hands-on. At the same time, the nature of block-IO storage is finely granular and inimical to data sharing and portability. It is literally hard to move LUNs around on the storage, and to restructure mounting on servers.

The combination of these factors deprecate SANs as the solution for the scale-out storage farms we need going forward.

Product pricing, and cost, also lose to commodity-based alternatives. SANs require specialized gear, and the vendor base is limited. The core technologies around FC are limited to four host adapter makers (Avago, Atto [23] and QLogic [24]), and two FC switch vendors (Cisco [25] and Brocade). This has to be coupled with array vendor practices, with high price points for very proprietary equipment. Even disk drives were marked up over 10x, though in recent years, competition from iSCSI and Object Storage has lowered hardware markups considerably.

THE FUTURE OF SANS

Technologically, RAID has reached its limit of usefulness. Very large capacity drives challenge the data protection model, since the time to rebuild such a drive after replacing a failure is now so long that a second, data-fatal, failure has a significant probability. RAID 6, an approach to add a second parity system orthogonal to the standard parity, has had a lukewarm reception due to the slow performance resulting from its complex calculations.

At the same time, the performance of *Solid-State Drives* (SSDs) is now so high that even the fastest RAID controller is unable to keep up, except in RAID 1 mirroring mode, and even then, can service just four drives. This is leading to new approaches to data integrity, and RAID is obsolescent. The technical issues of RAID are covered in more detail in Chapter 11.

From a business perspective, too, RAID arrays and SANs are losing ground to other forms of storage. iSCSI arrays and Object-Storage systems are taking market share from FC SANs, with cost, ease of use, and a wider range of vendors and products all contributing to the change. The cost issue is a backlash for many years of users paying very high prices for RAID gear, while seeing the rest of the IT market commoditize.

With high prices the norm, we have a repeat of the UNIX revolution of the 1980s, but in the storage world. The combination of inflexibility, lack of scalability, tight vendor base, and high prices is forming a perfect storm for the SAN approach. We can expect that same result as with the mainframe. Array sales will drop away and low-cost commodity-based solutions will thrive. We even have "Linux", in the form of open-source software stacks like Ceph and OpenStack, and there is a strong drive to separating software from truly commoditized hardware altogether, in the shape of *Software-Defined Storage* (SDS).

Some of those new storage solutions address the raison-d'etre of the SAN itself. We see software like Ceph offering a pathway to "universal" storage, where gateway software allows an object store to be presented to hosts just like a block-IO storage device (usually iSCSI not FC), or as a filer. With low-cost ODMs operating on single-digit margins and building huge volumes for the likes of Google and AWs, commodity "white-box" storage will become the norm as platforms for this software and storage prices can be expected to plummet through 2017. The larger vendors acknowledge the coming change. Most of them are moving toward a software-and-services model, with the aim of escaping the results of the drop in hardware pricing.

iSCSI can't save the SAN. Even though it ties in to low-cost software and uses Ethernet, the limitations in scaling will take the block-IO solution out of the equation in favor of object solutions.

Overall, then, the future of the SAN looks bleak. It stood as the "rock" of storage for nearly three decades, but its time has come. With those three decades having made storage IT staff somewhat complacent and conservative, we shouldn't expect an overnight change (I'm betting there'll still be SANs in government 30 years from now), but the incredible rate of capacity and performance improvement represented by SSD may speed up change in the commercial sector, especially as storage is expected to grow by at least an order of magnitude in the next 10 years.

FILER (NAS—NETWORK-ATTACHED STORAGE)

Around the time the first PCs were entering the market, in 1982, a couple of companies came up with the idea of moving the file system onto the shared storage appliance, resolving the issue of keeping all of the changes being made by the using servers in sync with each other, while making the data available to multiple users. Those companies were Novell and NCR, Wichita (where I led the team that developed the "Modus" file-server). Both companies released products at the same NCC show, and even had adjacent booths.

Filers like this were able to handle one user with write privileges to a file, with multiple users able to read, but multiple users could work at the same time in the same directories, since the file map was under control of the filer. The concept of users having their own private spaces was another innovation. There were limitations; Ethernet wasn't an option for a few years, for example, and Novell used a star-topology network that limited connectivity to just PCs.

Filers have become a mainstream storage solution. They are Ethernet-based today, but use COTS-server technology as a base. Filers come in a range of sizes, from two-drive desktop units to rack-stacked enterprise filers such as those that NetApp delivers.

HOW FILERS WORK

When a server accesses a BlockIO SAN device, it runs a file system stack just like it would if the SAN logical unit were local. The file server moves the file system control to the filer, making it much easier to share data among users.

The difference is actually quite subtle. The server on a SAN reads the file system on the LUN and asks for a specific "physical" block. The requested address is converted to the real physical address in the SAN array.

A filer (Fig. 3.5) does much of the same thing. The server also can see the file system on the storage share available to that particular server. All the requests for

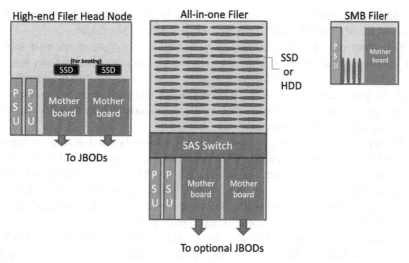

FIGURE 3.5

Filer structures.

blocks are abstracted to one of several Ethernet protocols and are translated from file name and offset type of addresses into physical storage addresses on the filer itself.

Because the filer controls changing the file directory, it can allow multiple users to access the same data. Write locks are executed at the file level, so several users can work in the same directory simultaneously.

With storage looking just like mounted drives with the same file system structure as a local drive, filers are easy to set up. Often they are used as backup space for desktop computers and workstations, where they also serve the purpose of shared repositories. This creates one of the downsides of filers, which is the creation of multiple copies of a file, versioning of those copies and a lack of lifecycle management, all of which cause confusion and use space.

At the low end of the spectrum, we have "freeware" code that is bundled with every Linux distribution that supports basic file-server operations for the two primary interface protocols NFS (*Network File System*) and SMB (*Server Message Block*). This code is perfectly adequate for a no-frills file-server solution suitable for storing data in small offices, and almost all small- and medium-size companies take advantage of this approach if they file share by either buying a file server with a couple of drives or, for larger shops, adding the freeware to a server.

The result is that we see boxes with just a couple of drives providing shared storage and backup for a few users at the bottom of the networked storage tree (Fig. 3.7). It says a lot about the stability of the solutions and their ease of use that they are so popular.

Larger businesses apply some discipline to filer use, and multiple filers are typical with varying degrees of governance applied. Production storage for server farms is usually controlled with strong data-management rules and limited access.

It is possible to self-integrate quite large filers using standard servers and external JBODS (Just a Box Of Disks) containing a large number of drives, using SAS external connections between the servers and the JBODs. With JBODs holding up to 80 drives readily available, quite a large storage pool can be created.

For enterprises and the mid-market user, preintegrated solutions with servers and JBODs are available from a number of vendors, but most notably from NetApp [26]. Although of essentially the same type of hardware as the "do-it-yourself" filers above, prices are much higher. The difference is that companies like NetApp are offering proprietary code solutions that are highly featured. These vendors also have a track record of quality solutions.

NetApp (Fig. 3.6) includes features like filer-level data redundancy, compression, and deduplication and cloning [27], the last being a very powerful feature when distributing data to server farms or virtual desktops. This code is well tested before release and that extra stability has some value. Even so, the quality gap has closed up considerably with the open-source code available, leaving vendors the challenge of proving that their features are worth the extra price to be paid.

Because of the directory tree structures, and the inherent inability of NAS to spread across multiple filers, simple NAS does not scale well. This has led to the introduction of scale-out NAS solutions at the upper end of the market, overcoming the address space limitations and allowing bigger installations. Typically, though, cluster sizes are still limited to one- or two dozen filers, which work for a small server cluster but not for a corporate or public cloud.

FIGURE 3.6

NetApp filer.

FIGURE 3.7

Small filer.

COMPARING NAS WITH SAN

In the early days of the Storage Networking Industry Association [28], representing most aspects of the storage industry and providing a strong mechanism for creating consensus and standards, the NAS and SAN camps fought hard to keep each other out of the SNIA umbrella. Clearly, they saw the other team as a challenge to market control and profits.

That polarization has been in the industry since the inception of both approaches and it manifests itself in strange ways, both important and petty. FC has been the SAN protocol of choice since the mid-1990s, while NAS has followed Ethernet for its whole history, except in the very early days when proprietary LANs still existed.

Reality is setting in, and development costs have forced convergence of all the core technologies, while IEEE, which regulates Ethernet, has bowed to the industry and allowed 2.5× and 5× developments in parallel with 10× work. The result is that filers and SAN boxes can be compared on a level playing field and as suspected, there isn't much performance difference (Fig. 3.8).

The most significant difference between the two approaches is the location of the file system metadata and its associated processing (See Fig. 3.9). In a SAN system, the metadata are permanently stored on the disk drives, but it is read into the using servers to allow them to figure out which data block on the disks actually contains the data. That creates file-opening traffic on the network, and may also add to write overhead if a new inode is opened up.

In a NAS system, the metadata is always kept in the filer. From a host-application perspective, the file commands look exactly the same, and the directory tree can be viewed, too. Normal IO, however, doesn't need the metadata to be copied and cached in the servers using the filer, reducing LAN traffic.

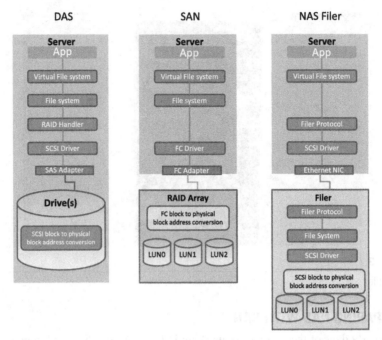

FIGURE 3.8

Comparing SAN and filer.

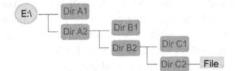

Filer Directory Tree Structure

This doesn't scale well or cross boundary between filers

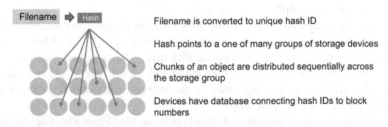

Object Store Flat Address Space

Filename ➡ Hash   Filename is converted to unique hash ID

Hash points to a one of many groups of storage devices

Chunks of an object are distributed sequentially across the storage group

Devices have database connecting hash IDs to block numbers

Inherently scales and was designed ab initio to cross boundaries

FIGURE 3.9

Filer storage versus object storage.

At the low and middle tiers of IT, filers rule the roost. SANs, with their own interface, networking and management software require a couple of storage administrators to run things well, and smaller shops don't want to spend the money and add the complexity.

The enterprise class is a different kettle of fish. SAN has a majority share of the market, though this is on the decline, as seen above. By far, the dominant vendor is EMC and their effectiveness in sales and support, more than technology, has cemented the SAN in place for so long. IBM, highly respected still in the 1990s, also supported the SAN approach, though with a proprietary version of FC called FICON. The fact that SAN controllers ran simpler code also helped SANs, and the fact that SAN piggy-backed to a great extent on existing DAS software and processes (Direct-Access Storage means the prenetworking method of having drives in the servers themselves.).

NFS, CIFS, SMB, LINUX, AND WINDOWS

Filers (often called for *Network-Attached Storage* [NAS] [29]) typically either use Linux or Windows Storage server as a base-operating system, with the most notable exception being NetApp, with their proprietary Data ONTAP operating system. Linux supports both NFS and SMB/CIFS.

Originally a Sun Microsystems [30] product dating from 1985 and substantially upgraded through several major revisions; NFSv4 [31] was open-sourced by being handed over to the *Internet Engineering Task Force* (IETF) [32] in 2000.

The *Server Message Block* (SMB) [33] protocol dates back to IBM in the late 1980s, but was picked up by Microsoft and incorporated into Windows within a couple of years. In 1996, Microsoft renamed SMB as CIFS and released some of the specifications to IETF, in an apparent attempt to head of SUN and NFS as a de facto standard in networking. Begun in 1991, a reverse-engineered version of SMB 1.0 was released as Samba, for use on UNIX and Linux systems.

SMB has evolved rapidly since 2006. Release 2.0 addressed performance problems by reducing the command set by 80% and introducing pipelining. SMB 3.0 entered the market in 2012 at the time of the Windows 8 release, with substantial changes that have left other storage vendors playing catchup. There is some relief from the slow market start of Windows 8, but SMB 3.0 is supported in *Windows Storage Server* (WSS) 2012 v2, which is offering a formidable alternative to other proprietary storage software stacks.

It's probably fair to say that Linux shops tend to use NFS and Windows shops tend to go to WSS and/or SMB, but both operating systems support either protocol. Uniformity of operating systems tends to be the rule, so an all-Windows IT operation would generally choose WSS and SMB, for example. Today, it is relatively easy to port WSS to an appliance; this is used requiring Microsoft to agree to a project and then test and bless the result. The result is WSS appears on a wide variety of storage solutions ranging from all-flash arrays to small appliances.

Which one is better? SMB 1.0 ran slow, due to message passing and other issues. The latest versions have fixed that problem. NFSv4 has generated comments about feature bloat. Reality is that the underlying hardware platform and the networks used have more effect on performance. Most of the controversy is moot anyway, since it started when HDDs were king. With SSD set to replace the hard drive, the issues will be much more complicated for a while. It is worth noting that the SMB Direct feature in SMB 3.0 does support RDMA transfers, over either iWARP, RoCE, or InfiniBand.

FILER USE CASES

Filers are by far the most common form of networked storage for the *Small/Medium Business* (SMB) (not to be confused with SMB the protocol!) market. Ease of use, low price, and a low level of skill required for administration give filers a distinct edge over SAN systems. Adding storage is also cheap, since most users will opt for consumer drives available on the Internet.

The primary use cases for low-end filers are as shared storage pools, where disk space is allocated by department, and as personal backup space for PCs and other servers, where each client gets a disk allocation. Each space is set up with owner and password information, with the capability to share directly with other name users, or to use null passwords for shared areas.

With drives reaching 15 TB or more in size today, low-end filers usually have just a few drives. This makes RAID 1 mirroring the preferred data integrity scheme. Some cloud gateway boxes are touted as alternatives to filers, with built-in backup and archiving capability to low-cost cloud storage. These may not be as protected as their hype suggests. If data stored, even temporarily, in the gateway is not protected against a drive failure, there is a risk of losing data, and with the rate data is produced today, it could be a lot of data! The issue is the time between receiving the data into the gateway and sending a copy on to the cloud—that could be minutes, which is forever in computer terms. A drive failure in that window could mean the end of the only copy.

Filers are often used as primary storage in the enterprise, though less frequently than SAN systems. The enterprise filer is a sophisticated product with advanced software features such as deduplication, compression, and extensive cloning and snapshot tools, as epitomized by NetApp's product line. Access authentication can be linked to *Windows Active Directories*.

Microsoft's WSS is providing a good alternative to NetApp. Not only is it well-featured (though not yet up to the level of all of NetApp's offerings), it uses commodity hardware and the parts all seem designed for virtualization as a major play for SDS. Since WSS uses the same Windows server software, it is particularly attractive to Windows shops, providing unified management.

UPSIDES OF FILERS

Filers are really easy to use. They don't need admins with three hands typing complex CLI. Many users take the pablum distribution and use as is. Security and authentication is easy, with ties to Active Directory [34]. Clients can go to a filer and log in once their share has been set up, and then they themselves can authorize access to others for their own share. Windows users see the shared spaces as just another disk drive.

Low-end filers use commodity gear and are inexpensive. This is true of WSS filers in the enterprise and mid-market, though NetApp charges a substantial premium over their COTS-based internals, justified by performance and reliability, customer support, and well-featured software.

Being Ethernet-based, filers fit the existing network-administration team better than FC SANs, which is a major reason why iSCSI boxes have done so well, too.

The mid-market sees a good many home-grown filers, where older servers are repurposed by adding some larger drives and Linux/NFS. Again, the low support cost and simplicity of integrating hardware and software makes this very attractive.

DOWNSIDES OF FILERS

Filers were conceived as free-standing independent storage nodes. While they can use the same RAID functionality as SAN arrays for data integrity, they are not designed to have redundant pathways through the server to the drives, so loss of the server motherboard can make all of the storage unavailable. NetApp is the exception to this, using a separate head-node and storage JBOD approach. Some scale-out NAS boxes, notably Dell Compellent/EqualLogic units, have dual-server redundancy built in to the appliances.

Filers are easy to work with but the lack of server redundancy makes recovering from problems a tough task, especially if the failed product is no longer available. This is another reason for the eventual replacement of the filer in the low-end market by the cloud.

The simplicity of control on filers is one of their great benefits, but at the same time a cause of much pain. Simply put, filers encourage data copying and file sprawl. Most filers have duplicate copies of the many files and these often are then independently revised and different versions end up with the same names. With many independent users at different skill levels, most filers have a mess of older data that can't easily be separated into the valid copies to be kept. This can be minimized in well-run datacenters by good data management processes.

Filers intrinsically have directory tree structures. These become limiting when very large-scale configurations are needed, and are far from the ideal of having a pool of available disk space. Name duplication is potentially unmanageable at scale, and the problem of finding files in an environment of regularly failing drives and nodes is daunting. Scale-out file storage is better handled by Object-Storage systems.

So-called "scale-out NAS" for the enterprise is intended to address the finite size of any given box by providing a way to add more filers to create an expandable pool of storage. This addresses the size issue, and provides a benefit of allowing buyers to start off with smaller filers and grow them as needed. It doesn't address the file and directory naming issues, and most solutions have limits on expandability. With space bridging between machines, locating a file can be an issue, and large files can cross the intermachine boundaries adding extra IOs to navigate to blocks.

FILER MYTHS

A great deal of effort has been expended over the last two decades to show that SANs are faster than the filer for enterprise use, and vice versa, but the reality was that hard drives had more impact on real performance than the interfaces. This fact was masked by the mismatch of line speeds that resulted from the FC decision to double performance roughly every 3 years, while the Ethernet faction looked for 10× performance every 10 years. Some minor issues fell out of the choices of connectors and cables, as well as the bit mapping used to avoid baseline shift (64b/68b is better than 8b/10b!)

The bottom line is that there is not much to choose in performance. On the other hand, we've a broad set of vendors for filers, compared with the near-monopoly and limited vendor choices for SAN. The result is filer prices tend to be lower than SANS, and also have quite a spread. One myth is that you get what you pay for and higher prices equal better filers. That isn't true at all! Though NetApp is very richly featured and priced accordingly, not buying unneeded software modules can bring the price a ways down, for example, and filers from some of the crop of startups acquired by the big companies of the industry offer good value too.

The most crucial myth is that somehow filers have less data integrity than SANs. That's true of low-end products, but today's enterprise filers have very similar architectures to SAN arrays, with dual pathing to data, file copying across the storage pool, and even some more advanced features SANs can't match such as the extra level of integrity on file trees in the Panasas boxes.

A new myth is that scale-out storage is, well, scale-out. Read the small print. Most products have upper limits to cluster sizes. These limits vary all over the place and can be as low as 500 TB, which is not large in today's world and couldn't handle the expected data expansion we face.

FILER FUTURES

Filers are generally cheaper than SANs on a $/Terabyte basis. In the enterprise, drive prices still remain high for filers. These leave filers as vulnerable as SANs to object storage systems based on commodity gear, especially if they offer filer access methods such as NFS and SMB. Vendors are countering this by enriching software, but the inexpensive suppliers are catching up in features, and, at the same time, we are running out of new meaningful features to charge for.

The gateway approach poses a challenge to the low-end NAS market, by usurping its backup role. Services like Drop Box add a challenge to the sharing benefits of NAS and the bottom line is that we can expect the low-end NAS market to shrink in favor of the cloud over the next 5–10 years. The combination of low, pay-as-you-go cost, someone else managing the gear, much higher data integrity, and disaster protection combined with sharing is irresistible.

In the enterprise, many arrays, especially all-flash arrays, are providing filer interfaces. That might generate a burst of sales activity for filer oriented versions, but it is much more likely that object storage will evolve and eventually absorb the filer completely. One might point out that object storage is slow, but that is definitely old news ad companies like SanDisk [35] and DDN bring fast solutions to market.

Object storage has to create replicas and distribute data, which increases network traffic considerably, but this issue is being tackled and any gap will close.

There is a class of "universal" storage moving into the market. These are software or appliance products that provide file, block, and object access methods using a single box. These are Ethernet-connected solutions, which more reflects the belief that the future doesn't include FC than a lack of capability to interface to FC. Open-source leader Ceph is a universal storage package, with filer and block gateways added to a native object store API and a standard S3-compatible REST interface.

Universal storage will resolve the transition to a much simpler storage topology, with the same appliances, the same Ethernet network, and the same software, allowing *software-defined* space utilization and access methods on even a single appliance. Ceph supports data service distribution, so it could grow to be a distributable package with great flexibility.

The bottom line is that the filer is doing well, but is ultimately doomed as a free-standing device by object storage and SDS. The transition will gain momentum over the next 3 years, to the point that the majority of new installations are universal solutions on commodity hardware. Still filers do a great job, and it will be a decade or more before the last one stops spinning its disks.

SCALING TO INFINITY—OBJECT STORAGE

As a storage approach, object storage is a new kid on the block. The first serious efforts in the area began at the start of the century, with work by Carnegie-Mellon and early commercialization by Replicus. The intent was to abstract storage management from the very structured and inflexible systems then in use, which involved directory tree structures and the inability to work easily across multiple storage nodes.

In concept, object storage allows extensive metadata to be kept for any object, allowing for metadata-driven policies such as compression and tiering, and also for advanced search approaches, aimed at finding objects in very large-scale configurations. In practice, this is still embryonic, but the advent of SDS should make this a powerful feature of future storage systems.

Object storage is flexible enough to support the other access mechanisms, filer, and block-IO. Several implementations of object storage offer gateway software that presents the data as block or file storage, making possible to offer all the storage modes in a single "unified storage" package. Note that this doesn't allow block-IO access to filer data or vice versa. The access processes are too complex and mutually orthogonal to allow this. The filer and block-IO spaces are essentially large objects.

HOW OBJECT STORAGE WORKS

Object storage is a very different way of looking at storage. Much of the data we generate today moves around without ever being modifies. Examples are web pages and movies. In fact, most of the growth in data over the next few years will be in static data. With no need to alter individual blocks, static data can be treated as an entity, an object, rather than the SAN method of just looking at individual blocks.

Objects are easier to handle in huge quantities compared with blocks and also files, although the latter shares some of the whole-entity characteristics of objects. Files are typically stored in a structured tree of directories, which limits the number of files that can be stored, and more importantly retrieved again. Fig. 3.10 compares the two approaches.

Files lead to duplicate data in a system, as anyone who has looked in detail at what's stored on a filer will tell you. This can make figuring which of many copies is the most current an experience!

Object storage uses a process called hashing to create an ID for each file ingested (written) into the system. The hash is based on the name of the file and other information, which are combined using a hashing algorithm to create a unique number, which then becomes the ID for the object. This hash code determines where the data are stored in the storage pool.

Schemes for deduplication using a hash of the whole file exist, crossing the bucket boundary and deduplicating the whole storage pool, and these offer substantial space saving opportunities, but these schemes are still early in development. With this level of deduplication, all the copies of the same data would be replaced with a single copy and a list of pointers to it. For office files, for instance, this can be a huge saving of space.

Objects are stored in a flat-file system, which is usually one of the recognized Linux file systems such as ext4, BTRFS, or ZFS. There are no directory trees. All the

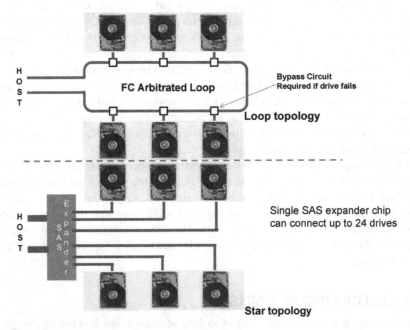

FIGURE 3.10

Drive connection in RAID arrays—Arbitrated loops and SAS extenders.

files are on the same level, indexed by their IDs. At the user level, there is a concept of "buckets", which hold objects. A typical user will have a number of buckets. The bucket name is concatenated with the object name to form the hashed ID described above, and the physical storage is in the flat file system with no concept of the layers and branches we see in a traditional file system.

The flat-storage space approach means that the size of the storage space is only limited to the number of unique hashed IDs that can exist. Hash values up to 512 bits are supported with SHA-3 (*Secure Hashing Algorithm*), so there are 2^{512} possible values, more than enough for the foreseeable future. SHA-3 guarantees that no two hash values are the same.

The hash value is used to determine where in the storage the particular object will reside. Various methods are used to do this. Ceph [36], the popular open-source object store, uses the CRUSH (*Controlled Replication Under Scalable Hashing* [37]) algorithm to determine a Placement Group of OSDs (*Object-based Storage Devices*) based on the hash value. This is deterministic, and it allows an agent in the client to know how to access the storage pool. There are other algorithms, such as Scality's Ring [38], that are used for the same purpose.

Once the placement for a given object is worked out, the data for that object are broken up into chunks (typically 64 KB each) and sent off to the members of the selected storage set. Replicas are made and sent to other storage nodes. All of this is determined by the original hash and the CRUSH or other algorithm used.

The distribution algorithms automatically spread the data over all of the available storage, keeping capacity usage and traffic loading close to level. Adding or removing nodes causes a redistribution of the storage to level it again. This is done as a background job, and may take some time to complete.

When an OSD node fails in Ceph, data from the failed OSD is instead recovered from the second or third replica of the data. A spare OSD is built with data from replicas in background. In a system with many *Placement Groups*, data are read from many, if not all of the OSDs present to speed the rebuild along. An alternative is to rebuild across existing OSDs by spreading the data evenly, as would happen if an OSD were purposefully removed.

USE CASES FOR OBJECT STORAGE

Object stores are aimed at handling whole objects, making them ideal for any data that are unchanging. Add in cases where data are changed by replacing files or objects and the stage is set for object storage to be the preferred mechanism for storing those file objects. Handling whole objects simplifies where data are placed, usually being written from where the last write ended.

Uses cases for archiving and backup fit this profile, and the original emphasis for object stores in enterprises was these use cases. Geo-dispersion of replicas added to the attraction of the approach, since it built disaster recovery into the solution for little cost. Today, public clouds using object storage are the preferred archiving solution.

For many smaller businesses, object storage provided a low-cost storage solution compared with block-IO and filers. This is especially true for companies buying compute services in the public clouds. With a good portion of their workload being rarely changed web pages, the object solution again is the cheapest pathway.

Outside of the cloud, object stores fulfill the same purposes. They are also attractive for large volumes of unchanging or slow changing data, such as the huge DNA databases of genome projects, where the data again are write-once, read-mostly.

Ironically, Big Data shares this characteristic. In the main, Big Data is written, read a number of times, and computed on, but not changed. Object stores make good key-data repositories. With large placement groups, even the very large files of *High-Performance Computing* (HPC) apps such as simulations and oil and gas geology can be dispersed over a lot of OSDs to level load the system.

Object stores are beginning to enter mainstream computing, though most primary storage is still block-IO or filer. As we move to a new tiering system with hot data in all-flash arrays and vSANs and cool data in bulk secondary storage, object storage will become the vehicle of choice for the bulk tier. This implies that the largest capacity by far will reside in object storage.

UPSIDES TO OBJECT STORAGE

Object storage is aimed at using cheap COTS components throughout. This will drive the price of object storage units to levels below home-made filers, especially as we are on the leading edge of Chinese ODMs moving en masse into the US market.

The object paradigm connects well with many use cases, and especially well with the hot all-flash/cool bulk storage tiering model. It also seems to fit SDS ideas well. Ceph, for example, is a modular design that could easily support Ethernet drives or appliances acting as OSDs, while using x64 COTS servers (or virtual instances) for functions like compression, deduplication and file replication, and erasure coding.

With ease-of-use and a simple structure even when scaled to very large levels, object storage is a low-maintenance, low-complexity storage solution well positioned for the coming data explosion.

One common thread in object-storage software is having wide-open metadata [39] capability. This allows files to be tagged heavily to ease future access. Unfortunately, operating systems are slow to change, and API definitions for metadata manipulation are a bit weak, so access-by-attribute methods have been slow to arrive.

With the coming wave of distributed data services in SDS, we should see the metadata tags used for routing objects through compressors and encrypters and such making data objects self-routing and systems more flexible. It's worth noting that, at scale, metadata searching is essential in finding objects in a flat pool that might be petabytes in size. Perhaps we need a standard taxonomy for metadata.

DOWNSIDES TO OBJECT STORAGE

One barrier to transitioning to object stores as mainstream tier 1 is the need to change applications to use REST [40] APIs instead of traditional file operations. A solution lies in having universal storage approaches, which overlay an object store with block-IO and filer gateways, but in some ways this dodges the bullet of moving to an actual object store.

The problem is that current implementations make the REST interface slow. REST is also less flexible in append and insert type operations. One issue is that adding a block of data into a stored object messes with the sequence of OSDs in the CRUSH algorithm or its equivalent. Either all the subsequent blocks have to be shuffled across OSDs or there has to be a mechanism to map an exception to the standard OSD sequence created by CRUSH or its equivalent.

Object storage has also been slow to adopt SSD and all-flash structures. It might be argued that the perception of object storage as an archiving environment drives this, but the reality may be more a performance issue. Object storage has back-end traffic that tends to saturate networks. This is one environment where faster disks don't actually help much.

The issue is the message passing involved in replicating blocks, and in recovering failed drives. Because data are dispersed over the whole drive set, there is $N \times N$ communication almost all of the time. Breaking objects down into 64-KB chunks multiplies the traffic. The process of moving these around between OSDs creates requests and statuses galore, as well as pressuring the malloc memory allocation routine no end.

There are some obvious fixes that might work. Using larger chunks will reduce messaging, as does erasure coding. Fundamentally, though, there has to be a better way to handle setting up chunk transfers. Perhaps NVMe over fabric is the answer. Creating a large, self-managed buffer scheme rather than using malloc seems like an obvious speedup, too.

Small-object handling needs finesse. With chunk sizes of 64 KB or 256 KB, a naïve system needing to write a small file could leave a lot of empty space if the object was required to have exclusive ownership of the chunk. The same is true of the last chunk of any object, which would partially fill a chunk. The fix for this is to allow more-than-one object to inhabit a chunk. The upside of this is that chunk sizes could be much larger, into the megabytes, and this would further reduce backend traffic.

OBJECT STORAGE MYTHS

Object stores don't have to be huge to be efficient. Think of them as filers on steroids. Unlike filers, however, there is a high limit to the scaling that we can get with object stores. For someone starting with a small storage farm, but planning future growth, object stores are ideal secondary storage.

The question of *using object stores as primary storage* is thornier. Many implementations of object stores were designed to match the secondary storage mission, making them low-powered HDD units. These aren't capable of a primary storage role. Today, we see companies like Coho Data offering tiered storage solutions ranging from flash-accelerated units to hybrids with SSD and HDD. The higher-performance versions of these fit the primary storage target for capability. It remains to be seen if the benefits of a single storage structure knock out block-IO.

There are considerable *differences in features and design robustness* between object-storage software stacks. Open-source products tend to be a bit slower reaching good quality levels, probably because bug-fixing isn't as much fun as feature design, especially when you are doing it for free. As an example, Ceph, considered a good open-source solution, had 7296 bugs fixed in the Kilo release, according to the release notes.

Proprietary products usually meet better quality standards earlier in life, but over time, the large user base will bring open-source into line. Linux is a great example of this!

Not all object stores are inexpensive. EMC's ATMOS priced up with traditional storage arrays, for instance. With software-only and open-source solutions having most of the same features, high-priced solutions don't appear to be winning many customers. With object stores from the start having been built around COTS gear, it's hard to make a case for proprietary unit pricing models.

HARD DRIVES

RAID arrays, as boxes of drives with SAN controllers are called, make up a large percentage of storage installations in the enterprise. Arrays can contain dozens of drives, originally using fast, but very expensive, FC drives linked on a network loop that went from drive to drive. This *"Arbitrated Loop"* had counter-rotating FC rings designed so that the failure of a drive did not block the data flow.

Today, RAID arrays use SAS or SATA protocol drives, connected via a switch board commonly called a "SAS extender", while Enterprise-class FC drives are obsolete and only sold as spares for old equipment. Two form-factors are standard— 2.5-in. diameter disks, used in notebook drives and some enterprise drives, and 3.25-in. diameter disks, used for high-capacity bulk storage drives.

Hard drives are usually classified as either enterprise or commodity consumer-class products. The enterprise-drive specifications look more robust than consumer drives, though much of the increase in measured reliability comes from never turning these drives off, which also would give a longer life to commodity drives. This is important as we move toward the use of commodity drives as the bulk storage tier in the new view of SSD/flash primary storage and HDD bulk secondary storage.

Enterprise drives are significantly more expensive than consumer drives and usually only available from the original array vendor, who, with a captive audience, could mark them up heavily. It is worth noting that the distinctions between enterprise and consumer drives are blurred in SSD, excepting PCIe-interfaced SSD, which are of very high performance.

Drives are also differentiated on rotation speed. FC drives rotated at 15,000 rpm to reduce latency, but this required expensive components and complicated cabinet design to avoid vibration problems. Hard drives today are mainly 7200 or 5400 rpm for bulk-storage drives. The lower speed drives use less power, which fits a profile for "cold" storage of archived data.

RPM	Latency mSEC	Av. Seek mSEC	IOPS	Optimized IOPS
15,000	2	4.6	150	300
7,200	4.2	8	82	164
5,400	5.6	10	64	128

FIGURE 3.11

IOPS per drive.

The difference in rotation speeds impacts access latency. When all we had were hard drives, 15,000 rpm drives were roughly twice as fast as 7200 rpm drive, but access latencies were still in the 5–7 ms range. Fig. 3.11 shows the IOs per second (IOPS) for each type of hard drive and compares them with SSD.

The advent of serial storage interfaces (SAS/SATA) and the resulting smarter drives allowed some steps to be taken to speed up access. Buffering was added, and "ladder" seek optimization allowed the time to move to the next track to be reduced, via schemes that took a stack of commands and executed them in the optimum order on the drive to maximize IOPS (the total number of read and write IO operations that a drive or appliance can deliver per second). The schemes are called "native command queuing" on SATA drives and "tagged command queuing" on SAS drives.

The way optimization is achieved is that the drive estimates the time to reach the start of transfer for all the commands in the queue (typically up to 32) and chooses the sequence of commands that will complete all the commands in the shortest time. Tag queueing also allows the host to specify that certain commands must process in sequence relative to all the other commands, though this is of limited use. The net of all this was still milliseconds of latency, compared with a few tens of microseconds with even the slowest SSD, and an upper limit of 300 IOPS was the best achievable, using 15,000 rpm drives.

The 15,000 rpm drives are fading away fast, but 10,000 rpm drives are still available today, though the market that all of the enterprise and fast rotation drives serviced is being rapidly replaced by SSD. The SSD vendors project that they will achieve capacity parity with bulk drives in 2016 and price parity in 2017, which will cause the HDD to rapidly lose market share to this new 3D NAND flash technology.

HOW HARD DRIVES WORK

Hard drives are built around a set of spinning disks. Each disk is coated with a magnetic material and is polished to a very high degree of smoothness. This is because a recording head flies within a couple of microinches of the surface, and any roughness would destroy it.

The heads are fitted to actuator arms that are moved in and out by a specially designed servo-motor. The heads all move together, to simplify the design. The servo-motor can position the head to microinch accuracy (Fig. 3.12).

FIGURE 3.12

Hard disk drive.

Source: Wikicommons

When a drive is built tracks are written using a special servowriter drive where the positioning is controlled externally. The tracks that are laid down allow the servomotor electronics to center the head over the track. Sector labels written on the track identify the track and the block number on the track.

Subsequent operations use a coarse seek to place the head roughly in the right position and then the head settles on track using the label data and the fine mode of the servo. Seeks use a fast acceleration and a highly damped deceleration to optimize the time to change tracks.

Each track holds as much as a few megabytes of data, and track density can be very high on high capacity drives. When a head arrives on track, it is often not over the data to be read or written. It has to wait for disk rotation, and that's why the time to access data is so long. Typically, an access is a combination of seek time, rotation time and transfer time. Seek time varies between drives, with enterprise drives being a bit faster, simply because they usually have lower capacity, due to fewer disks and heads. It's just mechanics—lighter weights can move faster with the same force applied.

The average access time is computed as the average seek measured over all possible seeks plus the average latency, and the time to transfer a block. This is often inverted to give the number of random IOPS a drive can achieve. This number ranges from 120 to around 250 IOPS today, which is very small compared to SSD and hasn't changed much in many years.

For decades, file systems have broken their IO streams into 64-KB to 256-KB chunks, aiming to allow all processes a fair share of IO time. Even sequential IO would look like a set of random IOs. In early drives there wasn't enough speed in the various processors in the system to allow the drive to do contiguous operations, so each 64-KB chunk meant a full rotation of the disk, making things pretty slow.

Frankly, the chunk size was empirically chosen back then and didn't keep up with the change in track length or transfer speed of the drives. The small IO size increased the number of IOs way beyond what it should have been.

Once FC, SAS, and SATA drives hit the market, IOs could be queued up to 32 deep in the drive while the drive had data buffers and its software had the ability to join contiguous IOs into a single IO for better efficiency. These drives also address the positioning latencies by optimizing the pattern of operations to take the minimum time. Even so, 300 IOPS is about the limit for today's 10,000 rpm drive.

All drives today have a private segment of storage for maintenance data, and for replacements for damaged blocks. Disks can have thousands of flaws, but the drive takes this in stride, and recovery is transparent to the user. These flaws, and the fact that they increase over time, are the reason for needing RAID or other data integrity protection.

When a drive is first built, it is scanned a number of times using different track patterns to detect flaws in blocks. These are logged to a table in the private space and the block is marked as flawed. A new block is allocated, either from spare blocks specifically for that purpose on each track, or if these run out, from blocks in the private space.

In operation, when a read error occurs, the drive rereads the data as many as 100 times, attempting to get a clean transfer. Often, the error is an electrical or mechanical transient and the reread works. If the block can't be read, it is flagged as a new failure. A rapid increase in unrecoverable errors signifies the impending failure of the drive, being usually due to head damage or contamination on a large scale. There is technology to warn of this, allowing data to be moved to another drive, but it is possible that the time from warning to disaster is too short to do this. If so, the option is to use RAID or replicas, or a backup, to recover the data to a spare drive.

SAS AND SATA

A wise observer might ask the question, "Why do you have two interfaces doing the same job?" It's a good question. We have to go back to the origination of SCSI to understand the rules of the game. When SCSI first came to market, it was intended as a solution for external 25-m links, and had electronics designed for that purpose. The arrival of 8-in. internal hard drives for servers happened a year or so later, and it quickly became clear that a cheaper solution made sense, so SCSI split into two camps, one aiming at the enterprise and one aiming at the desktop computer.

Moving forward from the mid-1980s to 1999, SCSI evolved into serial links for drive interfaces and a formal split ensued, with SAS aiming for enterprises and SATA focused on the consumer market. SAS has a more complex command structure, but the two protocols share many things. Electrically, they are identical, which proved advantageous when designing switches, since it made it possible to connect SATA drives and tunnel SATA data through the SAS protocol, using the aptly named SATA Tunneling Protocol (STP) to do so.

Complicating things, Intel threw support for SATA into its motherboard chipsets, while SAS needed a separate controller. This has since been fixed, but for a while,

SATA *had* to exist. The result is we ended up with motherboards with various combinations of SAS and SATA ports, and adapters for SAS internal connections.

So do we still need two interfaces? The short answer is no! It looks like the SSD is the clear winner against the HDD. SSDs typically use a SATA interface, though there are some performance drives that use SAS. A new interface is starting to take over the performance SSD space. This is PCIe with the NVMe protocol, which is much faster than both the SCSI-based SAS and SATA. The SATA *Special Interest Group* (SIG) saw the writing on the wall and formed a joint effort to merge the electronics, with the result that drives are coming to market with a single SATA-Express [41] connector combining SATA and PCI/NVMe, together with host side electronics that can detect which protocol they are dealing with. In that sense, they've combined the two interface approach into a single interface and also sunk SAS in the process.

As of the time of writing a similar SAS+PCIe/NVMe effort was underway, but the SATA-Express solution seems to have achieved mainstream status, making the SAS idea moot.

UPSIDES TO HARD DRIVES

Manufacturing hard drives is a well-understood science and capacity for a huge volume of production exists, mainly in Thailand and Malaysia. Flash-memory capacity is still building and the level that could replace hard drives won't be reached until 2017 or perhaps a year or two later.

The technology is well understood and well characterized. Data integrity and drive reliability are generally well understood. There are no real surprises!

Drive capacity is amazingly cheap. The original drives cost as much as US\$50,000 for just a few Megabytes, while today's commodity drives average \$30 at the 1TB entry level, and offer less than \$30/GB in bigger capacities.

DOWNSIDES TO HARD DRIVES

The primary hit that hard drives take today is that they are slow, really slow. At 150 IOPS for fast 7200 rpm drive, the HDD is typically 1% of the performance of a single solid-state drive. That gap is hard to offset by saying that hard drives are much cheaper than SSD.

Drives use 9–15 W of power, which is a lot in today's "green-seeking" society. Drives are heavy, too. Given all of this, the only thing really holding SSD back from capturing the whole market is capacity per drive, and 3D NAND has fixed that.

Moreover, SSD capacities are now bigger than HDDs can achieve and still growing. These huge drives are in the small 2.5-in. footprint, too, which means two can fit in the same space as a lower capacity 3.5-in. HDD.

HARD DRIVE MYTHS

There are many myths built up around drive *reliability and durability*. The belief in quality organizations, both on the vendor and user side, is that the drives follow what is called the "bathtub" curve [42] of reliability. In a nutshell, this means that the failure rate is high at the start of use for a drive, then rapidly drops for the next 6–8 years, and begins to increase as drive wear becomes the dominant factor.

An implication of this view is that those drive failures occurring in mid-life are random and infrequent, which impacts the durability of data in RAID arrays. Anything that accelerates failure can reduce data integrity dramatically. The problem is that the bathtub curve is a good model [43] except when there are latent design defects or poor component controls that cause a "cohort" of drives built around the same date to be flaky.

When a cohort of drives begins to fail at a high rate, the chances of more than a single drive in a RAID set failing balloons are there, placing data at risk. *Annual Failure Rates* (AFR) as high as 40% have been seen on batches of 3-yr old drives, so this is a real but rare phenomenon. Anyone with lots of hard drives needs to track failure rates [44] against drive installation date and watch for this pattern. Even RAID 6 would have an exposure with a 40% AFR.

Another reliability myth, which was touched on above, is that enterprise drives are more reliable than consumer drives when used in servers. The evidence tends to bust this myth.

Data integrity numbers for enterprise drives tend to be better than for consumer drives, usually by a factor of 10 in UBE (*Unrecoverable Bit Error*) rate specifications. The reason is not that the consumer drives are poorer in quality. It is simply that consumer drives have much more data typically than an enterprise drive. For example, a 10,000-rpm drive with 1 TB is the top of the line for enterprise drives, compared with 8 TB for consumer drives.

Assuming the disks had the same physical flaws, the number of blocks affected would be much higher on the consumer drive, both from the number of blocks lying over a typical error, and from the small size of the much denser recording tracks being affected by smaller but more numerous flaws. In other words, this is FUD (*Fear, Uncertainty and Doubt!*) and another busted myth.

More complex myths hinge around the SAS versus SATA interface [45] question. SAS enterprise drives often have dual SAS ports, which allow the connection of the drive to two different controllers via two independent SAS extender cards. The idea is that if anything in the SAS link fails, one can switch automatically to the other link. This active–active model is a selling point for SAS, though the logical extension is an expensive drive (rather than commodity) and a proprietary cabling and controller scheme.

In reality, the extra port shares electronics with the first port, since both are controlled by the same ASIC. There's a single small chip, the PHY or Physical Interface driver chip, between that ASIC and the port connector. That's not much that can go wrong, and likely most of the failures would be in the ASIC, killing the drive anyway! Now one could argue that there's an extra switch in a redundant architecture, but that's just one ASIC, too. The bottom line is that dual porting is more a safety blanket than a real benefit. It will become moot as we move to just using hard drives for bulk storage, since these will be SATA, but there are rumblings of "enterprise SATA" drives (with suitable upward adjustments in prices!).

Is SAS faster than SATA? SAS drives can have larger command queues, which might give them a slight edge. Raw data rates are identically and both interfaces use the same PHY electronics and transmission schemes, so there's no advantage there. SAS is full-duplex in operation while SATA is half-duplex, but there aren't any SAS commands that take advantage of this, so this is one for the spinmeisters! The bottom line is that there isn't much to choose between the interfaces, especially in array usage.

SAS drives are quoted with better *Uncorrectable Bit Error Rates* (UBER) than SATA drives (10^{16} versus 10^{15} bits transferred per error). That sounds important, but RAID and other, better, protection schemes are designed to cope with errors like this. In reality, this number doesn't matter.

A final myth is that an HDD is cheaper than an SSD [46]. Usually, when this is said the commentator is comparing a $30/TB commodity bulk drive to the much faster SSD. This isn't even a fair comparison, since it's about as sensible as lining up a golf-cart and a Ferrari and then talking about relative specs! The best comparison ought to be between an enterprise drive and the SSD which is replacing it. There SSDs have a 2 to 1 edge over the HDD, with $250 versus $500 distributor pricing (Of course, your favorite array vendor may have huge markups on SSD that make them cost several thousand dollars more than that HDD!). In 2017, however, we should be able to make the comparison with a commodity bulk drive and find that SSD wins on price there, too, at least in distribution.

THE SOLID-STATE REVOLUTION

In 2007, after 40 years of the spinning hard drive reigning supreme in storage, the first flash memory SSD appeared on the scene. It had tremendous promise—high reliability, ultrafast access (about 4000 IOPS in those first units), low power and no mechanical constraints such as vibration protection.

It took around 2 years to get the design right and characterize the product. It became clear that NAND flash had a wear-out problem. The number of write operations on a given chip was finite. Even with that, there were applications such as rugged computers where SSD made sense.

Since then, we moved forward on many fronts. SSD are approaching the same capacity as hard drives, well into the terabyte range, while performance is typically near 100x that of that early SSD, and 3000x the performance of hard drives.

This is a game-changer, though an industry with such a long history of designing for hard drives is very slow to change. We still use the same form factors. Interfaces are just beginning to evolve to take advantage of the much faster operations, and software is still living in the slow-IO past.

New ideas have appeared, with all-flash specialized form factor arrays creating IO rates in the millions of IOPS range. Specialized drives are reaching 2 million IOPS using the new PCIe/NVMe interface. The enterprise hard drive is obsolete and only a few current models still ship. RAID arrays are a casualty. They couldn't keep up with SSD data rates—controllers could only service four to six drives—and so new appliance structures and software approaches such as "SDS" are entering the market.

It's fair to say that SSD was the trigger for the Storage Revolution, and storage will never be the same again.

HOW DO FLASH AND SSD WORK?

SSD use NAND flash memory chips. These chips have millions of addressable "cells" that are designed to trap electrons—think of them as tiny bottles (in geek-speak, floating gates) that have an inlet with a valve transistor and a way to measure how much charge is contained in them. All of the cells start off drained of charge. When a controller wants to load up the cell with data it opens the inlet transistor to let a charge enter the cell. The charge remains there in an almost leak-proof state. The result is that cells with no charge can denote a one state and those with a charge denote a 0-state (Fig. 3.13).

Electrically, NAND flash is a sophisticated mixture of digital and analog electronics. Fig. 3.14 shows how a typical storage cell is configured. The key is the floating gate used to trap electrons for very long timeframes, perhaps into decades. The NAND transistor design supports "writing" to the floating gate by choosing suitable voltage for the wordline and bitline. Some of the electrons flowing across the transistor tunnel into the floating gate and remain there when voltage is removed.

NAND flash cells are connected in a chain, complicating how reading is done. The chain is used to keep the cell to a single transistor thus increasing chip capacity. Reading involves placing a vREAD voltage on all the wordlines in a page, with the wordline needing to be read at an even lower voltage. vREAD turns on all the

FIGURE 3.13

SSD with the covers off.

Source: Wikicommons

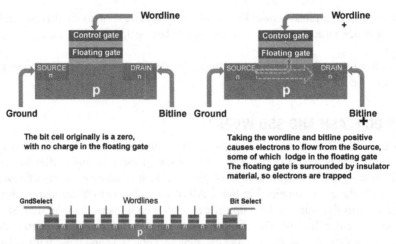

Real-world NAND devices have a set of these transistors connected in series, reducing the number of transistors needed and so increasing capacity

FIGURE 3.14

How a flash drive works.

transistors in the chain, irrespective of whether a 1 or 0 is stored, but the lower voltage on the desired wordline allows the electrons stored in the floating gate to determine if the cell conducts or not.

Erasure of all those zeroes requires the flash to be treated to a process called tunnel release, where a high negative voltage is applied to the wordline, pushing out the electrons stored in the floating gate. This is done in pages, typically of two or more megabytes at a time, which is one of the uniquenesses of flash. Because erasure on a single block of data is not possible, another mechanism is used to create an empty block ready for writing data. The address pointer for the block is changed to point to an empty block inside a chunk that has been erased previously. The discarded block is left until enough of the blocks in its page are discards, at which point the remaining data is moved and the page is erased, clearing any data, and made part of the empty free space pool.

Internal architectures of SSD are quite complex. Chips and segments of chips are treated almost as disk drives in a RAID-like structure using Reed-Solomon codes to protect against bit errors. This type of protection is essential, since flash is prone to higher levels of errors as it gets written many times, as well as random bit errors due to electronic noise. This approach also protects against whole die or segments failing, which extends the MTBF of flash considerably.

The parallelism of the flash devices improves speed, but needs a sophisticated controller to act as the traffic cop and move data to the right places. Part of this controller is a RAM buffer, which speeds up write operations, provides caching for reads and stores the block map while in operation. When power is lost, this map is stored to a space in the flash, or else a persistent memory class is used to protect this key data.

IMPROVING FLASH CAPACITY

To improve capacity, a number of approaches are used. Because the bit sensor is detecting the level of charge in the cell, it is possible to store more than 1 bit in the cell. 2 binary bits earn the flash device the title of "MultiLevel-Cell" or MLC, which is the most common flash configuration at this time. 3 bits (TLC) are also storable, but this is a more difficult technology to build reliably, since the voltage levels between each of the eight storable states become very close. Single-level cells are still the most robust electrically, but chip density suffers accordingly.

Another approach commonly used in SSD is to stack the memory devices on top of each other using special sockets. This adds some expense and takes space too. More recently, a 3D wafer fabrication approach allows 32 or even more layers of NAND cells to be built on the same wafer. While this increases wafer processing time and cost considerably, the savings over any of the other approaches is substantial. Moreover, economics allow reuse of older fab facilities at a larger "node" level, since capacity can be realized by adding layers rather than by shrinking transistor size. The larger node level improves yield tremendously.

All the vendors are moving to the 3D process. It allows capital to be diverted to building less expensive facilities as well as bringing older fabs back into service. The net result is a rapid expansion of SSD capacity and a dramatic reduction in price.

Predictions of price and capacity parity between SSD and hard drives in the 2017 timeframe are based on 3D NAND flash.

DELETION PROBLEMS IN FLASH

When you delete a block on a hard drive, the data still remain in the block, but the pointers to it in the file system are disconnected and it is moved to the free pool. If you want to clear the data you do a secure erase, which overwrites the data pattern and makes the data unreadable.

That process won't work with flash devices. When a block is written in flash, the old block still remains with its data unchanged. All that is achieved with a secure erase is to create seven or eight blocks labeled as deleted, but containing the original data and the overwrite patterns.

These blocks are not visible to applications, but utilities and operating systems can easily read them, which raises an issue in a multi-tenancy environment using hypervisors, which have many copies of operating systems. It also creates an issue for commercial disposition of old SSD. They either have to be completely written a couple of times, or else incinerated.

PACKAGING FLASH

Today, NAND flash comes in a number of packages. AT the top of the line, we see large PCIe daughter-boards with 4–8 TB capacity and millions of IOPS. These were pioneered by Fusion-IO, now part of SanDisk, but now are available from many vendors. Challenging these are PCIe drives in a standard 3.5-in. form factor. With the advent of the SATA-Express interface, these drives are taking market share from the PCIe cards, since they are more consistent in use with drive storage.

Most of the lower performance drives are in 3.5-in. or 2.5-in. form factors, though a module format exists. There are some proprietary formats, too. A new standard that is gaining interest is packaging of flash in a memory DIMM. In early adoption, there are at least two competing architectures, aiming at different parts of the market.

THE NVME REVOLUTION

Can you have back to back revolutions? NVMe is upstaging SSD a bit. This is a new type of interface protocol, designed to operate directly over PCIe links and take advantage of their DMA capability to speed up IO. By using a looped queue system with aggregated interrupts, NVMe reduces the time spent making decisions and state-swapping in the host. It also bypasses the creaky old SCSI stack with its many layers of indirection.

NVMe is turning up on PCIe flash cards and on high-end SSD drives. In both cases, performance is very good, with random IOPS in the million-plus range being achieved. NVMe looks to be a long-term wine in storage, with the adoption of a hybrid SATA-express connection scheme that allows SATA drives and PCIe-NVMe drives to share the same interface plug on motherboards and adapters. There is also a move in SNIA to create a longer-haul fabric version of NVMe.

NVMe stack and beyond is covered in much more detail in Chapter 4, Section 6.

UPSIDES OF FLASH

Flash and SSD units are lightning fast compared with disk drives. They wipe out three decades of stagnation in IOPS. The potential impact to computers is tremendous, though apps written around slow HDD tend not to reach their full potential. A rewrite may be needed in some areas of the app.

We are transitioning rapidly toward a two-tier model where flash and SSD form the top tier of storage and are used for all the hot data. Cool and cold data are stored on HDD arrays or object storage, with the latter expected to be the winner as current gear is replaced.

SSD are more reliable than hard drives. Intrinsically, solid-state solutions are more robust than mechanical assemblies rotating at high speed with components relying on microinch gaps. This is particularly noticeable in shock and vibration specifications as well as ambient temperature limits. Most SSD are ratable for ruggedized use, while HDD struggle with high temperature when ambients reach 45°C. HDD also need protection against rotational vibration, where multiple drives seeking interact with each other to stress the servo electronics and cause data errors. This isn't an issue with the SSD.

The combination of ruggedness and high-temperature operation means that SSD enclosures will be much cheaper to make, drives can be stacked closer together, and systems can be run at 50°C ambient with a little care in design. The impact of this last item is that we will see the end of chilled air datacenters, with major savings in power and equipment costs.

SSD/flash allows new software/system approaches to be built. We see analytics engines that chomp data at fantastic rates, where PCIe drives are used to keep up. All-flash arrays overcome VDI boot storms, though Docker and similar containerization approaches may make that moot in a year or so.

Flash units save in operating power, which becomes significant as we look at the billions of HDD installed and figure that we'll save 12 Watts each on average by replacing them with SSD. There are perhaps 5 billion drives running in total and 12 W is equivalent to 96 KWh per year, so the saving is around 500 billion KWh, or more than 25 billion dollars in power annually!

DOWNSIDES OF FLASH

Many applications are designed for slow HDD. IO is often single-threaded, and designed to wait for each individual IO to complete. It takes a bit of experience to speed IO up, and this is yet another reason for moving on past legacy applications.

The problem exists in operating systems too. Functions such as disconnecting from the IO system and switching to another application were fine when it took 20 ms on average to get a response from storage, but SSD can get down into the 5-μs range, making operating systems sound a bit creaky. Operating systems also struggle to keep up with the interrupt rates SSD and flash drives generate.

Generally, SSD and flash drives are a poor match to SAS and SATA drive interfaces. Designed for lower operating rates, these interfaces generate to many messages around the actual data payload and are out of balance with performance needs for Tier-1 fast storage.

The wear-out issue is mostly behind us. We still have to be careful not to use a low-endurance drive in a high-write-rate environment, but the good news is that there are drives with adequate performance for the most demanding loads available now. These are dropping rapidly in price due to 3D NAND reaching market, while 3D NAND uses larger "process nodes," which increases durability of the devices, so the wear-out issue is effectively behind us.

The deletion problems of flash still need work, otherwise security could be compromised both on drive disposal and on usage as local instance storage in the cloud. SNIA has a working group addressing the issue and a solution will be forthcoming.

MYTHS OF FLASH AND SSD

Write Wear-Out

The most important SSD myth is the wear-out issue [47]. This problem was recognized early in SSD development, before the first drives reached market and caused a concerted development effort by SSD controller and flash device vendors to extend wear life.

Flash has an inherent physics problem. Repeated writing makes the cell leaky and unable to retain data. This is a problem within relatively few write cycles, especially with higher bit count cells. A good deal of work to prevent this being an issue has made the problem mainly a historical foot note, though it limits the use of TLC even today. There is also a much less serious problem with leakage on reading.

One result of the wear-out problem is that drives are overprovisioned. A typical drive might have as much as 300% extra space hidden away from applications. At any time, this will be a pool of erased superblocks plus any unerased superblocks, plus "deleted" or "overwritten" blocks scattered across the whole pool of memory.

Adding extra blocks gave enough headroom for practical operations and this was adopted before the first SSD hit the market. Controller improvements allowed wear life to be stretched out and we now see even 1 TB consumer drives with lifetimes of 70-plus complete writes. My system, for example, saves around 1 GB per day, making me a heavy user. 70-TB write capability gives me 70,000 days (200 Years) of writing before the drive begins to croak, which is plenty good enough.

Server-class drives have lives from 2 to 10× this level, so for all but a few corner cases, wear-out is no longer an issue.

The wear-out problem was the main FUD leveled at SSD for the first few years in the market. It was poorly understood and often overblown for effect, but in hindsight it slowed market acceptance of a much faster memory solution by a couple of years.

HDD is Way Cheaper Than Flash

The argument goes that flash memory is as much as five times faster than HDD, but this is a case of Ferraris versus golf-carts and isn't a fair comparison. In reality, SSDs have been as cheap as enterprise hard-drives for two or three years. This is a fairer comparison than matching SSDs against bulk consumer drives. (Comparing an enterprise HDD to a consumer HDD would get HDD salesmen hot and flustered!)

This was the case up to the start of 2014. By 2015, SSD pricing was below enterprise drives and the advent of 3D NAND is bringing prices down further. Effectively, the enterprise HDD is dead. Why would you buy a family sedan when a BMW is cheaper?

HDD is about to get a real drubbing on price. Vendors hit the market in 2015 with SSD equaling or exceeding bulk drive capacities and these will be in a price free-fall during 2016. By 2017 we should see SATA SSDs at price parity with bulk hard drives, while the cost of mid-range server SSD will not be much higher. This will cause a massive transition to flash across the board.

Not Enough Foundries

With the advent of 3D flash memory, the SSD vendors are projecting that they'll overtake HDD in capacity in 2016 and that price parity will occur in 2017. A rebuttal of this often is that there isn't enough foundry capacity worldwide to make all the flash needed, while the HDD vendors are already geared up.

This is way oversimplistic as a view, and perhaps a bit disingenuous. 3D NAND has a silent pay-back. Many older foundry setups can be turned back on to produce 3D NAND devices, while using larger "nodes" will increase yield dramatically. Add in capacity expansion planned over the next few years, and there will be enough flash to kill the HDD.

Meanwhile, the HDD guys don't get a free ride. The two hot HDD technologies are helium-filled drives and shingled recording. Both of these need more capital investment to match the new manufacturing processes used, while higher track and bit densities also impact facilities. Even the testers need to change, with Ethernet interfaces on the rise instead of traditional SATA.

Not Enterprise-Ready

The idea that SSD are somehow not enterprise-ready surfaces regularly, often in commentary on all-flash arrays versus hybrid type arrays. In large part, this is because the SSD companies tend to ignore the decades-old stratification of the HDD industry. We are accustomed to enterprise and consumer hard drives, but there is a much less crisp boundary between classes, almost to the point that they overlap to a great extent.

The distinction in the HDD world has always been artificial. It is a way to charge much more for a drive by adding "features", using SAS versus SATA, having dual-port interfaces and such, and careful specsmanship on reliability figures.

Until recently, most of the SSD vendors were new to storage drives. Perhaps this has led to the blurring of categories, but it is worth asking if "enterprise" SSD really exist. The answer is more that there are fast and really fast drives today. "Fast" includes all of the SATA drives and many of the relatively few SAS drives made, while "really fast" is mostly PCIe or SATA-e territory, where IOPS range from half a million and up.

Within any drive type, we see ranges of wear-life or use case descriptions as recommendations. These are much better guides than the old class system. You do have to characterize your write patterns a bit, but many use cases that would have needed "enterprise" HDD can be serviced by lower-priced drives. A major example is all cold storage usage. The write rate is low, because data is written once and rarely rewritten. Facebook, for example, is looking at the least reliable multicell NAND, consumer TLC, because it is cheap and fits the use case model.

PCIe drives are still expensive, but we are yet to see the effect of SATA-e on the market. If this becomes ubiquitous, there is a good chance that lower-priced PCIe drives will be a mainstream solution.

THE FUTURE OF FLASH AND SSD

With flash-based technology just hitting its stride, why talk about "futures"? There is a desire to get faster and closer to the system DRAM, avoiding the IO bottlenecks and latency delays that plague coding. To put this in perspective, comparisons of before and after performance moving standard apps like Oracle to an all-memory-based solution show speedup of as much as 150×.

This needed a code rewrite and some expert tuning, but it highlights the potential for systems if the persistent storage got closer to DRAM. *This* is the biggest threat to flash on the horizon. Several nascent technologies are faster than flash. These are *resistive RAM memory* (Re-RAM), spintronic memory and *phase-change memory* (PCM). These are discussed in Chapter 14.

None of the new technologies are quite ready for prime time. There are early units being tested and characterized, but we are at least a year from a useful product. At that point any competitor has to break into a market that is dominated by a rapidly growing, heavily capitalized competitor. Moreover, the use case and packaging technologies will be different (PCM looks like it would be best used as slow, bulk, persistent DIMM DRAM, for example).

Flash-based storage looks like it will be around for a good many years. We can expect it to evolve, especially in packaging approaches, such as the NVDIMM approach of packaging flash on a DIMM and using the memory bus as an interface. Longer term, say in 2017, it looks to have a home in the Hybrid Memory Cube architecture for next-generation DRAM packaging (See Chapter 13). Flash speeds will change how computing systems are configured, and will necessitate rewriting of apps to get the best performance, but this is a small price to pay for the offset in system costs and the increase in business agility that speed represents.

RDMA—THE IMPACT OF ALL-FLASH AND HYBRID ARRAYS

RDMA is a concept that allows two computers to share memory spaces over networks. The idea is to have one computer send packets of data directly into application buffers in another, so bypassing layers of protocol stacks and complicated buffer shuffling.

First implemented in *InfiniBand* (IB) [48], the idea of RDMA has spread to Ethernet, where two standards are currently vying for leadership as the industry-preferred solution. These are RoCE (*RDMA over Converged Ethernet*) [49] and iWARP (*Internet Wide Area RDMA Protocol*) [50].

IB has by far and away the largest installed base of RDMA connections, with first installations in 1999. iWARP was standardized in 2007, though first shipping a year or so earlier, while RoCE is new, surfacing in 2013.

The RDMA products have sold into niche markets, in part because the cost of NICs and switches has been relatively high, but also because InfiniBand required its own support expertise. Each protocol excites a high level of partisan support, though the operational differences tend to weigh against each other to cancel out advantage.

HOW RDMA WORKS

RDMA is a memory to memory protocol. The end-points involved set up a session where each defines blocks of its memory for the other to write to or read from. When an end-point is ready to write data it packages up the data with information identifying the memory addresses to be written. The NIC pulls the data directly from the source's memory and sends it through the network. The receiving NIC moves the data directly into the destination addresses (see Fig. 3.15).

Typically, the memory spaces involved are inside applications, allowing all of the normal stacks to be bypassed. This maximizes transfer speed and minimizes latency. The data passed can be short messages, via a *Message-Passing Interface* (MPI) or

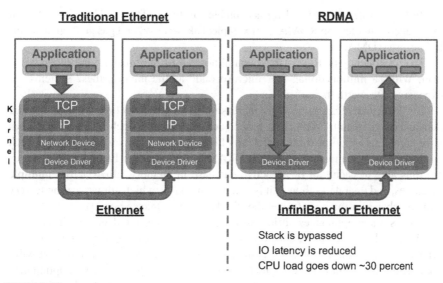

FIGURE 3.15

RDMA in operation.

storage data blocks or other longer packets of data. Intrinsically, RDMA does not notify the receiving node of the transfer, so another mechanism is required to do that.

In many ways, RDMA is a simple concept, but the devil is in the details, and very fast NIC chips are needed to keep track of addresses etc., putting price points up and limiting the number of vendors in the market.

RDMA reduces latency tremendously, by both removing a complex communication stack and by reducing the message passing associated with transfers. IB claimed that its switches were faster than Ethernet switches, but this gap has closed and the latencies achievable are close for all protocols, though IB may still have a small edge.

Electrically, IB and Ethernet have converged to be much the same. Using the same PHY elements to drive the lines, and similar signaling schemes, all of the implementations offer the same line speed options. In fact, one major IB vendor offers chipsets that can drive either IB or Ethernet.

Likely this alignment of the protocols will continue into the future, at least for a couple more generations, but the advent of inexpensive, but faster, Ethernet solutions probably means that IB will be sidelined in a few years in favor of Ethernet RDMA.

Today, speeds of 40 and 56 Gbps are available (56 GbE is not a standard speed, however). 100 Gbps product is to be available in 2016. IBM and other mainframe makers have used a 12-lane variant of IB for internal interconnect.

USE CASES FOR RDMA

RDMA is a favored interconnect in HPC, where it is seen speeding nuclear bomb simulations, complex fluid dynamics calculations and such where very fast interlinking of clustered systems is critical for acceptable run times. The US National Labs run their supercomputers on RDMA, for example. Likewise, oil and gas geological simulations use RDMA.

The low latency of RDMA has won almost all of the financial trading systems over. With "a million dollars per microsecond" as the mantra, these systems are expensive, but worth their cost.

Big-Data analytics solutions are increasingly using RDMA links to load in stored data and output results. With GPU-based parallel number-crunching, these machines have voracious appetites for data. RDMA links the servers to very fast storage, such as all-flash arrays, and also allows the DRAM in the system to be pooled. Databases are thus able to cache all of an active database in memory, albeit across multiple machines, and operate as though it is a unified memory, which allows scaling to very large databases in-memory (remember the 150× performance boost!)

With storage appliances shrinking in size due to the rapid growth in capacity per drive and the need to balance the compute power of the appliance with the SSD drives in it, the number of LAN connections is physically limited. Using 40-GbE connections is common, but demand for bandwidth may make RDMA an option here too. The driving force for this would be an extension of Intel's motherboard chipset Ethernet capability to support RDMA transfer.

COMPARISON OF INFINIBAND, IWARP, AND ROCE

iWARP uses standard Ethernet link systems and can be routed, which simplifies large-scale cluster operation. IB has its own ecosystem, while RoCE uses Converged Ethernet, which requires expensive switches.

Software-Defined Networking will give iWARP an unfair advantage, since iWARP can live with standard Ethernet gear and is easy to scale.

UPSIDES OF RDMA

As we've said above high transfer efficiency and low latency make RDMA attractive in a niche set of applications. Industry support has created interfaces to the RDMA system that mimic standard non-RDMA LAN operations as much as possible. An example is a Sockets interface.

Latency tends to be much more predictable with RDMA. Usually, all values of latency will fall in a tight band. This can be very important in HPC, where the whole cluster is tuned together. In the financial arena, knowing that latency will not exceed the average by much is a major plus, since "microseconds cost million".

DOWNSIDES OF RDMA

Applications need to be tuned to RDMA to get the best performance. Program flows are very different if data is accessible in just a few microseconds versus the milliseconds seen in standard Ethernet.

RDMA is an advanced form of communication, which adds to the support skills burden. This is especially true of IB, since a large installation will require additional staff just for IB support. RoCE has some of these problems. It is reportedly difficult to configure, laying extra requirements on the Ethernet substructure in which it resides.

Overall, RDMA adds cost to a cluster. NICs work out at about $150 per port for 10-GB iWARP Ethernet, while the cost of the same function in the motherboard chipset (10 GbE without RDMA) is perhaps $10. RoCE forces the use of CE switches, which more than double switch port costs, and IB is a separate infrastructure with pricing similar to RoCE.

THE FUTURE OF RDMA

RDMA usage will tend to expand with the growth in Big-Data analytics and the expansion of HPC-on-Demand in the cloud. We are just beginning to see HPC virtualization being offered as a service billable by the hour. Similarly, we are seeing graphics processing and other compute-intense applications move to the service model. In all of these cases, RDMA has a place in tuning performance. The issue will be port cost and support complexity, and here iWARP has a distinct edge.

As we move to all-flash/SSD storage over the next few years, and as hard drives go away, we can expect the storage appliance to become desperate for the fastest network bandwidth. RDMA will certainly help this along and one could make a case for pervasive use of RDMA—for iWARP, at least, there are no major operational negatives.

RDMA is likely to appear in photonic interfaces as a way to best match their very high speed. Once we begin to build clusters around 100 Gbe, we'll begin to look for ways to simplify the network traffic and reduce CPU overhead, with RDMA being a good solution for both issues. Photonics, in the form of silicon devices able to be fabricated as part of a CMOS chip, hold tremendous promise as a future interconnect scheme both for chip-to-chip communications and between appliances or servers.

OPTIMIZING THE DATACENTER

With so much change occurring in IT, planning a direction is challenging. IDC and Gartner, who love to package IT into discrete areas, try to describe storage networking in terms of data tiers. In current thought, we have two tiers of storage. Primary storage is the networked storage nearest the server, containing the hot data, while secondary storage is the bulk storage tier, using cheap commodity drives with large capacity. Cloud is the cold storage tier for offsite, disaster protection. This replaces tape in older tiering schemes.

This tiering scheme is replacing the older worldview with "enterprise" SAS or FC disks as primary storage and "nearline" or "enterprise SATA" disk drives as bulk storage. There are some flavors of the tiering concept, with DRAM as the pinnacle, or with NVDIMM as the top persistent storage tier, but these overcomplicate things and are not generally agreed to, anyway.

Unfortunately, these neat tiering schemes suffer from confusion when it comes to details. Primary storage today can consist of all-flash arrays, hybrid RAID arrays (or filers) with a mix of a few SSD and a lot of disk drives, or all-SSD appliances. Secondary storage can consist of object stores, filers or even re-purposed RAID arrays.

SOME USE CASES

I'm Running Out of Storage Space!

With the growth of data faced by IT, what is the best answer to the need for more space. The answer will depend on whose gear you currently have, but there are some factors to be considered first. Storage is seeing a number of major transitions. Prices are falling due to whiteboxes, open-source software and a move to COTS appliance hardware and cheap drives. Technology is shifting to solid-state, with prices rapidly dropping and performance soaring.

These are incentives to eke out the existing installations for another year or two, until directions stabilize and the new approaches are solid and trustable. The obvious solution is to add compression to the storage farm. This can be done with boxes that are placed in the SAN between the servers and the storage appliances. Compression will expand capacity anywhere from 2 to 10× for general data, but there are some datasets, such as photos, that are incompressible, so characterize your data and check with the vendor before you buy. Compression technology is available on the filer side, too.

The downside to compression is that it can add some latency to read operations. Writes usually go to SSD journals, which speeds them up, and using that SSD as a read cache can help too, but average latency may take a hit because data not in the cache has to be fetched, with the overall read operation taking longer.

Compression doesn't work out for all-flash arrays and fast SSD in hybrid arrays. The algorithms just don't keep up. Those fast solutions that do offer compression of flash/SSD do so after the data has been journaled in the appliance or else they take a serious performance hit.

Performance brings up the next issue in this use case. Usually, more server power is being added to the datacenter. Compression shortens write and read operations on the actual disks, because less data is being moved. This won't compensate for the increase in capacity in most cases... there will be fewer IOPS per terabyte on a compressed system.

The answer is to look at the primary storage for the cluster. In looking to repurpose the hard drive arrays already in use, there is no real performance advantage of the old "primary" tier enterprise drives over the secondary slower drives. They are both really slow compared with solid-state! The next section addresses the performance question.

I Need to Boost Performance

Many IT shops moving to virtualization or the cloud see a need for more storage performance. This is a good point in time to consider adding all-flash arrays (AFA) [51] to the SAN. The AFA is a lightning fast box designed to slot into a SAN between the server and

2015	Capacity	IOPS	IOPS	Capacity	2017
Primary Enterprise HDD	500 TB (500 HDD)	100,000	2,000,000	200TB	Primary All-Flash Array
Secondary Nearline Storage	500 TB (250 HDD)	37,500	3,200,000	800 TB (80 SSD)	Secondary SATA SSD Bulk Storage
Total	1 Petabyte	137,500	5,200,000	1 Petabyte	Total

Note the size reduction here. Today's solution is a full rack (or more) of gear, while the All-Flash solution is just 7U

FIGURE 3.16

Old tiering versus new, using AFA—the capacity IOPS story.

the rest of the SAN, just like the compression box above. (In fact, some all-flash arrays have the capability to compress data being auto-tiered down to hard drive arrays.)

There is an abiding myth that all-flash solutions are very expensive for the size of primary storage they are replacing. In reality, there is little need to match sizes. The AFA can be quite a bit smaller, with just hot data being cached in fast access storage. The result is that with AFA and compression, a typical installation will transition as shown in Fig. 3.7 with a shrink of primary capacity, a massive increase in primary IOPS and a large increase in total storage capacity (Fig. 3.16).

Compared with adding on more primary storage and buying more arrays and drives for bulk secondary storage, the compression approach combined with all-flash arrays means a large saving in space and power, and the avoidance of considerable acquisition costs. This buys two or three years of extra useful life for the existing configurations, without that pain and expense of a lot more storage boxes.

I Need to Replace My Installation

Even with the delaying tactics of compression and all-flash arrays, there is a point in time when the old gear reaches the end of its useful life. What you should do depends very much on when this happens—today or a couple of years into the future when next-generation storage (SDS and open-source software on COTS hardware) is mainstream, stable, and inexpensive.

Let's look at replacement choices today. If it is only a small part of an installation, the answer is probably to buy similar, but more up to date, gear and maintain the status quo in management tools and processes. If a large portion of the installation is being replaced, this will change the rules. No-one wants to be exposed to an 8-year life on current generation gear when competitors are becoming much more agile at much less price with SDS or whatever.

For all but the most risk-averse, this is the moment to begin transitioning to the modern world of storage. There are a couple of parts to the equation. Primary storage replacement must be solid-state, and the solution is to add a (smaller) AFA to replace the portion of primary storage that needs to go.

Replacing secondary storage today leads to the question of object storage very quickly. This is the right solution and there are a range of products to answer the need, depending in the main on the sophistication of your IT team. These range from a ready-to-go installation, through off-the-shelf and easy to install commercial solutions, to Ceph or Swift and inexpensive COTS boxes from any of a number of vendors (Note that in 2 years or so, the hardware choices will be easier, just as in building Linux servers).

Looking forward a couple of years, the emphasis in vendor choices is the agility of the configuration. Many IT shops will be considering SDS solutions, which increase the vendor base enormously, but makes the "Lego" of storage infinitely more flexible. There's a whole chapter on SDS solutions later in the book so I'm deferring the details till then.

Q&A
IS THE APPROACH TO STORAGE DIFFERENT IN THE HPC/BIG DATA WORLD?

The short answer is yes. In many ways, these are into new approaches more than any other area. We'll cover this later in the book, but the good news is that most of these classes of installation have admin staffs with advanced training.

HOW DO FALLING SOLID-STATE PRICES AFFECT PLANNING?

There will be a point, probably around 2018, when it no longer makes sense to buy HDD. When SSD "cross-over" HDD capacities and pricing, the storage game changes in many ways. Crucially, secondary storage is no longer slow storage. Compression technology will need to be 10× to 100× faster to keep up, for example, while appliance controllers will find themselves performance challenged.

It's worth asking vendors what they plan to do about this. Mostly, I suspect you'll get lots of 5-syllable words that really don't make much sense when looked at rationally. Some vendors will understand the problem and give a plausible answer. These likely are your best choices for future-proofing your storage buys.

The Million Dollar Question to ask the vendor is: "I will be buying only SSD after 2017. How does your product handle the performance and power issues that SSD imply?"

WHAT ABOUT HYBRID ARRAYS?

A hybrid array is a standard HDD array with SSD in some of the drive slots. Blow aside all the hype about "balancing primary fast storage and bulk slower storage, etc." and the real reason for the "few" SSD is that the RAID controllers can't handle the drives at full speed. Most of the SSD drives in these arrays can reach 400,000 IOPS. Most RAID controllers choke below a million IOPS. This is in RAID1 mirroring mode. Using any of the parity mode, such as RAID 5, slows things down a lot, since the CPU in the head node has to crunch all the data to generate parity blocks.

This makes the "best" configuration for the hybrid array 4 SSD and the rest HDD. If the hybrid array can auto-tier between SSD and HDD using internal SAS buses, a bunch of these arrays might match up to an AFA in performance, but the AFA likely has the edge on total capacity.

AFA's have the big advantage of being drop-in solutions into existing arrays. With ease of installation, speeding up the whole SAN quickly is worth a lot. It could be done with hybrid arrays, but the complexity is higher and it would take a lot longer to install.

Economics should win, but it isn't just acquisition price to worry about!

SHOULD I CONSIDER ETHERNET SANS?

iSCSI SANs are well worthy of consideration, simply because they merge the storage networking "silo" in IT with the rest of the network admins. FCoE perpetuates the separation, since there will be FC legs on any such SAN. Moreover, iSCSI can coexist with SDN, while FCoE likely won't, at least for a while. Unifying the network saves on training, additional admins, extra gear and the implicit costs of managing a separate ecosystem.

Remember though that iSCSI SANs have an inherent barrier to scaling. They will also drop price slower than object storage, simply because most iSCSI products come from traditional vendors, though this will be less true as universal storage units mature.

REFERENCES

[1] Storage Area Network. http://searchstorage.techtarget.com/definition/storage-area-network-SAN.
[2] Redundant Arrays of Inexpensive Disks. http://www.webopedia.com/TERM/R/RAID.html.
[3] Fibre-Channel over Ethernet. http://www.fcoe.com/.
[4] iSCSI. http://searchstorage.techtarget.com/definition/iSCSI.
[5] FC switches … Brocade company website. http://www.brocade.com/.
[6] Host-Bus Adapters … Avago company website., http://www.avagotech.com/products/server-storage/fibre-channel-host-.bus-adapters/.
[7] Just a Bunch of Drives. http://www.aberdeeninc.com/abcatg/jbod-storage-expansion.htm.
[8] Two ports on each drive. http://serialstoragewire.net/Articles/2007_07/developer24.html.
[9] Typical drive caddies. http://www.newmodeus.com/shop/index.php?main_page=product_info&products_id=199.
[10] EMC's ViPR. https://en.wikipedia.org/wiki/EMC_ViPR.
[11] Open-e company website. http://www.open-e.com/.
[12] Block-IO definition. http://searchstorage.techtarget.com/answer/What-is-block-I-O.
[13] Logical Units definition. http://searchstorage.techtarget.com/answer/What-is-a-LUN-and-why-do-we-need-one.
[14] EMC company website. http://www.emc.com/.
[15] HPE (Hewlett-Packard Enterprise) company website. http://www.hpe.com/.
[16] HDS (Hitachi Data Systems) company website. http://www.hds.com/.
[17] Fujitsu company website. http://www.fujitsu.com/.
[18] IBM (International Business machines) company website. http://www.ibm.com/.

[19] Dell company website. http://www.dell.com/.

[20] DDN (Data Direct Networks) company website. http://www.ddn.com/.

[21] Dot Hill company website. http://www.dothill.com/.

[22] Filer out-performed SAN. http://www.computerweekly.com/feature/Block-vs-file-for-Hyper-V-and-VMware-storage-Which-is-better.

[23] Atto company website. http://www.atto.com/.

[24] QLogic company website. http://www.aqlogic.com/.

[25] Cisco company website. http://www.cisco.com/.

[26] NetApp company website. http://www.netapp.com/.

[27] Cloning description. http://www.netapp.com/us/media/ds-2837-flexclone.pdf.

[28] Storage Networking Industry Association (SNIA). http://www.snia.org/.

[29] Network-Attached Storage. https://en.wikipedia.org/wiki/Network-attached_storage.

[30] Sun Microsystems. http://whatis.techtarget.com/definition/Sun-Microsystems.

[31] NFSv4. http://www.snia.org/sites/default/files/SNIA_An_Overview_of_NFSv4-3_0.pdf.

[32] IETF. http://www.ietf.org/.

[33] Server Message Block (SMB) Protocol. https://msdn.microsoft.com/en-us/library/windows/desktop/aa365233(v=vs.85).aspx.

[34] Microsoft Active Directory. https://msdn.microsoft.com/en-us/library/bb742424.aspx.

[35] SanDisk company website (Note SanDisk has been acquired by Western digital Corp.). http://www.sandisk.com/.

[36] Ceph object storage software. http://www.ceph.com/.

[37] CRUSH algorithm (Controlled Replication Under Scalable Hashing). http://whatis.techtarget.com/definition/CRUSH-Controlled-Replication-Under-Scalable-Hashing.

[38] Scality's Ring object storage software. http://www.scality.com/.

[39] What is metadata. http://whatis.techtarget.com/definition/metadata.

[40] REST protocol. http://searchsoa.techtarget.com/definition/REST.

[41] SATA-Express interface. https://sata-io.org/sites/default/files/documents/SATA_Express-SV2013.pdf.

[42] Drive reliability "bathtub" curve. https://www.quora.com/What-causes-the-bathtub-curve-failure-rate-in-hard-drives.

[43] Bathtub curve is a good model. https://www.quora.com/What-causes-the-bathtub-curve-failure-rate-in-hard-drives.

[44] Need to track failure rates. https://www.backblaze.com/hard-drive.html.

[45] SAS versus SATA interface. http://www.networkcomputing.com/storage/will-sata-express-dethrone-sas/1120840364.

[46] A final myth is that an HDD is cheaper than an SSD. http://www.storagenewsletter.com/rubriques/market-reportsresearch/capacity-ssds-cheaper-than-capacity-hdds-in-2016-wikibon/.

[47] The most important SSD myth is the wear-out issue. https://www2.wwt.com/wp-content/uploads/2015/03/10-Myths-About-Flash-Storage-TechTarget-NetApp-WWT.pdf.

[48] InfiniBand. http://www.infinibandta.org/content/pages.php?pg=technology_overview.

[49] RoCE (RDMA over Converged Ethernet). http://www.mellanox.com/page/products_dyn?product_family=79.

[50] iWARP (Internet Wide Area RDMA Protocol). http://www.networkworld.com/article/2858017/ethernet-switch/iwarp-update-advances-rdma-over-ethernet-for-data-center-and-cloud-networks.html.

[51] All-Flash Arrays (AFA). http://searchsolidstatestorage.techtarget.com/essentialguide/Flash-storage-Guide-to-enterprise-all-flash-storage-arrays.

Storage Software

4

Most of this book is about storage software and how it impacts complete solutions. Storage is evolving to a component-off-the-shelf (COTS) hardware base with software delivering the secret sauce value-add. In this chapter, we look at the historical storage picture and how it is now rapidly evolving into a new, more exciting, and useful, but daunting and challenging environment. Today we face the most rapid evolution in storage in IT history, driven primarily by what we can achieve in code, complimented by the immense step in performance achieved by flash-based technologies.

Software-based value opens up the market to open-sourcing both hardware and software. These two aspects of the future of storage will bring about a major revolution in purchasing strategies, much like the UNIX/Linux revolution [1] that toppled the mainframe. The realization that the world's great clouds are built on commodity hardware at commodity prices, all without suffering any material consequences, is building confidence that a new world of open-source and "whitebox" hardware is the future of the industry.

Needless to say, the large storage vendors see both a challenge and opportunity in what is happening. The challenge is that both their hardware base and high markup business models are at serious risk of being demolished by low-margin, high-volume product. This is a reality already in the cloud, where the traditional vendors such as EMC and HDS have been squeezed out of the bidding for Exabytes of storage appliances. With Red Hat [2] aggressively supporting open-source–based solutions the large incumbents are challenged to find a future game plan.

The opportunity is to join the open platform movement, though in typical juggernaut fashion this typically is in the form of "umbrella" solutions that allow open platforms to be merged with proprietary gear. An analogy would be for Company X to offer "Cloud software with an OpenStack feature" rather than "OpenStack Cloud with a strong support infrastructure." The umbrella approach will work with some conservative customers who want to hold on to their legacy storage as long as possible.

The new approaches have opened up a great vista of storage change over the next decade. That is primarily this book's topic, but we need to know where we have come from, where we are, and why we need to change. The rest of this chapter looks at these three topics.

Network Storage. http://dx.doi.org/10.1016/B978-0-12-803863-5.00004-2

TRADITIONAL SOLUTIONS

The traditional network storage software package follows one of the two models. Either a soft-RAID stack resides in the host server operating system, allowing the server to create and access a RAID array of internal drives and external JBODs [3] as direct-attached storage (DAS) [4]; or some form of SAN or filer is used, with just enough interface in the server to talk (through Fiber-Channel, iSCSI, NFS, etc.) to storage appliances. We've discussed the platforms and protocols involved in this, but it's worth building a perspective of how these choices are deployed at this point.

Soft-RAID and alternatively RAID cards built into the server are clearly small-scale solutions, insofar as they are not designed for clouds of servers accessing the same data. This doesn't mean that they are small-scale solutions. I've delivered petabytes in a single solution using this type of architecture. The key is to back off from the SAN model of low-level connectivity trying to scale to large capacity, and consider that today's storage "Lego" is often a small server with 12 or 24 drives. Scale is achieved by using many of these identical "blocks" to achieve Exabyte-sized configurations.

The SAN/filer approach is the traditional storage solution for mid-to-large companies, allowing sharing of data between servers over what amounts to a Storage LAN. Connectivity limitations and software constraints make large-scale versions of the SAN difficult to manage and operate. This is one reason for the evolution to new approaches.

With 25 years of maturation, both the DAS and SAN models are robust and slow-changing. This has contributed to a malaise of interest in the storage side of IT, and this is reflected in the slower than expected uptake of new technologies such as SSD. This is much like the UNIX phase of the "revolution" back in the 1980s. The vendor base hadn't changed much and a UNIX system was still proprietary and somewhat expensive. The Linux phase really brought change, as the customers had learned the new approaches and lost their fear of change. This second phase is underway already in storage—UNIX/Linux didn't have the cloud to accelerate change!

Each traditional SAN/Filer solution comes with a host of software tools that add value to the core code. These tools ease integration and management of large configurations, coincidentally providing the ability to handle multiple types of hardware from the same vendor and, more recently, hardware from other vendors, too.

The early tools focused on data integrity and availability issues, such as creating alternate pathing through the connections to remove single points of failure. Tools to automate setup and management of large clusters followed, with compression and deduplication tools next.

A separate thread of development has focused on backup, restore, and archiving. Initially delivering disk-to-tape solutions, these evolved to speed up backup windows by backing up to disk and then to tape. This same approach has been in use for two decades, though today's focus is to backup to the cloud, or to inexpensive bulk disk, more than to tape.

POOLS, LAKES, AND OCEANS

On the management side, most traditional tools have evolved features that bridge hardware vendors. The Symantec/Veritas products [5] are an excellent example, being very vendor agnostic. EMC created vIPR to be all encompassing, capable of bringing all of their various filers and arrays into a single storage space, and even accommodating recent gear from major competitors and the "whitebox" market.

This evolution occurred in response to a demand for simpler control, without boundaries in all of the storage being managed. Users wanted a single, apparently homogeneous, address space. This, they felt, would allow for better space utilization, as well as future automation of data positioning and manage-by-policy approaches to data governance and compliance.

This need is best described today in terms of storage pools being formed from all those traditional storage lakes. In its simplest form, each block of storage is virtualized to another level, where it is addressed in a large flat file space. Addresses would be sequential so that one pool seamlessly merges with its neighbors. When blocks are needed, just choose from the next set of free virtual addresses.

Reality tends to be a bit different. First, it's necessary to deal with data integrity properly, so with pools made up of RAID arrays that underlying RAID LUN structure will still exist. Moreover, tiering means that not all storage is equal. Solid-state drives (SSDs) are way faster than hard disk drives (HDDs) [6], while PCIe flash cards and Non-Volatile Dual-inline Memory Modules (NVDIMMs) are faster still. Good management needs to accept this and steer data to the proper storage tier, or else archive data will pollute the all-flash array and sink the system.

Essentially, each independent lake has policies for integrity and metadata describing performance. This is considered when data volumes are opened up in the larger pool, so it isn't truly homogeneous. This complicates overall management, since data has to be shifted around between lakes as it ages. Auto-tiering and archiving software does this today, giving a balance between solution cost and overall performance.

With the success of the cloud, terms like storage "oceans" are sometimes used. I personally deprecate such usage. Big pools are just that. They need no special treatment as yet. Maybe when we see single pools in the zettabyte range we should get excited. Microsoft has ventured into the oceans [7] of storage, too.

The cloud does have some very big spaces, incidentally. These are typically broken down into physical "zones," allowing replicas to be in different geographical areas for disaster recovery. Each zone is its own independent pool of storage. This is an approach that fits with the large corporation as well as the large Cloud Service Provider (CSP). The set of geographically dispersed pools can be joined into a single address space, of course, but metadata and policies must maintain the benefit of physical separation.

COMPRESSION, DEDUPLICATION, AND ALL THAT

The realization that not all storage is equal, and just as importantly that data ranges from hot and active to cold and slow, led to the exploration of ways to save used space. RAID 5, often built around 6-drive sets, is typically only 85% capacity efficient due to the use of parity, while RAID 6 drops to 67%. With a complete copy needed as a minimum for disaster recovery, the real numbers are 40 and 33%.

DEDUPLICATION

Real-world systems retain many more copies, however. These are duplicates of the files stored in different places, sometimes with small changes, and sometimes with none. File deduplication [8] arose out of the idea that you were better off having a single copy of each file, with replicas made by policy to protect integrity and availability.

Depending on the environment, the space savings can be huge. NetApp is particularly proud of their cloning software that allows many copies of a file image to be created, just by making pointers to the single real image. This is extremely useful in dealing with virtual servers and desktops. One advantage of the approach is that the single real image can be stored in DRAM or flash, allowing much faster transmission to using servers or desktops.

Deduplication only works in filers and object stores. You have to know what an object is to know if it is a duplicate. Not to be left out, the block-IO types got into the act. What they do is strictly speaking "compression" and should be called that, but it's possible that the roaring success of deduplication in the filer (at least on paper) created something of an inferiority complex in the block guys and they often use deduplication instead—a case of bad FUD?

There are those who argue that deduplication is just a use case of compression (or vice versa). The subtle difference is that deduplication ought to just be the process of removing duplicates at the object or file level. The process here begins with comparing metadata for files of the same name, which are candidates for condensing to a single copy. More importantly, when many users want a copy of the same file, creation with a deduplicated system is just building a pointer to the file, without any data movement. The same processes in compression involve identity tables and a lot more steps, so, really, these are not identical terms.

COMPRESSION

Compression [9] works by finding repetitive segments of data. These can be replaced by a marker and a pointer to a standard plain text equivalent. Doing this can save substantial amounts of storage space, perhaps as much as 80+% in the typical general storage case.

Some file types don't compress well, and you should know what these are in advance. Jpeg and Mpeg are already compressed heavily. It is possible to use advanced compression [10] approaches to shrink these further and the FaceBooks of the world are very interested in this. Other intractable forms are scientific data such as that from simulations. Unfortunately, these are file types that we really need compression on!

Compression and deduplication are complimentary. There is no overlap between the savings that can be achieved as long as they are always applied in the same order. They are both compute-intensive. Compression requires multiple passes through the data looking for replaceable data macros, while deduplication involves a complex hash calculation followed by a data search through a large number of objects. This means the process may be implemented iteratively. For example, a hash of the filename and some metadata may allow a fast check to see if the object is already present, avoiding any full data hash. (The latter is necessary because filenames and metadata can be identical while the data is different).

In the best case, compression and deduplication can reduce storage needed by more than 99%. This is not typical of the general environment, but the savings there can still run to the 70–80% level.

PROBLEMS WITH COMPRESSION AND DEDUPLICATION TODAY

The best place to compress (and encrypt) is in the originating server. This is because the LAN connections from that server are the major bottleneck in today's system and will become truly catastrophic choke points in all SSD/Flash environments such as we'll see by 2017. The compression applies to all that network data too!

Deduplication has the same issue, insofar as a search is needed after the hash calculation. Doing the "hash over metadata" approach described earlier cuts the hash creation time down, but the search is still an issue. Having the search execute in the storage appliance saves server load, but it adds round-trip delays to the latency for a write operation. At this point it seems likely that deduplication will be a background job in the storage appliances for a while, as opposed to a real-time operation.

Unfortunately, the general consensus is that compressing in the server will use too many server resources and take too long, adding enormously to latency and slowing the server to a crawl. This applies to encryption, too. Intel is looking at coprocessing some of this, but it will still be slow.

Some very smart entrepreneurs are looking at alternatives that will resolve these issues and make compression and encryption in the server more real time, so this may change for the better soon.

OPEN-SOURCE SOFTWARE

For most of the last three decades, the key ingredient of a storage solution has been proprietary storage software that runs arrays, filers, and lifecycle management. This has been the element creating a market for the traditional vendors, providing a barrier to entry for start-up companies and a lock on the customer who has devoted substantial license fees and training hours to a particular product line.

Storage, as well as computing generally, is in the process of a sea change as open-source software takes up a significant market share. This software is created by communities of interested parties, and the members of that community represent a heavy time investment as well as a potential customer base and evangelical group for each open-source project. Open-source software is intended to run on really inexpensive commodity (COTS) hardware, reducing the total solution costs by very large factors.

The major plays in open-sourcing that impinge directly on software are OpenStack [11], a complete cloud solution with block-IO, object, Big Data, and database projects; Ceph [12], which brings a powerful object and universal storage solution; and GlusterFS [13], which services the storage needs of high-performance computing and Big Data. Packages that impinge more on Big Data, such as Hadoop [14], are covered in a separate chapter of this book.

OpenStack has modules developed to match the storage options of AWS, with the exception of archived data, which generally today is considered a part of the public cloud. There is broad support for OpenStack across the industry, with a view to it being the de facto solution for the in-house portion of private clouds. It has some competition from proprietary alternatives in this area, with Microsoft Azure being offered as an in-house cluster solution and VMware pushing a cloud to protect their installed base. OpenStack is also seeing Ceph take a good deal of market share from its own object storage solution.

Ceph is appearing in the market as a software stack to build onto "Lego" storage boxes, small modular appliances with very high scalability. It has deficiencies, especially in performance and in handling SSDs, but Red Hat is acting as a support resource, much as they do for Linux, and is correcting these issues aggressively. Ceph integrates all of the storage access modes into one "universal" storage solution, which could make it the preferred storage approach a few years from now.

GlusterFS addresses the scaling issues of traditional filers and file systems, having a similarly large scalability as Ceph. It is more akin to traditional access methods for storage and has a large user base in the high-performance computing market. The advent of Big Data has opened up new opportunities, but it competes to a great extent with Ceph, which has notable superscale supporters such as CERN.

Software and hardware infrastructure is building rapidly around each of these open-source initiatives. This will ensure that they enter the mainstream. The impact of that happening on the traditional vendors has already driven a merger between Dell and EMC [14], while IBM is widely expected to sell-off the remains of its storage hardware business, much like PCs and servers went to Lenovo. As open-source gains market share, we can expect a spate of consolidations and perhaps even some bankruptcies or exiting of the storage market by the older vendors. In compensation, storage is becoming a lively place for start-ups, with software-defined storage charting the way storage will look in the future.

Let's look at the three major open-source initiatives in a bit more detail.

OPENSTACK

Looking to find a lower-cost solution to build clouds that could come close to matching the mega-CSPs such as AWS and Google, the OpenStack Foundation picked up on extensive work by Rackspace Corp. and NASA that has now become a major open-source program.

OpenStack [11] consists of a large number of modules (currently around 30) that together are intended to run in a virtualized environment on top of the hypervisor. Storage is supported by the following:

- **Swift**, which provides object storage capability,
- **Cinder**, providing block-IO,
- **Manila**, a shared file system,
- **Trove**, the database service.

These are all designed to run on low-cost COTS hardware (component-off-the-shelf solutions based on very standardized, high-volume and nonproprietary designs), aiming especially to the use of commodity, off-the-shelf drives rather than high-priced proprietary versions such as those needed with traditional RAID gear.

Having said that, many established vendors are supporting OpenStack while adding their own proprietary code. This will almost certainly lead to tweaks to drive interfaces or "configuration verification" tools that will attempt to sustain the proprietary drive approach. This is something to avoid if possible when buying hardware.

Swift

Swift is in essence the equivalent of AWS S3 object store. It is designed to provide data integrity by replication at the appliance level. This avoids the RAID failure mechanism where a whole array goes off-stream and access to data is lost. With simple appliance structures, the cost of this approach is much lower than the specialized hardware of RAID arrays.

The ability to scale Swift horizontally by easily adding more appliances is supported by software that integrates the new appliances and redistributes data. Likewise vertical scaling with additional drives is easy. The software is designed for hyperscaling and has no central file database or directory tree.

Swift provides a REST interface and supports AWS S3 APIs. This limits the ability to edit files without creating completely new versions, but this is, of course, common to all REST approaches at this point in time.

Writing Data in Swift

Data pass through one of a set of proxy servers that distributes chunks of the storage to a set of storage nodes. Replication occurs here. The proxy server also executes erasure coding if appropriate.

The distribution scheme used by Swift is called a "Ring." Hashing the new objects metadata gives an address in the ring. The ring structure is complex, being aimed at maximizing the distance between replicas to improve data integrity. Concepts such as zones are used to aid this. When rings are created, the storage devices are broken down into many partitions, possibly in the range of millions per drive.

The hashing process determines the partitions to be used for any given object. For objects less than 5 GB in size, there is no fragmentation of the object. Larger objects are broken into fragments that go to different partitions. This limits hot-spots during write to a good extent.

It appears that the proxy server approach creates a bottleneck in the system, especially as proxy servers have no spooling support. This contrasts with the Ceph approach which does speed up write operations, though with the cost of a lot of messaging.

Swift uses separate rings to manage accounts and containers. It supports an extensive storage policy system, which can define how many replicas are needed or if erasure coding is to be used.

Problems With Consistency

To deliver newly written data to several replicas prior to flagging a write IO as complete would impose a significant performance penalty on the system. This becomes a much bigger issue if the networked storage attempts to store a replica at a geographically distant location for disaster protection.

This can be handled by either writing the local copies synchronously to protected storage and then writing to the distant storage later (asynchronously) or all the replica generation is made asynchronous. Swift chose the latter route (Ceph went with the former method). Because the proxy servers have no journaling file, there will always be a short exposure period when there is only one replica of a file in the system. There will be a longer period, perhaps of seconds, when there is no distant copy.

This creates a risk of data unavailability or even total loss. Swift has mechanisms to handle loss of access problems, such as a zone outage, where the data is finally updated when the zone returns onstream. This process is called *eventual consistency*. Data is safe when at least two replicas are created and disaster proof when the distant copy is made.

The window of risk is likely to be just a second or so for local replication and a few seconds to minutes for distant, but it is a risk.

Ceph and others journal writes in a single node prior to replication. This guarantees data integrity, but if that node failed the data would become unavailable for a time. This forces additional labor to remove the drive pair from a failed node and remount it to recover data availability and eventual replica distribution. Even so, it would take a fire to destroy data!

Neither solution is perfect. The issue will become much more serious as object storage migrates to being the mainstream solution for all storage over the next few years.

Problems With Swift Performance

Swift is generally a good, highly scalable storage solution, but it has a few major and possibly fundamental issues, especially in performance. These are just surfacing as issues, which is to be expected given the lack of deep experience with OpenStack. (Note that Ceph has a set of its own bottlenecks and this is generally true in all object stores now available).

First, Swift stores data on any one of several standard Linux file systems. This is an economic shortcut, but it smacks of the problems you get when you put a bus on railroad tracks—there are mismatches in function everywhere.

Object storage is database oriented. Perhaps the biggest issue is parsing the inode trees to find and access object blocks. Object stores often have hundreds of millions of small objects on each node and the flat-file nature of storing data means that having the inodes in memory works best by far. The problem in this means a lot of DRAM is used up for the inode cache, which still takes a significant search time even if it is all in memory. The problem is compounded when the inode trees are hit for every block.

Currently, a typical installation will likely use less cache and will find systems slowing drastically as they fill up.

Second, Swift has a messaging problem, just like Ceph. It can easily generate enough messaging to bring a typical system to its knees. There are a couple of hacks to help get around this, but the underlying complaint is that there is no pooling, which means connections are built from scratch for each communication. This is a pretty naïve design.

Third, in common with all the other object stores, Swift struggles with using SSD. This is a major problem already, but will mushroom as we move away from hard drives to all-SSD systems in 2017–20 timeframe. The competition has figured this, at least to the point of speeding up write operations by journaling onto a pair of SSDs. One can only say in mitigation that the early mind-set on object stores was to use it as the slow but very scalable cold storage for systems, and the interest in using it as universal storage has caught the architects by surprise.

Swift tends to be delivered in low-end servers, with 1 GbE links, for example. That smells strongly of fundamental performance problems, and the arrival of all-SSD systems will crack this wide open. For example, losing the underlying file system and using a key data store or something similar will shrink inode size from 1 KB each to perhaps 8 D-words, saving a lot of memory and making searches much faster.

Fixing messaging by supporting permanent links and pooling will solve another major problem and beefing up the CPU will help too. SSD spooling will be essential in the proxy servers if the data rate moves up significantly; else they'll become the bottleneck on write operations.

Since Swift is getting a great deal of corporate attention as well as the open-source communities' help, we can expect these problems to come under the scalpel and be corrected over time.

Swift Features

Swift is well-featured and includes the ability to read data from the fastest available source. This is particularly powerful when replicas are made across WANs for disaster protection. Because it uses HTTP, it also allows platforms such as Scality and Cleversafe to be easily adapted as Swift storage nodes, and even could support storage into AWS S3.

The Swift REST API is a superset of the AWS S3 REST interface, reflecting the deficiencies in handling updates that are seen in the older design. With Swift reaching a substantial installation level, one can assume that REST will move towards standardization, probably via SNIA and the differences will disappear into a common spec. This is in the interest of all the players.

Cinder

OpenStack has a block-IO storage system called Cinder. This module allows volumes to be created from the storage pool and attached to virtual instances. Cinder supports a variety of hardware platforms including Ceph- and GlusterFS-based appliances; EMC, HDS, HP, IBM, NetApp; and products from start-ups Nexenta, Pure, and others, as well as Linux servers. This allows large storage configurations to be built.

Cinder is the OpenStack equivalent of AWS EBS. It provides block data operations and is geared to allow editing of files, just as in a local DAS configuration. At this point in time, the comparison with DAS is generally much closer than with true networked SAN storage.

Each array or appliance has a Cinder driver that establishes connectivity, much like any disk drive or appliance directly hooked up to a server.

The Cinder API provides the ability to create and manage volumes, generate snapshots, and clone volumes. Most of the configurations use iSCSI or perhaps NFS. Fiber-Channel is rare, both being expensive and not conducive to large configuration scale-out. It is possibly to use thin-provisioning and to oversubscribe the raw storage as needed.

It is possible to use Cinder volumes to boot instances. Cinder is flexible in how it handles the storage back end, too. It can configure volumes via NFS and GlusterFS as well as via iSCSI connections (which are the most common connections). Support is available for multistorage solutions such as EMC's ViPR. All of these make Cinder very flexible from a hardware perspective and, importantly, older storage gear can be used with the system as long as a driver of a pooling node is available.

There are tools to backup and restore volumes using snapshots to freeze the backup image. These tools also migrate volumes between back-ends. This isn't auto-tiering, as yet, since it requires manual intervention, but logically auto-tiering may become a feature in the near future.

Problems With Cinder

A Cinder volume can only be mounted to a single instance at any one time, limiting data sharing somewhat. It also prevents active–active operations, meaning that a server failure could cause loss of access to data.

The broad hardware spectrum for Cinder allows the creation of data sharing capabilities by presenting multiple volumes from the same data set and managing any conflicts. The Kilo release of OpenStack, for example, moved to an SQL database supporting atomic write operations. This prevents operations from getting out of sequence and corrupting each other and will allow active–active operation for high availability and extend to data sharing of volumes.

Cinder supports the concept of consistency groups, where a group of volumes can be snapshotted at the same point in time to maintain consistency between them.

Kilo also corrects serious problems in recovery that occur when servers or processes crash. It removes the need for manual intervention to restart by rolling back database changes.

Performance is still a challenge with Cinder, mainly with accessing the metadata database. This is clearly an area where SSD of flash would speed things up, with the alternative of making the database run completely in-memory.

It may be necessary to throttle bandwidth on copy operations, including when a volume is initially created. This feature isn't currently available for remote files system back-ends.

Manila

Manila, the shared file system, may be better positioned to handle the data sharing issue. It can connect hardware from a broad spectrum of vendors to deliver shares much like any filer. Manila is vendor-agnostic and supports a variety of file systems such as Red Hat's Gluster, which can be used to build low-cost file storage.

OpenStack's ability to tie into Ceph, which is a "unified" storage system providing object file and block access methods to its data pool, is a double-edged sword. Ceph can interface directly to OpenStack instances, with the result that it is supplanting Swift in popularity in the OpenStack space and will challenge Cinder and manila, too. In part, this is due to the maturity of Ceph and the strong support of Red Hat, who bought out the leading Ceph infrastructure vendor, InkTank.

Whether Ceph is the ultimate winner isn't yet clear. As always, the different approaches have their own supporters, and ideas take a long time to converge, but one has to recognize that in storage Ceph maps to the OpenStack efforts pretty well exactly.

OpenStack and VMware

VMware has recognized the power of the cloud movement somewhat belatedly. While OpenStack can be run on any hypervisor or as a bare metal configuration, VMware is tying OpenStack-over-VMware together as a somewhat proprietary solution, since OpenStack itself poses a serious long-term threat to not only VMware's new vCloud but even virtualization itself. This is because OpenStack is demonstrating that complexity and high license fees are not basic to a viable IT environment.

CEPH

Ceph [12] is a neat solution to the need for inexpensive, nonproprietary storage. It is open-source and well-supported and is rapidly gaining popularity. Many low-cost storage appliances have Ceph on board, and that is a telling sign of the future.

Ceph started out as a university programming exercise to create an object store by Sage Weil in 2006 and has since grown to become a comprehensive unified storage solution. It now provides an object store, RADOS, which can (see Picture 4.1) be accessed by a native API, or by REST/S3 (object), NFS/CIFS, etc. for filer mode or by a block-IO interface. These are not multiple ways of accessing the same data, at least not yet, but allow the total storage pool to be segmented and used for the specific type of storage needed. For instance, a block LUN volume would in fact be an object in RADOS.

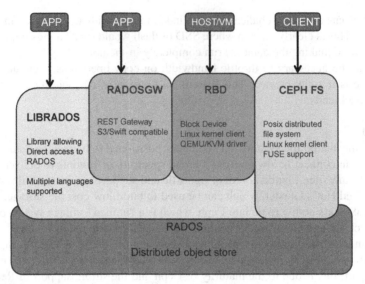

PICTURE 4.1

Ceph high-level architecture.

The object storage modes are the most mature part of Ceph, while block-IO is somewhat newer but also mature and the file system service is still maturing. Nonetheless, Ceph is known to suffer from excessive internode messaging and too many data transfers, which means a rewrite of the basic mechanisms for storing and replication are in the pipeline. The aim is a substantial speed-up, together with the use of SSD across the whole spectrum of storage rather than just in journal files.

To understand this, we have to go under the hood on Ceph. In doing so, please note the elegant modularity of the architecture (see Picture 4.2), since this will have a bearing on the discussion of software-defined storage later.

Writing Objects in Ceph

When a write operation is executed in a Ceph object environment, the source server identifies where the data object is to be stored using the "CRUSH" algorithm. This is done by calculating a hash value from the object name and metadata. With CRUSH being identical on all the server and storage nodes (it uses a map of the space stored in a redundant pair of nodes) in the cluster, applying this unique hash tag will specify a placement group of storage nodes. Data is transmitted to the primary storage node for that group, which determines how to disperse the object in typically 64 KB chunks.

The primary node, called the "primary OSD," then makes either a set of replicas (typically two) and sends them to other placement groups to protect data integrity. Lately, this has been superseded by erasure coding, which adds a sort of parity code to the data, then divides it up and sends it to a set of storage nodes. This avoids replicating

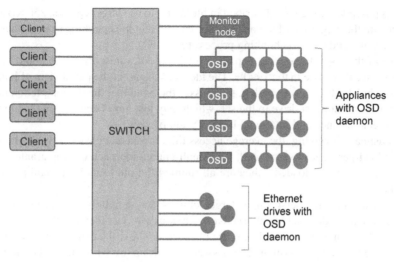

PICTURE 4.2

Ceph node structure.

the data and saves a lot of network traffic and messaging, but erasure coding is compute intensive and typically is only used for archived data going to slow hard drive storage.

The need to protect data while it is being distributed out to other nodes is satisfied by using a pair of drives as a mirrored journal file in each primary node. (Because there are many placement groups, this effectively means every storage node usually acts as a primary node for some part of the storage).

Read Operations in Ceph

Reading data in Ceph is essentially the reverse process. Knowing the hash tag for the object identifies its placement group and allows the server to request data. Currently these go through the primary OSD node of the placement group, which allows erasure coding or replication recovery for lost blocks.

CRUSH and the placement group approach evenly distribute data across all the drives in the cluster. However, as we'll see later in this section, the approach results in poor performance, since it generates lots of small IO operations.

Mechanisms exist to handle the loss of a primary node. A secondary node is identified for each placement group to recover from the loss of the primary. When drives or nodes are added, CRUSH is updated and data is redistributed as a background job to level-load all the nodes.

Chunking Issues in Ceph

Ceph is an elegant system and it can handle massive scale. The distribution of what, in today's parlance, are small chunks of 64 KB each is very problematic from a performance viewpoint, since it doesn't allow any real use of sequential IO on any storage drive. Since the storage drives are rarely SSD today, this is a major performance hit. It is possible, though not described in literature, to use larger chunks, 256 KB and maybe into the megabytes, but one has to be careful that the operating system doesn't get smart and add its own chunking process to any IO.

Use of the 64-KB chunking approach is a result of a misconception about drive performance that arose in the 1990's. The idea was to garner the parallelism of lots of drives to bolster IO rates. In reality, this misses the point that the IO completion now depends on the slowest drive in the set, which may just have been poorly positioned from a seek distance and rotational latency point of view.

Statistically speaking, the average access time increases considerably. Moreover the payload per seek is very small. The small-chunk approach does guarantee that the drives are evenly loaded—they are all running flat out to move a small payload of data!

From a chunking perspective, larger chunks are definitely better for today's ultrahigh-density drives. One alternative is obviously to just increase the size to say 1 MB, but this may cause inefficient use of space on the disk such as would occur if say a 1.1-MB file were written. The answer is to group the writes into a continuous stream in the final storage node and then write a large chunk of that each time around. Partial chunk writes like that above go away, though addressing may be slightly more complex, and a scatter gather operation needed when data is erased to recover the unused space.

We need to modify the chunking discussion once all-SSD appliances store data. The difference in performance between sequential IO operations and random I/O is much smaller in SSD, due to the lack of mechanical positioning latencies. The difference is not zero, but other factors more strongly point to the need for care in chunk management.

The small chunk size adds to the messaging issues in Ceph by simply increasing the number of targets hit. There are other crucial defects in the handling process, not least of which is the need to send all data to the primary node, where it is then forwarded to the storing nodes. More transfers and more messaging ensue.

Ideally, the data should be chunked in the server, either with erasure code added or for replicas. This is a migration of a data service in the best traditions (a little tongue in cheek! SDS is still being defined) of software-defined storage. Of course, there needs to be enough horsepower to perform the service quickly, together with compression, deduplication, and encryption if needed, so this implies that some form of acceleration for these processes will be needed. Note that the method currently employed of postprocessing these services during the transition of data from SSD to HDD no longer works when all the storage is SSD, as it will be beginning in 2017.

Ceph Future Directions

Red Hat and SanDisk have addressed a good part of the SSD shortcomings of Ceph with an announcement in March 2016 of extensions to take advantage of SanDisk's All-Flash Array. Whether this is enough depends on benchmarks being run as this is written. Most likely, further tuning in networks and operating protocols within Ceph will surface and more will still be possible.

All of this means that Sage Weil and his open-source team have a handful of problems to fix with the next rewrite of the OSD code, but this creates a great opportunity. Speculatively, if the data services are split from the OSD so that they can be virtualized as modules a la SDS, the drive appliance becomes very dumb and inexpensive. In fact, simple appliances with a converter from say SAS to Ethernet storage protocols would be enough for the drives, instead of expensive proprietary arrays or even modified COTS servers. It's even possible that the drives will direct connect to Ethernet—Kinetic drives already do that—though the interface may not fit well with a general solution, and it may be that HGST's approach of a Linux mini server on their Ethernet drive is better.

At the same time as the OSD service is split and virtualized, addition of needed compression, etc. can take place, making Ceph the base of a powerful SDS architecture. Red Hat appears to recognize that vision and may veer their guidance of Ceph in that direction. If so, storage will be very interesting in the future.

Hopefully, more emphasis will be seen on documentation, which is generally inadequate in Ceph. It is out-of-data and uninformative and leaves a lot to be desired. Against that, support from Red Hat's Ceph team, formally InkTank, is good.

Ceph and Networking

Ceph also benefits from faster networking. Mellanox [15] has driven hard to apply their RDMA products to Ceph, to good effect. They have sped up the basic messaging enormously, by using 56 Gbps InfiniBand links instead of 10 GbE. Ethernet is close behind InfiniBand with RDMA [16], and we can expect cheaper single-link Ethernet connections to move rapidly in performance, with 10 GbE already being superseded by 25 GbE and with 50 GbE perhaps one or two years away.

Storage appliances typically go for quad-lane Ethernet connections today, so 100 and 200 GbE are in the offing at affordable prices. With compression, we would be looking at effectively 6× to 10× that rate, for a lot of data classes, with correspondingly fewer IOs in the storage appliances. This makes for an all-round win.

Ceph and OpenStack

Ceph appears to have a very solid and important future in storage, and may be considered one of the most important innovations in years. There are a couple of competitors that are worth watching. Scality has a different distribution method, which they call a Ring, but this appears to behave much like CRUSH in spreading data and load evenly. Caringo has a software solution that is very heavily featured and mature, and it was the first to be introduced in market as a fully tested product in 2007 compared to Ceph's 2012 release 1.0.

With all these solutions available and objects stores from the appliance vendors to boot, the object storage user has plenty of options. A relative latecomer, OpenStack's Swift is a competitor [17] too, but Ceph is winning minds and the need or ability for the industry to have a pair of strong open-source solutions is really in question.

OpenStack itself is a large target, though much of the opportunity hinges around projected market size rather than actual installations. Realizing this, object storage products offer OpenStack compatibility and API support, negating the value of Swift as an open-source solution.

We are still some time away from the market finding its level, so it's hard to call winners and losers at this point. One determinant may well be the migration to an all-flash environment, when object store vendors will be much more focused on competitive performance issues. Most of today's solutions are targeted at bulk HDD configurations in the appliance and not focused on performance at all. Ceph suffers from this, among others, and is getting a performance-focused makeover. The future success of any given package will depend on how well optimized the SSD/flash versions are.

GLUSTERFS

Today, GlusterFS [13] is an open-source scale-out file system, offering NFS, SMB, and HDFS. With more than 8000 user-developers at the time of writing, it has a solid following in the HPC market segment. The software was designed to address the problems of scaling out file and NAS systems, where crossing the boundary between appliances presented a severe roadblock to petabyte-sized configurations.

GlusterFS is also discussed in File Systems for Big Data section of Chapter 8, where the emphasis is more on software structure.

GlusterFS is deployed on COTS servers, either within virtual instances or on bare metal. Scaling capacity is achieved by adding more appliances to the cluster, while performance scaling can be controlled by spreading data out across the appliance pool. Clusters with several petabytes of storage are achievable and multitenant environments with thousands of tenants can be created.

Gluster avoids the scaling issues of centralized metadata by distributing that data across the nodes. It copies from the RAID concept to mirror stripe and replicate data for integrity purposes, but it does so at the appliance level rather than at the drive level. This is critical in large-scale storage, since the failure rate of appliances is sufficiently high that data availability would be at risk if only drives are involved.

GlusterFS is a Linux user-space file system, a deliberate choice allowing faster integration into systems. It utilizes a Linux kernel file system to format the disk space. It can be deployed in environments such as AWS as a result, and this is a good way to get started with the approach. Networking is very well supported, and since January 2015 it has been possible to connect clusters with RDMA for low latency and high performance. iSCSI is supported, too. In common with object storage, replication control is well featured and supports geodiversity.

GlusterFS supports Hadoop seamlessly without the need for application rewrites. This brings fault tolerance to the Hadoop space and allows the choice of file or object access to the data. In fact, APIs have been created to allow objects to be accessed as files and vice versa.

It is also possible to install GlusterFS as a file system for Cinder, the block-IO access model in OpenStack.

GlusterFS Use Cases

Cloud storage can be built around GlusterFS, as virtualized systems, and large NAS systems can be created. These constitute the bulk of GlusterFS deployments, according to Red Hat.

The file system serves the analytics market particularly well, with strong Hadoop compatibility on the big data side and Splunk support for machine analytics. Rich media and data streaming can take advantage of performance tuning and scaled-out capacity.

Gluster Futures

GlusterFS, under Red Hat's direction, is adding features rapidly. The 3.1 release, "Everglades," adds in erasure coding, keeping up with the object storage companies, data tiering, and also SMB 3.0 support.

In common with many storage solutions, GlusterFS is destined to become much more automated, with provisioning by users and more policy-based management, with terms like File-as-a-Service and NAS-on-Demand being used by Red Hat. Being a Linux-based solution, it's unlikely to ever lose the CLI control process, which makes large-scale operations more error-prone.

Additional features are planned such as deduplication and compression. Performance tuning is on the table, though there are questions about how best to handle all-SSD clusters, as with any software stack in storage today. Planned support for NVMe acknowledges that the issue is understood to some extent.

Data integrity issues still exist in GlusterFS, due to the way data is replicated. Rack-level awareness is on the roadmap, to better distribute replicas and erasure coded data sets.

Why Use GlusterFS Rather Than Ceph?

There's no good answer to this question, at least for now. Both Ceph and Gluster have strengths and weaknesses, but not enough to give one model a decided edge. The fact that Red Hat drives both of them also reduces competition between them. Generally, Ceph addresses the object space very well, while Gluster might be the choice for data centers focused on more traditional file server networked storage.

Ceph is still coming to terms with the world of filers, and the file access gateway is still evolving towards full production. GlusterFS came to the object space late and it shows. Still, it seems likely that the overlap between them will increase as time goes on and the feature sets converge. This may not matter to Red Hat—they get paid either way and both products are leaders.

Performance is something of a mystery. At time of press there were no published articles on relative performance that had real credibility. Configuration setup and software tuning have a big impact, and it seems that this is still an area needing more study.

VIRTUALIZATION TOOLS
VMWARE

Hypervisor software vendors such as VMware [18] have tools to control storage and to allow orchestration of the virtual machine pool to be integrated with storage management, instance transfer, access controls, etc. Recently, the focus has shifted towards backup and disaster recovery mechanisms, perhaps both as recognition of the impact of the cloud in that area and the increased scale of virtual server farms.

VMware's vStorage is typical. It takes DAS, FC SAN, iSCSI, or NAS storage and creates datastores, which are virtualized storage pools that can span multiple physical storage units. Tools are provided for adding more space or for moving the storage to other storage devices. These datastores are presented to the tenant virtual machines as SCSI devices on a virtual SCSI controller, and so are completely abstracted from the physical storage devices.

VMware provides a proprietary file system, VMFS, to represent that data stored in the physical devices. VMFS is a clustered file system, allowing for sharing across hosts, with a lock system to prevent multiple servers addressing the same data simultaneously. The file system also allows raw device mapping, which gives direct LUN access.

Strictly speaking, these tools are not networked storage software at this time, but there appears to be increasing overlap in functionality between the solutions and the functions delivered in the storage pool. Examples are the unification of the pool, whereby appliances from diverse vendors are made to look as a single address space. Policy-driven data placement is another area where there is already an overlap.

The VMware approach requires a strenuous test prior to receiving approved device status. This limits flexibility and vendors tend to certify only a few configurations. This is good for VMware, reducing support, but it takes a good while to test and process through approval and it limits competition.

Economics will tend to further converge the functionality. The goal of tighter control is laudable, but it's intent is to lock in paying customers and increase the sales value of any deal. This is exaggerated by the close relationships of a couple of companies. VMware and EMC are tied together by ownership, for example, while Red Hat has KVM and both Ceph and GlusterFS in its portfolio. VMware has moved into direct competition in storage offerings, too. Its EVO:RAIL software delivers a virtual SAN using local drives in the virtualized servers. This is gaining traction in the converged system segment of the market.

Though modular, OpenStack shares some of the same vision of a complete solution, with new top-level modules being surfaced frequently. While VMware strives to improve its (late-to-market) cloud solutions, it seems likely that OpenStack will enter vSAN territory and also enhance storage management tools extensively.

VIRTUAL SANs

Discussing VMware naturally leads into the question of virtual SANs, where VMware [18] is pushing their own offerings strongly. The idea of the virtual SAN follows from the capacity growth per drive and the realization that a large amount of storage can be provided by the 10 or 12 drive bays of the typical large server. With ultrafast drives, such as NVMe-PCIe units, it's possible to satisfy the local processing needs and then use the excess bandwidth for sharing data with other servers in the cluster.

This mitigates the need for external primary storage appliances, such as all-flash arrays, leaving us with just secondary storage in the free-standing storage pool.

The marketing spin jockeys have coined the terms "converged systems" and "hyper-converged systems" for these systems types.

Making virtual SANs perform well has proven to be a bit of a challenge, since network bandwidth is at a premium in today's data centers, and typically the network effectively throttles the drives, but faster networks including RDMA and real-time compression may fix that problem or at least reach a level of adequacy. Until that happens, it's likely all of those 12 bays will not be filled with NVMe SSD, but may have 8 TB hard drives or slow SSD to provide some colder storage.

These performance limitations highlight the issue of using generalized servers for data-intense task related to storage. It is definitely possible to build a better architecture to address the problem of storage bottlenecks in virtual SANs, but this will tend to knock "convergence" and "hyper-convergence" on the head. Still, virtual SANs are not very old in this current context and it will take time to see if the hype and reality actually converge.

Adapting the management tools to fit the virtual SAN context is a major chore with any solution. VMware appears to have a stronger position in this with EVO:RAIL, which ties the virtual SAN into the vSphere toolset. The downside is, despite claims to be "software-defined storage," that this is a closed proprietary system. The limitation common in VMware to use selected platforms for the software is still in force, which will not yield the lowest pricing. Competitors like Datacore and HPE may get an edge, especially if their code becomes truly SDS.

Longer term, the idea of the virtual SAN is itself challenged by the arrival of NVDIMM memories such as ReRAM and X-Point. Most likely all three layers (DRAM, NVDIMM, and NVMe drives) will be shareable across the network, putting even more strain on network bandwidth and latency.

THE OPERATING SYSTEM STORAGE STACK

In describing today's storage software environment, for the past three decades or more, we've executed storage IO in the OS via a slowly evolving SCSI storage stack. While a very mature solution, this stack has accreted many layers in indirection and is unable to cope with SSD that can reach more than a million IOPS.

The search for alternatives has homed in on NVMe, which is a queue-based system that dramatically reduces system interrupt frequency. Drives run significantly faster with NVMe but there is still some baggage from the old SCSI stack to deal with. There are discussions about bypassing SCSI altogether, which may well fit in with recently evolved drive interfaces that use key data models for data access.

The following sections address these issues in a bit more detail.

THE TRADITIONAL SCSI STACK

SCSI was created to separate logical addressing, as used by the file system, from the physical block addresses in the drive, allowing enhanced bad block management. It then incorporated the idea of logical addressing across a set of drives, leading to the RAID array that has been an industry mainstay for so long.

In a typical operating system, there are other levels of indirection, however (see Fig. 4.1 for more details Wikicommons has an eye-test chart! [19]). Linux has a virtual file system that in turn interfaces to the mounted file system (such as ZFS or ext4). The interface translates the file ID and byte offset of an application's IO request into logical block addresses on a storage device. Next the block requests are sequenced and queued on a fair share basis so that each application can get IOs.

Yet another level of indirection usually creeps in at this point. Data is typically stored as RAID blocks. If the RAID software is running in the server, the logical addresses are translated again to give new logical addresses on each of the drives in the RAID set, and new queues are formed for each drive.

If a RAID card is present, this translation is done in that card. Likewise, for networked storage the appliance modifies the address to generate logical block addresses for each drive in the appropriate RAID set.

These latest logical block addresses are transferred to a drive using SCSI's successors, SAS and SATA. In past times, there might have been an intermediate step to optimize access sequence, but today's drives do that themselves, after translating the logical block addresses into physical block addresses on the storage media. SSDs are a special case, since the physical block representing a given logical block address may move around as erased block recapture and error correction occur.

The transfers via SAS and SATA generate a series of interrupts as commands and data are sent and responses received. Each of these causes a system state change, which in itself consumes substantial system resources.

All in all, this approach to getting to a physical data block has become much too cumbersome, to the point that performance using ultra-fast flash or SSD units has been compromised. The industry looked beyond SCSI [20] for a new streamlined alternative and the consensus has focus in on NVMe as the solution.

Unfortunately, NVMe is only a partial solution, and a restructuring of the rest of the stack is long overdue. This is becoming even more important as software developers, trying to get to market quickly, address file systems optimizations such as Hadoop and GlusterFS by layering these on top of existing file systems, so creating even more indirection. In a world where IO performance actually matters and where SSD and flash give us the opportunity to do something about it, this short-cutting is short-sighted and leads to slow and overly complex systems.

THE NVMe STACK AND BEYOND

NVMe is a queue-based IO solution. The concept derives from the queues that are generated by the file systems in a typical server, providing a mechanism for drives or storage appliance to directly access queues without the complex sequence of operations that command-driven interfaces like SCSI require (see Fig. 4.1).

The essential magic of NVMe [21] is to make the queues circular, with pointers for the last entry made by the originator and the last entry accessed by the recipient. Software logic prevents the recipient from overtaking the originator. Now extend this to many queues. NVMe allows 64,000 simultaneous queues to exist, so that each drive can have a set of queues, allowing job priorities to be set. More than this, queues can be targeted back to specific cores in the server, or even to specific applications (Fig. 4.2).

NVMe uses the queues to flag new operations and to send back status at the end of an operation. The NVMe approach is coupled with DMA data transfers over PCIe, which ensures very high performance. Since the drive side of the connection "pulls" commands form the queue, it can manage throttling and priorities without need the

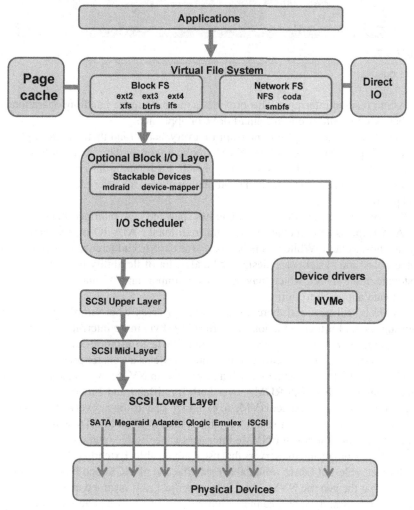

FIGURE 4.1

The Linux SCSI stack.

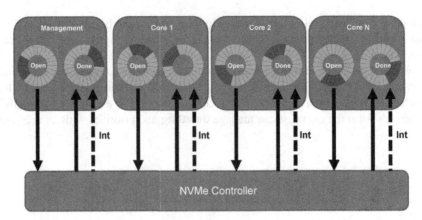

FIGURE 4.2

NVMe queues.

host OS to react to interrupts. This provides a mechanism for handling operations in parallel, which could occur in a smart drive or appliance.

Rather than create a system interrupt for every status (and there are multiple statuses in a typical SCSI operation) NVMe looks to consolidate interrupt to perhaps 1% of the frequency of the traditional approach. Each jumbo interrupt [22] triggers the servicing of many statuses in the completion queue, for a very low level of overhead per IO.

The combination of NVMe and PCIe has spawned new interface standards such as SATA-Express to combine NVMe and traditional SATA IO on the same drive bay in a host system. While this is bad news for the SAS adherents, it does simplify motherboard and system case design and adds a lot of flexibility to the configuring of storage in the server, which may be critically important if virtual SANs become a mainstream approach to storage.

NVMe is still new and there are a number of areas where improvements have been suggested. Further reduction in overhead [23] via more interrupt consolidation is one possibility, while the idea of extending PCIe to a fabric-level interconnect between systems is in part being tied to using NVMe as a transfer protocol.

Work on RDMA over Ethernet will allow us to run NVMe over standard Ethernet connections in 2016. With RDMA over both InfiniBand and Ethernet now a solid proposition, we should expect NVMe to extend to scaled-out networked storage, too (see Fig. 4.3). Long term, it seems very likely that SAS and SATA will fade away, since the incremental cost for NVMe interfaces is negligible, while the performance gains in both storage and the servers that use it are notable. Extending NVMe out onto an Ethernet scale-out fabric would also mean the end of iSCSI and Fiber-Channel.

Note that the generic NVMe over Fabrics project [24] is aimed at a broader solution set with IB and Fiber-Channel solutions, but Ethernet has an edge in being a required fabric in data centers and with converging performance should win the battle for next-generation connectivity.

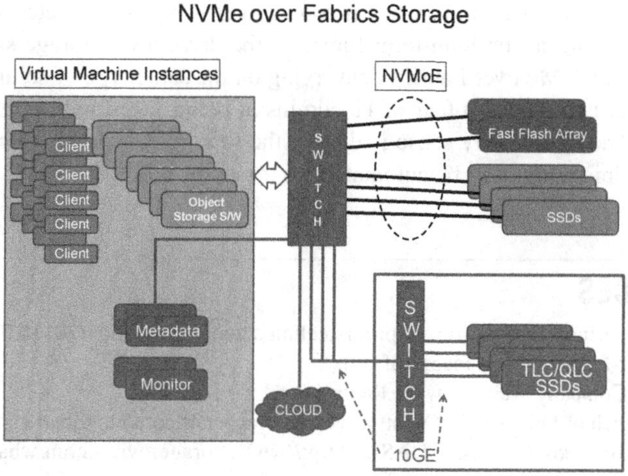

NVMe over Fabrics Storage

FIGURE 4.3

NVMe over Ethernet storage.

ETHERNET DRIVES AND KEY/DATA ACCESS PROTOCOLS

Another heresay is in the offing. The realization that drive CPUs were smart enough to run Ethernet is a bit belated. (Perhaps it owes more to vendors' special interests than technical issues, anyway!) Why not just connect directly to the drives? This allows a very large level of scale, with all the benefits of zoning and network management that Ethernet brings to the table.

With direct Ethernet connections a server can easily transfer data directly to the drive, speeding up operations dramatically, while reducing the cost of the appliance box a great deal. In fact, with this topology there is no longer a need for a controller in the appliance, which fits very well with the concepts espoused in software-defined storage.

While Ethernet drives are not mainstream yet, several large cloud providers are using them, implying that the cost and performance benefits are worth the rearchitecting involved. Moreover, Ethernet is by far the most rapidly evolving interconnect scheme, so these drives could leap ahead of the pack over the next few years, especially if NVMe over fabrics and RDMA Ethernet are deployed.

One of the two giants in drive manufacturing, Seagate, has gone a step further and deployed a key data mechanism to access data, clearly taking aim at the big data and object storage space. This approach has been incorporated into Ceph already, and it may become a mainstream approach in a couple of years. Most of the Ethernet drives reported sold to date have been of this type.

HGST, part of the other drive giant, WD, has put a full Linux server on some Ethernet drive models. This has been slower to take off, mainly, I suspect, because the integration of some storage services is more complex. We could see NAS and object storage code on these drives in the near future. These drives can also run the key-data code from Seagate's Kinetic approach.

NVMe shouldn't even blink when it comes to key-data access, etc., so I suspect we may be looking at the long-term future of the drive level storage system here, especially with NVMe over Fabrics converging on the same type of solution.

One caveat is the (real?) fear of IT admins at being faced with a huge number of discreet IP addresses. My sense is that by the time we reach this point, much of platform administration will be automated, so it may be moot.

REFERENCES

[1] The Unix/Linux Revolution. http://arstechnica.com/tech-policy/2011/07/should-we-thank-for-feds-for-the-success-of-unix/.

[2] Red Hat Company Website. www.Redhat.com.

[3] Just a Bunch of Drives (JBOD). http://www.storagecraft.com/blog/jbod-care/.

[4] Direct-Attached Storage (DAS). http://www.storagereview.com/what_is_direct_attached_storage_das.

[5] Symantec/Veritas Products. https://www.veritas.com/product/storage-management/infoscale-storage?s_kwcid=AL!4649!3!91706185265!e!!g!!veritas&om_sem_kw=veritas&ef_id=VWnhSwAABPg-ModJ:20160331230326:s.

[6] SSDs Are Way Faster Than HDD. http://itblog.sandisk.com/the-accelerating-economics-of-flash-and-the-retreat-of-hard-disk-drives/.

[7] Microsoft Has Ventured Into the (Storage) Oceans. http://www.citylab.com/tech/2016/02/microsoft-cloud-ocean-project-natick/459318/.

[8] File Deduplication. http://searchstorage.techtarget.com/definition/data-deduplication.

[9] Compression. http://www.data-compression.com/index.shtml.

[10] Advanced Compression. https://cran.r-project.org/web/packages/brotli/vignettes/brotli-2015-09-22.pdf.

[11] OpenStack Organization. http://www.openstack.org/.

[12] Ceph Special Interest Group. http://www.ceph.com/.

[13] Gluster File System Special Interest Group. https://www.gluster.org/.

[14] Merger Between Dell and EMC. http://fortune.com/2015/10/12/dell-and-emc-merger-official/.

[15] Mellanox company Website. www.mellanox.com.

[16] Chelsio Company Website. www.chelsio.com.

[17] OpenStack's Swift is a Competitor. https://www.openstack.org/summit/vancouver-2015/summit-videos/presentation/swift-vs-ceph-from-an-architectural-standpoint.

[18] VMware Company Website. http://www.vmware.com/.

[19] Wikicommons File Stack Eye-Test Chart. https://upload.wikimedia.org/wikipedia/commons/3/30/IO_stack_of_the_Linux_kernel.svg.

[20] The Industry Looked Beyond SCSI. http://events.linuxfoundation.org/sites/events/files/lcjpcojp13_wheeler.pdf.

[21] Magic of NVM-Express. http://www.nvmexpress.org/.

[22] NVMe Jumbo Interrupt. https://www.osr.com/nt-insider/2014-issue4/introduction-nvme-technology/.

[23] Further Reduction in I/O Overhead. http://www.snia.org/sites/default/files/NVM13-Wheeler_Linux_and_NVM.pdf.

[24] SNIA's NVMe Over Fabrics Project. http://www.snia.org/sites/default/files/ESF/NVMe_Under_Hood_12_15_Final2.pdf.

Software-Defined Storage

5

Software-defined storage (SDS) is the culmination of the storage revolution. It completes the journey from the ancièn regime of proprietary storage solutions to the new age of open sourcing and separation of data services from hardware that is now low-cost commercial off-the-shelf (COTS)-based.

PRELUDE

Most storage appliances built in the last decade have a common thread. Data services (what the appliance can do to the data) are provided by the appliance vendor and built into the appliance. This gives the buyer a dilemma, since one vendor may offer compression, encryption, and erasure coding, while another might have file dedupli-cation, encryption, and replication, but no vendor offers a complete set of services. Proprietary services don't talk to each other, so training up admin staff and writing procedures around a specific solution tends to lock-in the customer to that vendor. This leads to higher prices, as the after-market and existing-customer deals offer lesser discounts than the specials created to entice that first buy.

Vendor lock-in creates some profound pricing disparities. The cost of extra stor-age drives [1] is invariably much higher than the price on the Internet. High markups used to be nearly invisible to end-users, as drive vendors agreed not to sell OEM enterprise drives into the distribution channel or on the Internet. This is not the case with SSDs, where almost all drives can be purchased through distribution. The advent of SSD has also removed the need for the enterprise drive tier and firmly relegated HDD sales to the commodity SATA arena, where appliance-level redundancy is driv-ing the last nail into the 15K and 10K RPM drive business.

Even though the cloud has burst the bubble of the high-priced server from well-established vendors, replacing the platforms with low-margin hardware [2] from mainly Chinese original design manufacturers (ODMs) [3], storage has been resistant to change. In part, that reflects the fear, uncertainty, and doubt (FUD) and protectionism of the tradi-tional large vendors, who rightly fear drastic revenue shrinkage on the hardware side, but the underlying issue is the lack of software to run on COTS storage platforms.

Those same self-protecting storage hardware guys also own the software stacks and they won't give them up easily. However, the open-source community is rising to the occasion and products like Ceph and the storage modules of OpenStack have huge followings. For the first time, we can easily buy COTS gear, add freeware

Network Storage. http://dx.doi.org/10.1016/B978-0-12-803863-5.00005-4

(just like Linux…, it might be a supported distribution with an annual maintenance/ support license), and put together combined appliances that are stable, of good quality, and very cheap.

The obvious success for the mega-CSPs doing this "Lego" approach hasn't been lost to large enterprises looking to greatly expand their capacity but keen to lower the cost of doing so. As a result, we are seeing a huge swing in the server unit count toward the ODMs, which doesn't reflect so much in revenue share yet due to the much lower prices being charged.

Servers have gone one extra step. Usage is highly automated. Holding the virtual machines on the servers as a single huge pool, orchestration can easily allocate new virtual machines (VMs), replace failed VMs, and figure out all the billing. Server farms do have one tremendous advantage over storage. They use hypervisors to create the VMs, essentially removing dependency for both the bare metal and for the operating system (OS)/apps running in any one VM.

We need a similar utility in storage and networking to be able to orchestrate them with the servers. This leads us to the concept of software-defined infrastructure and particularly to software-defined storage.

SOFTWARE-DEFINED STORAGE

Software-defined storage (SDS) [4] is a new concept deriving from the success of virtualizing servers. The idea is deceptively simple—take all the data services and put them into virtual instances inside the server farm.

This transition to "virtual storage appliances" opens up the future of storage. Its benefits include the ability to scale easily, since more parallel instances of a service can be spawned as needed by traffic levels. SDS removes the vendor lock-in limitations of the traditional approach, and, as application programming interfaces (APIs) standardize, should allow mashups of different vendor services to achieve the desired feature set.

In the example above, one could obtain services of encryption, compression, file deduplication, encryption, and erasure coding from five different vendors and so get a complete, best-of-breed solution. If, later, a better or cheaper compression service becomes available from a new vendor, making the change should be easy. This will drive competition, to the benefit of the datacenter customer. I would note that this is where we will end up. There is at the time of writing a lack of standard APIs to allow intercommunication between modules, but the SNIA Cloud Data Management Interface (CDMI) subcommittee [5] and others are addressing this and we should see some convergence in 2016.

SDS encourages innovation, so additional services should become available, especially when the APIs firm up. Examples are content-indexing and search services, or services tied to specific data types, such as internet of thing (IoT) content.

Innovation by startups, coupled with a commoditization of the actual storage devices, will radically reduce storage costs. The traditional vendors will be unable to justify drive prices in the thousands of dollars range when drives priced in the low hundreds bought from the Internet or distribution work as well.

A COMPLETELY NEW APPROACH

SDS is a completely new approach to storage, derived from the great success of automated orchestration in virtual server farms and clouds. One part of the thought process is to make services flexible, so that they can be added or scaled as needed via similar mechanisms that add virtual server instances or repair failed processes. This places data services inside virtual instances or containers (Fig. 5.1).

The other part of SDS that dramatically changes the physical layout of a datacenter is the idea that the storage devices themselves can be bare-bones, inexpensive, and highly commoditized. The traditional appliance likely has a pair of xeon processors capable both of moving data and performing required services, while the SDS storage brick probably uses a low-power, low-cost ARM just to move data. In fact, we can expect drive boxes using Ethernet drives where the drives talk directly to the servers and there is no local controller (Fig. 5.2).

SDS encourages innovation. Data doesn't need to flow from the originating server directly to a storage box anymore. An object could be sent to a hash generator, which allows deduplication checks, then forwarded to a compression engine, which makes it smaller, encrypted in yet another engine, and then distributed via erasure coding. Do you need indexing? Just change the flow to add indexing after deduplication (Fig. 5.3).

These services might reside in the same physical server, or be spread over a virtual server farm. Both configurations will work, so it comes down to whatever works best in a particular situation at a particular time.

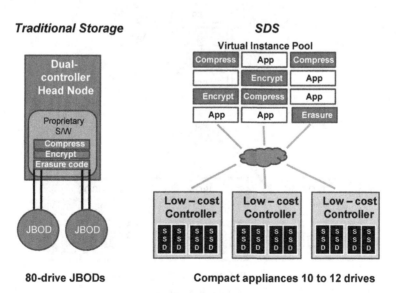

FIGURE 5.1

Traditional storage versus SDS.

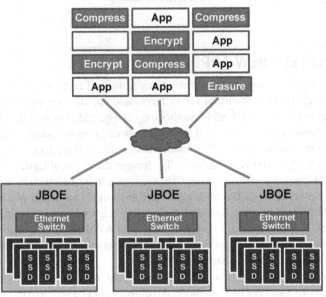

FIGURE 5.2

An *Ethernet Drive* solution.

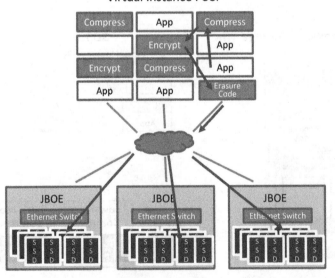

FIGURE 5.3

SDS dataflow example.

One consequence of this new freedom is that we'll see a lot more data-type specific services… databases, big data, etc. With standards coming from the likes of SNIA for the APIs and data formats, this should ease new features into the operational flow quickly, really enriching data management as a consequence.

One warning is that we are seeing some of the traditional vendors wrapping proprietary, appliance-tied code [6] as "SDS". This is likely a transient response to hide their evident confusion and lateness/weakness of their response, but beware of SDS that runs only on the software vendor's hardware… you'll pay through the nose.

WHO ARE THE PLAYERS?

There are two sets of players in the SDS game. On the one side, established vendors are laying claim to SDS-like features. Some have more credibility than others. EMC has ViPR [7], aimed at aggregating storage into a single shareable pool whatever the underlying platform. ViPR though is being moved to open sourcing as the "Copperhead" [8] project, which may be more internal EMC politics than good planning.

Dell is partnering, like crazy, with Nexenta [9] being a notable SDS add-on to the company's hardware platforms. In fact, many SDA startup vendors are looking to the traditional vendors as outlets for their products. One notable success story is Scality [10], who claim EMC, Dell, and other large vendors as resellers and partners.

Pure software plays like Nexenta and Scality are complemented by Datacore [11] and, perhaps surprisingly given their reputation for being a bit pedestrian, Microsoft's Windows Storage Server [12]. Open-source has jumped in with Ceph [13], which is close to being a distributable virtualizable resource, but isn't quite there yet.

Other startups are joining in the game, so this will be a crowded and somewhat confused field for a while. It isn't helped by some traditional companies stamping SDS on every piece of software in sight. Typically, these are closed systems and any relationship with "real" SDS ends at the PR department.

These products have taken the first step to becoming SDS by disconnecting sales from the hardware platform dependencies of the past, becoming agnostic to the platform as long as it supports Linux or Windows as appropriate. The next step, of achieving interoperability between software modules, still seems to be ways away as of writing, although the open-source fraternity likely will work the "glueware" issue out. SNIA will be a venue for interoperability efforts to move to standardization, perhaps as part of the DCMI effort.

"LEGO" STORAGE

The commoditization effect of SDS is to make storage very much like Lego. The Danish magic [14] that Lego brings is that all the pieces use the same "API", the circular locking mechanism, while the variety of basic bricks unlocks a huge spectrum of creativity; add some specialized pieces and you can build a Star Wars toy or a fairy castle.

Storage bricks will be much the same. The basic commodity of storage will be the 12-drive small appliance, capable of being racked and stacked to huge capacities. For backup/archiving, the sweet spot may be 60-drive units, but the economics at high volumes are complex and not always intuitive, so the large capacity box may end up costing more than the small brick.

These bricks will be simple. If there is a controller, it will be an ARM, but I expect we will move toward zero-controller bricks that connect the drives directly to Ethernet. There will be no redundancy in the brick. Data integrity is provided by a data service that either replicates the data or uses erasure codes to spread it over many bricks, so the loss of one brick or a single drive is handled on the cluster level, not on the appliance as in traditional RAID systems.

A countervailing approach is to have primary storage drives in each server in a cloud or cluster, so that IO rates can be maximized. In this situation, data are shared via high-performance remote direct memory access (RDMA) links in a virtual SAN. The "brick" in this case looks remarkably like the 12-drive brick above, except that a large XEON server is used for the compute side. Which of these approaches will win in storage isn't clear yet, and possibly they'll coexist serving different aspects of the system need.

CONNECTING THE PIECES

The key to effective SDS, as in Lego, is the interconnection scheme. It must be possible to easily connect (or disconnect) services to operate on any given data object or class of objects. The obvious way to do this is to use extended metadata to identify service flows for each object or object type. The structure and APIs that make this happen will need to be standardized by the industry.

SNIA is offering the metadata systems built around the CDMI [15] as one way to achieve standardization. We can expect pseudo-open solutions from a couple of the traditional vendors being offered as alternatives, if history is anything to go by.

UNIFIED STORAGE APPLIANCES

SDS is network agnostic and doesn't enforce a single storage networking protocol on the industry. However, it's pretty obvious that the paradigms all work better with Ethernet, since this is (with the exception of some InfiniBand) becoming the standard scheme for clouds and clusters.

This single factor tolls the passing bell for other connection schemes. Fiber-channel is destined to fade away, for example. If drives with Ethernet interfaces catch on, SAS and SATA will follow fiber-channel.

Even so, there is a need to handle block-IO, file, and object environments. Several key software packages, including Ceph, recognize that the access protocol can be abstracted from the drive data handling itself. The result is "unified storage" where a single software package can handle all three protocol classes in parallel, allowing them to share the same pool of data.

Unified storage removes the decision on protocol type from the IT table. It's possible to do what is convenient. More importantly as we transition toward a universe where one single approach is used (almost certainly an extended version of object storage protocols such as REST), the unified approach creates a transition vehicle.

We can expect the traditional storage vendors to offer unified solutions of various sorts. EMC already has ViPR, which can pool some heterogeneous systems together, but as of the time of writing, there were some signs of conflict inside EMC over its strategic positioning. The debate probably hinges on how much proprietary locks matter, versus the ability to use third party and whitebox gear.

AGILITY AND FLEXIBILITY

SDS offers agility in building configurations to match demand, both to central IT and to departmental users. Accepting that "slow-moving, rigid IT structures are part of ancient history" will take some time, but that's the reality of the near future. Much of the "learned best practices" around storage will need to be revised, or even abandoned.

Examples are "RAID for integrity", "fibre-channel for performance", "enterprise-class drives", "redundant controllers", etc. At another level, how data storage is doled out, recaptured, and monitored in a cloudy environment is very far apart from CAPEX-focused storage buying. Old loyalties to vendors will be broken, cost structures will change radically, and methods of acquiring capacity will move from buying to renting... not 100%, but certainly by a substantial percentage over time.

A benefit of all of this is that the new IT operational paradigms will be much more flexible. New ways to allocate storage to meet needs will surface, billing will be based on what is actually used at a given point in time rather than amortization of fixed assets, and access to new technologies, both to try out and to rent, will be much faster, encouraging entrepreneurs to innovative further.

THE IMPLICATIONS OF SDS TO THE DATACENTER

SDS is not just a new and agile way of doing storage. By separating storage into hardware and software "Lego", many of the proprietary lock-ins are demolished. With multiple vendors offering any particular service and a real commoditization of the hardware, the resulting competition should drive low prices. This will have a notable effect on drive pricing, as the concept of "enterprise storage" evaporates away before commodity bulk hard drives and low-cost SSD units.

Over the next few years, the traditional vendors such as EMC + Dell, NetApp, and HP will need to adjust to this model or become irrelevant to the mainstream storage.

This is a major challenge for them, given that they have built the whole companies around selling high-margin proprietary gear. In effect, their challenge is to migrate to a software/services model within a relatively short time period.

For the datacenter, the evolution of the large companies will tend to break old buying relationships. As it becomes clear that the Chinese ODMs are underselling the US vendors with high-quality SDS-compatible products, the old reliance on brand-name and organizational inertia will dissipate, leaving the field more open to a transition to the new vendor set.

SDS AND THE CLOUD

SDS is a good match to any cloud approach. With all the services virtualized, where they run is a function of dataflow efficiency and instance cost more than any desire for localization. Most likely, we will see companies deploy SDS in hybrid clouds as a way to tie in-house storage to the public segment of the hybrid, but it should be remembered that the mega-CSPs favor the approach within their clouds, too. In fact, altough they are tightlipped on what may be a set of major competitive advantages, the mega-CSPs are well along in their own proprietary versions of SDS already.

It's a matter of time before the public and private cloud worlds homogenize on an SDS environment, but that seems to be inevitable. It's in everyone's long-term interest to have homogeneity, but in the short term, any attempt by a CSP to deliver their solution to, say, OpenStack, will have lock-in overtones. This won't last... the user base is to savvy and experienced in bringing a workable consensus.

THE CURRENT STATE OF SDS

We've passed through the hype phase of SDS, for the most part. Claims of proprietary solutions being software-defined are diminishing, so one can expect some reality soon. We are seeing some moves by startups toward a software-only business model and this is accelerating. The year 2016 should see a rapid evolution and a number of ab initio SDS companies will reach market.

Hardware from the ODMs is available, and the low-cost, 12-drive appliance class is available from many vendors, ranging from large ODMs to startup operations.

We can expect 2017 will see SDS enter the mainstream in a big way. This will drop price points, even with the US vendors, but the datacenter will be talking more to distributors, especially on the question of buying drives, since the ODM products are much less restrictive on drive models and allow self-sourcing.

SDS is about software, and here the picture is just starting to take shape, at least outside of the mega-CSPs. A number of vendors have already declared themselves to be software companies and now describe their proprietary approaches as "software-defined". Looking beyond the hype, there's precious little "defining" going on as yet. This is software lifted from COTS-based appliances and each package exists as an island in the storage pool still.

Now I'm not saying that these packages haven't got the makings of becoming SDS. There just isn't the multivendor framework to tie these independent modules into a dataflow, or to publish a structure metadata that announces service characteristics and availability. That 's still a goal to be reached in 2017, I think.

There are some signs of a larger world-view in the industry. Notably, IBM is quietly amassing a powerful IP portfolio by buying up companies with specific storage-software solutions. They picked up Cleversafe [16] in 2015, which gave them object storage and erasure coding. Put 2+2 together and it seems like IBM is creating a dataflow solution and a framework for SDS to be built on.

Companies like Symantec [17] and Datacore are also well positioned to create an SDS framework. EMC appeared to be heading in much the same direction with ViPR, which is being released into open-source as "copperhead", but not only is this in a state of flux due to internal politics and now the merger, ViPR/Copperhead has a more proprietary intent, insofar as it will tie in most EMC products early in its lifecycle, while the rest of the industry will take some time to interface up.

Whether Copperhead can or should be rescued and made more general is a debating point. Functionally, it is described as creating a single storage pool out of diverse EMC, whitebox and third-party vendor product, which sounds like a good management tool to have around what will be a diversified SDS pool. It also addresses the transition to SDS by providing a vehicle to reuse legacy storage boxes, which will weigh heavily in any SDS transition plan.

In putting together a nascent SDS story, it is worth mentioning that cloud gateway companies are paying attention to the opportunity, too. Bridging the private–public boundary will be crucial to the cloud growth and SDS has to service that need, rather than getting in its way. Indeed, done well, the SDS common framework may ease a lot of the boundary problems, so there may be some room here for entrepreneurial opportunism.

In sum, the state of the SDS art is that the hardware is basically available, but software is missing on a unifying framework standard, and as a result, SDS claims, to date, lack some credibility, being independent "data service islands". This is being addressed, both by standards groups like SNIA and companies like IBM and perhaps EMC. It might better be a part of (heavily supported) OpenStack as yet another project aimed at storage virtualization, since hybrid clouds will be a major early user of both SDN and SDS techniques.

THE FUTURE OF THE STORAGE INDUSTRY

The storage industry is about to change radically. With the FC SAN going away, filers converting to object storage and price points dropping like a rock, vendors with an end-user sales model based on large gross margin will struggle to stay afloat. Many will migrate into software/support models over the next few years, but this place them in a competitive market against open-sourced solutions and new startups. This is a tough arena in which to be a top dog. We can expect mergers and fallout. Dell+EMC think the market favors the big battalions, but they are both high-margin operations (with EMC much higher than Dell, of course) and will be settling out a mega-merger while the industry transitions to a low-margin model.

NetApp [18] is clearly the leader in filer software, but they've denied the object storage model more than any traditional player and are very unprepared for a transition away from the filer. NetApp also faces challenges from Windows Storage Server and the new SMB 3.0 protocol.

Hewlett-Packard Enterprise (HPE) [19] is floundering in storage and lacks a focused direction, while IBM, to their credit, is getting out of the commodity hardware space altogether and is focused just on delivering just the software for storage. With the notable exception of DDN [20], who has developed high-performance object and block solutions based on COTS, the smaller fry will be in even tougher straits and will probably search for a merger or acquisition.

Who will step up to the plate? On the hardware side, expect SuperMicro [21], Quanta [22], and Lenovo [23] for starters. Mitac [24] also is likely to join the pack of new leaders. These all have a low-margin, efficient business model and should do well. Notably, years of working high volumes through tough operations like Google have honed their product, and they know the cloud market very well. Huawei also wants into the game.

What they currently generally lack is an efficient go-to-market presence in the United States and Europe. They do have access to all the mega-CSPs, of course, but those companies are gun-shy about releasing internal architectures and vendor relationships. SuperMicro and Lenovo are both well-known and trusted for quality, so that will give them a decided edge moving forward, but the others will catch up within a couple of years in the recognition stakes.

The situation is somewhat like the TV industry. Asian brands took over the supply side, while some of the old names, such as Magnavox, continued to be used for their brand value. This is bound to happen to the storage industry. Will NetApp become a front for Lenovo, for example, or will NetApp merge with HP just as EMC and Dell have joined up on the principle, possibly very misguided, that bigger is better.

This changeout of vendors isn't an overnight event, and the established players will fight back tooth and nail. Most probably, they will attempt to reestablish themselves as software companies and try to cash in on the SDS revolution. As I've said previously, IBM appears to be exercising a strategy to do this and is making the right moves... buying storage software companies, while discarding COTS-based hardware operations.

Commoditization will have an impact on the supply chain. Likely, much more hardware product will be obtained via distribution, including the all-important drives themselves. SDS should mask most of the bare-metal differences in hardware, while the concept should allow vendor-specific software to cover the rest (sort of like drivers, but at a higher level).

The exception will be large enterprises, which will follow the CSP model of going direct to the ODMs. We can expect a portion of the market to be averse to integrating hardware and software, so integrators and VARS should do well in the SMB space and the low end of the enterprise market.

The focus on COTS for SDS means that hardware support is a simplified good deal. Frankly, most solutions will be identical or near-identical to Intel and other reference design. The tendency will be to avoid building in any proprietary features, just as in the PC industry, with the result that support expertise will be both portable and widespread.

Software support is another issue. This will necessarily be vendor-specific, and there will be conflicts or issues between data-service software packages, especially in the early days. This could cause the conservative IT shop to consider buying from one of the old vendors as a way to avoid building new support channels and to dodge interoperability problems. This would be a very short-sighted approach, since the price premiums involved outweigh the benefits of the single vendor, while keeping you locked-in to a proprietary solution set that misses the opportunity to join the flow of new features that SDS will bring.

The future of the old storage companies can be summed up as, having "globalized" and migrated hardware manufacturing to the lowest cost third parties, they are now seeing the inevitable result of their strategy, which is those third parties have figured out that the middle-man no longer adds enough value. Survival in an SDS-centric software world will be a challenge for them, especially as their code is in the main very monolithic and not designed for an agile virtual environment.

REFERENCES

[1] The Cost of Extra Storage Drives. http://www.storagenewsletter.com/rubriques/systems-raid-nas-san/five-things-storage-vendors-are-not-telling-you/.
[2] Low-Margin Hardware. http://www.forbes.com/sites/greatspeculations/2015/07/13/odm-storage-vendors-gain-share-from-giants-emc-hp-ibm-netapp-lose-market-presence/#40841d6d173e.
[3] Chinese ODMs. https://www.ventureoutsource.com/contract-manufacturing/focus-odm-quanta-it-shift-cloud-infrastructure-leaving-dell-hp-traditional.
[4] Software-Defined Storage (SDS). http://www.networkcomputing.com/storage/software-defined-storage-deeper-look/617535779.
[5] SNIA CDMI Sub-Committee. http://www.snia.org/cdmi.
[6] Traditional Vendors Wrapping Proprietary, Appliance-Tied Code. https://blog.osnexus.com/2013/11/27/what-is-software-defined-storage-sds/.
[7] EMC ViPR. http://www.emc.com/products/storage/software-defined-storage/vipr-controller.htm.
[8] Copperhead Open Source Software. http://www.emc.com.mt/about/news/press/2015/20150505-02.htm.
[9] Nexenta Company Website. http://www.nexenta.com/.
[10] Scality Company Website. http://www.scality.com/.
[11] Datacore Company Website. http://www.datacore.com/.
[12] Windows Storage Server. https://technet.microsoft.com/en-us/library/jj643303.aspx.
[13] Ceph Special Interest Group. http://www.ceph.com/.
[14] Lego's Danish magic. http://www.topspeed.com/cars/car-news/this-lego-porsche-911-gt3-rs-looks-amazing-video-ar173138.html.

[15] Cloud Data Management Interface. http://www.snia.org/sites/default/files/SDC15_presentations/cloud/DavidSlik_Using_CDMI_ Management.pdf.

[16] IBM Picked up Cleversafe. http://www.networkcomputing.com/storage/why-ibm-bought-cleversafe/1349563859.

[17] Symantec Company Website. http://www.symantec.com/.

[18] NetApp Company Website. http://www.netapp.com/.

[19] HPE (Hewlett-Packard Enterprise) Company Website. http://www.hpe.com/.

[20] DDN (Data Direct Networks) Company Website. http://www.ddn.com/.

[21] SuperMicro Company Website. http://www.supermicro.com/.

[22] Quanta Company Website. http://www.qct.io/.

[23] Lenovo. http://www.crn.com/news/storage/300076946/lenovo-enters-enterprise-storage-market-without-emc-ibm-help.htm.

[24] Mitac. http://www.mic-holdings.com/.

Today's Hot Issues

6

Storage today has a number of areas where fundamental questions remain in dispute. Often, this is a struggle between the entrenched giants of the industry and a set of forces that threaten their growth or even their long-term survival. These debates tend to devolve into "Fear, uncertainty, and doubt" (FUD) exercises on the part of the defending incumbents, combatted by overhyped claims on the part of the upstarts.

It's not possible to hit all of the hot issues in storage, although some have already been touched on in earlier chapters. There are three, however, that hit at the foundations of what storage is, or will be. These are the debates about:

1. NAS versus SAN versus Object Storage
2. Ethernet and the End of the SAN
3. Commoditization and the Network

Let's take them one at a time.

NAS VERSUS SAN VERSUS OBJECT STORAGE

Talk to any older group of storage engineers or admins about what the best storage protocol is and you'll usually find intensely held opinions and a somewhat dogmatic view of the storage game. Probably the most heated debates come on the issue of whether to use network-attached storage (NAS) or storage area network (SAN), and lately the representational state transfer (REST) protocol for object storage has gotten into the act.

The NAS view is that sharing data by having its metadata stored on the network appliance makes most senses, while the SAN adherents firmly believe that block level operations are the most efficient. The debate often rages over performance levels, but it must now be admitted that protocols and access methods are much less relevant to performance than underlying drives and storage software efficiency. In any case, the differences are just a few percentage points, although discussions of that point rarely were qualified by the extra price to be paid for that small increment of performance.

The consequences of the NAS–SAN debate were profound. Two complete streams of development occurred, with no attempts to cross over between the camps. By 1998, EMC was synonymous with SAN, while NetApp led the NAS camp, and companies followed one or the other. Open-source NAS complicated the issue somewhat

Network Storage. http://dx.doi.org/10.1016/B978-0-12-803863-5.00006-6

by offering a do-it-yourself path to a networked storage system using an off-the-shelf server. Many companies used this approach for sharing files between PCs.

Some of the innovation in those early days looks a bit bizarre in hindsight. Making a SAN file-space shareable by multiple servers requires some complicated locking and access control systems, something that came naturally to NAS systems. NAS also lived on Ethernet networks, which even in the early days of NAS were ubiquitous. The flexibility to attach anything from a PC to a landline connection didn't overcome the entrenched SAN worldview, which continues to demand HBAs and separate cabling.

Even so, a lot of duplicated effort occurred in the storage industry as vendors matched the new data services from the other camp. Eventually, though, buyers settled into NAS or SAN camps, typically driven by an installed base of one or the other, with the result that poaching between SAN and NAS slowed and the speed of innovation in storage dropped.

Another element of the NAS-SAN debate is Ethernet versus *Fibre*-Channel. The fibre channel (FC) community defends their operational advantages, such as a better bit-mapping scheme, vehemently, but the reality is these are not significant in the big picture. We'll get into that debate in the next section.

Perhaps the kindest word that can be said about the NAS–SAN debate is that it may actually have mattered more back in 1994, when Ethernet evolved more slowly. A suspicion that job security is somehow involved might also have validity.

Irrespective of the great debate, object storage happened as a result of the realization that neither NAS nor SAN could scale to any serious size. In the case of NAS, redundancy and data integrity were localized to the individual NAS appliance, while, in the case of the SAN, the difficulties of controlling multiple access at the block level and addressing of data made for problems. Along comes the object store. It is designed from the start to be easy to scale… mostly a "just-add-boxes-and-we'll-handle-the-rest" approach. The evidence is that this goal is well met, so it's worth asking why the other methods of addressing storage haven't been supplanted [1].

Partly it's FUD again. The large NAS/SAN vendors didn't want erosion of their business, especially in the early days while having no object stores of their own. The result was that a recognizable pattern emerged. The entrenched vendors bunkered down and dissed the object storage idea rather successfully for several years.

The object storage guys didn't help themselves by having a verbose and complicated back-end between nodes that ran slowly and defied performance tuning. The result was that object became somewhat synonymous with backup storage—a good place to put objects that won't be altered.

In addition, the object storage camp created its own access protocol, REST. It might be designed for scale-out addressing, but REST is different from FC, SCSI, NFS, or SMB. It requires a substantial modification to application software and some new expertise in using it, so that was another block to object acceptance. In hindsight, a translator from the traditional protocols to REST running in the server would have been a simpler path to acceptance and convergence.

The FUD level is starting to diminish as the traditional vendors add object storage units to their line-ups. This may be premature. It looks like that the proprietary products are very expensive compared with open-source + whitebox, which is not surprisingly reducing sales. A telling point is that not one of the traditional vendors has a major object storage win with the mega-cloud-service providers (CSPs).

We are seeing convergence in storage today in the form of unified storage appliances, which provide all of the access methods under one roof, usually hosted on an object store. Strictly speaking, the protocols are not converted to REST, but use internal APIs to achieve a compatible access. This doesn't mean, however, that any one data object can be addressed by the three access methods, which in turn implies that the applications will continue to have REST or block or filer calls. Someone, somewhere, needs to write a REST stack that is invisible to the Linux and Windows file system and applications.

The discovery that more and more of our data fit this write-once model is changing the picture. Images, video, emails, and unstructured big data are all candidates for object storage, as are web page elements. In this respect, Amazon's S3 has demonstrated how huge scale can get and has proven to be robust, easy to use, and very economical. In the end, scale-out capability may force the migration to an object-storage-only environment, but this looks to be a few years away. In the meantime, yet another high-speed protocol, NVMe over Fabrics [2], is entering the market and 3× the effort will be needed to match it to the access methods.

The object world is changing. Today, the performance issues are being addressed. Data Direct Networks (DDN) has especially high-performance object stores in their WOS family and it's a matter of time before the object storage generally catches up with NAS and SAN performance. That will leave a dilemma for the chief information officer (CIO) to decide which to use. The application rewrite required for REST will likely get fixed within a year, so that roadblock to object will disappear, leaving mostly the performance issue to resolve.

Open-source software and low-cost COTS appliances are driving the object storage market, with the result that low price per terabyte number are hard to argue with. The advance of software-defined storage (SDS) should accelerate this trend, and in the end, economics should bring the industry to convergence, even if the price paid is supporting NAS and SAN within the object storage framework.

Generally, I think the industry would have progressed better if the "War Between the Access Methods" hadn't occurred. Cooperation on methods would have increased competition in boxes and features and perhaps even prevented the stagnation of the 2000–10 period. In sum then, this debate is over now minor issues but it has been a major stumbling block in evolving storage.

ETHERNET AND THE END OF THE SAN

Ethernet and Fibre-Channel became part of the NAS–SAN debate early on. Ethernet was the fabric of choice for NAS, while FC was originally the only way to connect SAN elements together. The fact that Ethernet used copper connections while FC used Fibre tended to separate them in the price point as well as technology. It was claimed that Fibre gave FC a transmission quality advantage, which was certainly true in the 1-Gbps days. However, cost got the better of the debate and copper FC links were introduced.

An aside: One architectural difference of note was the ability to talk to drives over FC as well as appliances. Coupled with a pass through switch, it was possible to create a token-ring type of structure that cheaply connected lots of drives. This approach lasted until drives got faster and the cost premium for FC drives became too high to sustain, at which point FC to SAS converters became the norm. With Ethernet drives just hitting the market, it's possible some of these lower-cost approaches may see resurrection, especially given that the new Ethernet drives are pretty smart. The drive may even end up as a self-contained appliance in the SDS constellation, with some interesting impacts on topologies and packaging.

With Ethernet running on a "10× in 10 years" performance design cycle and FC running on a "2× every 3 years" model, there was plenty of room for leap-frogging hype. FC enjoyed a period of leadership on performance up to the point where 8-Gbps FC beat 10 GbE to market by a year (in 2005/2006) just as we entered a recession that slowed 10-GbE's deployment down tremendously and kept 10-GbE network gear price points as high as FC's (Fig. 6.1).

I think the 10-GbE slowdown was the primary motivation for a rethink of the "10× in 10 years" IEEE Ethernet strategy. As the recession abated in 2012, we saw first

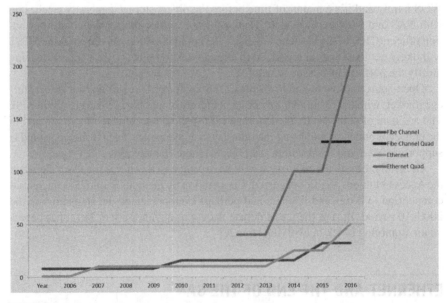

FIGURE 6.1

Evolution of Ethernet and FC line speeds.

40-GbE solutions, followed by 100 GbE, and just recently 25-GbE base links and a much lower cost 100-GbE solution. There are other Ethernet happenings that change the leadership position totally. RDMA over Ethernet is beginning to replace Infini-Band, and will see a lot of mileage in storage.

One might argue that the Fibre-Channel community has a strong roadmap. 16-Gbps FC is here, 32 Gbps (which will actually be 28 Gbps) is coming in early 2017, and a 4-waylane aggregation system just like 40-GbE uses will take 4×32 Gbps lanes to 128 (really 112) Gbps in 2017/2018. RDMA and NVMe of FC are also being talked up for 2017/2018.

The problem is that all of this is already available on Ethernet [3], and their community also has an aggressive roadmap. The result is that FC is destined to play catchup technically, and be at least 2 years behind.

In the protocol stakes, Fibre-Channel's attempt to bridge over to Ethernet [Fibre-Channel over Ethernet (FCoE)] is not strongly supported [4]. Ethernet-based iSCSI (Internet Small Computer System Interface), which is a long-standing alternative for block level traffic, is flourishing. It's this that has and will continue to weaken FC's hold on block-level storage, especially as there is ample evidence that performance, stability, and data integrity are within statistical error or the vagaries of configurations in both types of appliances.

In some ways, though, the issue is no longer technical. Who is the fastest no longer matters so much. We are in an era where server and network virtualization is being automatically orchestrated in clouds, at tremendous efficiency levels and with huge cost savings. With Ethernet having performance and cost advantages over Fibre-Channel already, orchestration is the key factor that pushes storage networking to Ethernet.

The orchestration story is strengthened by the likely migration to SDS. The mega-CSPs are already driving down this path, given the scale of the operations. The implication is that we need to be able to deploy storage data services in an agile manner across the pool of virtual machines, which in turn implies an Ethernet network rather than a Fibre-Channel one [5].

So far, in this section, we've been addressing Ethernet and Fibre-Channel. FC is nearly synonymous with SANs … it has no other use … but the opposite actually isn't true. FCoE was a failed attempt to break free of FC; it failed because it required a "converged" Ethernet topology in the datacenter, which generally meant expensive router boxes from Cisco and FCoE NICs (Note that iWARP is beating out RoCE [6] for just the same reason. Expensive networks to gain a small percentage of performance just aren't worth it).

But there is more. We have virtual SANs emerging as an alternative to the other storage methods, which complicates the question of just what is a SAN no end. Virtual SANs aim to share the storage in each server with the network. The concept is that the direct-attached drives provide a pool of storage that is managed, usually by a proprietary data service. These drives are made available on the Ethernet network to all the other servers in the virtual SAN cluster.

It's still too early to figure whether virtual SANs [7] will be successful, and if they are what form will they standardize to. We can expect object storage to virtualize data services too and also allow instantiation of those services on virtualized servers, so virtual SANs have a strong competitor in the wings.

It isn't clear if this is the future of storage or a stopgap, either. Both WD and Seagate have Ethernet hard drives, making it possible to argue a future where drives are just nodes on the cluster network. NVMe over Ethernet fits well into that picture. A further complication is the likely evolution of servers in 2016 as 3D X-Point memory [8] arrives from Intel/Micron, bring fast persistent and DRAM extensions coupled with the potential removal of any need for local drives. In this situation, the idea of a virtual SAN of 3D X-Point DIMMs as the only storage doesn't hold up to scrutiny and some other networked storage appliances will be needed.

We've digressed a long way from the "traditional" FC SAN concepts. The virtual SANs are SANs in name only, at least at this point, and it's clear that there are competitive alternatives that dilute the SAN concept further. This likely is the end for SANs as we know them, based on FC, although we can expect FC to fade away over as much as a decade or even more.

I confess to some personal nostalgia over this. Randy Meals and I had some deep discussions over using fibre with SCSI when he was Director of Research and I was GM at NCR in Wichita. Randy later led the division of HP that brought the first Fibre-Channel to market. Neither of us suspected it would do so well and for so long.

COMMODITIZATION AND THE STORAGE NETWORK

The last few years have brought a quantum shift in the structure of servers. With the cloud demonstrating that the use of a common architecture makes for the lowest cost and for seamless replacement, the rest of the industry has been forced to follow suit.

This in many ways is one of the roots of the *Storage Revolution*. The traditional vendors all have moved to commodity platforms. We no longer see specialized CPUs for storage controllers. In the main, these are ×64 architecture today, with ARM 32 for the low-end market. Typically, these units have a Linux operating system. There isn't much real hardware differentiation between vendors.

Moreover, most of the older vendors moved manufacturing to China, to take advantage of low wages. Putting all of this together, we have a highly commoditized industry on the hardware side [9], which is ripe for penetration by the very original design manufacturer (ODM) suppliers who were set up to keep the industry cost-effective. It turns out that the ODMs have figured how to grow huge annual sales volumes by working with big CSPs such as AWS and Google, and they are now parleying this into cutting out the middlemen such as HPE, EMC, etc.

The impact on the traditional vendor base is immense. Companies like EMC with a business model based on a markup (at list) in the range of 10× the component cost find themselves competing with essentially the same hardware they sell from vendors living off 10 to 20 percent gross margins. The response from the old guard is as expected, with concerted efforts to emphasize software feature, support, and product quality. The problem is that their own supplier base (the ODMs) is cutting out the middleman, while open-source and SDS software matches and sometimes exceeds the best the old guard can offer.

That leaves support as a value proposition, but, in a commoditized environment where there are no real mysteries involved in system integration, support is no longer the arcane art it used to be. The result will be a good portion of business will migrate to the new suppliers and their associated fulfillment and integrator partners. While this still leaves the traditional supplier base with a segment of the market, the price pressure associated with the ODM-selling model will force revenue per unit way down, amplifying the stress on the traditional supplier.

The second key to the storage revolution is the advent of open-source software packages such as Ceph and OpenStack. These provide the features needed for competitive storage appliances, a necessary step to change the storage game radically. There is now a strong trend (SDS) toward abstracting data service software form the hardware base, making it more agile and competitive.

The move to COTS and the software trend have called into question many cherished sacred cows of the IT industry. Why do any maintenance? Just move the failed workload to another virtual machine instance. Why have warranties? Just buy a few extra machines as spares. Do servers all have to be the same? Do I need a video port on each server? Do I need a local drive?

The list of questions is very long, but the point is that we are heading toward minimalist server designs, where proprietary architectures and features add no value since they fall outside the common denominator of the cloud cluster. This has led us to *Software-Defined Networking* (SDN) [10], where network data services are abstracted from the switch gear and instantiated in an agile manner in server virtual machines. Switch hardware is becoming a commodity merchant chip, with standard APIs to communicate.

This concept is spilling over into storage. The realization that COTS JBODs (just a bunch of discs) and appliances are good enough for today's distributed data integrity systems and that drives bought from distribution are of pretty good quality means that old vendor lock-ins to proprietary hardware and vendor-delivered high-priced drives are on their way out.

This is what AWS and Google have been doing for years. Of course, they buy enough gear to go directly OEM to the drive makers and the server ODMs, but they've built up the quality systems and the cost model that makes this easy for the rest of us mere mortals.

Commoditization is now inevitable, with all the impacts on traditional vendors that a major revision of their business model implies. Margins in the single digits on hardware, low maintenance revenues, cutthroat competitors using price as a selling point, migration away from direct-sales…it's a long list and the transition is coming fast. The FUD machines will be running at full speed, but the newbies will be able to say "Google already has a million of these", and much of the debate is over.

Remember too that most of the traditional vendors buy from Chinese ODMs rather than build their own units. They use fulfillment companies [11] to tailor the systems to customers' needs after they arrive in the US or EU. This is a low-value add to the ODM product, which means that traditional vendors are very vulnerable to the ODMs moving directly into the space, just like what the TV business has seen [12].

There is some risk that we will migrate to a deep reliance on the Intels of the world for reference designs, slowing innovation tremendously, but in many ways we've already reached the point where most designs struggle for any differentiation. The SDS/SDN approach should at least open up the doors for innovative data services, and also for creative ways to assemble the Lego together (As that company would tell you, the profit is no longer in the bricks; it's in the boxed sets!)

As this book is written, more and more storage companies are breaking the bonds of hardware specificity. This is a result of the centering of the industry on x64 architectures for the smart platforms in appliances, which has occurred over the last few years. The result is that they already work on COTS platforms and just need to be virtualized and interfaced to each other. With this as last, the common interface or API still eludes the industry, but it's early days.

Mostly, these are small companies, with little to lose from the hardware side in revenue, a value add that is primarily software and no rigid support structures for hardware in place. The only major player to overtly recognize the need for COTS is EMC, whose ViPR storage consolidator is stated to handle "whitebox" commodity designs as part of a total storage pool. It isn't clear that EMC generally has accepted this approach as mainstream; however, ViPR is now being made available as an open-source product called "Copperhead" and looks more and more like a way to make EMC legacy gear useful in pools of SDS.

Object storage appliances are beginning to look like compact 12-drive servers, as an example of COTS impact on the product lines. It may well be that servers and storage will look more like each other as we go forward, but the migration to shared storage may make drive-less servers even more attractive.

The advent of the so-called hyper-converged clusters [13] confuses all of this, but these configurations appear to be vehicles for increasing prices a bit, coupled with old-fashioned vendor lock-in. We may see the ODMs delivering similar converged solutions…they already have the server units with say 12 drive bays. The issue is that the ODMs will not demand sourcing of drives and other components from their price list, so overall costs will drop a lot.

With changes in the structure of the server motherboard coming with *Hybrid Memory Cube* [14] or its variants, we can expect a diskless or 2-drive SSD unit to be very compact. A quarter-U design is quite possible and, with these being much faster than current servers, a datacenter shrink based on these compact boxes is attractive, leaving the virtual SAN/object store appliances to a more tailored solution.

Even with divergence between servers and storage being as likely as not, the internal "Lego" of these COTS units is essentially identical. The remaining differences will mainly be in the metal-work of the server or appliance. With highly reliable SSD replacing the HDD, the industry is leaning toward not replacing failed drives until the unit is swapped out at its end of life, when it might be sold on to a third party. An implication of this is that costly items such as drive caddies will disappear from systems as a way to save both acquisition costs and the cost of admin staff.

The COTS-based revolution is the most profound driving force in storage today. Users will benefit tremendously, but as Pat Gelsinger, the President of VMware said in late 2015, perhaps half of the top 100 tech companies will disappear [15] in the next few years. We will see an industry more like television, where the hardware comes from mostly China, while the software and content are generated locally. The new shrunk-down server motherboard of 2016 might be built locally too…that will depend on Intel.

A comment on the International Data Corporation (IDC)/Gartner view of the trends highlights the impact of the revolution that is beginning in storage. Because there is a dramatic price difference in whitebox or ODM gear, it doesn't typically get the emphasis it should in the pundit reports. The low-cost boxes will have a much higher percentage of unit sales than unit revenue, possibly three to one different. The real impact is that the units sold by the low-cost vendors replace units offered by the traditional vendors, so their effect on total revenue for storage is significant, and as that whitebox unit share increases, the traditional server vendors' revenue stream will begin to drop, especially when they begin trying to compete on prices. This is already happening fast in servers, and storage will follow in 2016/2017.

To sum this up, COTS and open-source code have triggered an unstoppable revolution in the storage industry. Though in its early days, we can expect the winds to blow strongly over the next few years, with the result being a playing field full of new approaches, new vendors, and much lower costs to the IT buyer.

After 30 years of essentially stagnation, storage needed a major shake-out and we are certainly seeing it begin.

REFERENCES

[1] Other methods of addressing storage haven't been supplanted. http://searchstorage.techtarget.com/feature/Object-storage-vendors-push-NAS-out-of-the-enterprise.
[2] NVMe over Fabrics. http://www.tomsitpro.com/articles/nvme-over-fabrics-qlogic-brocade,1–3064.html.
[3] RDMA, etc already available on Ethernet. http://www.mellanox.com/blog/2015/12/top-7-reasons-why-fibre-channel-is-doomed/.
[4] FCoE not strongly supported. http://www.theregister.co.uk/2015/05/26/fcoe_is_dead_for_real_bro/.
[5] Ethernet network rather than a Fibre-Channel one. http://www.networkcomputing.com/storage/sinking-fibre-channel-san/110754926.
[6] iWARP is beating out RoCE. http://www.hpcwire.com/2015/11/30/roce-fails-to-scale-the-dangers-of-sliding-down-the-roce-path/.
[7] Virtual SANs. http://searchservervirtualization.techtarget.com/tip/NVDIMM-and-RDMA-offer-significant-virtualization-advantages.
[8] 3D X-Point memory. http://www.eetimes.com/document.asp?doc_id=1328682.

[9] Highly commoditized industry on the hardware side. http://www.networkcomputing.com/data-centers/server-market-under-siege/2095215192.

[10] Software-Defined Networking. https://technet.microsoft.com/en-us/library/mt403307.aspx.

[11] Fulfillment companies. http://www.nfsrv.com/what-is-a-fulfillment-company.html.

[12] Loss of manufacturing just like the TV business has seen. http://www.techhive.com/article/2955338/smart-tv/sharp-tvs-wont-be-made-by-sharp-anymore.html.

[13] Hyper-converged clusters. http://searchvirtualstorage.techtarget.com/feature/Hyper-converged-market-grows-but-is-still-young.

[14] Hybrid Memory Cube. https://www.micron.com/support/faqs/products/hybrid-memory-cube.

[15] Gelsinger: Half of the Top-100 tech companies will disappear. http://www.barrons.com/articles/vmware-ceo-half-of-top-100-tech-firms-may-vanish-1441306683.

Tuning the Network

7

GETTING UP TO SPEED

Often in storage we hear comparisons between systems based on capacity or cost per terabyte. Using just these two measures, we lose sight of the fact that getting the job done quickly [1] can save substantial amounts of money, ranging from needing fewer servers to reducing the number of virtual machines in the cloud.

The reason the storage industry is capacity-centric is that capacity was the only real differentiator for any storage solution for the better part of 30 years. Simply put, hard disk drives spin at 5.4K, 7.2K, 10K or 15K RPM. The only way to get notably better performance was to have more of them, while the costs savings came from bigger drives. The dialectic between unit count and capacity led to some interesting solutions, such as using just the outer 20% of a high-capacity drive for data. This allowed a much shorter seek (short-stroking the drive [2]) and effectively made the drive a bit faster.

We reached the point where 15K RPM drives, which were marvels of technology, were two generations or more behind slower drives in capacity, and substantially more expensive than those slower capacity counterparts. Market economics forced the end of fiber-channel (FC) 15K drive development around 2007, and ironically in many ways it was capacity (or the lack of it) that made these drives unattractive.

Still, the storage industry was analogous to Victorian England, where a sense of complacency was considered proper and the storage teams labored out-of-sight. Between 1998 and 2007, nothing really exciting happened!

Then along came flash. At much faster data rates, one would have expected flash to be an overnight success, but like any technology, it had some weaknesses, such as write wear-out and the need for backup power to flush cached data to flash.

Here we are, a full decade after the first SSD reached market, and there are yet many IT staffers who believe that hard drives are still the right solution for their data storage.

LET ME REACH OUT TO THOSE PEOPLE NOW!

Compared with hard drives, solid-state drives (SSDs) are much more reliable, can run at higher temperatures, and are shock-proof. They use much less power. SSDs are much faster—random IO numbers range from 100× on up.

Yes, SSDs are more expensive, but if you do a fair comparison and match an enterprise drive against a (serial AT attachment) SATA SSD of the same capacity,

Network Storage. http://dx.doi.org/10.1016/B978-0-12-803863-5.00007-8

the SSD actually wins [3]. There may be some vendors who tell you to use "enterprise SAS SSD" (Serial-Attached SCSI SSD) at a much higher price, but that's not necessary. SATA is plenty good enough unless you want to change to "Non-Volatile Memory express" (NVMe) for the ultimate in performance. Most SSD behave well in use and even low-cost units can thrive in today's appliance-level integrity environment.

By 2017, we may be very close to or even at price-parity between SATA SSD and bulk storage drives. The first 16-TB SSD arrived in 2015 [4], beating any hard drive on the market for capacity by a healthy amount.

But that point of parity misses the real issue. With all of the other benefits, and especially performance, why would you not want SSD instead of HDD? The cost delta today is partly offset by power savings, but reducing the server count needed saves much more money and will likely pay for all those SSDs [5].

All-Flash Arrays (AFAs) [6] have added to the debate, making hard-drive arrays a secondary tier in the SAN and driving their sales volumes down considerably. An AFA, as they are affably known, sits between the hard drive array boxes and acts as either a new primary tier or as a data cache. With AFAs typically delivering millions of "Input/Output Operations Per Second" (IOPS), they give a real boost in SAN performance, while being easy to install.

Future evolutions of servers and close-up, NVDIMM storage [7] in those servers will change the picture again. We'll cover that in another part of this book.

So, the bottom-line question every CEO should ask every CIO or IT Director is

How much more agile are you planning to make us using SSD and Flash?

TUNING FOR FAST SYSTEMS

There are many things that can be done to speed up a storage setup today, much more than in the era of redundant array of independent disks (RAID) and hard drives. The key to new levels of performance is the use of solid-state storage. I'm somewhat surprised that the uptake of SSD and AFAs hasn't been universal, given the huge performance gains they bring to storage, but the FUD campaign of low write lives and high costs appears to have worked with many IT people.

I'll say it again for the record. There is no longer a wear-out issue [8]. Recent advances in flash and in controller design make SSD durable for any reasonable use, with some exceptions that require specially overprovisioned drives for a higher level of usage. Costs have dropped below "enterprise" hard drives, and many commodity class SSDs are durable enough to be their replacement.

There is thus no earthly reason to be buying enterprise SSD for any use case, unless your RAID gear is so slow it can't handle the data rates of SSD. (The answer here is the AFA of course!) SATA SSD should do the job well.

So let's assume we've bought into SSD and flash. Let's look at use cases.

THE (VIRTUAL) DESKTOP

Whereas this may seem to be out-of-place as a networked storage environment, the desktop creates an enormous amount of traffic in many companies. This ranges from booting up at 8 a.m. to backing up data.

Of all of these, the boot time is probably the most irritating of delays, taking several minutes to bring the screen to life with Windows. The PC community and Microsoft have worked to fix some of them. Tricks like staging the boot applications into a cache area on disk speed up the disk IO that occurs at startup, while adding a small SSD to hold the OS, really makes a difference. I personally tried this and put an SSD into my system as C-drive, with all my personal data kept on bulk hard drives. It works well enough that I haven't replaced my HDD completely even after 3 years.

Note that I didn't select a hybrid drive. All of these were too small to hold the OS and my key applications. That's being remedied in 2016, but the hybrid is a bit of a spent force and, with the desktop declining at an ever-increasing rate, any resurrection attempt is too late.

More complex operating environments need more sophistication, and this is where networking enters the picture. Enterprises are rightly concerned about security and attempt to sandbox their working environments on any desktop or notebook that is connected to their network. This is one variation of the Virtual Desktop. Here, boot storms are a common occurrence [9], and admins dread 8 a.m. A boot storm occurs when most of the desktops installed try and access their virtual desktops on the corporate server farm. The IO rate required, together with the network bandwidth demand, just slows down everyone's boot to a crawl.

There are a couple of solutions for this. One is to accept that most of the data are identical between virtual desktops. NetApp created an elegant clone system for their filers that stores one copy of those common files in a "Peripheral Component Interconnect Express" (PCIe) flash card and has the file system point to those shared files for each instance of a user's image. This is deduplication at its best. I did a joint development program with NetApp while at Rackable and booted 8K desktops in 4 min this way.

Another alternative for those who prefer SANs is to deliver the traffic needed from an AFA [10]. With fourmillion IOPS or so to play with, this is a brute-force solution to getting the data delivered quickly.

Both of these are somewhat stopgap today. The ideal solution is not to deliver the data in the first place. The way to achieve that is by moving to tablets with HTML displays presenting the output of server-based (software as a service) SaaS applications such as Microsoft Office or Google Apps. This gets rid of all of the OS and app loading, making the boot storm history.

This last highlights one aspect of tuning—you have to think at the system level big picture as well as solving problems in narrow areas such as networking or storage.

THE INSTANCE STORE

Do we need drives in servers? Ask that question in a pub full of admins, and glasses will start to fly!

This is a partly religious, partly mythical, and partly technical question in reality and it's a very important one right now. Let's zoom in on the virtualized server. Such a beast can have hundreds to thousands of virtual machines, and versions are now being created for specialty markets with big and huge instances with GPUs attached as part of the compute capability.

The concept of the virtualized system is that it has no persistent state. Power it off and all the data go away. That elegant concept is proving difficult to work with, since the loading and unloading of data are severely straining networks. Add to these difficulties the latency that slow networking and high loads generates and the situation is pretty untenable.

Enter the instance store [11]. This is storage inside the virtualized server that can be included as part of the instance configuration. Instance storage is either HDD or SSD, although it looks like SSD is by far the most popular. What you get is part of a shared SSD drive with multitenancy access fencing to keep data safe during operation. The instance store dies when the instance dies, which creates some problems in using it for permanent storage, but even this issue is being addressed by allowing the instance store to exist after the instance dies for a fixed period to allow data recovery.

SSD instance stores really do speed up instance performance a lot. Having 40K IOPS dedicated to an instance likely well beats out any networked solution in a virtualized environment. More important, latency is measured in low microseconds instead of 10s of milliseconds. This is critical for keeping app flow smooth and is an absolute requirement in some industries such as securities trading.

Such stores have some hidden dangers [12]. The first, and most serious, comes from the nature of SSD. All of these drives are overprovisioned by as much as 40% to extend the wear life of the drive. There is another reason for the overprovisioning, however. The way that data is erased on an SSD is to mark the block as dirty and use a block from the overprovision pool instead. This is necessary because the erase process only works on a macro-block of say 2 MB of data, rather than on individual blocks.

So, if an instance store is erased, it is really placed in that SSDs overprovision pool for later erasure and the data still actually exist even though the user thinks it is erased. That's seriously bad news, since there is a possibility that another tenant may get to see that data. I wrote on this subject on Network Computing a couple of years back and was astounded to hear of a case where over 20 GB of valid data from another tenant was read.

Overwriting the data simplistically doesn't solve the problem with SSD. Unlike HDD, the new data (all 1's say) goes into a different physical block to the old data that is being "erased". The CSP has to figure out a way to protect the old data. Azure claims to detect reads on unwritten blocks and force an all-zeros data response, for example.

The bottom line is that, if properly supported to prevent cross-tenant leaks, SSD instance stores can really boost the performance. As a place to store a copy of data or programs to support the instance, they can speed up the instance considerably.

This really gets interesting with containers. Since by design, these share operating systems and potentially application spaces, an instance store could service those needs very effectively.

With all of this, instance stores don't go far enough. If the tenant wants access to data after the instance is closed down (either accidentally or deliberately), another mechanism is needed. Today, this is the old virtual storage standby of writing the data to a network storage system. This involves some large latencies, so performance can take a big hit.

Ideally, the local storage can be made into a networked drive system, shareable to the other members of the virtual cluster. This could be a use case for virtual SANs, which we'll discuss later in this section.

One other solution is to revert back to a hosted model. AWS, as of December 2015, is offering permanent instances, which is basically hosting. While this doesn't make data 100% available, it does make the instance store dedicated to the tenant.

NETWORKED STORAGE—SAN

The mainstay storage of the cloud, and of virtualized server clusters, remains networked storage. Speeding this up is a bit more complex than replacing hard drives with SSDs. This is a result of older RAID arrays being design for the much lower bandwidths and IOPS that we get from hard drives.

With the RAID array being a bottleneck, what can be done to use the new technology in the existing installations? One solution is to go with new storage appliances, with a focus on Ethernet solutions being my preference. If this is too expensive (existing RAID arrays are relatively new or cost of process changes are too high), things get a bit tougher.

The answer doesn't lie in the so-called "hybrid" arrays [13]. Adding a couple of SSDs is a token improvement but it just delays the inevitable, while complicating operations with no end. The answer for SAN users is to add an AFA to the network as a cache or a fast tier.

Doing this gives quite a speed up to the whole storage farm, but there are a couple of things to consider that might save some cash. First, it isn't necessary to buy the same capacity as the primary HDD storage in the AFA. Much of the primary data are there because the secondary tier is too slow. The AFA obviates this problem by compressing data [14] before tiering it down to the secondary storage, which boosts performance on the secondary tier just because less data need to be retrieved.

Depending on the vendor, most AFAs use compression on the SSD data too. This is postwrite compression, where the raw files are stored temporarily in SSD before being compressed and stored in a more permanent address on the SSD. This further reduces the capacity needed in the AFA.

This raises the question of the size of secondary storage. With compression and deduplication [15], the secondary tier can shrink anywhere from 5x to 10x with typical data. Now there are data types that don't compress—video is an example—but typical office files will compress down. One conclusion is that secondary storage can be much smaller, too. That raises a few alternatives. One is to use the old primary storage in place of the secondary, although it might be better to sell that on. Another is to just stop buying secondary storage for a couple of years until the demand catches up.

So, we have significantly smaller AFAs and secondary storage to tune up. The first step is to recognize that four million IOPS from an AFA need a big network pipe to travel through. That means many FC connections…most likely 40 to 80 Gbps worth (alternatives include 40-Gbps Ethernet [16], increasing to 100 Gbps in 2017, or IB, and Remote Direct Memory Access (RDMA) is becoming common with these connections…these will be discussed later in the section). The network *will* be a bottleneck, so use all the ports.

Data integrity is a bit more complex with AFAs. Do we buy two and mirror them? Do we buy a unit that has internal redundancies and rely on those? It's a vendor-dependent issue and should be evaluated model by model.

With the configuration in place and running, what can be done to speed things up? The AFA uses some of the huge level of performance to tier data out to secondary storage and to handle compression. It should give priority to real-time traffic, though, so there should be much of the bandwidth or IOPS available for peak loads. If more performance is needed, more AFA units are the likely answer, unless the FC network is getting choked up with the level of traffic. This could trigger an upgrade to the next level of FC speed, but more likely a longer term view will indicate it's time to go down the RDMA link pathway.

Performance on the secondary storage is not a major consideration. Compression is essentially a bandwidth multiplier. Secondary storage should eventually all be SATA devices—low speed and cheap.

Clearly, this discussion doesn't leave much room for the hybrid RAID array. This type of product is a stopgap until the market sorts itself out around AFAs. We may see a last gasp of the RAID array divisions [17] in the form of higher speed controllers with faster processors and more access ports, but the topology the industry sees as optimal is being changed both by SSD performance and drive capacities. The model of one pair of RAID controllers to hundreds of drives is being superseded by a "COTS motherboard with 12 big drives model" creating small "Lego" bricks that support appliance level redundancy modes such as replication [18] or erasure coding [19].

Current Lego appliances [20] usually combine primary and secondary storages in the same box, allowing compression in-box and a much larger effective capacity. All-SSD boxes do ship, however, although this may mean some performance throttling. Most of these boxes sit on Ethernet and not FC networks.

This change of philosophies will accelerate with the advent of large, cheap SSD. The largest drive on the market at the time of writing was a 16-TB SSD unit, but it was still somewhat expensive. As prices of SSDs fall, we will see all-SSD solutions as standard in a couple of years, requiring appliances to have either a lot of ports or faster ports or both. This will increase pressure to consider moving over to Ethernet/RDMA and converging on a single infrastructural architecture for the next generation of datacenter.

NETWORKED STORAGE—NAS FILER

Network-attached storage (NAS) is in some ways easier to accelerate than SAN, and there are some low-hanging fruit in the tuning game. Any drive in an NAS box can be an SSD and provide acceleration. I would advise any CIO to make sure that the CEOs NAS share is on SSD!

Making a filer all-SSD may not work as well as expected, since the controller board or network ports may be too slow. At a minimum, the controller board (usually a COTS motherboard) should have two 10 GbE ports if SSD are deployed, while four ports would be even better if more than six SSD are in the same box. It's just a matter of bandwidth. In 2016, 25 GbE will start to enter mainstream and if this is in your datacenter master plan, from 2017 on, any upgrade of NAS networking and any new NAS boxes should have two or four 25-GbE ports [21].

The higher throughput of SSD may need some tuning on the controller, too. Slow motherboards (We often use hand-me-down servers for filers) won't cut it with a bunch of SSD, while DRAM may need some expansion as caches grow.

ARM-based filers [22] much like the Lego appliances talked about earlier are also a possible solution. Most datacenters already use multiple filers for a variety of reasons, so the Lego appliance fits in. With object stores (especially those based on Ceph) getting a filer interface, this might be a good time to transition to the new technology.

More complex filer configurations, such as NetApp F-series units, handle tougher challenges such as virtual desktop or virtual image booting. Since most of the data and apps in a desktop are identical over many users, logic suggests that a cloning/deduplication system would work well. If the virtual image is stored in a fast flash unit, such as a PCIe card, access can be very rapid indeed. NetApp has a cloning tool that allows images to be torn down and then rebuilt with new files in just seconds.

While the NetApp approach [23] can work with huge sets of images, it still transmits all of the data to the servers. That means the network is still a bottleneck. The solution of course is not to transmit the images and that has led us to the containers approach to virtualization. Here, the image (OS + tools + selected apps) is sent just once to each server, reducing both the network load and the bandwidth passing through the NAS controller by as much as 300×, or even much more.

Since the common image isn't tenant-dependent, it is possible to store it on a local small SSD [24] in each server, speeding boot even further and removing common image traffic altogether from the storage network. This will make container boot much faster than hypervisor network boot and likely will help push the industry toward containers.

AFA units haven't had anywhere near the impact on the NAS side of networked storage. Most filers don't share data with other filers, so having a sharable repository like an AFA doesn't work. Making the AFA into a filer is a possibility, and Violin has a product that aims at SMB3, but even there the bottleneck of a single filer engine handling all the file systems and protocol slows things down.

In sum, filers do benefit from SSD, but the limitations of motherboards in the controller and networks tend to limit the number of drives. AFAs are of little utility today, though this may change. Flash accelerators can, however, have huge impacts in specific use cases.

TUNING SSD

Now that we've added SSDs and flash to the plans for our next-gen storage solution, let's focus on getting the best bang for our buck. The SSD market is a little chaotic, as one would expect from a fast-growing, fast-evolving new area of technology.

The question of how to tune SSDs starts with the choice of the drives themselves, which of course depends on use cases. There are three classes of SSDs being marketed. The top of the pyramid is the "enterprise" SSD. These are expensive drives, with NVMe or SAS interfaces, and the clear hope is they will replace the "enterprise" HDD with a resulting super-premium price.

The mid-range drive is targeted at bulk storage in the commercial market. This means the drives are of high quality and have power-fail backup features needed for the server space. Most drives on the market, at least from the larger vendors, fall into this mid-range category. Pricewise, they beat the equivalent "enterprise" HDD by a substantial amount, and of course are much, much faster.

The third category is the consumer-grade drive. These are cheap drives that sometimes lack features. Fortunately, most of the vendors have dropped out of the market. The SSDs seen in PCs typically meet the mid-range definition.

There are just a few use cases that justify "enterprise" drive performance. Big Data is so data-intensive that NVMe drives [25] with PCIe or SATA-Express interfaces are needed. These can reach up to a million or so IOPS and 4 Gbps of data bandwidth, so there are serious considerations in interfacing. Direct connection to server motherboards is the usual solution, with no controller in between. NVMe reduces interrupt servicing dramatically and allows efficient data movement via RDMA. Four or six of these drives can saturate the PCIe system.

A bit cheaper, SAS "enterprise" SSDs are also slower than NVMe. Used in servers, most of their features, such as dual porting, are a waste of money. This is true in JBOD configurations, too, since we are migrating toward redundancy at the appliance not the drive level. If a hardware RAID controller is used, it will likely not have the IOPS capability to keep up with the drives. This can be fixed by connecting drives directly to SAS ports on the motherboard.

Note that all of this is relative to the full performance that can be achieved. A hardware RAID controller might deliver 700-K IOPS or even more, which is a heck of a boost from HDD even if something is left on the table. A better solution is to use an HBA or connect to the motherboard.

Don't use RAID 5! A major source of slowdown in RAID controllers is the exclusive-OR engine used to calculate parity. Use RAID 1 (mirroring) [26] instead. Writes benefit a lot, while reads can come from either drive in the mirror, increasing the performance.

- Each IO operation interrupts host on completion or exception
- Each interrupt causes host to halt current program and change state in base core
- Interrupts get priority – prevents lost interrupt
- A single point of control for interrupts
- This works for low interrupt rates, but is too much overhead and too slow at SSD workloads
- Other issues:
- Interrupts are non-specific
- Queue system is simple FIFO approach, though RAID controller and/or drives try to optimize IO sequence for hard drives
- RAID controllers do consolidate interrupts from multiple drives in a RAID operation

FIGURE 7.1

SCSI interrupts.

If anyone complains that RAID one is expensive, remind them it's a trade-off for performance [27]. One alternative is to buy SATA mid-range drives, at maybe half the price, and use those for the mirror. Mid-range drives run slower than SAS, with 400-K IOPS at the high end right now, but two drives are probably a bit faster than one SAS SSD drive.

Mid-range drives can fit a lot of use cases. Most use cases would benefit tremendously from say 10× HDD performance in random IO, and that is well within the range of the mid-range drive class. The best HDD gives around 300 IOPS today, while the mid-range SSDs sit at 40–80K IOPS [28]. That's up to 100:1, but file systems and poorly tuned apps limit the improvement possible, and in many cases these slower, and cheaper, drives will be fast enough.

That brings up the ultimate pain in the SSD game. A typical block in Linux sees as many as seven or eight address virtualizations, between the file stack in the OS and the convolutions in an SSD drive. These all take a lot of time to calculate, and that slows down the IO tremendously.

I did some analysis of the lifecycle of an IO, and figured that forcing a disconnect of the process to wait for the IO to complete and then to handle the interrupt and reconnect cost about half the systems compute power in a system trying to go flat-out (Fig. 7.1). The answer is NVMe. This consolidates interrupts, flattens the whole file stack, and uses queues to communicate directly with drives (Fig. 7.2).

We see only NVMe in the top end of the market today, but by 2017 there should be enough infrastructure to bring the technology to down-market. By 2020, it is possible that NVMe will have savaged SAS and SATA to death.

- Designed around RDMA system where downstream controls queues
- There are many job queues, linked to cores & apps on one side and per appliance or drive on other
- Queues are circular, allowing simple remote access without locks
- Completion queues corresponding to job queues are updated on completion or exception
- Interrupts to host are consolidated based on completion queues, reducing them by 10 to 100 x
- Each interrupt is vectored to linked core and causes host to halt current program and change state in that core
- Multiple points of control for interrupts
- This works for high to very high IO rates and <u>can</u> keep up with SSDs

FIGURE 7.2

NVMe interrupts.

Still, changing the OS radically and moving the market to a new interface is a giant task, and may or may not succeed. While NVMe is finding itself, life will go on and we will be thinking in terms of ditching HDDs altogether. That brings us back to using mid-range SSD for storing secondary data and in some cases acting as primary storage.

The secondary data tier is motivated less by horsepower than by life-cycle cost per capacity. Power, reliability, and space used all factor into that cost number. By 2017, we should be close to TCO parity for mid-range SATA SSDs compared with bulk SATA HDD, and have larger SSDs available. Remember that HDD technology is running into a wall at 10 TB per drive with evolution slowing rapidly.

This all say that we'll migrate to SSD in the secondary tier in the 2017–2020 timeframe. The resulting appliances will be 60–200 drive units that care little for performance and which are aimed at Nearline-class performance as archives, and also true secondary stores that are like the 12-drive Lego appliances referred to above.

With, say, 10 TB per drive being the sweet spot in 2017, the former box class will be 720 TB to 2 PB units of raw capacity and 5× that for compressed capacity—that's 10 PB in 4U of rack space at the top end! There will be customers for such huge beasts, but the volume sales will be in the Lego class.

These Lego units balance network speed and compute power with the 12 SSD, and should be able to deliver at least a million IOPS with dual 10 GbE links. If compression can be sped up to match SSD speeds, we'll be looking at 500 TB in a half-wide 2U unit, which is sufficient capacity for a lot of workloads. Four of these will make up a pretty good object store.

THE VIRTUAL SAN

Virtual SANs [29] use the fast drives in servers in a cluster as a shareable resource. The key to tuning virtual SANs is the network between nodes. This has to be as fast as possible [30]. The best solution, assuming very fast SSD such as NVMe drives, is to use RDMA over Ethernet. With many virtual SANs being enshrouded in "hyper-converged" clusters, this usually means iWARP, to take advantage of the standard Ethernet switches being used. Likely, a dual RDMA connection is needed on each server, just to minimize latency issues. InfiniBand is an alternative, but why add the complication of a totally new network for just a few percent of performance?

Things get complicated when in-memory architecture is used as well. That DRAM data needs to be pooled since it reflects the most active state of the cluster's data. An example is an Oracle database cluster using in-memory technology. Its very speed depends on data sharing between nodes. The virtual SAN needs to cope with in-memory sharing, too, which could be a major complication if the software for in-memory and the virtual SAN come from different vendors. In this case, it might be necessary to keep the two traffic streams separate on different Ethernet links, but my preference would be to share links, since this allows the in-memory and drive-based dataflows to dynamically find their own balance.

The virtual SAN issue is bound to become even more complex with the advent of persistent Non-volatile DIMMS. Now we have three tiers all looking to be shared across the cluster. These three tiers are so different in latency expectation that it's likely that the in-memory and NVDIMM traffic will need to be separate from the drive traffic.

Intel is pushing the idea of NVMe for X-Point memory [31], which makes good sense given the queue system and interrupt consolidation it brings to storage. NVMe fits the RDMA paradigm and should result in further speed-up [32] for virtual SANs. At the time of writing, it isn't clear if Intel has their own version of clustering into virtual storage pools in the pipeline. NVMe make this an interesting question, since in theory all of the data could be set up as a single pool within 64-bit addressing.

In-memory storage is byte-addressable and X-Point likely is too. This creates possibilities for network optimization and lower traffic levels, compared with traditional 4 K block IO. Intel's roadmap includes freestanding X-Point NVMe drives which may also have this capability.

Intel also talks about using OmniPath as interconnect [33], which would be a 100-Gbps RDMA solution. It will be in a horserace with 100-GbE RDMA/NVMe over fabrics and it's unclear how that will play out. Likely, there will be pushback on Intel introducing a new fabric [34] into the game that's proprietary, but it is possible that it will be tightly integrated with X-Point in some way.

TUNING FOR VIRTUAL CLUSTERS

A simplistic view of virtual clusters is that they consist of many of the same server, all divided up the same way. Big jobs are handled by adding more virtual instance to the workflow.

Sadly, it isn't that simple. Workloads can range from low IO rates to very high, low-latency response to IO requests. Similarly, some jobs don't fit the "standard" instance and need more memory, etc. One size does *not* fit all!

Reality is that clusters may be smaller and more specialized than the "cloud" concept would lead us to believe. A cluster for video-editing is not the same as an HPC cluster, which is not the same as a database cluster, and which is not the same as a general purpose server farm.

The impact on storage networks and the way storage is connected is wide-reaching. One thing to remember, though, is that often multiple needs can be served by the same storage appliance, especially if it has really high performance. An example would be serving stored data to a cluster from an AFA running SMB 3.0. As long as the network backbone is fast (say 40 GbE), different server pools could tie in with some branches of the network carrying much more traffic than others.

The following list of suggested configurations follows this thought-process:

1. The storage appliance: 40 GbE is optimal for connection of a fast appliance to the backbone of the network. It should be the uplink connection on the top-of-rack switches in the cluster.
2. In-memory databases: Here a virtual SAN might be the solution if fast NVMe drives are deployed in the server. Oracle and SAP may come with their own clustering software, which may or may not conflict with a third party virtual SAN.
3. Network storage for databases: Probably iSCSI block storage will continue to be a common solution, as well as FC SANs, but the latter require a separate network management team and that increases costs. 10 GbE is the solution of choice today, but 25 GbE will be eagerly accepted when available.
4. GPU-based instances: These instances need a lot of IO. Local instance stores may handle that, but there is still the issue of staging data to load into or unload from those instance stores. 10 GbE can be used in many use cases but a couple of ports might be needed or even a 40-GbE port, depending on network load. This category covers HPC, video-editing, oil and gas and medical simulations, so use cases can differ widely.
5. Web-servers: These should be the easiest instances to service, but we've fallen into the trap of using 1 GbE for low-power instances and this is defining the topology for the class. With containers and much more server power becoming available to us, 10 GbE is the right connection speed and the result will be fewer servers and lowered costs.
6. General-purpose servers: The network for new clusters should be 10-GbE based today, but 25 GbE is coming soon and this will definitely boost server performance and reduce the size of the required server farm. Buy as few servers as possible and wait for the new technology, then begin a rolling upgrade.
7. Virtual desktops: The dreaded boot storm [35] is about to become a thing of the past. Containerization reduces the image load size dramatically, since only one OS copy needs to be loaded for hundreds of VMs. This will take the pressure

for ultrafast pipes and cloning systems away. Even so, new VDI server farms will need decent bandwidth and 10 GbE can make sense for them. Removing the OS part of the boot storm takes away at least some of the need for AFAs, which have been a stopgap in solving the boot storm problem.

TUNING FOR BIG DATA

We used to have hundreds of drives and dozens of arrays to deliver the IOPS needed to drive our servers, but from the above, it's pretty clear that the mid-range IT shop is going to need a lot fewer storage appliances in the future. Obviously, this impacts datacenter size, etc.

There are some scenarios where this isn't true. Scientific operations such as the Square-Kilometer Array of radio telescopes [36] generate phenomenal amounts of data, while closer to home the retailing industry will soon be doing the same. What happens to these data types and how they are handled differ. Retailing and so on are often lumped together as Big Data, while the scientific experiments are labeled as HPC for High-Performance Computing.

Big Data is an umbrella for relatively unstructured data from many sources. Think of it as the Amazon that results from all those feeder streams in the Andes. Big Data is considered to be "unstructured", mainly because streams have different characteristics and formats, but are related to each other. Examples are my historical buying patterns [37], where I'm standing in a store, where my eyes are looking, what I am wearing—all related, all impinging on the blue-light special about to be displayed on a screen near me, but all over the place in structure.

Projections of massive growth in this type of data put it 10 or more times the size of traditional structured data in just a few years. Clearly, we need a mechanism to allow us to handle this type of data efficiently. The clue is in how Big Data is used. Mostly, Big Data is transient in value and doesn't need long-term storage. The downside is that its value typically decreases rapidly. This means that Big Data needs to be crunched quickly, a process that is very compute-intensive and one demanding very high bandwidth.

One solution is to follow the Hadoop paradigm [38] and build a storage system supporting the Hadoop file system. This system provides for a key-data storage method that allows almost anything to be "data." Another alternative is to use object stores to hold the data, since these too cater to unstructured object formats.

Whichever approach is chosen, this is a complex issue and still evolving. We'll cover Big Data in Chapter 8 and HPC in Chapter 9.

TUNING THE STORAGE NETWORK

There are a number of considerations when tuning the storage network. The first, and critical, issue is that Ethernet is the wave of the future in storage. Fiber-Channel basically is limited to replacing the fabric with the next generation and getting a "2×"

speed boost and we've talked about how Ethernet is moving faster and adding more features so as to become the interface of choice for storage in previous sections of this book.

Assuming the way forward Is Ethernet, the next question is how much bandwidth is needed for each appliance. By now, 10 GbE should be ubiquitous for storage networks, with some appliances, such as AFAs, being connected by 40-GbE backbones. Frankly, these speeds and feeds are Hobson's choice—100 GbE is too expensive and 10 GbE is the economic sweet spot for the appliance. In 2016, that starts to change. We will see 25 GbE and an associated 100 GbE using four lanes, which will begin to replace 10/40 GbE quite rapidly beginning in 2017.

The cost of installing 25/100 GbE will be lowered by the ability to use most of the same fabric. For larger clouds/clusters, this looks like a very cost-effective solution, avoiding adding more servers and storage nodes to offset the cost of the upgrade.

RDMA solutions [39] are still expensive compared to Ethernet-on-motherboard solutions. Intel and the industry in general appear to be leaning strongly toward iWARP [40] as a solution for Ethernet RDMA, which could lead us to it being a chipset feature in a few years. iWARP has the advantage over RoCE that standard Ethernet switches work with it and so RDMA traffic can share existing networks.

With RDMA reducing server load by as much as 50%, NVMe over fabrics [41] being an RDMA technology and the advent of much faster DRAMs, NVDIMM memories and high core-count CPUs, the likelihood that RDMA becomes a chipset feature is relatively high. Intel's intentions with OmniPath may cloud this, but this is not a mainstream alternative yet, and may fail to capture the markets interest.

A note on InfiniBand. RDMA over Converged Ethernet (RoCE) [42]) is an alternative to iWARP pushed by Mellanox, the leader in InfiniBand. While possibly being slightly faster than iWARP, it requires expensive switches with throttling and buffering (the "Converged" part) and essentially implies a separate storage network. This is proving a tough sell [43], except in the HPC market.

My suggestion in handling the rate of change in Ethernet is to buy the minimum amount of hardware needed at any given time. There are good reasons for doing this. Prices are falling on hardware, while performance continues to increase, but the main reason is to get into the mode of replacing a cohort of the server farm each year, with the object being to change the server farm out on a rolling basis using a 4- or 5-year cycle for achieving a complete update. Over time, this will give each cohort a roughly 4× boost in performance and keep the whole server farm at a high level of capability.

As long as the Ethernet community maintains the wiring structures, as they are doing from 10 to 25 GbE, the cost of upgrade on the rolling cycle should be just switch upgrades along with the usual cost to update to the server farm itself.

TUNING FOR THE CLOUD

Chapter 10 of this book is devoted to cloud issues, and we'll cover tuning there. Suffice it to note that this is an area with little information, quite a few myths and definitely opportunities to speed things up a lot!

THE NEW STORAGE TIERS

The rules of how and where data is stored are changing. The old tiering scheme of primary, "enterprise" hard drives and slower secondary bulk drives is crumbling in the face of flash and SSD and being replaced by a new tiering scheme with SSD (or flash) in the primary role and really inexpensive SATA drives as the new secondary tier.

Things are of course a bit more complex than this. The primary SSD tier can deliver huge performance levels, which allows part of the bandwidth to be directed toward data compression. Compression, as we've seen in the previous section, increases effective capacities in all of the tiers by typically 5× or so.

Part of a well-tuned system is taking advantage of compression wherever possible, making it important to select hardware with enough horsepower to deliver compression services. Another factor is to look at the balance between primary and secondary storage carefully. If the primary tier acts as decompressor for the data, horsepower is again a concern.

Assuming that the horsepower is available, a typical new-age storage tiering structure has AFAs or SSD boxes making up the primary tier, with delayed compression of data being the norm. To speed up write operations, data are journaled in the primary tier on a pair of mirrored drives and then the system takes advantage of the high SSD bandwidth to steal cycles and process data out of the journal, compress it and then store it in the other SSD or directly on to secondary storage. Reading involves staging data back to the journal in the primary and decompressing it.

This approach is a better solution than compression in the secondary, since it takes advantage of otherwise unusable IOPS available as a result of using SSD. Compression in the secondary most likely would involve journals on SSDs, too, increasing the cost. The main advantage of compression in the primary is bandwidth on the network. Compressed data needs much less bandwidth as well as much less raw drive space. With datacenter networking already strained, this isn't a minor issue.

Taking the thought process a step further, Software-Defined Storage (SDS) [44] migrates data services like compression and deduplication back into the server farm. Sending compressed data between the primary tier and the server farm cuts network bandwidth even further.

The problem is doing this at anything near a fast enough speed. The server wants to fire and forget on any write operation, but local compression with today's tools isn't fast enough for the job. That probably will change over the next few years, with hardware assist helping the issue along. When it does, servers will emit compressed, possibly deduplicated and encrypted, data to the storage pool directly. This will seriously boost effective network performance. This is especially important for the hyper-converged or virtual SAN approaches.

Storage tiering also has to cope with the cloud and the idea that irrespective of where computing is done, a geo-distributed ultra-cheap backup/archiving solution is necessary. Today's hot solutions are Google Nearline [45] and AWS Glacier [46].

While pricing is close on these services, Nearline has a 2-s window to the start of data recovery, while the tape-based Glacier window has 2 h.

With recovery often spanning multiple volumes and the ubiquitous expectation of instant gratification, it doesn't take a rocket scientist to figure Google has a real edge. AWS will likely fix the gap in 2016 or 2017!

It's worth noting that gateway software [47] (optionally with dedicated hardware) is used to move backups to the cloud. These packages have some distinct performance differences. These range from the ability to split the load onto parallel instances of the backup app to architectures that cache the data being archived or backed up on the basis that recently written data are the most likely to be recalled. These approaches might benefit your specific use case.

Looking at the future of tiers, there is a lot of activity on technologies close in to the CPU DRAM. One result is that the primary tier will probably move inside the server to be based on Nonvolatile DIMMs and/or ultrafast SSDs using say the Intel 3D X-Point memory. The pieces of this all solidify in the 2017 timeframe, which coincidentally is the point where Intel and others have stated that solid-state and bulk hard-disk drives achieve parity in price.

One result is that primary storage becomes in-server memory, while SSD-based secondary storage becomes the norm. Sharing that primary storage effectively across networks will be a challenge, and RDMA over the fastest available Ethernet is the likely, but possibly inadequate, answer.

The hard disk that gets displaced won't have much resale value, but tape units will be needed to recover the legacy backup tapes, primarily because most IT shops don't want the inconvenience of converting them to the cloud. A caution—support will deteriorate rapidly for tape gear. This is a used-equipment market and spares and expertise will rapidly evaporate.

CACHING DATA

We've just touched on caching in the backup/archiving appliance. The value of the approach there is use case-dependent, as is often the case with caching. In some ways, caching is a lazy way to take advantage of different speed storage tiers, rather than optimizing where data are placed in the storage tiers.

Caches work by detecting which data are most likely to be needed at any given time. Traditionally, that meant that data were not demoted to slower storage, on the off-chance that it might be used. Today's caching (which includes "auto-tiering" as well) tries to anticipate the need to promote data as well. Most caching software also supports forced tiering promotion and demotion using policies, which allow files to be moved out after a period of time, for example.

Examples of the substantial benefits of caching are easy to find. CPU cache speeds up DRAM access substantially, for example. Caching the key startup files speeds up boot on systems. AFAs give the SAN a new lease on life. The bottom line is that caching is a needed and useful tool in overcoming slower than desired data access.

Sizing the cache is a sophisticated art [48]. Too much cache can actually slow down operations, since the tables of contents need to be searched. Too little cache increases the miss ratio too much. In any case, balancing cache contents with demand and trading read cache for write cache is a dynamic process that depends on workload and the apps that are running. If we can accept that caching is an imprecise process that will *never* be exactly right, the best solution *is* to let the software figure out the trade-offs.

Could we/should we cache more? There are hidden caches all over systems. Hard disk drives try to overcome latency by beginning read operations wherever they land on a track. The data are cached until needed, and the drive may read ahead some number of blocks based on the fact that often IOs are quite large and that the OS breaks them down into 256-KB chunks to allow "fair access" to other users. This means the drive potentially moves offtrack between chunks and the read-ahead obviates that problem.

Caching is also evident in compression approaches; that's what the SSD journal files are doing. Write operations appear to run faster, whereas read operations, because decompression is much faster than compression, can use the cache for staging the expanded file.

Large, cheap NVDIMMs could add fast caching to the whole spectrum of storage appliances, from storage map servers to metadata delivery and data storage. An example might be streaming the latest Star Wars movie, where keeping the whole movie in memory might give the most efficient delivery system.

The most important thing to remember about all this caching is that you need to model the whole system and dataflow. That will identify the real bottlenecks, and where cache will help. This will save you money and a lot of frustration.

SSD AND THE FILE SYSTEM

One reason we don't get astounding performance from high-end SSD is that the operating system and applications are tied to a file system software stack that dates back to 1984. This stack is based on how SCSI works, which was a realistic approach when all file protocols—FC, SAS, and SATA, and SCSI itself—all derived from the SCSI command set (Fig. 7.1).

As we've added complexity to the software architecture, the SCSI stack has grown into a monster. It is layered up, to reflect the addition of services such as RAID or access optimization and heavily virtualized (See Chapter 4, Section 6). In short, the current file stack is very complicated, remaps addresses several times and takes a notable amount of time to complete.

All of them are OK when drives ran slow and spun lazily. With IO rates more than 1000 times faster, SSD causes most systems to choke. All those disconnects and interrupts eat cycles, and all the redirection uses up a good chunk of what's left.

It is clear a much sleeker alternative is overdue in storage, which is why NVMe (Non-Volatile-Memory-express) was created. The small "e" reflects its initial tight connection with PCIe, incidentally. NVMe is a queue-driven solution that strips back most of the overhead in the OS.

To overcome the limitations of the SCSI stack, NVMe is designed as a pull system, using RDMA, rather than the traditional push system. This removes some of the interactions in sending a command to a drive, including statuses and interrupts.

NVMe has circular queues, which can have many entries if necessary, and these queues are accessed via RDMA by the drives as and when the drive is ready for the next work item. This allows appliances with the ability to process many operations in parallel to access multiple queue entries. There can be many queues per destination, up to 64 K and queues can be tied to CPUs, cores, or processes. This becomes important on completion, as status is returned via a noninterrupting queue process where the remote drive or appliance uses RDMA to enter status. The system periodically scans responses in bulk, saving enormously on state changes compared with current interrupt-per-operation schemes.

With NVMe, we end up with a much flatter and efficient file stack. We already have drives in the terabyte class with millions of IOPS. Speed-up in PCIe and potential much faster solutions like OmniPath (from Intel) could make the performance jump much higher still, never mind the impact of X-Point or ReRAM flash alternatives.

This performance boost is all in the lower layers of the stack. The file system is still an issue, both from a performance perspective and from its ability to operate at a large scale; add in unstructured Big Data and this area is something of a mess still. We see long discourse about new data structures or file systems—Hadoop FS, for example or Ceph—only to find that there is a debate about which traditional file system to build them on.

This reflects a weakness of the open-source approach, which is the difficulty of addressing major strategic questions such as the rewriting of a file system for SSD structures. The whole issue of object storage begs this question. Converting an object ID to blocks in a traditional FS seems a bit pointless. Admittedly, features like journaling and bad block handling are intrinsic, and hidden portioning of metadata and data files may be useful to the higher-level design team, but it smacks of the top-heavy, layered stacks of yore, not the streamlined solutions we should be building.

Perhaps the answer is to move to a key-data model like Seagate's Kinetic. This approach has the advantage of being easily updated as blocks are consolidated during erased block clean-up, saving one level of indirection in addressing. This may not fit well with structured data such as SQL databases that tend to divide up space into much more granular elements.

Complicating this is the possibility that we will see X-Point and ReRAM as byte-addressable memories. This could complicate the file system question to no end. The answer here might be to just address all of memory, persistent or not, as a non-contiguous memory space with 2^{64} addresses. There'd be some fun mixing devices using the traditional 4-KB block with byte addressable units, but constructs for that should be easy.

Whichever way file systems finally go, we have to accept that change must occur if we are to maintain efficiency and keep up with the hardware. The software side of the industry has to stop the lazy approach of adding more layers as computer performance increases. That may sell more boxes, but it misses the value of hardware improvement, although trends like containers and SSD may have blown the lid of that mindset.

WHAT TUNING COULD MEAN IN 5-YEARS' TIME

Reader Warning! *With all the changes, prognosticating in detail where we'll be in 5 years is a challenge. Quite likely, what follows will be wrong on at least some points, as reality overcomes hype and technologies succeed or fail to deliver.*

The virtual server of 2021/2022 will most likely be running containers on 16 to 32 cores (and possibly with onboard GPU assists) while ultrafast HMC memory delivers 0.5 to 1.5 Terabytes per second. Such a beast will run thousands of small instances—the sort that drives the Web, for example. It will have a tier of X-Point or ReRAM memory on the HMC module to act as local persistent storage. Servers for in-memory databases will probably have a lot of X-Point, while small instance servers may have little or none. Note that CPUs with 128 or more cores will be in the market, but there's a heat problem with these monsters keeping out of the cloud mainstream.

There'll be a layer of SSD attached by NVMe and SATA-express running below this. This will be faster than today's SSD. Again database systems, including HPC and Big Data units, will use NVME X-Point/ReRAM drives for blinding performance.

The DRAM, NV-DIMM and on-board drives will be shared with the cluster by RDMA over Ethernet, which by then will be around 50 Gbps per lane for the mainstream. We'll still have secondary bulk storage, now consisting completely of SSD, and this will be transitioning to NVMe over fabrics and RDMA for consistency and ease of management.

What's missing? AFAs will be pushed out of this picture unless local virtual SAN structures fail to deliver enough performance across the network. The benefits of fast, proprietary flash architectures will lose out to the economics of mainstream SSD, although we will see some bulk storage plays using proprietary flash architectures that look quite a bit like AFAs!

HDDs will be fading into history (but not completely abandoned—IT is a bit conservative as industries go!). Heat-assisted recording (HAMR) [49] will prove expensive to manufacture and tricky to get right [50], delaying availability past the window where any HDD technology can catch up with the solid state. Remember, we'll have 20 to 30 TB per SSD in that timeframe, so the alternatives being discussed for adding platters or reverting to 5.25 in diameter disks (or bigger) would struggle to keep up [51], at best.

That defines the hardware environment we'll see. Software is much more exciting. Lots of new data service modules will be available, all running under an SDI/SDS environment. We'll have a solid way to join modules from different vendors together into dataflows, as well as tools to orchestrate the SDS services within OpenStack and other environments. It's probably optimistic to hope that this extends into all the major public clouds, but that will be a close-in objective for the industry, allowing real agility and flexibility with hybrid clouds.

We'll have addressed the file system mess that exists, and so will have a stream-lined solution for mainstream servers and a platform to carry the HDFS of the world forward. It isn't clear if the kinetic approach will get the buy-in to make key-data structures feasible, but the idea of smart drives will likely have reached the point where drives are directly attached to Ethernet and possibly running NVMe-over-fabrics. This changes the efficiency of scaling enormously, but creates needs to handle different drive types or classes—local versus distant storage (measured both in latency terms and also to cover the geo-distribution question for disaster protection).

One issue that will be on the table, but unlikely to be yet resolved, is the sharing of data files between Linux and Windows. On the fly translation looks like a data service whose time is due, but of course that's not trivial. We can do some of this today, of course, but it involves rewriting the files manually. Indexing data is another valuable service. Reality is that finding things in huge storage pools is not trivial and a good indexer and search engine system is needed.

Encryption will have finally found a home. Whether through hardware assists or some smart coding, all data are encrypted at source [52], which also means compressed, deduplicated, etc. at source, too. SDS is definitely needed for this! Specialized hardware solutions for accelerating these features are coming into the market, including an FPGA built into select Intel CPUs. These solutions will be competing with GPU technology, such as AMD's built-in APU or ARM/GPU hybrids from both AMD and NVidia.

Control of the data pool will be shared, like the server pool today, with the departmental units. Policy-driven management [53], including orchestration and billing, will allow easy access to the pool, with storage becoming just another on demand resource. Tuning the storage cloud to be efficient here will win many brownie points with the user base that is now, in essence paying for IT directly.

One thing will be certain. Given the scale of the Storage Revolution, in 5 years we'll not have reached any final settled state. Changes in strategic and in tactical implementations will still be pouring from the startups. These will be exciting times!

REFERENCES

[1] Getting the job done quickly. https://www.tintri.com/blog/2011/12/when-it-cheaper-use-ssd-vs-hdd.
[2] Short-stroking the drive. https://storageswiss.com/2015/12/22/unintended-consequences-afa-shrinking/.
[3] SSD actually wins on price. http://www.networkcomputing.com/storage/ssd-prices-free-fall/1147938888.
[4] First 16TB SSD arrived in 2015. http://arstechnica.com/gadgets/2015/08/samsung-unveils-2-5-inch-16tb-ssd-the-worlds-largest-hard-drive/.

[5] Server savings will likely pay for all those SSD's. https://www.linkedin.com/pulse/how-ssds-can-reduce-server-costs-david-bernstein?forceNoSplash=true.

[6] All-Flash Arrays. http://www.networkcomputing.com/storage/will-containers-sink-all-flash-array/1185632646.

[7] NVDIMM storage. http://www.snia.org/forums/sssi/NVDIMM.

[8] SSDs no longer have a wear-out issue. http://www.networkcomputing.com/storage/6-ssd-myths-debunked/896126592.

[9] Boot storms are a common occurrence. https://www.techopedia.com/2/31844/enterprise/storage/the-vdi-boot-storm-why-it-happens-how-to-prevent-it.

[10] All-Flash Array and VDI. http://www.networkcomputing.com/storage/all-flash-arrays-vdi-solution/1983604525.

[11] The instance store. http://docs.aws.amazon.com/AWSEC2/latest/UserGuide/InstanceStorage.html.

[12] Hidden dangers of instance stores. http://searchservervirtualization.techtarget.com/tip/Local-storage-solves-some-problems-creates-others.

[13] "Hybrid" arrays. http://www.theregister.co.uk/2015/05/14/hybrid_storage_arrays_versus_allflash_will_disks_hold_their_own/.

[14] Compressing data. http://www.snia.org/sites/default/education/tutorials/2007/fall/storage/GerrySimmons_Benefits_Hardware_Data_Compression-rev.pdf.

[15] Deduplication. https://storageservers.wordpress.com/2014/12/23/a-look-into-data-deduplication-feature-and-its-advantages/.

[16] 40 Gbps Ethernet. http://www.ethernetalliance.org/roadmap/.

[17] Last gasp of the RAID array divisions. http://www.storagereview.com/emc_introduces_allflash_unity_for_less_than_18000.

[18] Replication. http://www.computerweekly.com/feature/Remote-replication-Comparing-data-replication-methods.

[19] Erasure coding. http://www.networkcomputing.com/storage/raid-vs-erasure-coding/1792588127.

[20] Lego appliances. http://www.networkcomputing.com/storage/going-all-ssd-side-effects/732249354.

[21] 25GbE ports. http://www.mellanox.com/blog/2016/03/25-is-the-new-10-50-is-the-new-40-100-is-the-new-amazing/.

[22] ARM-based filers. http://www.forbes.com/sites/patrickmoorhead/2013/08/28/arm-in-storage-servers-why-would-anyone-do-that/#5de72aa07afa.

[23] NetApp approach. http://www.netapp.com/us/products/platform-os/ontap/storage-efficiency.aspx.

[24] A local small SSD. http://www.datacenterknowledge.com/archives/2012/08/21/netapp-unveils-flash-accel-and-extends-technology-alliance/.

[25] NVMe drives. http://www.dell.com/support/article/us/en/19/SLN301149/.

[26] Use RAID 1 (mirroring). https://storageswiss.com/2015/01/13/which-raid-level-use-for-ssd-tier/.

[27] Trade-off for performance. http://lifehacker.com/pair-ssds-in-a-raid-0-for-a-huge-speed-boost-1602417386.

[28] Mid-range SSDs sit at 40K to 80K IOPS. https://www-ssl.intel.com/content/www/us/en/solid-state-drives/consumer-family.html.

[29] Virtual SANs. http://www.networkcomputing.com/storage/vmware-vsan-reality-vs-hype/1713768902.

[30] As fast as possible. http://www.datacore.com/.

[31] NVMe for X-Point memory. http://www.theregister.co.uk/2015/10/23/intel_planned_nvme_for_xpoint/.

[32] Results in further speed-up. http://wccftech.com/intels-3d-xpoint-memory-featured-optane-ssds-optane-dimms-8x-performance-increase-conventional-ssds/.

[33] OmniPath as interconnect. http://www.top500.org/news/The Dawn of a Next-Generation Supercomputer Approach from Intel/.

[34] Intel introducing a new fabric. http://www.intel.com/content/www/us/en/high-performance-computing-fabrics/omni-path-architecture-fabric-overview.html.

[35] Dreaded boot storm. http://www.zdnet.com/article/boot-storms-and-how-to-avoid-them/.

[36] Square-Kilometer Array of radio telescopes. https://www.skatelescope.org/.

[37] Historical buying patterns. http://retailnext.net/en/benchmark/real-time-data-drives-the-future-of-retail/.

[38] Hadoop paradigm. http://hortonworks.com/apache/hadoop/.

[39] RDMA solutions. https://www.zurich.ibm.com/sys/rdma/model.html.

[40] iWARP. http://www.networkworld.com/article/2858017/ethernet-switch/iwarp-update-advances-rdma-over-ethernet-for-data-center-and-cloud-networks.html.

[41] NVMe over fabrics. http://www.flashmemorysummit.com/English/Collaterals/Proceedings/2015/20150811_FA12_Overview.pdf.

[42] RDMA over Converged Ethernet (RoCE). https://community.mellanox.com/docs/DOC-2283.

[43] RoCE is proving a tough sell. http://www.chelsio.com/wp-content/uploads/resources/RoCE-Deployment-Challenges-for-Clouds.pdf.

[44] Software-Defined Storage. http://searchstorage.techtarget.com/video/The-different-faces-of-software-defined-storage-vendors.

[45] Google Nearline. https://cloud.google.com/storage-nearline/.

[46] AWS Glacier. https://aws.amazon.com/glacier/ Cloud gateway software.

[47] Gateway Software. http://www.enterprisestorageforum.com/storage-technology/cloud-gateways-in-the-enterprise.html.

[48] Cache sizing a sophisticated art. http://www.yellow-bricks.com/2016/02/16/10-rule-vsan-caching-calculate-vm-basis-not-disk-capacity/.

[49] Heat-assisted recording (HAMR). http://phys.org/news/2016-03-storage-density-tbin2-heat-assisted-magnetic.html.

[50] HAMR tricky to get right. http://www.theregister.co.uk/2015/08/31/muted_hamr_blows_coming/.

[51] HDD alternatives struggle to keep up. http://hexus.net/tech/news/storage/85769-hamr-hdd-capacities-scale-4tb-2016-100tb-2025/.

[52] Data encrypted at source. https://www.veeam.com/backup-files-encryption.html.

[53] Policy-driven management. http://www.slideshare.net/VMWitacademy/softwaredefined-storage-for-dummies-guide.

Big Data

8

The advent of cheap storage and analytics hardware and software is making it possible to gather and utilize much more of the data that we threw away in the past. This is often called "Big Data [1]", but Big Data is really a misnomer. It should be "Lots of Little Data", but that's a mouthful. The term describes the results of recording all sorts of small things, such as where your mouse is on a screen, or where your eyes are looking at any instant, then moving all these so-called unstructured records to be analyzed for meaning. In one aspect, though, Big Data is the correct name. There's going to be a lot of data [2] processed and stored—perhaps 100× today's data per year.

The term "unstructured data" is, well, unstructured. A movie file is unstructured, but it conforms to tightly controlled rules of formatting. Likewise, a text file is structured, but can contain gibberish text. The reality is that the term "unstructured" is a bit vague. In reality, it applies more to the flow than the data. In sum, Big Data can be described as "volume, velocity, and variety"!

Big Data is described somewhat like the Amazon. Lots of little streams feed big streams that turn into ever-changing rivers of data flowing into the datacenter. There are other models, though, wherein an effort to reduce WAN bandwidth needs the data is distilled at or near its source to reduce it to meaningful content.

An obvious example of this is data from a set of surveillance cameras. Likely, nothing will change for hours in the scene that's being watched, so why continually send 4 Mbps of data to a distant datacenter. Just process the data near the cameras and send a 'Nothing-has-changed" message.

ADDRESSING BIG-DATA BOTTLENECKS
NETWORK BANDWIDTH

Bandwidth is a serious issue in the Internet of Things (IoT) [3], as all this sensor stuff has become known. IoT will strain many installations, in part because of the reluctance of telephone companies (telcos) [4], especially those in the US, to create adequate bandwidth between endpoints and exchanges. Likely, this will not be solved quickly, as the slow roll-out of gigabit fiber in the US attests. The result will be a strong tendency toward the distillation model, which will lessen the impact in the datacenter.

In either model, once the river of data enters the datacenter, it has to be stored and then delivered to some extremely fast processing units. We are migrating away from traditional servers to in-memory databases [5] with very high-speed and high-bandwidth DRAM and persistent memory on the DRAM bus. These units, using GPUs to process the data in parallel, will create a major performance problem for networks and particularly networked storage.

SPEEDING IN-MEMORY COMPUTING

DRAM buses will morph into very parallel, but independent, access paths, much as the Hybrid Memory Cube (HMC) [6] architecture. This envisages DRAM and non-volatile (NV) memory sitting on a silicon module close to the central processing unit (CPU), so speeding up transfers while making them much more parallel and able to avoid the wait-cycles associated with traditional DRAM. Debuting in 2016 with perhaps 5× the bandwidth of existing memory, bandwidths in the terabytes (TBs) per second are likely within 5 years.

Having persistent memory inside the HMC architecture makes a good deal of sense, since it expands the effective memory size dramatically, while providing a place to write results with nanosecond latency. It's very likely that the NV portion of these memories will be byte-addressable, which creates some major challenges for the whole storage architecture.

Byte-addressability [7] is very fast compared with traditional block-IO. Data can be stored directly from a "write-to-memory" instruction in the code, rather than having to be processed into a 4-KB block and moved through the very cumbersome file IO system. We are talking nanoseconds versus milliseconds here. Moreover, the writing process doesn't have to disconnect and wait for an interrupt saying the IO is complete.

Not only is latency reduced by byte-sized processing, but also the bandwidth across whatever bus or LAN connection is much lower. This probably will be a feature in future tiered memory systems, although it may take some time to evolve just because of the code changes needed in the operating systems and applications.

KEY/VALUE STORAGE

In a similar way to traditional file systems versus Non-Volatile Memory express (NVMe), the way that data are stored has to change. Many of today's storage questions hang on how best to store Big Data. It's best to look at the stream model again. Data arrive along a timeline, but unlike traditional data, the records are a jumble of different types. Moreover, they reference different contexts—my keyboard data versus your camera pictures.

The best way to handle this is to prepend a key that defines the context of the data element, such as type and source. This key becomes searchable for, say, all records relevant to me. This defines a key/value store [8], where the pair of items constitute a record and where the data can be freeform in size and content.

Handling large quantities of unstructured data is further complicated by the time value of the data. We aren't accustomed to thinking much about how time affects the value of the data we store, but this will change dramatically in the era of Big Data. As an example, a ceiling camera detects my position in a retail store and which way I'm facing. Based on where I look most often, the ad display screen nearest to me starts displaying the blue light special that would interest me most. This type of targeted ad needs superfast responses and so for a minute or two, that data are very valuable, but then the data are not worth much when I leave the store.

Remembering I liked ugly Xmas sweaters might be an analytics result worth keeping for a month or so before year-end, but the raw camera data likely won't need to be kept for more than 30 min. Any storage system has to look at this question of value, distillation, and disposal to make sense of the storage flow.

This is a lifecycle management process that's still in its infancy. Disposal especially has a long way to go. The reason is that this is a dynamic, not static, policy-driven process. The need to keep a data-record type can easily change with circumstances. Retention becomes a much bigger issue if a known terrorist is spotted on surveillance cameras, for example, but it can be an issue in almost any data stream.

The following sections examine some of these questions in much more detail. Just remember that the whole Big Data question is relatively new and rapidly evolving, so follow the subject on the Internet to keep up to date.

BIG DATA STORAGE

Any system for storing Big Data has to cater to its unstructured nature and to the very large number of record objects that result. Block or file systems are too scale-limited and don't match the concept of large flat spaces that are needed for rivers of data. This has resulted in specialized solutions such as the Hadoop Distributed File System (HDFS) [9]. With Hadoop so common, the next sections will use it as an example and look at how storage platforms and Hadoop interact. We can expect these issues to spill over into other Big Data approaches.

Platforms for HDFS

HDFS is the most common file system used with Hadoop. Today, HDFS is implemented on a variety of platforms, ranging from local direct-attached storage (DAS) drives networked across the cluster to NAS and SAN [10] networked storage. Tuning for optimum performance is still in its infancy and all of these approaches have pros and cons, and some partisan rhetoric. Add to these, the cloud-based versions of Big-Data processing highlight the limitations of moving data round in clusters.

HDFS is somewhat unusual in having a strong sense of locality [11]. HDFS grew out of an idea at Google that bringing compute to where data are stored makes the most sense from a network bandwidth and latency point of view. Each compute node should map or reduce the data most local to it. Irrespective of whether the data are local or networked, the best architecture is the one with the fewest delays between compute and its data. With networked storage, an implication of this is that most of the server's data should be on a storage appliance connected directly to the same top-of-rack switch. While it isn't a formal requirement of Hadoop today, locality makes sense for better performance and is an idea that incidentally fits many applications.

In selecting an approach, it's necessary to figure out the data lifecycle of your data. If most of the data are ingested into the server then accessed over long periods, with perhaps dozens of accesses to any one record, the answer probably lies with local DAS. On the other hand, if the data are very transient, with a total lifecycle in minutes, the better solution is likely to beef up DRAM (and/or add NVDIMM to effectively expand it) and use networked storage. In either case, a fast network, preferably with *remote direct memory access* (RDMA), is needed.

With SSD drives reaching 16-TB capacities [12] in 2016, way exceeding the largest HDD, the logical conclusion is to build servers with several ultrafast drives in each (local DAS), and find a way to share them within the Big-Data cluster, essentially in some form of virtual SAN. The sharing part is still a challenge, since networks are never fast enough, but having part of the data local to the server allows it to load into its own memory with very little latency when needed.

Hadoop processing on local DAS generally is designed to limit the intracluster traffic by having each server processing its data as mapped to its internal drives. This leaves the loading of data into the local drives as a major network load and it also emphasizes the importance of disposing of old data in a timely fashion, both to make room for new data and to avoid having to write it onto to secondary storage.

Given the need to load almost all the data from "outside" into each local DAS, compounded by the tendency to use each record anywhere from once to only a few times, the benefits of the local DAS approach on network traffic compared with network storage are much less than one might initially surmise. Given the need to move data through system memory from the inbound LAN port onto the storage drive, then later to retrieve it from the drive back into memory, other methods may be more efficient.

The simplest of these is to increase the size of DRAM substantially. Servers capable of holding as much as 12 TBs are available. Keeping the data received from the LAN eliminates the need for a write and a read on the drive, plus two large memory operations. When we add persistent memory on the DRAM controller/bus, we can expand the total fast-access capacity by perhaps 3× to 10×, putting us in the range of 20–100 TBs of DRAM equivalent.

This is being put to the test with available technology, using non-volatile dual in-line memory module (NVDIMM) memory [13]. This is flash-based technology, much slower than Intel's now-announced X-Point [14] or SanDisk's R&D ReRAM, but there are notable gains in performance even so. This memory can be shared with the cluster directly using RDMA over Ethernet, and again uses a single access to DRAM/NV memory versus two accesses for a drive-based solution.

The bottom line of this thought process is that we are evolving in the direction of intracluster memory-sharing in the processing cluster and networked storage as the buffer storage that feeds data to that cluster. Networking will drive toward the fastest links available. Today that means 40 GbE RDMA links and we can expect either 100 GbE or Intel OmniPath (also at 100 Gbps) to be the hot choice by 2017.

The question of protocols will probably resolve on NVMe over fabrics [15] which should standardize early in 2016 and enter production by 2017. This neatly serves the issue of byte versus block addressing, especially as Intel is addressing both with an NVMe drive family using X-Point. The combination of RDMA and drive will allow for both modes.

HDFS can be mounted on other file systems, but there is a danger that data locality may be lost, since none of the traditional file systems have a mechanism that supports the approach. This can be costly in performance terms, so ancillary management tools are needed to add back the feature and properly distribute data.

HDFS provided high-availability data integrity options in Version 2.0. These allow replication of the data on multiple servers or data nodes, with a default of three replicas. If locality is working, this means two replicas in the same rack and one in an adjacent rack, so it doesn't meet the standards of geodiversity necessary for disaster protection.

Picking the Optimal Storage Model for Big Data

Many of today's users have taken the local DAS approach for HDFS. This follows from Google using that approach before Hadoop was released to the open source community and the strong dictate that data should be local to the compute. Many of those users complain about the system cost of loading and replication and are clearly less than satisfied by the state of affairs.

Another common complaint from the same group is that the Hadoop server with a large and expensive drive complement is heading diametrically away from their general philosophy of minimalist general-purpose servers.

These are the result of looking at the software side without taking a holistic systems view. Properly, the guiding point for the architectural decision should have been optimization of dataflow, rather than following a trade-off made in the early days of Big Data that has been superseded by large DRAM memories and GPU-based solutions.

Does this make the local-DAS option wrong? As discussed earlier in this chapter, it's somewhat dependent on data lifecycles and usage patterns. In Big Data, the hot area is stream processing, where the Amazon River analogy is really apt, although Hadoop is batch oriented and this involves breaking the data streams into large files that are then loaded onto the data nodes. At the same time, most of the data are obsolete once processed and can be discarded.

Replication to multiple servers in the local-DAS method results in 3× the number of expensive (often GPU-based) servers in the cluster, with all the other added expenses such as switches. An economy-minded admin might consider building the replication in relatively inexpensive self-recovering storage appliances such as Ceph boxes and having just a single server with more DRAM/NVDIMM instead of three servers.

This is a much cheaper solution, but has the obvious problem of downtime if a server fails. Some spare server nodes solve this (just a handful probably are enough for all except really big clusters). There will be a penalty for loading a server and restarting if a failure occurs, but that should be infrequent enough that the cost trade-off is worthwhile. Mapping the data to smaller files should help this along by reducing the load time during recovery.

Ceph units have the benefit of being compact. A 10-node pod of Ceph units can be built in 10U of rack, with 120 drives and potentially a petabyte or more of storage using 10-TB drives. This can be in a rack with a good complement of server nodes, following the "keep-data-close" guideline. With a four-lane Ethernet backbone, replication to nearby racks is feasible.

A consideration in such a design is the impact on the whole process if some data are dropped out of the processing effort for a while. Take a scenario where people are being tracked in-store. Ideally, everyone should be tracked all the time, but if a server goes down, it may not be the end of the world—just some lost revenue opportunity. Thinking along these lines may help clarify the thought process of having rollover servers and networked storage instead of replica servers.

We've touched on Ceph's current performance deficiencies [16] earlier in this book. Current revisions have the data from the Ceph cluster all go through a primary node that is unique for each distribution group. With Big Data, that's a bottleneck in reloading the large amounts (several terabytes) of data to a spare server. A better architecture is to recover the data directly to the spare, saving latency, processing, and storage steps. Other object stores may have resolved this question, although of course they aren't likely to be free.

In considering hardware costs, give some thought to whitebox class hardware. Ceph isn't difficult to set up and tends to administer itself. It really is designed for any COTS platform, although it needs to improve both networking and SSD usage, and Hadoop also is designed to run on COTS, including GPU cards. This opens up using whiteboxes for the whole cluster, especially if SDN is used to allow low-cost switches, and this provides admins a way to build a cluster with some serious hardware savings.

In summary, Hadoop can be built on server clusters using either local DAS or networked object storage, with trade-offs in latency versus operational overhead and cost. Since data persistence as a part of the data lifecycle in the servers has a major impact, modeling and/or sandboxing this should be a step in evolving a full Hadoop cluster. Whitebox hardware may generate substantial savings whichever architecture is chosen.

Future Hardware Directions

With the advent of X-Point memory and HMC-like architectures speeding up memory access and increasing capacity, the optimization of a Hadoop storage system has to evolve to keep pace. As the industry saw when we transitioned to in-memory databases, the greater the amount of data for a workload are stored in fast memory, the faster the job runs. Though improvement tends to be discontinuous in in-memory databases—they tend to be all or nothing—this is less of an issue with Big Data, simply because much of the data are flowing through the server and is discarded after analysis.

Even so, the scale of Big Data points to a need for Big Memory to match. X-Point memory offers a way to multiply the size of DRAM as we discussed earlier, while HMC-like solutions make the close-in memory complex much faster, lower latency and dramatically lower power, making for a major uptick in core performance, whether for CPUs of GPUs; add in the 3D stacking approach that HMC envisions and high capacities become possible. Let's call this the memory-centric architecture.

Thinking of X-Point as DRAM extender makes sense, since CPU caching and parallel access masks the lower speed of the X-Point memory. The net is that we are about to see a boost in the in-memory portion of the designs. When this happens (likely in 2016/2017), we face the same debate of local-DAS versus networked storage.

Most of the issues don't change, but the fact that X-Point is persistent *is* a game-changer! With both DRAM and X-Point shareable over an RDMA network at the byte level, local-DAS approaches, with their need for expensive server level replication, will be mostly deprecated in preference to the network storage model. There may be exceptions such as financial trading where data uptime is critical and server redundancy justified on the value that could be lost in the time to reload, but in most cases this will be hard to sell.

Another impact of the memory-centric approach is that the need to feed all of that capacity demands very powerful networks. Intel is talking up OmniPath [17] as a 100-Gbps solution later in 2016, although Ethernet using four 25-GbE lanes ganged together has already reached the market and Mellanox is talking 50/200GbE availability by 2017. Both support RDMA, and Ethernet has the support of many vendors, so it will reach market with a pretty complete infrastructure.

Intel knows this, so they must have some rabbits in their hat to make OmniPath more attractive. Possibly OmniPath between servers will be implemented with the very low overhead of the core–core links that it derives from. If I'm right about X-Point being byte-addressable, this could give OmniPath a substantial edge over Ethernet RDMA, which has a great deal of packet and processing overhead for small messages. The question then for OmniPath is how it scales to very large clusters and if it can be routed, both issues that have been raised with InfiniBand and its Ethernet surrogate RoCE [18].

With NVMe over Fabrics (NoF) [19] looking like a real option in 2016/2017, Ethernet should be able out scale out to large storage clusters based on NVMe drives. These may be discrete standard form factor drives or proprietary all-flash structures. Economics most likely will favor the drive approach, especially if vendors take NoF directly to the drive and give them an EthernetRDMA interface.

If they do allow NoF drives, the storage farm will change enormously, both in structure and usage. All the drives become directly accessible to any server, encouraging object storage based on distribution and collection directly from the server, rather than through some intermediate appliance. This is in line with SDS architectures and has the benefit of highly flexible scaling. The direct drive-to-server transfers will reduce latency and increase effective bandwidth, especially during a server recovery operation.

Applying NoF to the secondary storage in these systems will follow logically providing an efficient way of moving data that have grown cold but still retains value to cheap storage. The continuous RDMA connections allows direct restoration of this secondary data to the server, with potentially a high bandwidth if the data are distributed across a large drive set, or have multiple replicas.

Big Data Processing in the Cloud

You can run Hadoop in the cloud. How well it runs is a totally different question from in-house setups. First, the cloud has bandwidth limitations in its networks and IOPS or bandwidth limits on storage. Second, any notion of locality is a lost cause. Taken together, the conclusion is that today's cloud-based Big Data operations probably do better with a local-DAS model using SSD instance storage. There is some progress in resolving the performance issues, with companies like Velostrata [20] providing acceleration for intercloud data sharing.

If we now look at the hybrid cloud, locality takes a big hit and this complicates handling load surges in the public cloud, especially if the networked storage model is used in-house. In the US, transferring data from in-house storage to the public cloud is very slow, due to our poor WAN infrastructure, and with Big Data, this becomes a serious problem indeed.

Even the local-DAS model suffers from this during surge handling. It must be assumed that all the data are in-house initially, and has to go across a WAN to be loaded into the instance storage. Architectures where the data are stored in a telco service provider's operation so that it can be connected to the various major clouds via very fast fiber links only invert the problem. Here the link from the datacenter out to the telco is the bottleneck. Overall, this problem is bad enough to make a hybrid Big Data cloud cluster untenable, unless the dataflow can be restructured to reduce WAN loads.

An example of this is the store-tracking system we described earlier. Multiple sensors detect where I'm standing, which way I'm facing and perhaps even what I'm looking at. All of that sensing result in a largish stream of raw data. Let's add that it's the weekend before Xmas and our datacenter is in overload.

A solution that will work with surging to the public cloud is to divide up the dataflow aiming to preprocess the raw data to figure exactly where I am in the store and whether I've moved in the last 10 s. That can be done in the public cloud, and then the results passed into the in-house analytics cluster as somewhat refined Big Data. It's a tidy solution, since it doesn't add WAN transits for raw data, for example.

SERVER STORAGE VERSUS NETWORK STORAGE

The issue of which is better for Big Data processing—local-DAS storage or networked storage [21]—was touched on in some depth in the previous section. The key issue was the need to store parts of the data for extended periods measured against the extra bus loads and overhead this created when compared with a networked storage approach.

This is a complex issue and well worth more extended discussion [22], since it affects some fundamental choices in architecture for Big-Data processing. We have to recognize that bus cycles (memory bus especially, together with IO access cycles), system overhead and LAN load all are finite resources and, in fact, are all probable bottlenecks unless tuned correctly.

It is too easy in a software-centric environment to ignore the hardware operational details, with the result that we can be led to suboptimize our solutions unless we take the time to model the detail flow of data bytes in the system. I've seen this happen many times in the last few years as the details of how COTS gear operates are subsumed into discussions about the elegant way to write the code. The result is file systems that protect against all sorts of real or suspected evils, but perform like snails, for instance. Often the lack of dataflow knowledge messes up the efficiency of some of the operations involved, while the (natural?) software tendency is to assume next year's faster processors will solve the speed problem. This may be why it's always taken 2–4 min to boot Windows on a PC!

Let's look at today's flow model for an IO. In Fig. 8.1 we see the basic flow of a networked drive operation in a COTS server. Data flow into the LAN adapter (chip or card) and are transferred by DMA over the PCIe links to the memory control units. Here it is usually cached then transferred to the DRAM memory when cycles are available. That's pretty straightforward.

When we start buffering the data on local drives, life gets much more complicated. Data can't flow from the LAN directly to the storage controller (at least not yet; we'll come back to this later). The result, as in Fig. 8.2, is that we not only use up a portion of the LAN and storage link bandwidth resource, we use up two chunks of the DRAM bandwidth resource.

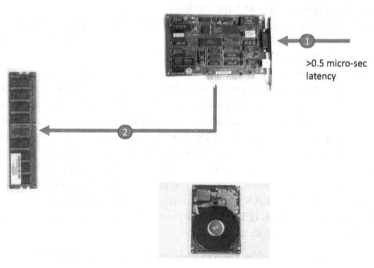

>0.5 micro-sec latency

FIGURE 8.1

Networked storage dataflow.

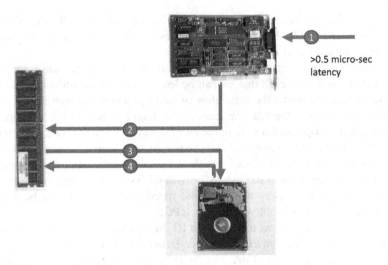

FIGURE 8.2

Virtual SAN dataflow.

But wait! There's more! We've parked data on the drive, but we need to bring it back to memory to use it. That's another chunk of storage link bandwidth and yet another chunk of DRAM bandwidth. That's a simple local-DAS storage data operation end-to-end. It takes one LAN, two drive, and three DRAM bandwidth chunks.

If we look at the networked storage model of Fig. 8.1, the operations stop when the LAN card DMAs its data into DRAM. The cost of the operation is one chunk of LAN and one chunk of DRAM bandwidth.

Sharing the data to another server has the same consequences. The local-DAS virtual SAN model requires one chunk of drive and one chunk of DRAM bandwidth more than the networked storage approach.

Clearly, the networked storage model uses less server resources, but there's a penalty for this. Transmitting a block over even the fastest RDMA network adds as much as $0.5\,\mu s$ of latency to the IO operation. This isn't a LAN bandwidth impact, since block from other servers can fill the time, but it does slow response to any one IO. Some business use cases for Big Data are very sensitive to this type of latency. Examples are trading systems in stock markets. We'll discuss low-latency structures in more detail in the next chapter, on High-Performance Computing (HPC).

Let's convert this discussion into a look at use cases. It assumes the best available technologies for RDMA LAN and SSD. There's a contrast between data that are stored on an extended basis (ED) (such as the results of previous analyses) and data that are streaming in for processing (SD).

1. If the ED can be held in the DRAM distributed across the cluster, we have the first necessary condition for an in-memory database. No local-DAS action is required, except perhaps to keep a loadable copy of all the results to speed up

reboots. This is best served by the network storage model, since it minimizes the DRAM bandwidth load to get data ready to be processed. All write operations will go to multiple storage nodes for data integrity purposes, although this could be achieved by the delayed replication used in, for example, Ceph or Scality.

2. If the ED is larger than DRAM can support, local persistent storage *is* needed. This can be NVDIMM. The storages in DRAM and NVDIMMs should be treated as a continuum, with software to promote or relegate data as needed. Any write operations to the NVDIMM must still be replicated to either other server node local-DAS or to networked storage before a write is considered complete.

3. If the ED is much larger than the available DRAM space, drive efficiency becomes of paramount importance. NVMe drives using PCIe are the solution, but the best choice of system is one capable of holding six or more drives with a motherboard with enough PCIe bandwidth to service them. Don't run the drives as a redundant array of independent disks (RAID) five set under any circumstances. RAID 0 mirroring can be used if there is a need to keep write operations short. Networked replicas can then be loaded on a lazy, asynchronous basis.

The last case has some variations to further complicate things. As noted, one of the weaknesses of Hadoop is that multiple replicas of data are normally created as protection. This costs enormous extra LAN bandwidth and storage space. It is possible to replicate to noncomputing storage nodes, and equally possible to send just a single copy to that node and let the storage node do the required replication on a different storage LAN.

This "hybrid" of local-DAS and networked storage approaches should be more economical and has lower loading on the cluster LAN. It also takes advantage of the higher port count typical of storage nodes.

TECHNOLOGY CHANGING THE PICTURE

There are some other considerations that should be borne in mind in looking at this. Suppose that there were a first line of defense—aggregation servers [23] with the sole job of creating streams of related data from the rivers flowing in. An example might be to aggregate all "Jim O'Reilly" traffic. These are Big Data servers, since they'll handle huge volumes of data using parallel computing. These are a variation of Case 1 above and would best be designed with the fastest LAN connections (dual 40 GbE pipes, for instance) and no local-DAS.

The coming tsunamis of Software-Defined Storage [24] add some alternatives to the mix of choices. It becomes less clear (again the purism of the software view) as to what are storage nodes and what are servers. From a computing perspective these are all virtualized server engines. From a dataflow point of view, performance optimization may dictate different LAN connections, such as more ports on storage nodes or having a back-end storage LAN on those nodes.

There may be different numbers of drives in the nodes. Servers in the in-memory model [25] use no drives and so can be compact, 1U systems. SuperMicro, for example, makes such systems capable of holding two or more GPUs, so these can be very compact clusters. Storage appliances can hold petabytes of storage, especially with compression.

As we move in the direction of terabyte-class HMC memory [26], and byte-addressable NVDIMM [27] as a DRAM extension, the effective size of primary memory can be very large indeed, moving solutions for Big Data toward the Case 1 model—ED all in-memory, no local-DAS and using networked storage mainly for cool and cold data to offload the DRAM/NVDIMM. Speed-up of LANs to 100 GbE for four-lane connections and 25 GbE for single-lane will accelerate this trend. However, the sharing of the DRAM/NVDIMM memory that will be a feature of this approach blends in some of the virtual SAN ideas—the result is a composite of the two models.

Note that I've avoided the evocative "hyper-converged system" designation in all of this. First, SDS effectively makes the term obsolete and whitebox units solve the need without resorting to expensive proprietary configurations. Second, the hyper-converged concept makes the nodes homogeneous and we saw above that a case can easily be made for drive-less servers and enhanced storage nodes.

Does this condemn hyper-converged systems to the shadows of oblivion? Like blade servers, a simple concept aimed at simplifying integration turned into a very expensive gold-plated setup where everything had to come from the original vendor. The result was a weak take-up of the blade idea, leading to hyper-converged systems as a replacement. The hyper-converged units carry much the same stigma of vendor lock-in and moreover they aren't cheap compared with whiteboxes. Reach your own conclusion as to whether hyper-converged systems have enough value to justify the extra cost!

BANDWIDTH AND SCALE

Over and above the questions of how much scale you need and whether your choice of file system can manage the scale level adequately, we have issues about LAN topology, placement of storage and servers, limits on rack power and cooling and management tools to understand.

The hardware issues related to the rack are the easiest to define and lead into LAN questions. Suppose I built a cluster of 1U 2×GPU units. Each of these consumes 800 W, so my rack, if fully loaded with servers, would need 42×800 W to run. That's roughly 34 KW and that's going to be one hot rack. In most datacenters, it's not possible to either power that level or cool it safely. Add to that, the noise level from the small fans in use in each server would be at high-pain thresholds.

The answer to this is to mix servers and storage in the same rack. That helps the locality issue and reduces latency, as well as lowering rack power to a tolerable level. But it brings a problem. In this top-of-the-line cluster we are hypothesizing, the storage nodes likely have 40 GbE RDMA links, which creates complications with the top-of-rack (TOR) switches. Most switches have all-40 GbE ports or just a couple of uplink ports and the rest are 10 GbE.

We want to feed data to those expensive servers as fast as they need and that means at least two 10-GbE ports on each server, which fits in with redundant pathing at least. What it doesn't fit is providing the best locality for data and servers. Let's try a model for this. Place 32 servers in the rack and fill eight RU with storage modules. There are TOR switches with 32 or more 10-GbE ports available to connect up those servers.

We need to look to the storage. There are two models for this. One has a few NVMe drives per 2U appliance (or an all-flash array) while the other goes for 4U units with a lot of drives. Likely, we'll want the 2U solutions for performance. That means 4 units each with two 40 GbE connections.

TOR Switches with eight 40-GbE connections for storage plus another eight or more to talk to the network spine just don't exist and anyway, the rack is still hovering around 25 KW. I think you see the dilemma!

In the end, the devil is in the details. How much storage in one appliance? Should I balance the system with one GPU per server so I can bring the per-server power down and double the number of LAN links per GPU? Do I need four TOR switches instead of two to get sufficient 40-GbE ports and does doing that impact locality in my data situation? What's my maximum rack power?

Impacting this is the question of needing a back-end LAN for efficient storage replication to take place. That's probably two more switches, since redundancy is needed. All in all, this is a complicated mess. It may well be that SDN will lead to some fast innovation in this area. The new approach should give us a good deal of flexibility in dropping the two-decade-old model of servers connecting to storage via a TOR linked to the network spine, which has determined the switch configurations we are currently seeing.

Scaling the whole system has its challenges, of course. The intrinsic file system that the cluster talks to has to be robust at very large size, while adding new nodes has to be easy. In fact, the best solutions just accept the new unit and integrate it automatically in background. Likewise, rebuilding after a node or drive failure has to be automated.

The file systems listed in the fourth section of this chapter have different scaling levels demonstrated. Most can go into the petabyte range, but be careful, since that isn't a large amount of storage anymore. With compression, a 12-drive 2U box using 10-TB drives can easily be 0.5 petabytes of effective storage capacity. Now, fast enough compression software/hardware to keep up with fast SSD isn't available yet, but we can expect this to be on its way to resolution in 2017.

In 2016, we have to re-examine the equations that balance out these types of system clusters. On the one hand, the DRAM side of the equation becomes much more important as X-Point memory begins deploying. On the other, we are going to enjoy a 2.5-fold increase on Ethernet performance. 25 GbE and four-lane 100 GbE will be compelling alternatives to 10 and 40 GbE. The fabric looks like it will be reusable, but, of course, we'll need new servers and switches.

Still, the Mega-CSPs all clamored for an intermediate step in the Ethernet family, rather than waiting another 5 years or so for 100-GbE lanes to surface. This reflects the stress on current networks. The power boost will be very welcome in the Big Data community.

There's been some debate about InfiniBand as an alternative to Ethernet. IB is established in high-performance computing, but the need for a separate fabric and all the skills needed to support it has caused most users to keep on the Ethernet path. Mellanox, who are the primary IB supplier, recognized this and proposed an "IB-over-Ethernet" solution called RoCE (for RDMA over Converged Ethernet).

RoCE needs to use expensive "converged" switches that buffer transfers and are capable of flow control. It is up against iWARP, a routable RDMA solution that uses standard switches and is routable over multiple LAN and WAN layers. It looks like iWARP is taking the lead in this battle of the protocols.

The final issue in this section is the scaling out of the Big-Data storage ocean across multiple, geographically dispersed sites. Even with data compression, this isn't easy to do economically. Partly, this is a direct result of the telcos not acknowledging the need for fiber connections for urban businesses. The impact is that getting the rivers of data to the computing centers will be impeded and the protection of processed data across sites will also be slowed. We can do better!

FILE SYSTEMS FOR BIG DATA

Even though unstructured and not suited to the fixed schemas of relational databases, there is a common thread in Big Data, the concept of key/data. Unfortunately, this fits databases but not traditional file systems. The result is the evolution of new filing structures better attuned to the key/data model. Premier among these is the HDFS, which is optimized for relatively static data, but there are a number of alternatives aiming to address perceived deficiencies in HDFS and to add capabilities for processing transient data flows.

The list of new file systems continues to grow, reflecting the newness of Big Data in the IT arena and the bottlenecks and issues that we still run in to. Even hardware is evolving, with Kinetic drives that store data in a native key/data model.

HDFS

Written in Java, HDFS [28] is designed for storing large quantities of quasi-static data. A storage cluster consists of a single Namenode and multiple Datanodes. HDFS stores its data in large (multigigabyte) files striped across multiple Datanodes and ensures data integrity by replicating the data across other nodes (the default is a total of three replicas). These large files reduce Namenode traffic, while replication removes the need for RAID.

HDFS clusters can have a secondary Namenode, used for snapshots of the Namenode as a way of recovering from failures without having to run through the full journal of file system operations. The Namenode itself can be a bottleneck as the cluster grows in size, especially if the majority of files are small. HDFS Federation is provided to resolve this problem by sharding the storage space into multiple spaces each served by their own Namenode.

As commented above, HDFS is locality-aware. The typical replication process aims to create two copies within the same rack, and a single copy in a remote rack. The file system and Hadoop's Job-tracker try to localize the processing of data into the same racks as the two copies, allowing better read-performance and the benefits of no performance loss if one of the replicas fails.

HDFS can be mounted to a system with the Filesystem in User Space (FUSE) method in Linux. This preserves the locality option. It can, however, be mounted to a variety of underlying distributed file systems provided by the operating system and here locality is lost. This almost always results in increased network traffic and lost performance.

Problems With HDFS

The weakest point of HDFS is the load process and subsequent replication of copies. In a networked model configuration, this could be done outside of the server cluster on a separate LAN, reducing the load on the server network tremendously. HDFS performs poorly in mostly transient data environments, which has stimulated development of alternatives.

HDFS is not POSIX-compliant, using an Append operation and other speed-up features. It doesn't support backup and archiving methods, or point-in-time recovery.

The one Namenode in each cluster is a major single point of failure issue. This is being addressed, with a backup Namenode being supported in Release 2.0, albeit with manual rollover. Automatic rollover is being addressed for incorporation in a later release.

Ultimately, Hadoop is a batch-oriented system and HDFS is designed around that model. It performs poorly with small files [29], since the Namenode becomes a bottleneck, as does the traffic associated with creating replicas.

The Alternatives

Hadoop isn't the only Big-Data solution. Oracle, for example, has added mechanisms for handling unstructured data. The emphasis is more on tying objects to the structured data framework than in handling them directly, although this is changing as Oracle deploys better tools.

The HDFS high-availability approach using replication is very similar to Ceph and AWS S3 both of which are used to feed Hadoop servers. These handle huge counts of small files better, while the constraints of cloud operations or general cluster structures are strong considerations in their use. Even so, there are bottlenecks that limit performance. Ceph, for example, brings all data through a single primary OSD. The exception is DDN's WOS system, which is a fully featured high-performance object store.

IBM has published code to run Hadoop on its GPFS (General Purpose File System). MAPR [30] has taken things a step further, writing their own POSIX-compliant file system for Hadoop that supports full read/write capabilities. Panasas [31], part of HP, has a proprietary file system solution, too. Scality's Ring [32] is a good object system, as is Caringo [33], and DDN [34] has WOS with very high performance.

In the more general market, the choices are extended scalable file systems such as Lustre and GlusterFS, a unified storage solution such as Ceph, with OpenStack Swift potentially a competitor, and PVFS and Quantcast, both of which support very large-scale solutions.

Briefly, their value propositions are:

Lustre: Designed for very-large-scale general-purpose computing, Lustre [35] is a good file system for unstructured data. It is claimed to be faster than Hadoop. Lustre supports erasure-coding, which reduces storage requirements by ~50% while improving data availability. Lustre can scale to tens of petabytes and thousands of client systems. Lustre is open-source, but supported by Intel.

GlusterFS: Advantages of GlusterFS [36] include a global namespace, compression on write and encryption. It can scale to petabytes with thousands of clients. It is open-source, but strongly supported by Red Hat [37].

Ceph: Unified storage and massive scalability into the Exabyte range make Ceph [38] very attractive. It supports both replication and erasure coding, though lacking inherent compression and encryption. Ceph is easy to deploy, and there are multiple sources of appliances ranging from inexpensive white-boxes to proprietary variations. Ceph is open-source, but leadership is provided by Red Hat.

OpenStack Swift: This project for object storage on OpenStack lags behind Ceph, which often supersedes it in configurations. Swift [39] is supported by the OpenStack SIG.

Quantcast: An open-source solution with no big sponsor, Quantcast's [40] claim to fame is roughly a 2× performance edge over Hadoop, combined with a choice of replication or erasure-coding, and a low memory footprint.

PVFS: PVFS [41] is a petabyte-scale open-source solution that is not POSIX compliant due to trading higher speed by not locking files.

There are a number of other solutions aimed at specific problem classes.

All of these share the common COTS hardware approach that should save so much cost in the future. It isn't clear where the dust will settle, as the file-system side of Big Data is an evolving area. Currently Ceph and GlusterFS look like the leaders in usage.

It isn't clear if these file systems meet the needs or capabilities of today's storage. Some rely on native Linux file systems to provide most of the underlying structure. While that might be elegant and a fast short cut to delivering a solution, it isn't likely that the result is going to be very fast, nor is it probable that features appropriate to Big Data will be developed optimally without underlying file system support.

Let's look at each of these file systems in more detail.

Lustre

Lustre [35] is a venerable product, having been created back in 1999. It was created for high-end scientific computing and is currently in use on many of the world's top supercomputers. Lustre has wide acceptance in the scientific/oil/gas markets. Today it is driven by the OpenSFS Forum, which contracts out development to, and works closely with, Intel.

As in any scale-out system, Lustre presents a single name space to the using clients. It goes about this somewhat differently to HDFS, avoiding the Namenode bottleneck. It does have a Namenode equivalent, the Metadata Server. There can be multiple MDSs in a cluster. However, they are only involved in pathnames and permissions, which remove the bottleneck caused in accessing chunk tables that point to actual data. MDS nodes store data in Metadata Targets (MDTs).

The other key elements of Lustre are the Object Storage Servers (OSSs) and Object Storage Targets (OSTs). An OSS stores file data onto some number of OSS units, using the underlying file system on the OSS node and making Lustre a user-space file-system. In an IO operation, the client obtains the layout of an existing file or creates a new file by accessing the MDS. Data transfers then are directly between the client and the OSTs (asymmetric pooling) thus removing any latency from intervening nodes and ensuring the fastest performance.

The layout information transferred is somewhat analogous to the inode tables in a traditional file system, but raised up a level. The pointers are now to files on OSTs, which can be read without direct knowledge of the placement of those files on the OST storage (somewhat like files in a NAS or object storage system). The OSTs may utilize RAID for added performance and for data integrity.

The access mechanism allows additional performance gains from striping the file over multiple OST nodes. Once the file layout data is in the client, it is possible to access chunks of data in parallel, multiplying the IO performance tremendously and reducing the time to load or write the data. Striping also allows files that exceed the capacity of a single OST to be stored, which is of tremendous value in Lustre's original target market, large-scale super-computers.

Lustre has extensive locking capability. Locking scales with the OSTs, so that it doesn't present a resource bottleneck as the cluster grows. Networking reflects the timescale of Lustre's genesis. While the front-end network from the MDS and OSS nodes out to the clients uses a fast connection such as InfiniBand, the OST connections use a SAN. While this could be based on iSCSI and so be Ethernet, the evidence is that no-one yet connects the OSTs with RDMA over Ethernet, though one could expect this to be changing.

If Lustre has a major weakness, it is the reliance on underlying file systems in the OST units. This adds a full OS stack to any transfers, slowing performance and adding to maintenance complexity. This offsets some of the gains made by asymmetric pooling and direct transfer of data.

Likewise, the approach to data integrity reflects the 1990s, with RAID-based solutions rather than node-level data dispersion and/or erasure coding. This brings home yet another set of maintenance complexities as well as all the problems of rebuild time and performance that make RAID unacceptable as a modern-day integrity method.

Vendors selling bundled computing and Lustre storage systems include Dell, HPE, Cray, SGI, and Fujitsu. Those selling Lustre support along with storage units include HDS, DDN, NetApp, and Seagate.

GlusterFS

Despite the similarity in name, GlusterFS [36] is a very different beast to Lustre. In some ways, Gluster ties in with virtual SAN approaches, insofar as it is designed to allow servers to export a local file system. These are consolidated together using stackable translators, which allow the exported file system or the consolidated virtual volumes to be mounted via a variety of protocols, such as SMB, NFS, or OpenStack Swift.

The stackable user-space protocol approach allows features such as mirroring, compression, striping, and caching to be added to the cluster. This is both a positive and a negative, insofar as it allows great flexibility but the software stacking is very reminiscent of the overhead built into operating system file stacks. It must be remembered that these stacks also exist in the exported file systems. The Gluster approach does, however, have the makings of an SDS-based approach, with the modules distributed across virtual servers.

Gluster supports InfiniBand and Ethernet connectivity and the native RDMA support makes it a streamlined performer in the pantheon of Big-Data filesystems. It uses a hashing algorithm, avoiding the problems of metadata servers altogether. Volumes can be added or removed easily, enhancing its scalability to several petabytes in size.

Gluster is an open-source project targeting mainly Linux environments and is heavily supported by Red Hat, providing distributions and support. GlusterFS supports Hadoop seamlessly without the need for application rewrites. This brings fault tolerance to the Hadoop space and allows the choice of file or object access to the data. In fact, APIs have been created to allow objects to be accessed as files and vice versa.

Ceph

Ceph [38] is primarily discussed in Chapter 4, Section 4b, "Ceph". Rather than rehashing what is discussed there, let's examine the interaction of Ceph and Big Data in a bit more detail. The first thing to decide if Ceph is chosen to store data is how many replicas are needed. If the answer is that the dataset is mission critical, the solution is like HDFS—two local replicas and one on a remote node, whether just in a different rack or even in a different datacenter is a matter of how important disaster protection is.

A lot of Big Data is "use once and throw away", and yet more is "use once, but keep it to comply with the law or best business practices". The former typically can survive its short time in the datacenter with just a single copy. That means that occasionally a server failure will cause some data to be lost, but if the lost data is just my eye movements in a store, that loss may be acceptable. The benefit, of course, is that all that nasty Ceph back-end LAN traffic is avoided and the Ceph cluster will run much faster.

Data that are in the second category can go out to cold storage. That might involve staging on a fast SSD-based unit, but slow drives can be used to hold the data. This is where erasure coding comes into the picture, using roughly half the space and offering much better failure protection even than three-way replication.

As noted, Ceph has some serious bottlenecks that need to be addressed as it matures and becomes the premier open-source object store. It needs to borrow asymmetric pooling from HDFS and avoid the ingestor bottleneck that currently exists. Back-end traffic uses multiple messages per IO operation and this also must be streamlined.

Ceph uses compact and inexpensive nodes. Some of the performance issues can be overcome by massive parallelism, but only for Exabyte-scale capacity systems. The reason for this is that drive capacities have grown rapidly, while compression and deduplication multiply the raw capacity of the drives. It is thus easy for a 12-drive, 2U box to hold 0.5 petabytes of data today in 2016, while we can expect that to reach 1.5 to 2 petabytes in 2020.

The result is a small footprint can hold a great deal of data. This leads us to several consequences. First, to maintain systems IOPS with the box count reduced so much, we need fast SSD in the primary networked storage. Second, we are going to have a network bottleneck unless we are careful. Even 25/100 GbE will be stressed in this environment, which will have an impact on the architecture of the motherboard and the number of network ports on the nodes. This may well stress ARM-based solutions beyond their bandwidth capacity and force the use of x64 designs with beefier IO and DRAM buses.

We can expect the intense interest in Ceph to drive the required innovation, so we should expect it to be a leader in cost, performance and market share from 2017 onwards. With Red Hat's purchase of InkTank, the guiding light on Ceph, the open-source code has gained an experienced and competent supporter and much wider market access.

OpenStack Swift

Swift [39] also was discussed in Chapter 4. Looking at Swift and Big Data, it's clear that Ceph is well out ahead at this point in time. Nonetheless, Swift development continues with strong support. There is a chicken-and-egg question involved; however, when it comes to Big Data, Openstack has attacked the Big Data issue in two directions, allowing HDFS, Cassandra, and PostgreSQL to cover the gamut from noisy big data to columnar databases to relational data.

In a sense, this mirrors the Google discussion about bringing compute to the data versus bringing data to the compute. That leaves Swift trying to solve a problem that may well be solved, leading to the question "Why?" and unavoidably to the next question, "What's the value proposition?". Even so, there are many people and organizations involved in Swift development.

Swift is somewhat slower than Ceph in a single datacenter configuration, but the fact that Ceph uses a master-slave model for replication and requires a quorum of writes to complete means that Ceph writes can be held up if remote datacenters are added to the picture. For example, if 4 datacenters are clustered and a quorum of three replicas is needed to complete a write, that remote write operation will extend write latency by as much as 0.2 s and run into bottleneck problems that will really slow large writes. Swift doesn't suffer from this problem, since it defaults to just requiring the two local stores to complete.

The quorum problem is real, but for how long? I can see the Ceph team figuring out a fix already! The reality is this is a minor tweak to the code. More fundamental is how Ceph partitions traffic on LANs. The connections to the client servers are shared with the back-end, unencrypted replication dataflow. A compromised client would allow access to the data being stored and potentially allow erasure or modification.

The security issue has some in the Swift camp pushing for a split system with local fast storage on Ceph, but multi-site storage based on Swift. This seems rather pointless. The solution is either to fix the Swift performance issue or the Ceph security problem. The industry will succeed with the latter faster than the former, since the LAN issue requires in the main the addition of an extra LAN with additional ports in each storage node. A virtual LAN (VLAN) would address the issue, too, but it wouldn't be as secure and, anyway, Ceph's back-end traffic is verbose and the private storage LAN would be a great help.

Overall, it looks like Ceph will be the eventual winner in the OpenStack stakes. Its issues are trivial compared with Swift's performance shortfall, although even Ceph needs to get moving. It's worth noting that many of the comparisons between the two emphasize that this isn't a competition, rather it's complementation, but these come mostly from Swift supporters and tend to sound defensive!

Quantcast File System (QFS)

Designed as a Big-Data storage vehicle for Quantcast analytics applications, QFS [40] is now in the public domain. Architecturally, it is similar to other files systems above, with Chunk Servers storing the data, and a Metaserver holding the information about where the chunks reside.

It presents the storage as a single huge ocean. Redundancy was a day-zero focus and QFS solves this by encoding the data using Reed-Solomon codes so that six chunks become nine. These are distributed over nine Chunk Servers, with recovery of data if any six can be read successfully. Essentially, this is erasure coding.

Parallel Virtual File System (PVFS)

PVFS [41] began life in 1993 and development is now being funded by NASA, Argonne National Labs, and several other government agencies. Primary development is being done by Clemson University, the Ohio Supercomputer Facility and Argonne.

PVFS is similar to Lustre and Panasas FS in having a key/data model for metadata, with the pairs being stored separately from the data itself. The design needs just a single access to a server to get metadata pointing to the chunks on the data servers. IO to each data server is managed by a routine in that server (Trove), which supports the Trove-dbfs, storing metadata in a database structure and the data in files.

PVFS is now also known as OrangeFS.

Other Storage Solutions

There are a lot of niche products and solutions that fit classes of Big Data. Several of these are associated with the Apache open-source group (Spark, Cassandra, and Kudu). These may gain in importance as Big-Data evolves, so let's look them over.

Apache Spark

Spark [42] is an Apache open-source project to support in-memory databases. In this respect it is very different from the file systems we've discussed, and is essentially a MapReduce alternative, but Spark supports memory sharing across the cluster and, with nonvolatility coming to the DRAM bus in 2016, is legitimately a form of networked storage.

Spark consists of several components. The Spark Core handles task dispatching, scheduling and data distribution. It creates Resilient Distributed Datasets, logically related sets of data partitioned across the nodes in the cluster. Spark Streaming ingests data in mini-batches, allowing very fast processing of "rivers of data". Spark SQL provides support for structured or semistructured data, and there is a Machine Learning Library that provides a framework for ML analytica.

In-memory operation is as much as 100× faster than traditional cluster analytics and, with the current trend toward much faster and higher-capacity DRAM memory on a given server, combined with Intel's plans for nonvolatile X-Point storage on the DRAM bus, this number is bound to increase significantly.

Apache Cassandra

Cassandra [43] is a distributed database management system. It is designed around high throughput and can support clusters across multiple datacenters. It is written in Java and runs on commodity servers. There are no metadata servers and all nodes are functionally identical. Replication is configurable and new nodes add nondisruptively to the cluster.

One downside of the high-throughput approach is that latency tends to be high for both read and write operations, so this is not applicable to many use cases, but it is proving to be a popular solution with a growing user base.

Apache Kudu

Kudu [44] is a clustered approach to storing data. It is currently "in incubation" within the Apache community. Kudu has a very simple data model, avoiding blob creation and other issues seen with many of the Big-Data approaches. As a result it is a low-latency storage system, as opposed to a file format.

Google File System

This file solution is unusual [45] insofar as it is the only one in this list that's proprietary and in fact just used internally to Google. It has, however, influenced many of the other approaches to Big-Data file systems and, moreover, is probably the single largest Big-Data file system deployment, so it would be unfair to ignore it. GFS is implemented in user space.

In GFS, files are chunked into 64-MB segments. The Google data characteristically is rarely overwritten, if ever, so file operations are reads or appends and the file system is optimized on this. GFS clusters have two elements—a single Master Node and a large set of ChunkServers. Each chunk is labeled by the Master Node when created and these chunk mappings provide the means to read data.

Data are replicated with three or more copies, the higher numbers being used for faster access or for protection of critical files. Locking is not used. Instead "leases" are created and flagged in the Master Node to allow data changes, with a fixed finite expiration. The modifying ChunkServer must update all replicas before a change is tagged as complete.

GFS is a work in progress. Google is a massive manufacturer of SSD and uses them to speed up operations. The architecture allows for huge scale, but there appear to be some architectural bottlenecks, and the Master Node approach looks to be a single point of failure.

REFERENCES

[1] Big Data. http://www.mckinsey.com/business-functions/business-technology/our-insights/big-data-the-next-frontier-for-innovation.

[2] A lot of data. https://en.wikipedia.org/wiki/Big_data.

[3] Internet of Things. http://www.networkcomputing.com/wireless/internet-things-not-so-scary/1614867224.

[4] Reluctance of telcos. https://www.washingtonpost.com/news/the-switch/wp/2015/02/06/google-is-serious-about-taking-on-telecom-heres-why-itll-win/.

[5] In-memory databases. https://www.oracle.com/webfolder/s/delivery_production/docs/FY16h1/doc5/baORCL1503-Infographic-v14.pdf?elqTrackId=195d86caa49d45f3942819e189163c2e&elqaid=24915&elqat=2.

[6] Hybrid Memory Cube. http://www.hybridmemorycube.org/.

[7] Byte-addressability. http://research.microsoft.com/apps/pubs/default.aspx?id=81175.

[8] Key/value store. http://www.enterprisestorageforum.com/storage-management/is-key-value-data-storage-in-your-future-1.html.

[9] Hadoop Distributed File System (HDFS). https://hadoop.apache.org/docs/r1.2.1/hdfs_design.html.

[10] NAS and SAN. http://searchstorage.techtarget.com/opinion/External-storage-might-make-sense-for-Hadoop.

[11] Strong sense of locality. http://www.hadoopinrealworld.com/data-locality-in-hadoop/.

[12] SSDs at 16TB capacities. http://arstechnica.com/gadgets/2015/08/samsung-unveils-2-5-inch-16tb-ssd-the-worlds-largest-hard-drive/.

[13] NVDIMM memory. http://www.vikingtechnology.com/nvdimm-technology.

[14] X-Point memory. http://www.intel.com/content/www/us/en/architecture-and-technology/3d-xpoint-unveiled-video.html.

[15] NVMe over Fabrics. http://www.snia.org/sites/default/files/SDC15_presentations/networking/WaelNoureddine_Implementing_NVMe_revision.pdf.

[16] Ceph's Current Performance Deficiencies. https://www.mellanox.com/related-docs/white-papers/WP_Deploying_Ceph_over_High_Performance_Networks.pdf.

[17] OmniPath. http://www.intel.com/content/www/us/en/high-performance-computing-fabrics/omni-path-architecture-fabric-overview.html.

[18] RoCE. http://www.chelsio.com/wp-content/uploads/2011/05/RoCE-The-Fine-Print-WP-1204121.pdf.

[19] NVMe over Fabrics. http://www.flashmemorysummit.com/English/Collaterals/Proceedings/2015/20150811_FA12_Overview.pdf.

[20] Velostrata company website. http://velostrata.com/product/.

[21] Local-DAS storage or networked storage. http://www.infostor.com/disk-arrays/hadoop-storage-options-time-to-ditch-das.html.

[22] More extended discussion. http://blogs.vmware.com/vsphere/2014/08/big-data-design-considerations-hadoop-storage-choices.html.

[23] Aggregation servers. http://searchsqlserver.techtarget.com/definition/data-aggregation.

[24] Software-Defined Storage. http://www.snia.org/sds.

[25] In-memory model. http://www-01.ibm.com/software/data/what-is-in-memory-computing.html.

[26] Terabyte-class HMC memory. https://www.micron.com/products/hybrid-memory-cube/all-about-hmc.

[27] Byte-addressable NVDIMM. http://nvmw.ucsd.edu/2010/documents/Nightingale_Ed.pdf.

[28] HDFS. https://hadoop.apache.org/docs/r1.2.1/hdfs_design.html.

[29] Hadoop performs poorly with small files. http://apmblog.dynatrace.com/2013/07/17/top-performance-problems-discussed-at-the-hadoop-and-cassandra-summits/.

[30] MAPR. https://www.mapr.com/.

[31] Panasas company website. http://www.panasas.com/.

[32] Scality's Ring. http://www.scality.com/.

[33] Caringo company website. http://www.caringo.com/.

[34] DDN company website. http://www.ddn.com/.

[35] Lustre. http://www.lustre.org/.

[36] GlusterFS. https://www.gluster.org/.

[37] Red Hat. http://redhat.com.

[38] Ceph. http://www.ceph.com/.

[39] OpenStack Swift. http://www.swift.openstack.org/.

[40] Quantcast. https://www.quantcast.com/about-us/quantcast-file-system/.

[41] PVFS. http://www.pvfs.org/.

[42] Spark. http://spark.apache.org/.

[43] Cassandra. http://cassandra.apache.org/.

[44] Kudu. http://www.cloudera.com/about-cloudera/press-center/press-releases/2015-09-28-cloudera-launches-kudu-new-hadoop-storage-for-fast-analytics-on-fast-data.html.

[45] Google file solution is unusual. https://www.quora.com/Does-Google-have-its-own-file-system.

High-Performance Computing

9

High-Performance Computing (HPC) is a group term for high-powered computing that addresses scientific, oil and gas, and other very large-scale tasks. Clearly, there are enough similarities with the Big Data environment that many concepts are shared, but, at the same time, HPC has unique characteristics.

Critical to success with HPC is the handling of data properly and here, there is no one-size-fits-all solution. Each data set, especially in the scientific space, has unique characteristics. For example, astronomy data are generally considered incompressible, although recent work on the Square Kilometer Array (SKA) program is achieving as much as 10% compression. At the other extreme, sparse data are exactly that, though it's still huge until the active data elements are identified.

HPC varies from Big Data [1] in that the process of computing tends to expand the data to be stored by large amounts, while Big Data tends to have smallish output files. An example is a nuclear reaction simulation, where each cycle of the simulation generates a full memory dump from the cluster. Deciding on which memory the images get stored, and when, is a major architectural challenge. An example of the problem is a nuclear weapon simulation that takes 30 min to load into a single-tenant supercomputer, then computes for an hour and then takes 30 min to unload. That effectively doubles the cost and time of the compute work.

Historically, HPC systems tended to be one-off solutions with peculiar hardware and task-specific software. We are seeing a transition to COTS-based solutions, albeit mostly highly tuned and high-end. One new trend in HPC is the creation of HPC clouds [2]. These allow multitenancy, which means much better utilization of the compute resources, but they add to the challenges of configuration and optimization. Nonetheless, this is a crucially important trend in HPC, since it allows even individual investigators access to simulation and analysis tools that previously were unaffordable, with the result that, in many areas of science and medicine, the pace of research has doubled or tripled.

Multitenant clouds create security concerns; enough that nuclear weapon simulation currently won't be running on a cloud—it will have the super computer to itself. Getting the load/unload time down assumes a critical priority in such a situation.

One common thread in trying to optimize HPC environments is that classes of resources such as DRAM bandwidth or LAN connectivity tend to be totally consumed during the computing phase. Adding more resources to speed up loading, for instance, can run into a conflict between using those resources to make computing even faster and focusing somewhat on better IO. This is a dilemma that tends to be solved use case by use case.

Network Storage. http://dx.doi.org/10.1016/B978-0-12-803863-5.00009-1

One extreme use case usually classed as HPC, not Big Data, is high-speed financial analysis in stock or currency trading operations. Here, the cost of decision-making is quite literally measured in millions of dollars per second and enormous effort is put in to ensure fast communications across the clusters and fast storage operations. This is where low message latency is most critical.

Another characteristic of HPC applications is that they have huge amounts of data. The SKA program is expected to generate an Exabyte of data every day, for example. This makes the cost of storage gear an issue, but it also throws into highlight the problems of networking that data to consumers who might be on other continents. In this case, many issues remain unresolved, including whether computing will be done near the consumers or at the array end of the network (Even in the latter case, the antennas are thousands of miles apart).

The result of all this is that there is no single use case for HPC. Rather it's an agglomeration of task types loosely defined by the characteristic of lots of data (typical streams with well-conditioned structures, such as telescope data, simulation cell values and such) and the need to compute those streams very heavily.

Common to HPC applications is the benefit they receive from parallel data transfers. This means the optimum solution for storage is a scale-out system with a high ratio of network bandwidth to the storage capacity of the box. Object storage appliances and COTS-based GlusterFS solutions fit this bill and likely will be the solutions of choice for the storage farm. Which will be prevalent is a matter of debate. Gluster is incumbent, but operations like CERN are very bullish about Ceph object stores.

Let's look in detail at some of these use cases.

MAJOR SCIENTIFIC EXPERIMENTS

Poster child HPC examples are the SKA [3] and CERN's LHC [4]. These experiments generate huge amounts of raw data, typically in the Exabyte range. The raw data are usually converted to more useful forms. For example, radio-astronomy data are turned into independent patterns for each radio source and then the center peak of those patterns are identified. The radio-astronomy approach is similar to synthetic aperture radar, but at a much finer resolution.

The Large Hadron Collider at CERN converts particle tracks detect in cloud chambers and other sensors into information about the origination of a particle, its energy and electric charge, and other quantum measurements such as spin. In many ways, CERN computing is a bit like looking for needles in a very big haystack, with billions of interactions masking the occasional prize such as a Higgs boson.

Both operations have remote sensors, but SKA has blocks of telescopes distributed over thousands of square miles, while CERN's distant sense for neutrino experiments is currently only tens of miles away. Needless to say, there is preprocessing of data before transmitting it to the central computing facility. Data are digitized. These are high noise environments from a signal to noise perspective and the digitized data resolution has to be high enough to cope with that. Sampling also has to be very frequent or the telescopes' resolution falls off.

The bottom line is that preprocessing here likely increases the amount of data to be handled at the data center. The raw data must be stored for a period of time, and a good deal of debate must go into retention periods. Since there is always a chance that scientists will want to look at the raw data from a year or two back to see if there are any other Higgs bosons, say, most data must be retained for a long time. The result is that data storage for these mega-projects tends to be the largest on the planet.

At the same time as creating huge capacity, we have to move the data into the storage system, then deliver it for computation and then store the results. CERN does this with Ceph [5], using cheap whitebox appliances. Ceph scales easily and can store very large files. CERN has becoming a bleeding edge user of Ceph and this has played back into Ceph development.

SKA is still embryonic and the computing approaches are being held closely by the various contenders for the work. There is still a debate about GPU versus hardware acceleration, for instance. Two groups are vying to get the SKA operation, one with a site in Namibia and the other in Australia. Both are characterized as being a long way from the end-customer—the science community, distributed worldwide. This implies that the results data probably need multiple copies on multiple continents, which again points to a Ceph type of approach. Ceph could also handle the raw data streams, and the fact that it supports erasure coding as well as asynchronous replication is a real positive.

From a hardware point of view, none of these mega projects will use traditional big vendor gear. These will likely be built on purpose-built whiteboxes, avoiding the huge markups on drives and DRAM.

BIG SIMULATIONS

One reason that we got Test Ban Treaties in the last 50 years is that computer simulation got well ahead of practical experiments in figuring how to optimize the bang for the buck. As a result, we can design subcritical ordinance that can get a bomb into a packing crate. I suppose that's progress and it's definitely better than the hundreds of Big Bangs we would have needed.

Simulations for this type of model are just very scaled up versions of the simulations run to tune airflow over a car hood, for example. Still, they require extremely large supercomputers, which until the advent of SSD tended to be very IO starved. Getting the data in and out stalled on the slow speed of hard drives and the scaling limitations of SANs, with the result that loading the initial simulation state and then saving periodic results files took up much more time than actual compute.

Today, storage tiering with SSD and bulk HDD has improved the drive speed problem, while Remote Direct Memory Access (RDMA) links using IB or Ethernet have helped speed up the LAN interlinking everything. Data compression at LAN speed isn't yet available, but the national labs that tend to be the owners of these systems are looking for ways to achieve that.

Simulation using supercomputers is also broadly used in academia and in segments of the commercial market such as airframe stress analysis and drug design programs. The advent of cloud approaches in HPC complicates the storage issue, since workflow has moved from a single huge project at a time to multitenancy with small short-run projects. This has led to a higher bandwidth to storage, attained with more LAN connections and access to higher bandwidth through IB (at 56 Gbps).

Next-gen solutions will likely migrate to 100 GbE links, with all-flash or all-SSD primary storage. Power considerations in these huge facilities are a major issue and will increase pressure to be early adopters of the all-flash data center model. Likely, X-Point type DRAM extensions will prove very valuable for in-memory speedup, with the result that there will not be a trend toward servers with local drives.

Hardware will, within security constraints, be inexpensive whitebox class products. Sensitivity over international hacking, primarily directed at China, could create an opportunity for onshore fabrication of systems and storage.

SURVEILLANCE SYSTEMS

Some of the largest computing clusters in the world are dedicated to surveillance. Just ask the NSA! We know from Edward Snowden, that the agency listens to all the phone calls coming into the United States and a whole lot more. We do know that NSA keeps huge amounts of data as a result—they are building a monster data center in Utah [6] to store even more data.

While the agency is remarkably tight-lipped on how it does things, we can guess that speech is compressed before use, then run through a variety of recognition programs with the resulting data compressed prior to archiving.

The results of all of this consist of millions of small data objects—2 min of speech compresses into a few kilobytes. This is the nightmare of very large-scale storage systems. Object striping algorithms such as CRUSH (in Ceph) tend to break down under these conditions and become very inefficient. Similarly, Gluster and Lustre will clog up on metadata lookups. Most likely, there is file concatenation with a proprietary indexing scheme (stored in a structured database) to make this all tractable and accessible.

A key to productivity in any surveillance system is recovery time. There's no room for the 2-h waits of Amazon's Glacier [7] here. We need a disk- or SSD-based solution, though a case might be made for the fiber-optic cable storage system the CIA created. Likely, SSD is the best solution, being fast, low-powered and very fast to start up compared with hard drives, but the agency may just be getting there in terms of cost justification.

Video surveillance has its own challenges. The need to look for the proverbial camel tracks across the desert is very real. This means that bulk archived storage probably needs to be staged to much faster near in storage to allow the back and forth of searching and comparing. That near in storage has to be SSD or flash, while hard drives are the likely archive store today. Looking out a couple of years, space in the data center will be saved and maybe a tier of storage eliminated by going to an in-memory approach for the tasks being currently worked, and bulk SSD at perhaps 30 TB for the archives.

Facial recognition [8] is a key element of any surveillance system. (I wonder if they have a database of camel jaws at NSA!) This is a Big Data type application that may benefit enormously from parallel processing using GPUs. Again, in-memory architectures make the most sense.

On a more mundane level, there are millions of surveillance cameras in the world. Britain, for example, uses roadside cameras to track license plates, and in British detective fiction on PBS they appear to solve one crime in five. With street cameras and cameras in public places, the United Kingdom has a camera count [9] reaching perhaps 6 million, or one for every 11 Brits. Part of this count includes private cameras, but the number is large and growing.

Any system like that suffers from the Amazon River comparison data flowing in from many small sources creating a giant flow. Of necessity, data storage needs to be closer to the cameras, and technology to dedupe and compress is very useful at the source or near it. This is a dataflow problem more than a storage issue and removing unchanging parts of the stream should relieve the capacity problems associated with huge numbers of hi-res cameras.

The ideal storage for this class of surveillance data is an object store, since the scale of many storage systems has to be very large. To put this in perspective, a major airport likely generates enough data to fill a container full of high capacity drives. With 10 Tb drives, we are looking at 6 Petabytes per rack and at 28 racks in a container we only have 168 Petabytes of space, which is probably just enough for 60 days of operation. This means that holding 6 months of historical raw data means 3 containers and there is probably a need for extra containers for backup operation, etc., Big Storage!

THE TRADING FLOOR

Stock and currency trading bring a whole new meaning to the time value of money. Microseconds matter, since estimates give roughly a million dollars per second for the cost of latency [10]. The result is that storage for these use cases has to focus on end to end and not just storage box latency. We have to figure out how to minimize network latency, too.

Needless to say, this tends to be a "money-is-no-object" environment. We see expensive PCIe (Peripheral Component Interface express) flash drives in servers and multiple InfiniBand connections between servers, workstations, and storage. The InfiniBand is still the lowest latency solution for networking, though RDMA Ethernet [11] is poised to challenge that, and RDMA reduces the server overhead for managing the LAN from 30 to 50% down as low as 3%.

This market segment will probably lead in the uptake of 25 and 100 GbE links, which reached mainstream in 2016. RDMA currently means special adapter cards in the servers, so this will be easy to replace, while the cabling and such is still usable for the higher speed links. New switches and router cards will be needed of course.

In 2017, we'll likely see storage connect via an NVMe-over-fabrics [12] scheme of some sort, using RDMA with NVMe (Non-Volatile Memory express) to further speed up storage access. This may bring some changes to the file systems uses to store the data, perhaps making it directly readable into the servers, rather than going through a layer or two of storage appliance controllers.

Even with all of this, trading floors will continue to be a challenge, especially as the data environment moves from local to global. Keeping current is the name of the game and long-haul systems are particularly challenging in this respect. The solution is to find a protocol that doesn't rely on handshakes for each read or write operation; much like NVMe does for interrupt handling in a server CPU. This is the rationale for the NVMe prediction in the previous paragraph.

One further challenge is to achieve data compression in real time on the streams transmitted over WANs both intra-continentally and intercontinentally. We weren't even close to that in 2015, but start-ups are looking to fix the issue and if they succeed they should improve the synchronicity of the whole system.

Within the trading operation, we likely will see a move away from distributed workstations at the traders' desks to centralized, cloud-based virtual desktop solutions. This simplifies the distribution of stored data and reduces LAN latency by as much as 50%. The approach has the benefit of allowing agile resource usage to be applied to typed queries, which should allow much faster processing.

HIGH-PERFORMANCE COMPUTING CLOUDS

The idea of using supercomputer to provide shared tenancy to the cloud is still somewhat embryonic. Mostly, this is because the tuning approaches used to speedup specific applications aren't easily generalized to a broader spectrum of applications and workloads. Specific challenges occur in networking and in dataflow optimization which involves storage in a major way.

Generally, instance types in HPC clouds are large compared with the standard cloud, since it's better to process as much as possible within an instance to reduce interinstance communication. This puts quite a bit of stress on the storage LAN with the need to load and unload more data per server, suggesting RDMA as the best solution for connectivity to storage.

Security is clearly an issue in these use cases, but the capability to encrypt still lags the performance needed, and the result is data often is unprotected at rest. Faster encryption technology and hardware acceleration are definitely needed to make operations secure.

Traditionally, HPC supercomputers, especially in academia, use a scale-out file system such as Gluster or Lustre for managing storage. This is probably not the optimum solution for a multitenant cloud, given the sprawl of files one can expect from the lack of optimization and the relative IT skill set of small users. An object storage approach would work better for this. An early example of this approach was Johns Hopkins Genome Project [13], which used a Caringo object store back in 2007 to control the main database and all of the experimental shards in the system.

The creation of HPC clouds has brought HPC way down market, making it available to individual scientists for small projects at an affordable price. The result is that experiments are sped up significantly, perhaps as much as 3×. This suggests that the HPC cloud approach will grow rapidly in the market, as issues of security are resolved.

Another HPC approach comes from a mainstream hardware provider, Nvidia [14], making a GPU-based cloud available. This allows sandboxing as well as production work and is generally aimed at allowing users to try out the GPU approach before buying into large volume buys of GPU cards or GPU cluster appliances.

VIDEO EDITING

The video market took a major upset when Adobe abandoned the licensed software model for a SaaS approach using a private cloud [15]. Overnight, the entry price for professional video editing dropped from 5 to 10K range required to buy licenses and a graphics workstation to as low as $10 per month with only a cheap PC or tablet at the user end. This has made graphics editing economic for many more users and Adobe has increased overall revenue as a result.

More generally, video editing involves joining data stream together and snipping out unwanted scenes. The process is very manual and used to be slowed by poor storage response time. Fortunately, we've made huge progress in this area. Whether the data are processed on a local workstation or in the cloud, this is a high bandwidth application. We are already converting Hi-Def raw data to 4K compressed streams, and 8K is on the horizon, so the raw streams tend to be very large indeed.

A rationale for the cloud approach in video editing is that the workload is episodic. There are periods of review after an edit, and jobs have different compute load requirements as they are processed. The flexible capacity of a cloud is ideal for this type of workload.

The cloud approach makes collaborative editing relatively easy since the data are all in one place. It gets tougher with local workstation approaches, since the speed of operation requires a local copy, which involves transferring data into the workstation. Usually, the workstation approaches share data across a SAN, but the advent of geographically dispersed editing and effects work makes that a slow process over a WAN or even slower by physically transferring data tapes.

A partial solution is to colocate video-related businesses and serve this group of users with a private cloud. This is being tried out in several places in Europe. This means that the various specialist effects and editing operations can collaborate as businesses on the project, rather than the traditional method of independent work, which allows layering of effects, etc.

Needless to say, professional-class video postproduction work requires strong security and encryption is a must for any moviemaker using such a facility. In reality, though, that's true of any movie data set—stealing a copy of Star Wars would be worth a fortune! It's especially an issue with small private clouds and that should be a consideration before using such facilities.

OIL AND GAS

With compact GPU-based systems clusters, it's possible to take a lot of computing out into the field, with the result that the need to transmit raw data is reduced considerably. The rigors of computing in rough terrain suggest strongly that SSD is the right storage solution for these field units. This matches up better than HDD for compute speed on the raw data.

Most of the raw data need to be archived for years. An HDD solution is the way to go today for archiving, rather than tapes, just because of the time to mount a particular data set. As SSDs get larger and cheaper, they'll replace the HDDs, moving from existing RAID arrays to object storage appliances in the process.

Let's now look in more detail at some of the technology issues in storage networking for HPC.

LATENCY IS KING!

In HPC, latency—the time elapsing from starting a communication to getting a response or block of data—assumes a high level of importance, but the reason for that depends on the use case and even the definition of what is an acceptable latency will vary. Latency has two measurements that matter—the average latency seen over a lot of transactions and the largest latency seen.

Latency has two main sources. First, for all messages in the system including storage, is Round Trip Time (RTT). The total time from when we send out a message until we get a response is RTT. RTT consists of delays in the NIC cards and the operating systems at both ends, plus the line delay in each direction, plus the switch delay. When switches are layered up, as they usually are in big clusters of servers, we incur extra delays at each switch and extra transmission delays on the connections between the switches.

In typical Ethernet systems RTTs add up to several microseconds of delay, but remember that there are quite a few messages involved in any transaction and this causes the delays to mount up, too. This matters because time really is money in these environments.

An alternative is to use RDMA. Today, that means faster speed connection, based on raw line speed, and it also means that we chop the operating system and NIC time down by a bunch and, because the largest vendor has optimized for this, also reduced the switch latency into the one-tenth of a microsecond level.

Latency-sensitive use cases like trading floors have bought heavily into the InfiniBand approach. This may be the largest single market for the technology and possibly the savior of what is generally considered a niche product. The advent of 25 GbE and Ethernet RDMA likely will pose a challenge to IB's supremacy as the low latency solution. Switch silicon in the Ethernet space has caught up with IB on the switch latency issue and NIC and OS latencies are essentially the same for both technologies. Ethernet has one big advantage over IB—Ethernet scales to very large clusters simply because it can be routed. It's also the backbone of choice for the rest of any data center.

As mentioned, the other network latency issue is the maximum latency for any message. This turns out to be far more complex issue than average latency. To financial institutions, it is also a very important measure of system adequacy, since time is money. Excursions into the millisecond range cause problems, especially if they happen during multimillion dollar transactions. Estimates range up from 1 million dollars per second of delay so a burst of excursions to 50 ms could turn out expensive indeed. Debates about maximum latency have died down, indicating that developers in both Ethernet and IB have a handle on the issue, so that lets us move on to the storage latency question.

The second source of latency is compute time and data access time. This is the time the target computer takes to create an answer to a message and is usually a function of horsepower in the CPU, or, in the case of storage, the speed of the drives and the amount of cache. In the last several years, we've gone from HDD to PCIe flash cards to PCIe SSD and all-flash arrays. All have changed the way that low-latency configurations like trading systems talk to storage.

PCIe SSD is the likely winner in the race, for the moment, since it can be parallelized up better than PCIe flash cards, but there are and will continue to be adherents of both approaches. Even so, the storage question is about to be thrown into some confusion as Non-Volatile Dual In-line Memory Module (NVDIMM) and Intel/Micron's extremely fast X-Point memory hit their stride in late 2016. We'll see in-memory architectures coming to the fore, with persistent backup in the addressable memory space. This will lead to a dramatic reduction in the storage portion of latencies, though it won't impact messaging. Data to be read will be in memory and data being written will be put into the NVDIMM space at near-DRAM speed.

Any need for multiple copies for data protection will be handled via a DRAM-sharing scheme similar to that of the virtual SANs. Most likely, this will be an extension of NVMe-over-fabrics, or perhaps a dedicated RDMA process. Because NVDIMM will ultimately support single-byte write operations, the transfer time for storage operations should go down considerably using this protocol.

NVDIMM with byte addressability are already available. They are one of the two classes of NVDIMM agreed by JEDEC (Joint Electron Device Engineering Council) and Storage Networking Industry Association (SNIA). The technology allows each address to be written to or read from using standard CPU register to memory operations. This makes the writes blindingly fast compared with any other storage device. X-Point is actually slower than this, because the data have to go into the cache and then into the non-volatile memory, and this takes around 20× the time for a DRAM write, but if technology to save the cache is added to the CPU this may not be an issue and the result will be faster even than an atomic write to memory.

Having persistent DRAM requires a great deal of software to change, including the operating system, compilers, link editors, and management tools for memory. More importantly, the application has to become aware that it is writing or reading persistent data, which probably involves a considerable rewrite and some tuning of performance. For any of the HPC sectors where needing to keep results of calculations or transactions safe is an imperative coupled with low latency or high bandwidth, this set of changes would bring huge gains and we can expect a high level of take up in the next generation of HPC systems.

Overall, with Hybrid Memory Cube architectures in the offing for both CPU and GPU, much faster and bigger DRAM and increased core count, together with the technology changes we've just discussed, HPC will be a hot spot for storage and networking, just to keep up.

CONVERGING REMOTE DIRECT MEMORY ACCESS

RDMA is clearly important in HPC and likely will become an absolute requirement within a couple of years. The question is what form it will take—InfiniBand, Ethernet, OmniPath, etc. There's certainly plenty of spin, hype, and FUD being tossed around by various players.

In the commercial market, we can expect Ethernet using the internet Wide Area RDMA Protocol (iWARP) to win handily. It will take a few years, but the convergence onto a single LAN infrastructure and, moreover, one that is friendly to SDN makes this inevitable. Just like Fibre-Channel, the cloud of the future will have no room for InfiniBand or any other alien connectivity.

This argument in favor of Ethernet doesn't hold up as strongly as it does in the HPC world. The supercomputer boffins are used to InfiniBand, the majority of existing supers in the top 500 use it, though not by a huge margin, and we can expect a tendency to stay with a trusted solution that can easily link to existing gear.

Comparisons between IB and the two RDMA over Ethernet protocols, iWARP and RoCE (RDMA over Converged Ethernet), tend to favor the author's view of the world rather than being purely objective, but the fact that the protocols use essentially the same electronics and the closeness of the results indicate, first, that physics is in charge of the race and, second, that we essentially are getting the same result for any of the three.

This makes the choice of LAN more of a decision based on nontechnical factors such as pricing and buyer's experience. Volume of sales has a big part to play in NIC pricing, for instance, but even more important is the inclusion of a technology in a motherboard chipset, where the incremental cost is essentially zero. A decision to add RDMA to the next generation server chipsets (Ethernet) or a focus by Intel on OmniPath to the exclusion of others will make pricing of the network connections a major issue, especially if the technology enters the mainstream commercial segment. Whoever wins the commercial segment will have a big edge in the HPC RDMA stakes too.

There are several Big Science installations on the horizon. We've mentioned the SKA and CERN a few times earlier and we can add obvious NSA activity. The United States will bid to get back the title of fastest supercomputer from China, and the National labs are very active [16]. With the widespread benefits of supercomputer clouds, we should see more systems installed in academia, though oil and gas will probably cut back on purchases.

Putting this together, there are some flagship programs that will tend to define approaches into the 2020's. It's possible they will all move toward object storage and if this happens we should see a lot more Ethernet as opposed to InfiniBand. OmniPath could spoil all of this, but it will need strong features and performance to win against two strong incumbents.

A further competitor for the intercommunication crown comes from silicon-based photonics [17]. Deriving from experiments to reduce the power used to drive a CPU chips interfaces, silicon photonics promises low power and direct interconnection of CPUs without intervening PHY chips. (PHYs are the circuits that convert low-level internal signals to higher power or to optical beams that then drive the interface connection). This makes the CPU much cooler and removes the hot PHYs from the equation, too.

Photonics requires fiber connections directly to the CPU or the motherboard equivalent, an optical light-pipe. Both of these are real challenges in technology, with the basic materials and techniques well understood, but the complexities of attaching them to the CPU and routing them being very difficult. Photonic switching is needed for flexibility, and scale and repeaters are needed for any join in the fabric. The state of the art today is that it's possible to build small configurations with a point to point connectivity scheme, but scaling beyond a dozen or so motherboards is still in the research stage.

REFERENCES

[1] HPC varies from Big Data. http://www.nextplatform.com/2015/10/27/the-hpc-big-data-difference-its-at-the-bottom-line/.

[2] Creation of HPC clouds. http://www.admin-magazine.com/HPC/Articles/Moving-HPC-to-the-Cloud.

[3] Square kilometer array. http://thenewstack.io/ska-telescope-may-change-computing-as-much-as-astronomy/.

[4] CERN's LHC. http://press.cern/press-releases/2005/11/cern-awarded-high-performance-computing-prize-supercomputing-2005.

[5] CERN does this with Ceph. http://www.slideshare.net/rwgardner/using-ceph-for-large-hadron-collider-data.

[6] NSA building monster data center in Utah. http://www.wsj.com/articles/a-top-secret-nsa-site-draws-swipes-shrugs-1430523735.

[7] Amazon's Glacier. https://aws.amazon.com/glacier/details/.

[8] Facial recognition. http://www.forbes.com/sites/bruceschneier/2015/09/29/the-era-of-automatic-facial-recognition-and-surveillance-is-here/#7533e1e0edd8.

[9] UK camera count. http://www.telegraph.co.uk/technology/10172298/One-surveillance-camera-for-every-11-people-in-Britain-says-CCTV-survey.html.

[10] The cost of latency. http://www.sciencedirect.com/science/article/pii/S2405918815000045.

[11] RDMA Ethernet. http://www.networkcomputing.com/networking/will-rdma-over-ethernet-eclipse-infiniband/1893518522.

[12] NVMe-over-fabrics. https://www.openfabrics.org/images/eventpresos/workshops2015/DevWorkshop/Monday/monday_10.pdf.

[13] Genome project. http://searchstorage.techtarget.com/feature/Content-addressed-storage-CAS-explained.

[14] Nvidia company website. http://www.nvidia.com/.

[15] SaaS approach using a private cloud. http://www.adobe.com/creativecloud.html.

[16] National labs are very active. http://www-03.ibm.com/press/us/en/pressrelease/47318.wss.

[17] Silicon-based photonics. http://www.hpcwire.com/2016/03/22/mellanox-reveals-200-gbps-path/.

The Cloud

10

The cloud is a massive move away from the concept of companies owning their own datacenter. An idea that would have been launched at in the 1980s is now taking over IT, and it's not clear where the boundaries between in-house operations and public clouds provided by the likes of Azure [1] will settle down. A case can be made for "hybrid" clouds where the workload is split between an owned operation in-house and a leased operation in public clouds, while an opposing view that everything will migrate to the public clouds also is worth considering.

The cloud has created many new technical approaches. Perhaps the most profound is the use of huge volumes of COTS gear purchased directly from the manufacturers. This is fueling the storage revolution too. It is making life miserable for the large traditional OEMs (Original Equipment Manufacturers), who can't compete with people who, if truth be told, are their manufacturers too. It's a classic case of cutting out the middleman.

In the early days of the cloud, 2006–09, start-up operations such as Verari [2] and Rackable [3] challenged Dell and HP by being very flexible and taking low margins. By 2009, Google and gang were dealing with the Chinese ODMs (Original design Manufacturers) [4] that fed the whole industry. The mega-Cloud Service Providers (CSPs) had learned enough to specify their own products in detail. Moreover, they had figured out the issues of putting large configurations together, come up with new maintenance protocols, and were well on their way to specifying minimalist designs to save cost and space.

Azure had containerized storage appliances in 2007—I designed and delivered 70 PB worth of them—and Google had their own contribution to the art of containers too. The idea of installing and decommissioning a huge compute cluster just by using a big forklift was a major innovation in how fast the CSPs could react to market changes. Containers reduced the time to going live from 6 months plus the build time of a datacenter (a total of maybe 18 months to 2 years) to just 3 months.

That agility came with efficiencies in operation. Instead of repairing a failed unit as soon as it failed, the CSPs either delayed repairs until a few units in the same container needed work or, they didn't bother to do any repairs at all. In either case, the issue is whether the servers had any unique data stored in them and this was a no–no from the start of the cloud. As a result, a failure was recovered by starting up a set of new instances on other servers. On the scale of a cloud datacenter, zero repairs can be tolerated easily. Likely, the CSPs paid for the cost of some extra servers by negotiating away the product warranty by the server vendors.

Since those early days, the cloud has added new features and capabilities far beyond what was available. Drive capacities have grown 10-fold and continue to increase—13 and 16 TB SSDs have been announced as of writing. Flash and SSDs have altered the performance profiles of virtual servers and the availability of large memories (into the terabytes) and GPU (Graphics Processing Unit) parallel processing have made "big instances" popular, with the capability to run Big Data analytics and HPC tasks demonstrated readily.

Security in the cloud has improved to the point that many experts believe the cloud is safer than most in-house datacenter operations, and recent hacks seem to prove that—none of them have been in the cloud.

For all of this, the cloud is still a work in progress. Deficiencies in networking have led to acceleration of development of 25 GbE technology, while instance stores using an SSD in the virtual servers are proving very popular especially in the high-performance end of the market.

One result of all of this is that Google, Azure, and Amazon Web Services (AWS) do almost no business with Dell, HPC, or in fact any of the US-based "manufacturers." They buy direct and save a lot of money. Google pays $30 per terabyte for hard drive storage, comparing really well with the price charges by EMC in its arrays or even Dell in its server storage.

Needless to say, with those cost advantages, the cloud is growing rapidly compared with the rest of IT. This is paving the way for the ODMs to enter the US and EU markets [5] and compete head-to-head with the traditional vendors. Since the ODMs make *all* the equipment, the middlemen have no opportunity to compete on price and face a very bleak future [6]. Most likely, these companies will be forced out of the hardware market altogether and will either consolidate or find a niche as a software and support company.

The ODMs are using the Internet, coupled with their existing expertise in handling very large deals, to expand from a base of CSPs to the largest enterprises and then down market. There may come a point where the economics of the public cloud will outweigh any benefits of an in-house operation. Most of the "M" and all of the "S" parts of the SMB market segment will end up using the public cloud and will no longer have in-house computers. This will coincide with the expansion of software-as-a-service (SaaS), and the simultaneous downturn in legacy computing.

In a nutshell, the cloud is much more than just a cloud. It is creating its own IT microcosm and this is spilling out to impact how we do any IT. At the same time, like a black hole, the cloud is sucking in more and more work from the rest of the IT universe. There is no sign yet of any equilibrium, while the datacenter has to learn the harsh lessons of "adapt or die" very quickly over the next 5 years. The serene bliss displayed by legacy (COBOL) users, with 35 years of enjoying obsolescence, is very much a thing of the past. We have the COTS barbarians at the gates!

For staff and budgets, and corporate management, the next decade will have enormous challenges. The cloud is bringing them, but it isn't the enemy. Become agile and go with the flow!

WHAT IS THE CLOUD?

We've been virtualizing systems since 1998, when VMware arrived on the scene. This company enjoyed unprecedented success, gaining a high percentage of the market and converting the value proposition of servers in the process. VMware was joined by Microsoft, Citrix, and Red Hat in the market.

In 2006, several companies started delivering "cloud" services. The leader in this pioneering bunch was AWS, with Microsoft Azure, and Google following on their heels in 2008. The fourth major player was Rackspace [7], who had been an ISP since 1998, entering the cloud stakes in 2009/2010.

So, what is the cloud and why should we get excited about it? The cloud takes the concept of virtualized servers and extends it to be an agile and flexible pool of computing. Basically, orchestration software is added to virtualization to allow elastic response to demand. New virtual instances can be added by a user (usually called a tenant) on demand and the use of that instance paid for by the minute, hour, day, week, or month. Tenants can disconnect an instance quickly too.

With an automated billing system, clouds can deliver the instances on a pay-as-you-go basis. Tenants only need to pay for what they use. Since most computer workloads are very spiky, this allows the tenant a way to optimize costs.

The most important thing from a tenant's viewpoint is that there are no hardware acquisition costs. The days of sizing a datacenter for the heaviest workload, or scheduling work to load balance the available gear are a thing of the past. Now jobs can be run when it's most convenient and if apps are written to automatically react to demand, new instances can be created and unneeded ones closed down within a minute or so.

Of course, the cloud concept needs more than just starting instances and billing. Storage has to be handled, and the ability to create Virtual Private Networks (VPN) between instances is essential if instances are to do more than just exist as islands of computing. The various mega-CSPs (the top three CSPs are AWS, Azure, and Google, with Rackspace having fallen into the next tier) all provide object storage offerings, which by a miracle of IT science all use the same REST interface to communicate with instances or with the outside world.

In addition, they provide a block storage service that can be mounted to instances as a raw block device, which can be formatted with a file system and used just like server drives. There is one difference. The block or object storage isn't in the server mounting the virtual drive in a virtual instance. The cloud model relies on a stateless server instance to permit a restart on another server if an instance fails for any reason.

With hundreds of instances in any one server, the networked IO model places a huge burden on the networks. Both image traffic, related to the operating system and applications running, and data are carried on the network. Achieving adequate bandwidth on the networks is pressuring the cloud providers to demand 25 GbE as an early intermediate step in the Ethernet roadmap. With roll-out in 2016, this goal has been met with alacrity, reflecting the size of the problem and the leverage the CSPs can create.

Another way of reducing the pressure on the network is to remove the image traffic. The original "purist" cloud had instances that are able to support any operating system, so a server could have Windows, Linux, and Solaris instances simultaneously. This can only be achieved by treating each instance as a virtual server, complete with the whole operating system and app set.

Some damn fools ask the question, "Why can't we just segregate the various operating systems, dedicate a server to them and then just have one copy of that operating system shared by all the instances?" The result is the container (not to be confused with containers for racking up systems) which is a virtual machine running under the control of a single copy of the operating system along with many other copies. The leading container solution is Docker [8].

This reduces the DRAM memory footprint of the instance, since the instances can all share the static code of the operating system. We are seeing this extend to shareable applications too, which should make a huge difference in repeated instances for say web servers or indeed any repetitive instance situation. It's worth noting that AWS runs many instances of web-store software for its online shopping business, while Google runs identical search and indexing jobs on hundreds of thousands of servers. Clearly, both environments will see costs plummet by a factor of three to five times.

Speaking of cost, we are in the fourth year of a massive price war [9] for web services, with the three largest CSPs playing a race to the bottom for instance pricing. The reductions have been massive and continue to be so. This makes the ability to change vendors quickly and cheaply a must for any tenant, though it must be said that threatening to leave may be just as effective in getting equivalent pricing, without the pain of an actual move.

It's worth looking at the pricing models for the moment. Instances are priced roughly according to how much of a CPU is being used, how much memory, and any guarantees on storage IO rates. There are special GPU instances now, as well as huge instances for Big Data, and services built around various databases are also offered.

Storage is charged both in situ and while it is on the move. There's a fee for reading data from any storage, but no fee typically for writing it there in the first place—the more you write the happier the CSP gets. Prices for storing data are very competitive against typical OEM prices. We are at 1 cent per gigabyte per month, and it still continues to drop.

Still, you have to get deep into the details to figure out what it will cost to use the cloud. As an example, the cost of moving data from your cloud storage to the Internet can reach 8 cents per gigabyte transferred. This makes moving all that data to another CSP, an expensive proposition ($50–80/terabyte), though there are volume discounts and tape- or disk-based offload options to reduce the cost.

Cloud storage services now come in tiers, too, with high-frequency access storage at around 2× to 3× the price of the infrequent access storage tier (but with higher service charges for reading data from the latter). There are also archive storage services about 30% cheaper still.

To better understand the cloud, we need to look at the detailed anatomy. The following sections look at how a cloud is built, both hardware and software, and the anatomy of a typical cloud datacenter. Next we'll see how a typical datacenter is run. Then we'll overview the various instances and how they interact with application use cases. Then we'll discuss the issues of moving and accessing data in the cloud.

CLOUD HARDWARE

The major cloud providers are the biggest IT customers in history. They buy literally millions of servers and Exabytes of storage each year. They also get rid of old, obsolete gear in huge quantities, too—typically working to a 4-year useful life instead of the old-school 8+ years.

The CSPs use COTS products, but not quite what you'd get from a Dell or HP. Generally, the CSP unit will be free of any nonrequired features. This almost always means no keyboard, video, and mouse connectors and may also extend to not having front bezel or drive bays. The reason for not having KVM ports is that repair on units is rarely performed, and never on a per-unit debug basis. It's replacement only. Losing bezels falls out from the same thought process. They really aren't necessary in static configurations, while racks or containers of units are usually preconfigured prior to shipment and so limiting handling.

Fans are built in at the rack level. Big fans are much more efficient at moving air than little fans. They are also more reliable and one big fan is cheaper than two dozen small fans. For those admins with sensitive ears, there is also the benefit of a quieter datacenter! Losing bezels and other extra parts helps cooling, too, by removing blockages to airflow.

Servers and storage appliances are often completely customized. The reason is that these are purchased in 100,000 unit quantities, so the ODMs that manufacture them are very willing to customize. Most likely the volumes are so high that there is no penalty for doing so. It's worth noting in passing that efforts such as the Open Compute Project [10] only go part way down this path. The idea of a CSP-like unit is a good way to reduce gear costs, but it lacks the flexibility that the CSPs enjoy and it lags their internal state-of-the-art by at least a couple of years.

Servers typically have a boot device, since this makes bringing up a unit in a cold-start much faster. The boot device is likely to be a small SSD drive, just capable of booting the hypervisor. As we move to Docker-like containers, this will expand to a larger drive with the operating system and standard applications. With instance stores becoming popular, there is a need for one or two drives to be shared among the instances. These are today a mixture of HDD and SSD, but will be SSDs in new gear as we go into 2017.

Networked storage is a bit of a spectrum, ranging from iSCSI SANs to object storage. The SAN boxes tend to be HDD and have a high drive count per unit, while the object stores more closely follow the small Lego appliance approach.

The storage boxes are bought from the ODMs, too. Drives are bought in huge quantities from the OEM vendors, WD or Seagate, but SSDs are a different story. Google makes their own drives and in sufficient quantities to be a major enterprise SSD player at #2 or #3, AWS and Azure still buy on the general market. Because of the appliance model for data integrity, expensively featured SSDs aren't needed for the object stores and as these migrate away from hard drives, the volume will shift to inexpensive SSDs.

There is a lot of interest in saving costs in the controller part of the appliance or array. ARM-based solutions look attractive, especially as high-core-count 64-bit ARM processors hit the market. One downside to the ARM is that PCIe connectivity is low compared with the x64 server designs available, limiting bandwidth out of any given box. This is not an issue with all-HDD boxes, but most definitely is a concern for all-SSD appliances.

The drives used in these configurations can be the most inexpensive around. I've estimated that Google pays around $30 per terabyte for hard drives, which means bulk 3.5″ SATA drives are the predominant storage. This is also true for their Nearline archive storage, which likely employs spin-down controls to save operating power. Most likely, as main storage transitions to SSD, the archives will soak up the bulk HDDs that are released, at least for a while.

With maintenance based on a no-repair approach, drive caddies are no longer necessary. This is important, since a typical caddy can cost as much as a 1 TB drive. CSP servers often have a fixed drive, and this will become almost ubiquitous with SSD due to their higher reliability. Storage is a bit more complicated in this area. Caddies are still a way to assemble lots of drives, but I've designed units for the CSPs where the drives mounted on U-shaped plates that clipped into the chassis as well as direct-mounting drives to pizza-plate appliances, which are just drilled flat sheets of steel.

Drive power in arrays and appliances is still typically redundant. Power supplies are the single most unreliable module in a unit, with MTBF around one-eighth of a typical HDD. As we move to low power solutions—SSDs—I expect solid-state power supplies [11] will become much more common. These are expensive today, at perhaps 2× to 3× the traditional supply, but at 99% efficiency and 2 million plus hour MTBFs they are very attractive and prices will fall dramatically with CSP volumes.

Input power into units has run the gamut from 12 V DC to 800 V DC, with 288 V AC and 120 V AC most common. There is a strong argument for converting AC to some other DC voltage and then distributing that DC voltage across a rack, since the AC-to-DC converters can be connected for redundancy. Large converters are also more efficient than smaller supplies. The advent of cheap DC–DC converters makes delivering a single DC voltage to a server or storage box a good way of distributing power economically. This is a large topic and is tied in with cooling systems and overall rack design, all of which have a separate subsection later on in this section of the book.

Whether unit or rack fans are used, cooling a lot of DRAM and one or two hot CPUs is tricky. Air-ducting can make a big difference, but requires a good deal of testing and simulation to get it right. I've used air-ducting to raise ambient temperatures in COTS servers for the US nuclear submarine fleet into the 45–50°C range. We are going to hit this in more detail later in its own subsection, since it impacts on how datacenters are built and how units are cooled in some major ways.

THE FUTURE OF CLOUD HARDWARE

With the various price wars and competitive scrambling between the big CSPs, it's hard to get a definitive sense of direction for their hardware. We do know they are pushing hard for 25 GbE availability. Once that's in place, the next network issue will be to get that on the motherboard as part of the chipset, followed by the extension of networking to RDMA, at least for part of the server farm with big instances and GPUs.

Networking performance is an issue with the advent of Docker-style containers, since they increase the effective number of instances in a server by a factor of 3× to 5×. While there is a reduction in the IO related to the operating systems, the extra instance increase overall demand on networked storage—the increase to 25 GbE just about keeps the status quo.

Servers themselves are about to see a major revolution in design. It will take a while to fully deploy, but the concept of Hybrid Memory Cube architecture is to remove the separation between DRAM and CPU by mounting them all on one module, removing the high-power off chip drivers and thus speeding up the DRAM significantly while dropping power. One result is that servers will have a lot more storage, which will lead to memory sharing. By adding persistent X-Point memory on the DRAM bus, the typical server gets smaller in physical size, but with much more horsepower.

This will impact both the server design and both storage and storage networking. As pricing works out towards commodity levels, X-Point will become THE server persistent storage. Some servers may still need a local drive, but X-Point fits instance storage much better than an SSD can. Use cases such as databases will interlink servers, though likely not in a virtual SAN model. Rather, memory mapping across a cluster may fit RDMA at that level much better.

Moving to this model, even if a local large SSD is added for instance storage, fits the single DC power supply model better. Most likely we'll home in on 12 V DC as a compromise between adequate slew rate for voltage conversion and keeping current low in the rack-level distribution. Overall, then servers should become more compact and simpler. This will apply to storage appliances too.

Over time, we'll migrate away from block storage to an object model. This won't be a binary shift and for the commercial market at least will go through a "unified storage" approach much like Ceph where block and file services are provided on top of an object store.

This migration will mean smaller appliances with say 12 SSD, allowing speed matching between the performance of the drives and the need to get it onto the LAN. There may be alternative architectures, depending on whether drives migrate to a native Ethernet interface. With high-core-count ARM processors, the horsepower to make a drive an Ethernet-connected OSD for Ceph [12] is well within reach, which removes the bottleneck seen at the appliance controller. We may therefore see boxes, called variously either EBODs (Ethernet-Box-Of-Drives) or JBOE (Just-a Box-Of-Ethernet-Drives), with 60 Ethernet drives or more all talking directly to the network backbone. SSDs can incidentally be packed much tighter, especially if they don't have an outer case as in M2 form factor drives, making these boxes smaller than their hard drive predecessors. This also loses the latencies associated with queuing in the controller, so potentially this is a faster solution.

As the zero-repair mindset of large cloud players like Google becomes more common in datacenters, we may see a migration away from the traditional "swappable drive in a caddy" approach to a more embedded solution. SSDs without covers in the M2 standard form factor are readily available and should allow tighter packaging and more compact appliances. Note that this is a bit different from all-flash arrays, where the flash cards are proprietary form factor.

With Ethernet switching getting pretty compact, with just a chip or two, these EBODs could present a high interface performance in the form of say four or even eight 100 GbE ports. That fits in with a compact, very high-performance storage system that fits both small random IO and the bandpass needs of Big Data and HPC instances.

Ethernet storage would fit into both public cloud and hybrid cloud strategies. We still need a meaningful level of support on either the Kinetic [13] or HGST [14] (a division of WD) solutions or an alternative and we need Ethernet SSD to make this happen. One potentiator for this, and a powerful one, is the idea of NVMe over Fabrics, making the drives RDMA. This would give us a very efficient interface, which could be easily enhanced for key/data or other access methods if needed. There's still a great deal of room for creativity here.

In the end, we are converging on a flavor or two of software-defined storage, with all of the agility, flexibility, and cost benefits we expect it to bring. It appears that Google and the other big CSPs are already there, though their internal implementations are neither public nor standardized.

CLOUD SOFTWARE

The three largest CSPs deploy their own software solutions and consider them a part of their proprietary edge. The fourth largest, Rackspace developed a cloud suite with help from NASA, of all people, and have now moved that code (OpenStack [15]) into the public space, where it is being aggressively touted and supported as the cloud software for a private or hybrid cloud. We need to understand the implications of this and how OpenStack interacts with the other providers and with VMware to figure how the cloud will shape up on the software side.

Let's examine the basic elements of a cloud suite. All of them have Orchestration, which is the tool that connects tenants with instances and allows those tenants to create or destroy instances as they need to. All vendors surround Orchestration with a variety of other services. AWS, for example, provides a complete online retailer experience, which dominates the online store business. Microsoft positions Azure as a way to migrate MS Office and Exchange email into a SaaS environment. Google has search and its own collaborative document system and other apps.

In the operating software arena, it's necessary to look after security, so authentication is a service. Both block and object storage is offered and networking, in the form of a way to create VPNs, is a staple solution to linking instances together. All the services offer a way to load data in or read data from cloud storage, and they also offer a bulk transfer system based on disk or tapes to avoid the huge delays from loading lots of data via the Internet.

It's useful to look at OpenStack to see how the modules are structured, and then compare AWS, Azure, and Google with this to see the service "Lego blocks" involved in a sophisticated and trouble-free environment. VMware, both as a heavily entrenched hypervisor vendor and as a latent cloud provider rounds out the current serious contenders.

OPENSTACK SOFTWARE

Originated by Rackspace and NASA, OpenStack is a set of open-source projects. Companies and individuals are making IP and development time donations to various projects to expand the reach of the tools. This isn't altruistic. Without the software, it is unlikely that a cloud could be built, and vendors are looking to get their proprietary approaches embedded in the designs at an early date.

OpenStack is aimed at private clouds and the private segments of public clouds. Interoperability is still in its early days, but will get to a point where the pain goes away. Vendors such as HPE, Dell, and IBM are OpenStack backers, aiming to offer services and support, plus their hardware, to users not yet sophisticated enough to build their own cloud.

A look at the current project list for OpenStack [16] is revealing.

There are six core modules, four of which are fully mature. These four modules include the following:

Nova	Compute service which manages instance lifecycles.
Neutron	Networking tool which connects instances. This tool has a pluggable architecture to allow extension of features.
Cinder	This is the block storage system on OpenStack. Storage survives instance destruction, and data can be shared between instances and across the Internet.
Keystone	Authentication and authorization service.

The two-core modules that rate a four out of five maturity are the following:

Swift	Object storage using the REST API.
Glance	Used for storage instance images, Glance speeds up provisioning new VMs.

There are many optional modules, which indicate the scope of interest in OpenStack, and also the complexity of defining a full cloud suite.

Manila	Shared file systems
Trove	Database
Magnum	Containers
Heat	Orchestration
Horizon	Dashboard
Barbican	Key management
Ceilometer	Telemetry
Congress	Governance
Designate	DNS service
Ironic	Bare metal provisioning
Murano	Application catalog
Sahara	Elastic map reduce
Zaqar	Messaging service

The first four have a good deal of impact on OpenStack storage.

Manila, the shared file systems module, aims to allow a variety of file systems to be deployed on top of Cinder and so bring data sharing within the operational structures commonly used in scale-out bare metal configurations.

Trove allows relational and nonrelational databases to be deployed as a service. Sitting on top of cinder storage, this will create traffic that looks like standard databases. It isn't clear yet how Trove evolves with in-memory databases and persistent DRAM.

Magnum is intended to bring the density of containers to OpenStack. With a likely fast uptake, due to new approaches for security between container instances, we will see the impact in IO demand and in network load.

Heat does for applications what Nova does for basic instances, allowing apps to be combined and loaded efficiently when starting instances.

As we move to Software-Defined Infrastructure (SDI), OpenStack will evolve to automate many of the tasks needed to run workloads efficiently. This is essential if the suite is to support agility and flexibility properly. SDI will have an impact on the tools in the suit, mainly because interfaces move closer to the hardware, on the one hand, allowing many more features, while new software modules will bring new data services that can be called on-demand in virtual instances as needed.

Clearly, the other modules will also impinge on storage at various points. Governance can't avoid controlling encryption issues, for example. Sahar carries implications of Hadoop-friendly file systems and Murano, the app catalog, likely will index available SDS software services as they become available. In a nutshell, OpenStack will evolve to embrace SDI approaches and code.

Openstack is clearly a work in progress and its supporters acknowledge that fact. The modules that are mature are seeing useful service, and we can expect support and deployment to strengthen rapidly over the next few years. This will be in the face of competition from Microsoft, who has begun pushing Azure as a private cloud environment. Even AWS is not immune to the private cloud opportunity and has created private clouds for the CIA. AWS is talking about hosting instances on a permanent or long-term basis, in an attempt to nullify the need for a private cloud. In doing so they are capitalizing on the low WAN speed most users see in the US, which, with long latencies and SDN-like bandwidth is a real chokepoint for cloud-bursting and other data heavy hybrid cloud operations.

AWS

Since inception in 2006, Amazon Web Services [17] has been the leading cloud provider. Today it has massive amounts of compute and storage distributed in some 15 datacenters in the US, nine in Europe, nine or 10 in Asia, and two each in Brazil and Australia. A couple of the East coast US sites deliver AWS GovCloud. These datacenters are organized as regions with "availability zones," which are important in the S3 storage replication model.

AWS toolset is very rich compared with OpenStack, both as a result of a longer existence and by having a substantial cash flow to fund development. For example, storage services include not only S3, the object store using replication for integrity and elastic block storage (EBS), the block store service. We have Glacier, which is an archive storage system that is very slow to retrieve first data compared with Google's Nearline Storage equivalent, due to likely being tape based.

AWS now has an elastic file system to put on top of EBS. There is a tool for import/export of data in bulk and a service called CloudFront for media delivery to the Internet. A new and interesting tool aims at the hybrid cloud market. Storage Gateway connects on-premises software appliances with S3, using a cache in the gateway to reduce latency. This tool also allows primary data to be stored in the gateway and asynchronously copied to S3.

AWS has Compute services that provide strong support for Docker containers. Lambda, another service, provides a way to make apps run on events. The database services include ElastiCache, an in-memory caching system, as well as SQL and No-SQL models of database. The Analytics suite includes Hadoop support (EMR) and Kinesis provides real-time streaming of data.

With management tools, access controls and desktop apps with email, AWS is a well-rounded service that continues to expand features. In many ways, it provides the standards and benchmarks for the cloud industry, forcing Google and Azure to match them on capability and making a tough arena for new players in cloud services. In fact, we've seen some shakeout already as both HPE and Rackspace moved out of direct competition in 2015.

It's worth looking at the life cycle of data being sent to the cloud and retrieved, then deleted. In the S3 service, data objects are stored as objects striped across a set of storage appliances, in some ways similar to Ceph or Scality. To get the data to the cloud, the server writing the data uses the REST protocol to send the data to the appropriate bucket on the storage system in AWS.

Upon receipt, the data is journaled and then the journal is broken up into chunks that are distributed across a set of storage appliances. Once that is done, the appliances create usually two replicas of the data on other appliances. One of these replicas is within the same datacenter and is like an appliance-level RAID mirror in being close in with low latency. The third copy is usually sent off asynchronously to a storage appliance in a different control zone, usually a nearby datacenter, but not the one where the two primary copies are kept. The tenant can specify zones, aiming for stronger geographical separation, but fees may apply.

S3 comes in flavors. There is "Standard" – general purpose storage, Infrequent Access – for low access data, and Glacier for archiving. A tool for lifecycle management is available to move the data to lower tiers based on policies.

Block storage, EBS, operates more like a RAID system. Data is mirrored locally in the same zone, likely at the appliance not drive-set (more like replication than RAID from an AWS perspective, but not from the user view). Tenants can choose one of three services. Two general purpose and provisioned IO are now SSD based, while the third is "Magnetic" HDD storage. Pricing differs between the options, of course.

To get a sense of cloud performance a general purpose EBS volume is designed to deliver three IOPS per gigabyte on a consistent baseline level, with a limit of 10,000 IOPS. Even though these are SSD-based, however, the latency runs in the single digit milliseconds range rather than a few microseconds. Bandwidth is limited to 160 MBps, which is about that of a 7200 RPM HDD. Neither latency nor bandwidth is stellar!

Provisioned IO uses a faster IO system and can deliver 30 IOPS per gigabyte and 320 MBps throughput, but with the same latencies, reflecting that this is networked storage and not local. The last class, Magnetic, is limited to around 100 IOPS on average.

Clearly, getting really high performance is a tough task. It really needs a faster network, less storage protocol overhead, and perhaps local buffering in instance storage or in-memory caches.

When the data is written to storage, it should be encrypted. In fact, the best encryption occurs back at the originating server. Unfortunately, the cost of encryption and decryption using the CPU is too high and much of the data stored is plaintext and so exposed to hacking risk. Techniques for storing data on drives that can encrypt it using their own key set have been embarrassing failures, since the small number of available keys in the drive can be handily discovered by the black hat squad.

AWS has had a couple of notable outages, taking out whole zones for as much as 24 h. These appear to have been caused by inadequate pretesting of software upgrades, coupled with poor process control in orchestration that triggered point failure recovery processes such as disk rebuilds for every drive in the failed data-center. These occurred some years back, and it would seem that AWS has properly addressed the issues.

AWS has a "side" business, acting as host for countless online stores. They offer a bundle of prepackaged services from website design to access to their online store-front, basically a search engine and all the way to handling inventory and fulfillment. This business is decimating the high streets [18] of the world, as bricks and mortar retailers find they can't compete. We likely will look back in 20 years and see the effects on retailing as one of the defining moments in history, since the ramifications extend far beyond the closure of stores and changed buying patterns. For one thing, the rapid rise of Chinese industry would not have occurred without AWS (and eBay) giving them a way to sell easily.

MICROSOFT AZURE

Microsoft leans somewhat naturally towards Windows users, putting a heavy emphasis on Office apps moving to Office 365 in their cloud, as well as other apps such as Exchange email. Given the 60% server market share Microsoft enjoys this is no surprise, but Linux support is strong too (and getting stronger) and Azure competes well with AWS, sitting in the number two position of market share.

Feature-wise, Azure [19] matches AWS pretty closely. Terms may be different—Microsoft has "blobs" of storage—but once past that services match up line for line.

Microsoft has some strategic visions that AWS is only beginning to share. MS pushes the idea of managed clouds (by vendors like Rackspace) and even private and hybrid clouds all based on the Azure and Hyper-V software environment. Rack-space is worth discussing a bit more. They offload the installation and management of Azure clouds to their datacenters, so accessing fast data links to the public Azure cloud.

Microsoft's intention to migrate users to their cloud probably will doom the desk-top/laptop PC. With Office 365 and the collaboration tools that are inherent to a CSP solution, the economics of a computer at the desktop that can be easily hacked versus a tablet or smartphone will doom PCs, and relatively quickly.

Like AWS, Microsoft is rapidly expanding its Dockers container environment to be able to run both Linux and Windows in high-density virtual machines. Given the speed this has come about, it's clear that Microsoft also shares the view that contain-ers are a major mainstream force in the cloud.

Looking into the future, one has to ask if the existing Microsoft base will assist them in competing with AWS. In and of itself, I don't think it makes a lot of differ-ence, but coupled with MS having a lead on AWS in making a version of Azure for the private/hybrid market and the support of Rackspace for hosted private clouds based on Azure, MS may gain ground. AWS has to respond to the private cloud question and doing so may grip OpenStack, and its supporters like HPE, IBM, and Dell, in the pincers of a price and feature war that may make their life a bit miserable.

However this evolves, at the end of the day Microsoft will look much more like a SaaS company than the original Allen/Gates model of selling software. Most probably, AWS will extend its pay-as-you-go method to pricing private, hybrid, and hosted versions of its cloud code and the industry will follow suit.

On the storage networking side, there is little differentiation between MS and AWS. However, as part of it's evangelizing of Azure, MS entered into partnership with NetApp and Verizon to make storage available in Verizon datacenters and POPs that are privately owned and in full compliance but connected to high-speed dedicated fiber links to Azure datacenters.

This type of storage positioning solves the public cloud latency issues, but leaves the in-house private cloud a bit starved on performance, since most companies don't have the nearby fast fiber trunks to tap in to. Verizon may emulate Rackspace and add managed Azure cloud clusters to the mix.

GOOGLE

Google is a search company that also sells cloud services. It's #3 in the pecking order after AWS and Azure. Google [20] has made much of esoteric cooling systems, containerizing their datacenters and changing maintenance approaches and they are pioneering a lot of what will be datacenter of the future. For instance, they came up with the idea of keeping data storage and compute close to each other, advocating mixing the tow in racks to offset the backbone latencies in a large switched cluster.

Underneath that is a good deal of the same thing that AWS and MS Azure buy. Detailed packaging, such as cabinet shape, cooling fans, and the position of components may vary from the other guys, but at base the hardware is mainly the same.

Google has proven itself to be willing to pioneer. The company builds its own flash drives and is, by IDC's reckoning, the third largest maker of enterprise (fast) drives. They have pioneered a good deal of the thinking behind SDI and have deployed their own private versions of SDN across their clouds.

Google also is heavily into Big Data. Their search engines grind enormous amounts of information each day, both ingesting new web pages and searching the huge amount of data they store. Because of this, they may be the leading storers of data in the world.

They clearly use a multitiered storage approach. Hot current data is probably kept in those flash drives, while the older colder storage resides on HDD. With just a planned 4-year unit lifecycle, Google obsolesces a lot of gear each year, and slow HDD storage coming off mainstream use makes for cheap secondary bulk storage. At some point, the migration will have to change over to SSD/flash as all the HDD storage is committed to the secondary pool or obsoleted out of the company. Based on the age of flash gear, this trend to flash/SSD secondary storage will likely occur in 2016/2017, but there are enough 1 to 10 TB SATA hard drives in use that a complete transition to SSD is some years away.

The reuse of drives probably won't keep up with storage needs, and so large quantities of additional storage will be bought. This may well be ODM-sourced boxes using cheap high-capacity SSDs as their capacity and price improves.

Google keeps tight counsel on their internal operations, but one might figure that the flash cards/drives reside in their servers, while secondary bulk storage is in storage appliances with high drive counts. These are distributed among the racks to balance the complement of servers and bulk storage and to avoid the latency and traffic bottlenecks of extra hops across the clusters backbone. This will probably still be the shape of new configurations, but with faster LAN (25 GbE) interconnections.

VMWARE

VMware [21] spent the first 8 years of cloud history in denial. Here was the giant of hypervisor virtualization with a huge locked-in customer base and perhaps they considered themselves unassailable. After all, the cloud seemed fit for just web serving and archiving!

Meanwhile, the private cloud idea made rapid progress based on OpenStack, opening up a challenge to VMware that saw much reduced growth from simple virtualized clusters. VMware finally woke up to the challenge in 2013, and began work on a cloud solution of its own, called VCloud Air.

VMware figures that it can capitalize on that huge installed base to seamlessly link virtualized clusters to private clouds, all running VMware products. There is a painful realization that others are already established players, so VMware is forced to interface to the public clouds, and worse, to be able to talk freely with Openstack.

The user in the datacenter now finds it possible to reach out from the VMware virtual cluster to any of the three major public clouds, all of which are heading into direct competition with VMware for the private cloud software market. Worse still, VMware clusters can talk to OpenStack, which many companies have embraced and are well advanced in early deployments.

This puts the VMware-installed base advantage into question. Moreover, VMware is pushing its own cloud service, vCloud, at its base, but it is way behind any of the other solutions in features and hardly registers in IDCs tables in terms of users. In fact, redundancies and other announcements point to VCloud's exit from this business in 2017.

VMware has shown itself to be a savvy and agile company, however, and might find a way through all of this that capitalizes on their strengths. There are hints, as the impact of the Dell–EMC merger works its way, out that VMware has decided to get out of the public cloud space, which would leave them free to concentrate on evolving VMware towards being a true private cloud environment.

VMWare has created NSX, a networking tool that bridges between private and public clouds to create a single virtual network space. This is already in the billion-dollar annual revenue range and may evolve to be a true SDN offering, giving them a strong position in that market segment.

This evolution of course won't happen overnight, but the erosion of VMware's business won't be instantaneous either. I just saw a January 2016 451 Research prediction that in 2 years, by the end of 2017, IT spending on the public cloud will have doubled, while in-house IT spend will drop 27%. If we add in the factors for in-house purchases of software from the CSPs, the numbers are probably stiffer. Even so, this would flatten VMware's growth—they have a lot of recurring income from licenses—without necessarily causing a large decline in revenues.

Longer term, VMware will adapt or else suffer a lot more decline. In-house spend, as we'll discuss in more detail in the subsection on Hybrid Clouds, will probably drop even further if the mega-CSPs get into the hosted private cloud business, essentially adding what Rackspace is doing to their portfolio and offering virtual private clouds in their datacenters.

THE REST

Life for the rest of the cloud providers attempting to find a place in the mainstream is utterly miserable. How do you compete with a well-established behemoth with 40+% market share, or with three big companies that own 90% of the market between them?

You either need some *very* good technology and some new sharp marketing approaches, or you are dead before you start. That's what is happening to the smaller CSPs. Rackspace was a pioneer of the space, and created OpenStack, enjoying #4 status for several years, but is now relegated to a hosted cloud model, and, as the first working it, is holding its own.

HPE is quietly getting out of the CSP business. Dell did this 2 years ago. Both had based their clouds on OpenStack. On the other hand, IBM is moving towards niche plays in media streaming and analytics, and looking to combine analytics with retail Big Data to serve the retail market. Verizon is more of a hosted services company and it's unlikely to try to be more.

Oracle and EMC have cloud services, but they are small compared with the mega-CSPs. These will need to find niche markets to survive much longer. The Dell-EMC merger may create a larger critical mass, but that could just mean cloud losses get bigger and last longer if a general cloud approach is followed.

There are some specialized clouds that are doing well. Adobe is offering its editing and postproduction tools in a SaaS model using their own cloud, and has converted its license model to a subscription basis and done so with spectacular success. NVidia has a GPU cloud for developers to use as a sandbox prior to investing (heavily one hopes) in GPU-based gear. Apple has iCloud, but this is more of a photo storage system rather than a compute-centric cloud and may be immune from the CSP wars.

The HPC arena still has cloud providers—we used to call the supercomputers! These fill special performance–focused niches and all the signs are that they will still be here decades from now. The funding of these by governments tends to separate them from the mainstream.

We might see a partnering between vendors such as HPE or Dell-EMC and telcos to open up a new CSP business. It will take that sort of scale to be viable. However, it looks late in the game for that to happen.

One area where there is a huge amount of room for becoming cloudy is government. Many agencies at a number of levels still use legacy dinosaurs for their work. This is no longer tenable and many countries have initiatives to move government computing to the cloud. This could be done in a segregated section of a public cloud, as AWS has done with their GovCloud service, or else the government(s) can set up their own private cloud to be shared among multiple agency tenants. In the latter case, they may follow the leadership of the CIA who had AWS build them a cloud. This type of evolution will further tilt IT spend towards the public cloud side of the ledger.

In passing, it's worth noting that the usually slow-moving US military is moving to the cloud at a rapid pace. Navy has a plan [22] to run all shore-side operations in clouds and the Army is close behind [23] them, and already considering such a move for logistics management.

THE CHANGING DATACENTER DENSITY, COOLING, AND POWER

The decision to build stripped-back COTS server to internal specifications led the three giant CSPs to experiment with cooling, power systems, and overall packaging. CPUs have an upper working temperature limit of around 100°C measured on the chip by a temperature sensor. Above this temperature they first slow down the clock and "throttle" performance, and then they shut down if things get too hot.

DRAM is another hot element of a server. Fortunately, the DIMM is designed to run at a higher temperature than the CPU and is also mounted vertically for optimal cooling.

On the downside, until 2014, HDD were limited to an incoming air temperature of 55°C, which meant that, from a cooling perspective, drives severely limited the upper end of the potential ambient temperature range for computer gear. The result, for years, has been a chiller-based solution for datacenter designs, with air precooled to below 35°C entering the servers.

Chillers use a lot of power. Measured by power utilization efficiency (PUE), most traditional datacenters [24] operate at 1.20 PUE or worse, meaning that 20% more power goes to cooling, etc. Google and the others aim for numbers better than 1.05 PUE [25] and this has led to some great inventions that should flow on into the general marketplace.

We have to begin with the fans in the racks. These traditionally were in the server units. Rack-level cooling fans proved to be very effective compared with the 1″ fans possible in a standard rack server. Typically larger than 7″ diameter, they moved much more air, use less power and run quieter. There proved to be downsides to very large fans, however. These have nonuniform air-flow patterns across the blades from center to edge. The solution is a mixing plenum, but this takes up too much space with really big fans.

An alternative is to group the servers into 4U or 8U blocks and build a set of smaller fans onto the block. This evens up the airflow and is a good balance of the efficiency factors and even cooling. Typically these are 4″–5″ diameter fans.

Having figured out the air movers, the next issue is to decide how they move the air. Ducting across the motherboard makes cooling much more efficient. I've used the techniques on standard COTS motherboards to be able to run them for extended periods with 50°C incoming ambient air. This impacts the rack level cooling and ultimately reshapes the datacenter, but more of that later.

Impediments to airflow should be removed from the design. The "connector stacks" for keyboard, video, mouse, USB, etc. can be removed from cloud servers, since the maintenance approach doesn't use them. Disk drive caddies proved much more of an air block and, with caddies being expensive and disk drives today being fixed rather than moving around for maintenance, losing the front-side row of cad-dies helps cooling a lot. The typical cloud server doesn't need many local drives, at least as long as the configuration of the day isn't a converged system.

Further clean-up of the designs comes from the avoidance of redundant power supplies in servers and the more advanced idea of distributed low-voltage supplies that we'll address below. PSUs take up a lot of space and use a good deal of air-flow. Typical server PSUs are less than 90% efficient. Using central large PSUs can increase efficiency to the 96% range, and also bring back redundancy.

The next issue in cooling is disposing of the waste heat from the servers and stor-age units in the racks. This is where innovation has led to some wild schemes [26]. Concepts built around chilled water are very common, but the sources of the water can be interesting. Water from the bottom of a deep lake [27] in mountain areas or the higher latitudes remains really cold all year round, so that's an obvious one. (The problem of getting data and power out to remote locations places some limits on site choices.).

Other systems use chilled water to cool the units, building the heat converters into the hot air side of the racks. This has been used in a number of containerized data-center approaches. This is about the limit of water cooling, though. I believe none is using water-cooled heatsinks for the CPUs. Feasible in theory, the number of and type of quick connections lead to leaks, which are disastrous in electrical equipment.

There are some interesting cooling approaches on the horizon, including combin-ing freon-type liquids and carbon nanotubes to make a much more efficient heatsink. Overall, however, the best solution seems to be to use normal outside air and blow it though the rack and exhaust it. This works best with containerized datacenters [28], but it can be done in a bricks and mortar datacenter too.

As mentioned above, CPUs and DRAM can handle this, with incoming ambient to 45°C, which excludes only Death Valley in the US, and then only on a few days of the year. The problem is the hard drive. Vendors have upped their specs in the last 2 years to standardize on 65°C incoming air temperature. This allows most cloud data-centers to move to a zero-chill model [29], and avoid all of the water cooling issues.

A zero-chill datacenter, with appropriately designed servers and storage, can lower PUE into the 1.03 range.

The key is to look at temperature profiles over a year on the selected site. In most days the temperature is below 40°C (103°F), which is true for most of the higher latitudes, the odd few days up to 45°C (113°F) will still leave margin in the servers if they are designed properly, and while hotter running will degrade hard drives, a few days of it aren't a killer.

Of course, the better solution is to use SSD instead of hard drives. Typically an SSD is rated to 70°C or even 80°C, but a key factor is that with the exception of ultrafast NVMe drives, most SSDs today dissipate less than 2 W when running and almost nothing in idle. This implies we can pack them closer together, especially if we accept that admins won't ever be swapping drives, drop the drive caddies, and so save a good few bucks and run them with 45°C ambient till the cows come home.

It's worth noting that there are mechanical advantages in the SSD world. Drives weigh a few ounces, and now M2 versions without the external case [30] are being delivered for embedded designs. These are much thinner units. At a guess, we could double up drive density in appliances over HDD designs, reducing storage footprint by another factor of two and also still save weight and power. Add this to the 30 TB SSD capacities predicted for 2020 and the case for SSD-only becomes awful strong.

SSDs are not sensitive to vibration. HDDs are prone to failure if there is too much "rotational vibration" [31] present, so fan noise and even adjacent hard drives can be a serious problem that requires careful design to damp vibrations. This limits the packing density for hard drives and may require special metals in the case structure and antishock mountings. SSDs can be delivered without outer covers and with lower heat dissipation the possibility of closer stacking is obvious.

Beyond cooling, power distribution in cloud racks is a challenge, too. From experience, a 12 V DC system with say, three high-wattage PSUs delivering DC power for a group of servers or storage appliances makes the most sense. The three supplies allow three-phase AC power to be used. These can be connected on a simple copper bus-bar scheme to each other and to the servers in their cluster. A little math shows that power losses are actually very small, especially if the cluster of servers is less than 20U tall (PSUs in the center, of course).

With this configuration we are protected against losing a phase or a single supply, which means that any two supplies need to meet the total power in the cluster. Motherboards today convert 12 V DC into the needed voltages and SSD can use 12 or 5 V DC, unlike HDD that need substantial amounts of both. The result is there is no need for a secondary supply in the servers or appliances.

A logical follow-on from these innovative approaches to cooling and power is the containerized datacenter [32]. The idea of prebuilding a large number of racks, with all the servers, storage switches, and cables, into a standard intermodal container is very attractive, once the issues of cooling and power distribution are adequately optimized.

The containerized datacenter doesn't fit well with preexisting facilities, but if building a green-field facility, containerized datacenters can save a great deal of money [33]. They are compact and inexpensive to build compared with bricks and mortar, but even more importantly, there is no long planning and permission cycle when building one. These modules can be built into container barns with a roof and walls to protect dozens of containers from the climate. Alternatively, they can be parked in the open and wired up to the central power and databackbones, though this complicates the zero-chill model a bit. Generally, the container barn model works best for snowy or rainy climates.

Most of these containers use a center aisle, dual row architecture, with a row of racks on each side. The center aisle is the hot aisle and air is exhausted from it through the roof of the container. Hot is not an exaggeration, by the way! The servers pump out a lot of waste heat.

LAN backbone connections come into a set of routers or backbone switches at one end of the container, and power is delivered, usually from two separate three-phase AC feeds, to a power failover box. Occasionally, a third feed comes into the container from a RUPS (rotating uninterruptible power supply unit, basically a huge spinning flywheel and generator) to guarantee no brownouts when a feed goes down. Containers also have environmental monitors and fire suppression systems.

The 12 V DC distribution system described above allows many servers to be 1U high and 1/2U wide, since they don't need an on-board AC supply. These are typically dual CPU servers, and the wattage of the CPUs is limited because of the heat-sink height to 45 or thereabouts Watts. These servers are used in huge quantities for web serving and the like.

Storage appliances in a private cloud should share the space with the compute servers. Storage units today will be a mix of 60 drive bulk HDD storage in the main today, probably with object storage on appliances that size out a couple of rack U high, and either 1U or 1/2U wide. The transitions to all-SSD solutions and perhaps to converged systems will change the configurations more towards the smaller boxes, though the drive count may increase because of the smaller size of SSD.

USING CLOUD STORAGE

One common concern for IT shops wanting to use the public clouds is data security [34]. This is discussed in Chapter 12, but it is important to preface this section with a comment that the public clouds are handling security issues well [35], so this issue is today somewhat less of an issue, especially for users with some cloud experience.

There are four broad classes of use case for cloud storage. These are the following:

1. Storing data for use by instances in the cloud
2. Transferring data to instances of storage in a private cloud
3. Feeding data to gateway units to be used by non-cloud server or desktops units
4. Acting as a backup or archive repository

The first use case, consuming the cloud-stored data within the cloud, treats block storage as it would a networked volume. A file system is put on the virtual drive and create, read, write, append, and delete operations are possible. A block can be modified and data blocks added or deleted in the file sequence.

Object storage is more constrained. The consistent choice [36] of interface across the CSPs and common to all object storage software is a (minor) variation of the S3 API [37], which is a RESTful protocol. This gives us "buckets" rather than directories, but there is a major difference in that buckets are not tiered, in keeping with a scale-out flat storage resource. Commands like PUT and GET are used to move whole objects around. One uses the PATCH command to create a new version, but this requires a great deal of care in structuring the semantics. Changing data in an object is thus much more difficult than with block storage.

It is indeed a great pity that the industry didn't provide an operating system file stack translator from normal file semantics to REST to make all this much more flexible. Such a translator would have removed the need for rewriting apps to use REST. We have plenty of examples of how to do this, including the file stack on Ceph and the myriad of cloud gateway appliances that look like file servers to the user, but the right place to do this is at the file system level in the operating system stack on the user servers.

The second use case, as we've touched on before, is victim to the poor WAN communications [38] offered in the US and to a lesser extent in Europe. The issue is reducing access latency to the data from hundreds of milliseconds into a few hundred microseconds and getting bandwidth to gigabit Ethernet levels [39]. This is discussed at some length in Section Hybrid Clouds.

Non-cloud access to cloud storage is of course a major traffic element in cloud storage. Protocols such as HTTP and FTP suck whole objects out of storage and send them over the web. As a way of providing safe, back-up storage to small businesses and remote offices, however, the cloud infrastructure gets a bit more sophisticated.

Gateway units sited in a remote office or business act as front-ends to cloud storage. These units have either hard drives or SSD as cache for the data being written or read, reducing apparent latency substantially. Data is presented to local systems typically as a file server, though REST is often supported. Software-only versions are available which run on customer-provided servers with a couple of internal drives.

A similar structure is used for backup and archiving. The better solutions use gateway products that cache the most backed-up data, as well as retrieved objects. Both gateway and backup/archive solutions compress the data being transmitted over the WAN to increase effective bandwidth and reduce latency.

HYBRID CLOUDS

The hybrid cloud is a step above the small business story, due to the intent to move computing between the public workspace and private cloud on a flexible basis. Data is like a boat anchor in these situations. Typically, you don't know what data you want until just before you need it, so latency from the public cloud to the private cloud becomes a major issue.

Obvious solutions, like keeping replicas in both clouds, can fail on the need to keep data tightly synchronized, but this is use case dependent. If most of the data is read only, synching writes may be an acceptable operating mode. Even so, with data locks and multiple write operations, the latency for a transaction can be very large. New start-ups like Velostrata [40] are addressing the issue with software to cache and sync data efficiently, which may ease the problem.

Added to this is the need to meet compliance requirements. Data at rest in the cloud might be considered vulnerable. However, data in transit also is vulnerable. If compliance is to be satisfied, data is always encrypted except when being processed upon and this security issue is moot.

That brings up the question, "If the public cloud is to be trusted at all, why can't we trust it completely [41]?" This is a very loaded issue, since it calls the need for in-house processing into question, at least for jobs that could overflow across the public–private boundary.

Some solutions have attempted to meet this question part way. One approach, by MS Azure, Verizon, and NetApp [42], is to site NetApp filer storage in Verizon's hubs. As Verizon now has high speed, dedicated fiber links to Azure datacenters, this storage is much "closer" to the public cloud. The downside is that it is further from the private cloud. If the model is to mostly process in-house and use the public cloud for cloud-bursting, the majority in-house operations incur an access penalty.

Realization that hybrid clouds are difficult to operate due to data transmission speed issues, coupled with acceptance that public clouds are safe for much of the processing workload of a business, could make the transition to all-public-cloud operations occur much more rapidly. After all, if they are cheaper and secure enough [43], why keep things in-house?

The telcos are belatedly deploying fiber connections on a selective basis in the US, after some well-received and necessary savaging by Google. Laws that the telcos supported banning municipalities and states from providing fiber services are going down like flies, and it looks that we will get fiber in cities over the next 5–10 years. Is it too late to save the hybrid model? Time will tell!

The hybrid issue is also a multi-datacenter issue. The S3 model, for instance, has a remote copy of data kept in another zone. Recovery works moderately well when there is a failure of some local storage. Even if both local copies went away, the rebuild wouldn't saturate the inter-zone WAN links. It would also be feasible in many cases to move the compute instances involved to the other zone.

When zone-level outages have occurred in the past, it's been clear that the normal recovery mechanisms don't work. Restarting instances in another zone gets bogged down with attempts to rebuild replicas of the data in that zone and a complete crash can happen. Any cloud deployment has to handle these problems in a different way from normal recovery mechanisms.

It's worth mentioning that these past failures occurred due to operator error, promulgating untested network firmware changes to the backbone routers in a zone. Clouds are hugely scaled, but this means that some mistakes or failures can take out a great deal of resources at one shot. Cloud construction has to protect against this type of mega problem.

Multizone or multisite operation could provide the tenant protection against this class of failure. Only part of a job stream might be lost when these (rare) events happen. Again, though, this brings up issues of synchronizing three or more copies of the data sets. Perhaps a "map-reduce" approach might work in some use case to segregate part of the active data sets and their associated computing to each zone.

Determining if the failure is temporary or if data loss might have occurred also can mitigate the problem. If the failure class is the former (and most failures will be) it should be possible to delay rebuilds until network and zone accessibility is recovered, leaving just a large, but tractable, resync operation.

EVOLVING CLOUDS

Speculating on long-term futures in the IT business is always a bit of a risky business, but examining where the cloud may go is worth the effort, since it will determine much of the direction of the business. As long as the reader accepts the warning that this might not be what really happens, it seems fair to continue.

Let's look at both hardware and software.

HARDWARE OF THE CLOUD OVER THE NEXT DECADE

In the server space, the upcoming battle is between ×64 solutions from Intel [44] and AMD [45], measured against multicore ARM64 processors [46] from a variety of vendors. Generally, the more robust PCIe IO complement and better DRAM interfaces make ×64 the solution of choice for highly virtualized systems, while ARM64 sits better with microservers with lots of independent blades, such as HPE's Moonshot, and in storage appliances.

Yet, in some ways, the battle is between the microserver concept and the traditional virtual server [47] approach. The microserver position is based on the premise that many independent processors can execute independently and together achieve more for the same price. The math can be a bit tortuous, but the advent of containers seems to tilt the cost per instance equation strongly in favor of ×64, especially comparing the relatively few microserver offering with whitebox, high volume ×64 solutions.

Going down the ×64 path, we can expect a move to Hybrid Memory Cube (HMC) architectures, reducing the power in the CPU/DRAM complex by as much as a factor of 2× or 4×, while making space for as many as 2× the processing core count. HMC, which will have proprietary names in Intel, AMD, and NVidia implementations, speeds up memory bandwidth to around 360 GB/s in 2017 and 1 TB/s by 2020.

Memory size will grow dramatically, too. Max DRAM should expand to around 1 to 4 TB on HMC by 2020, but remember, this is per **CPU**, so we'll see 8 TB dual and 16 TB quad processor solutions. Intel 3D X-Point persistent memory (now renamed

Optane [48]) could add 4 to 8 TB per CPU. This is great for in-memory configurations, and we can expect fewer but more expensive servers to be the norm for database and large instances.

Big Data and HPC will use the same memory structures, but the addition of GPUs will speed up analytics and scientific computing tremendously. This again is ×64 territory today, but ARM could get a foothold via NVidia or even AMD, both of whom have a worldview that the GPU is THE processor in these configurations and the ARM or ×64 is along just for housekeeping.

With big memories, what does storage look like? It definitely needs a rethink. Loading and unloading from the memory needs a good deal of storage bandwidth. Intel has announced RDMA in chipsets for the 2017 timeframe, with 25 GbE likely to be the base Ethernet for that. Servers with HMC, GPUs, and huge memories will likely need 100 GbE pipes, possibly four per server.

Likewise, networked storage bandwidth will increase disproportionally. Appliances with SSD need good bandwidth. Consumer SSD today can deliver 5GBps for 12 drives while NVMe drives can double that or more. This is important because NVMe over Fabrics (NoF) will be off and running in 2016/2017, allowing direct connection of NVMe drives via Ethernet. We can expect NVMe drives with RDMA over Ethernet (probably iWARP since Intel is putting that protocol in its chipsets) in 2017.

The drive picture has enterprise NoF at the performance end of the scale as the primary networked storage layer, with either NoF bulk SSD or SATA SSD with a front-end controller as the secondary cold storage. This will evolve to an all NVMe environment fairly quickly, as RDMA becomes standard in CPU chipsets.

What about storage drives in servers? The traditional model of stateless servers with networked storage has given way to local instance stores to reduce latency and increase effective bandwidth from storage. This led to virtual SANs, taking advantage of local storage to create a pool of data shared across the cluster.

With persistent memory and large DRAMs, sharing between servers is still required, but the model could be extended to primary SSD storage very easily using NVMe. This makes the near-in storage and primary storage a single pool with homogenized access, removing command and protocol translations and data routing. In the end, ease of operation will be the driver to extend this to the secondary storage tier.

Physically, datacenters will shrink [49] in many cases. Both servers and storage will be much smaller and performance per cubic meter will go up rapidly. As we've said elsewhere, packing density of drives will at least double, while 3D NAND technology or even X-Point will drive more storage per drive. Intel's forecast of 30 TB drives in 2020 will probably be reached, and that points to 100 TB bulk storage drives (low write rates) in 2025.

There are other magic tricks in the research labs for the second half of the decade. Carbon nanotubes are exotic, but look like they can support ultrafast transistors [50] and possible persistent memory devices. Graphene [51] also has a lot of research in the same direction. Room-temperature superconductors [52] might also debut in the latter part of the next decade, which would completely change the game on speed and density. Who knows?!!

SOFTWARE OF THE CLOUD OVER THE NEXT DECADE

It would be easy to say that the three big CSPs will march along with their proprietary solutions in feature lock-step while mere mortals all use OpenStack. A year ago in 2015, that would have been a reasonable statement, since those were the options available. VMware's cloud didn't look too healthy and was put on the block with the Dell–EMC merger. Even OpenStack lost adherents, as HPE decided to get out of the CSP business.

For all of that, OpenStack now has competition in the form of Azure private clouds and AWS and Rackspace cloud hosting. This should make the competition for private/hybrid cloud share more intense and that will lead to richer features and innovation.

What sort of things can we expect? OpenStack needs better security and more automation of processes. The advent of SDN and SDS [53] will allow for major improvements in this area. SDN is already moving networking from the manually controlled script era into one where policies determine what happens to vLANs (and so the storage networks and vSANs) in the cloud cluster. Policies make almost all of the work cookie-cutter and this reduces set-up errors enormously. One step further, with central IT managing the policy templates tightly, and departmental computing can control their own network configuration.

Storage will go down the same path, with services being decoupled from hardware boxes. Now, encryption, compression, deduplication, and indexing are all scalable tools floating around in the virtual instance universe.

The benefits of some localization will add some constraints on how this is done. Those data services need accelerators to keep up with the NVMe/persistent DRAM model described in the previous section, and accelerators are localized hardware. This could easily constrain the service to a VM in the server where the data is generated—it isn't pure virtualization, but it seems a reasonable compromise. I call it "vectorized virtualization" (VV).

VV should allow the output of any server to be deduplicated and then compressed, then encrypted prior to sending it over the LAN from the server. By doing this, we first, prevent unnecessary transmissions by deduplicating objects; second, make objects smaller by compression; and third, make the safe by encryption, which covers data both in transit and at rest.

Today, servers can't really keep up with hard drives, never mind SSD, with these services. I know of a couple of stealth start-ups addressing the problem and expect that a good solution will be in the market in 2017.

Where does this put storage appliances? The software is going to migrate out of the appliance into the cloud, so the appliance will dumb down. Assuming that the appliance has an Ethernet interface with RDMA, the key question is whether the drives talk directly to Ethernet [54] or are connected via a controller. The use of NVMe points toward direct connection for two reasons.

First, taking an interface protocol tuned for almost no overhead and adding steps through a controller and through protocol changes makes little sense. Second, NVMe is smart enough to handle direct access from a server to a data object on a remote drive. Now there will be some issues with authentication and security, which suggests that a service is needed to mediate setting up sessions between drives and hosts, but ultimately this form of asymmetric pooling is the answer to performance issues, as it easily achieves parallel access, even massively so for big data/HPC file sizes.

This could be the path Ceph evolves down. It is almost SDS-like today, and moving the distribution and replication functionality of OSDs back into the host servers looks feasible. If this were done, adding missing services and distributing data directly from the host would increase performance and flexibility tremendously.

Ceph is likely to become the preferred OpenStack solution [55] for all storage needs. As a universal store it provides the entire block and file needs as well as object storage. Ceph needs to better handle SSD to win that crown, but that rewrite is already underway. To me, it doesn't look like Cinder and Swift have any significant features to combat Ceph's ascendancy.

Using NVMe to interface all of the fast storage simplifies life tremendously. Fewer interrupts, a pull rather than a push system with no need for protocol semantics to accept commands and request data transmission and the ability to vectorize data and statuses by applications, cores or CPUs means that it is attractive across the board as a replacement for SAS and SATA.

Using it across Ethernet means drives with NVMe over iWARP Ethernet will appear in the market and there will be a flurry of start-up software companies around goat-herding the new product. Whether this goes so far as to allow media to stream directly from a drive to a home user, for example, is another issue, more a test of security systems than technical difficulty.

Where does this leave legacy gear (SANs and filers)? SDS allows for legacy gear to be used for storage, but it does so generally by ignoring the internal "bells and whistles" software that's proprietary. Otherwise we are back to vendor lock-in. Whether it makes sense to keep the older gear on until it reaches end-of-life, or adopt the 4-year life cycle of the CSP or even be aggressive and de-install after 3 years is a case-by-case issue, but with storage evolving so quickly, I suspect the legacy problem [56] will be short-lived and may not be worth a lot of innovation.

Clearly, one major issue in all of this is what happens with the major traditional storage vendors. They are seeing shrinking revenues already, but tend to deny that dropping per unit pricing is the reason. Yet, the traditional old guard is out of the CSP business already because they couldn't compete, so they are a bit behind the eight-ball when it comes to the next few years of evolution.

Like EMC appears to be doing, they are starting to migrate away from hardware-based plays to being software-and-services companies. IBM is perhaps the furthest along, getting out of PCs, then COTS servers, and doing poorly on the hardware side of storage while their software side is in better shape. Overall, IBM has seen declining storage hardware revenues for 18 consecutive quarters and the writing is on the wall.

VMware is also reacting to the changes coming in the market. NSX is a powerful tool for creating virtual networks in hybrid clouds, and should evolve into an SDN product. VSphere is, however, declining in sales as IT moves more to a cloud model, and it remains to be seen if the transition of product leads to a growing or shrinking company.

At the end of the day, can the traditional players make the conversion fast enough? This involves realigning R & D and then the sales force, which is no small feat, especially for box-focused companies such as EMC where the array was king for 30 years. More importantly, they've got to convince customers that they aren't attempting the old lock-in tactics and they'll have to overcome the harsh realization that comes from users learning that they could buy a $300 SSD from distribution and it would be as good as that $14,000 EMC drive. Likely, traditional vendor loyalty will prove elusive, and this especially if their "SDS" solutions are really relabeled proprietary, closed software.

With all of this, the storage software market will be more vibrant and creative than it has been for years. There are still huge problems to overcome, from rapid analysis of big data to gigantic HPC problems like supercolliders and Square-Kilometer Arrays. Just be prepared for different vendors to call on you!

NETWORKING FOR CLOUD STORAGE

Today's clouds use 10 GbE for networking. It's inexpensive, with switch sources other than Cisco available, and for the largest CSPs the ability to get stripped down semi-custom solutions from ODMs exists.

Networking has three major evolutionary threads going forward. RDMA is entering the mainstream and Intel is planning iWARP support in its chipsets. As with 10 GbE, this drops the per-port cost tremendously for RDMA and likely the protocol will become ubiquitous in a few years.

In parallel, we are seeing a transition to 25 GbE technology that will occur in 2016. I suspect that there will be some mutual exclusion of RDMA and 25 GbE until 2017, when the two will be available in the same chipset. With 4-lane versions also available, we effectively will see a 4× or more boost in overall network performance by the end of 2017, and also have 100 GbE links for storage appliance and backbone use.

The third thread is the evolution of software-defined networking (SDN), coupled with SDS. SDN is entering mainstream usage rapidly. It has the advantage of cutting the cost of switchgear down to bare metal levels, while adding scalability to data services such as VLAN setup and security.

Unbundling data services means that users will be able to choose service needs a la carte and even on a Data-Service-as-a-Service basis, paying for just what is needed at any point in time. We can expect this flexibility of choices to lead to expanded innovation and a new set of start-up companies.

These structural choices will impinge heavily on storage. First, it's no longer clear where storage ends and networking begins in this new model. Is encryption a networking service or a storage service? Is compression a way to save on storage space or a means to accelerate the LAN? It probably doesn't matter if the APIs are structured correctly. In fact, I would describe this as "stream processing" which homogenizes both sides of the equation, storage, and networking. Stream processing opens up the thought process of doing much more to the data, which may be a very good concept as we open up to the Internet of things.

As an example, my much referenced surveillance system will suffice. The data form a lobby camera should see almost always the same thing all night. Occasionally headlights will flash on a wall, and maybe a stray employee will cross the lobby. There isn't any need to send the raw data to a datacenter. A cheap processor in a box could be used to detect if images change, but that involves some maintenance of "yet another computer," so a better answer might be to float an encryption service in a local cloud datacenter or hoster and deduplicate and encrypt all the camera traffic back to headquarters on the other side of the country. Now we can use data services rather than an app, and only fire it up when surveillance is needed.

Back to the cloud environment, the impact of SDN is to bring services into the virtualized servers. Suppose now that every server has encryption, compression, and deduplication services available in VMs. Using these services means that all data is minimized and made safe before leaving the server. This is a huge step up from where we are today and will radically improve operating performance and security in clouds of any type.

The downside is that we don't yet have the accelerators needed to keep up with the network, but as I've stated elsewhere, I know of stealthy start-ups attacking that issue and expect a working resolution in 2017, if not before.

Those of you savvy in data flow modeling will comment that this means delays in write operations, but I would contend that one of the values of persistent DRAM bus memory such as X-Point is to journal write operations for the short time needed to apply data services to the object being written. This is almost the identical process we used for 30 years with RAID controllers in servers, which used battery-backed up memory, and then flash, to protect against loss while data was being converted for RAID writes, but it is of course a much faster solution, which will reduce write latencies to microseconds.

One consideration in networking in the future stems from that persistent memory usage. Data sharing from this memory will also be prevalent in future clouds. RDMA and fast networks will strive to keep up with the low latency requirements and bandwidth needs, but this is very fast memory and the cluster could easily be out of balance and not reach its potential if the network bottlenecks transmissions frequently.

There is a trade-off between delay in transmission and delay in compression and encryption. Depending on how good those accelerators get, traffic from the DRAM and persistent memory might or might not be compressed and encrypted. The latter is especially an issue. That raises the issue of whether or not data in that persistent memory should be first compressed—to save space and to speed up load times into the system cache. Certainly light compression, such as handling consecutive or common patterns, might be done, increasing the effective storage space in persistent memory by 2x or so.

NoE, NVMe over an Ethernet fabric [57], looks like a winner for storage. Intel plans X-Point NVM-interfaced SSDs. These will initially be PCIe products, since PCIe is faster for near-in solutions than using an Ethernet protocol conversion. Stepping up to Ethernet makes sense, however, since that takes the server hosting the drives out of the data path for cluster networking. They can connect direct to the LAN and be grouped within VLANs for access control.

RDMA Ethernet drives will be the fastest solution available in networked storage and also one of the simplest configurations. All of the networked drives will be on the network as peers. There won't be a need for controllers, translating protocols, and slowing data transmission and access down. That means that setting up access and deciding where data is mounted moves to SDS data services, which determine configurations, and SDN-created VLANs, which group drives together. That's huge flexibility and it's very agile, since configurations can be changed in just seconds.

Remote storage, in other zones or datacenters or in a hybrid cloud environment, can be mapped as Ethernet nodes, too. Likely, the gateway business will thrive, where data for a remote store is journaled locally prior to transmission then spooled at the receiving end before being written to the final drives.

There will be a battle over how to present Ethernet drives to the network. On the one hand, the current block-IO approach might morph to a Kinetic-style key/data interface, while directly building object stores onto each drive [58] is very attractive. Both Ceph and Scality could be configured with drive-level object stores.

Timelines for this look like 2016 for early NoE adapters and controller-based remote storage, with sharing of server drives in the same timeframe. 2017 should see the approach hitting mainstream [59] with multiple vendors and the first Ethernet drive solutions available. It will be 2018 before volumes really get going, but from then on the only thing preventing the approach from ubiquity is CIO complacency or major vendor mispricing and FUD. The bottom line is the NVMe approach which is like a Ferrari to a Model T compared with alternatives and will bring great performance benefits to any datacenter.

Somewhere around the start of 2017 we should begin to see early networking products in the 50 GbE range, effectively doubling network performance yet again. By that point we will need the benefit! Server horsepower, based on higher-core count CPUs, GPUs, and HMC/persistent memory will be pushing the bandwidth envelope again. There are breakthrough possibilities too, which might take affordable single links to 100 GbE levels, but like any nascent technologies, these are still "in the lab" and an end point is uncertain.

The Ethernet drive approach will stimulate quite a bit of packaging ingenuity. Bulk storage could end up packed 120 drives to a 3U box (assuming 2.5″ SSDs without caddies), giving one or more raw petabytes of data per rack unit (1U) as drives go beyond 30 TB capacity. Performance drives are more likely to be boxed up in smaller configurations, based on the bandwidth capacity of the internal Ethernet switch and external ports. With 24-port quad-lane switches common, configuration like 12 drives with three external 4-lane ports would be nonblocking, for example.

Dual port drives won't make any sense. Redundant power and switches or controllers are increasingly avoided by following the replication-across-appliances model, so having two ports for each drive in a box is just a way to up the SKU price!

Security concerns will push the idea of an independent storage LAN to the top of the precautions list. Raw drives, even with clever security and authentication systems, create a huge number of vulnerable end points to target, increasing the challenges of key protection and access control considerable.

Remember, encryption is not enough. If I can tell a drive to erase a block of data using plaintext or simple encryption, that drive is wide open for an exploit that hurts my datacenter, possibly fatally. We need controls on drive commands that offer protection against hacking attacks at this level. Encryption is a solution, but there is the problem of short blocks with guessable content stemming from the fact that command structures are published as industry standards. This is still a work in progress.

One benefit of moving to an Ethernet drive base is that we can realize highly parallel accesses very easily. Instead of getting data from just a couple of drives in a RAID mirror, we will naturally be storing across drives sets with large numbers of drives, allowing bigger transfers to come from 20 or 40 sources rather than just 1 or 2. There's some rightsizing involved in this and it will come down to use cases to determine the best configuration. There are also some intriguing things one could do with multiple servers being loaded in parallel, as in Hadoop.

With networking evolving so rapidly, we have some uncertainty about moving forward. The good news is that most paths will lead to great improvement, so being tentative is probably the worst choice possible.

BACKUP AND ARCHIVING

This is where the cloud really started for most people. Backing up and archiving in the cloud looked much easier than tape-based solutions, and so it proved. For the first time, "Tape is Dead!" [60] actually may be a true statement.

All of the CSPs offer a low-priced solution for cold storage of data. Pricing is set up to encourage loading (that's usually free) and penalize restoration. The services offered in early 2016 have some major differences. Google has disk-based Nearline Storage with a retrieval guarantee of a couple of seconds, while AWS Glacier service appears to have bought tape libraries and as a result has 2-h recovery latency.

With Google handling data protection by replication and using multiple zones, a disk-based solution is the clear winner. Nearline allows grazing for particular data items, where you begin restoration by searching for the item in various volumes. With Glacier, this involves a 2-h wait each time, and clearly is a nonstarter. Similarly, once an object is retrieved, there's a good chance that it won't be the version you wanted, especially in document searching. The result of this is that AWS will need to speed Glacier up if they want it to be competitive.

Actually running backups is not difficult. There are many tools, ranging in price from hundreds to tens of thousands of dollars that can do the job. Tools come in the form of software-only solutions for COTS systems, backup appliances and even specialized clouds (basically these are sublets from AWS or Google). Price is by no means a gauge of effectiveness. Some of the highest rated products are quite inexpensive. This is a fiercely competitive business and the picture changes constantly.

If I were doing a cloud backup setup today, I'd find a well-featured software backup tool that covered all my major environments including Linux and Windows, MS exchange, and databases. Then I'd buy a cheap whitebox server from distribution, shove in a couple of 3-TB drives and connect it to the network—not a complicated job!

One of the challenges that IT faces is the backup of users' machines—desktops, tablets, and even phones. All of these may contain important company data, but more important still is the loss of productivity that comes with the typical few days of downtime that most end users suffer when their desktop or portable goes down. Some of the newer software packages in the backup market cater to that and provide backup images for portable units in the cloud.

Where is cloud backup heading in the future? Power is a problem in large datacenters and backup systems spend a good deal of time just consuming it and doing nothing. One answer is to spin hard drives down when inactive and spin them back up on demand. This means it takes a few seconds to bring data to the requestor. Even spun down, drives consume a couple of Watts of power and not all drives support spin down anyway, since it reduces the drive life considerably.

Enter low-cost, high-capacity SSD. We are entering an era of 3D-stacked 4-bit-per-cell QLC flash, which won't be very durable on writes, but plenty good enough for archiving work. Here, the operating power of a drive is around 0.2 W or even less when idling, so power down is no longer an issue. Boxes with these drives could have huge numbers of drives, maybe as high as 120 or 160, since drives without covers can be used (the M2 form factor [61]). With SSD, response times of a second or better should be possible, which would more than satisfy latency-sensitive users on YouTube, for example.

HYBRID CLOUDS AND DATA GOVERNANCE

Designing and operating a hybrid cloud is a data problem [62] through and through. Figuring out which data goes where and which can be replicated to the public cloud is a mammoth chore. The reality is that a lot of data doesn't need to be tightly controlled. Web pages and such can live in either portion of the cloud and still be as safe (provided the data is encrypted and access authentication is in place).

Other data is subject to "crown jewels" status and may be under compliance to HIPAA or SOX or such. Generally, this data can go into a public cloud, provided it is encrypted and the keys are controlled by the data owner. This last is a very important requirement. Using drive encryption provided by a CSP doesn't qualify as compliant and has been shown to be very vulnerable.

The hybrid cloud brings the data issue to the foreground. To get performance, we need to avoid the latencies of WAN traffic [63] between the public cloud and our datacenter. Multi-second latencies would kill cloud performance.

We talked earlier about this latency problem, so enough said here. There are other dimensions that should be explored to fully understand the options. Evidence is strong that public clouds are at least as secure as in-house datacenters [64]. In fact, the evidence is that the public cloud does better, based on some serious hacks that have occurred. This colors what we can do about critical, compliant data management.

First, if any critical data goes into the public cloud, it has to be protected in a compliant way. No ifs or buts, it has to be encrypted and a key manager tool used to deliver keys to servers for decryption. It's critical to keep up with encryption trends—256-bit AES may be broken [65] as of the time of writing, for example.

Second, critical data is just that. There should be a consistent version of any record in that data on the system. An example is the inventory on items. If a server in the public cloud logs a sale, the database version in the private cloud must be updated too, or else overselling might occur. This means one copy of the data is designated the master copy (usually the in-house copy) and any changes that have implications like that inventory item need to be synced at *both* ends before the transaction is complete. That's onerous, but the slow links across WANs are the problem.

An alternative to this might be to take an idea from Big Data and formally distribute the database. Taking the inventory example, all of the shoe inventory could be managed from the cloud. This would take a few seconds to set up if there were database copies in both private and public clouds, this being enough time to complete any outstanding show transactions on in-house servers before the handover is made.

Not all traffic can be resolved that way. The decision as to moving work to the cloud may well then reside on the question of how much data must move to the public cloud to either work there on an ongoing basis or to just allow temporary cloud-bursting to occur.

Moving a lot of data to the public cloud will slow down any cloud-bursting dramatically. In these situations, it might be better to keep a copy in the public cloud and journal updates. By keeping a background write job operating in the public cloud, for example, it might be possible to keep the journal queue relatively short, and adding extra instances might cope with periodic higher write loads. When cloud-bursting is needed, the journal is completely processed and then the public cloud instances brought online.

Once the public instances are running, we face the dilemma of synching the copies of the data. Use cases determine if the sync has to be atomic across all copies, or if it can be applied asynchronously to the data. Clearly, making atomic as little data as possible is the best solution.

As said before, the data flow problem is a major issue with hybrid clouds and salvation, in the form of the telcos laying fiber, seems a bit distant, except where Google throws down the gauntlet [66]. Perhaps it's time for governments to take over the infrastructure business from the telcos?

Governance [67] is the other issue in this section and it is closely related to the data management question. Assurance that data is protected only comes from comprehensive audits of the public and private cloud operations, done regularly and with corrective actions being taken promptly.

This isn't an easy thing to do in the cloud, especially with a fluid boundary between public and private operations and operational and software efforts aimed at masking that boundary and simplifying operations. Moreover, the nature of cloud instances makes manual analysis difficult and one should look for tools aimed at automating that sort of process.

Life is much easier if storage traffic avoids the external traffic altogether. Keeping a separate storage LAN makes sense. It reduces the externally visible footprint of storage to just the connections between the private cloud and the public cloud and even there good practice and the extension of the VLAN across the cloud boundary should keep out most hackers.

Any management LANs need to be aggressively protected and monitored. As the cloud is essentially a flat space of servers and appliances, anyone getting access to the control planes of the cloud can do tremendous damage and steal a lot of data. In reality, these are the new crown jewels and compliance auditing should give them a high priority.

In all the data shuffling that a large hybrid cloud suggests, we have to be very careful that orphaned copies of critical data [68] aren't left behind when work moves or instances are closed down. This becomes a much bigger issue when persistent memory is provided in servers as "instance storage" and when departmental IT (who might be one individual doing IT part time and with little experience!) controls their own configuration.

Policy systems need to extend to destroying instances, etc. They also should be easily audited. A good policy system also ensures that all policies in a class are updated together to avoid versioning attacks. Again, there are tools to help do this and again, this should be audited regularly at all levels. Assume that departmental computing bods will look for ways to game the system, either to look good at budget time or just for kicks, and there is always the risk that they do some things so infrequently that they will make mistakes.

Likely, we will see the rise of governance service vendors [69], who provide a toolkit and processes and procedures for everything from security and authentication to auditing. This is certainly feasible given the similarity between private clouds, their operations with public clouds, and the few public clouds that matter. This may well be the profile of companies like Symantec in a few years, leasing a modular tool chain that covers the needs spectrum. That could make figuring a world-class plan and then implementing it a whole lot easier.

In sum, cloud security is really data security and that is still a much neglected area in many companies. Safe operation in the cloud requires a focus on correcting that situation quickly or the consequences could be very painful.

CONTAINERS AND THEIR IMPACT ON STORAGE NETWORKS

When virtualization first appeared on the scene, it was a religious mantra that all virtual machines were emulations of bare metal servers and that any operating system could run in one. Perhaps no one envisioned the grand beast that the cloud has become. We literally now have millions of instances running any operating system. Finally, the penny has dropped and next-generation virtualization is taking the market by storm.

The new approach, called containers (and sometimes Docker [70], after the leading approach), uses a single copy of a specific OS and all the container instances in that machine have to use that same OS. This is an easily handled operational issue in large clouds with huge numbers of instances, since there are so many instances of both Linux and Windows that separation on individual servers is not a problem. The memory that OS copies would have taken up in all of the other instances is freed up. This allows more VMs to be opened up and typically a server can host four times the VM count as the traditional hypervisor.

Security has been an issue [71] with the approach, which first appeared halfway through 2014 and is still maturing. Sitting a bunch of containers on top of an operating system negated some of the multitenancy protection built into the server CPU. Intel and others have figured out a way to resolve this using a light-weight hypervisor to hold the containers, and most users no longer are concerned that security is weaker than the old hypervisor.

Containers will have major impacts in IT. The increase in VMs may cause server sales to drop dramatically even in the face of an increasing workload, and units stretched to their limit may get a new lease of life. Long-term, we will see datacenters that are less than half the size they would be if everything had continued as usual, and that is before taking into account the physical size reductions from denser packaging and more powerful servers that we can expect.

Storage, too, is impacted by containers [72]. On the one hand, the bandwidth needed to load images to all the VMs in a server just shrank tremendously. In fact, that one copy of the OS and key applications may be the only load in that area compared with hundreds of images before.

This obviates the notorious boot storm issue seen mainly in VDI systems, which choke at the start of the workday. In general cloud usage, starting up a new instance can take just a couple of seconds if the OS and apps are already on the server, compared with the average of a couple of minutes with current systems. Image updating and making sure that all images are consistent also becomes an easier task.

The downside is that I now have thousands of VMs operating in each server as opposed to a few hundred. Random IO for these instances will go up, which isn't good considering that most VMs are already IO starved. Containers will increase the pressure on networks and networked storage to speed up and may well absorb the "bounce" from 10 to 25 GbE very rapidly.

Even RDMA and the following generation of network, 50 GbE, in the 2020 timeframe will not be enough. Using NVDIMM persistent memory as a write journal to level-load the LAN connections may also help somewhat, but servers will evolve much more horsepower in the next few years. Real-time compression is essential to balance the server/network/storage triad. This will boost LAN speed by as much as 5x, or even more in some cases, on top of any other gains.

Migration to Ethernet-connected NVMeoE drives will have a major impact on network storage latency as was discussed above. Another aspect of this is the possibility of making those drives visible on the external (storage) LAN. This would allow the drives in an instance storage scenario to be direct-loaded, speeding up operations. Extending this LAN connectivity to the persistent DRAM memory would certainly boost performance tremendously too, but that isn't a trivial engineering task.

Perhaps the simplest solution is to have more Ethernet ports on the server. This scales bandwidth readily, and with SDS/merchant silicon switches won't cost anything like the traditional datacenter network to implement. With RDMA, these ports will add a trivial additional load to the server CPU (3% per port at full load versus 20% with non-RDMA ports). Add compression and the 50 GbE factors and we would be at 50 or more times the effective bandwidth with four 50 GbE ports in 2021.

Containers will have disproportional effects on applications where the app code is large. Virtual desktops qualify, since the Window OS is quite large and large portions are normally paged out. Databases also have this profile, with Oracle, for example, having a lot of code modules. Running a single image of all of these is a logical step in container evolution and should lead to considerable efficiencies in use of DRAM.

For storage appliances, the single app image opportunity creates some possibilities. In a multitenanted server, each tenant gets copies of the same service, without incurring the penalty of having multiple copies of the code or OS. This makes for a secure, flexible environment that increases service density for just the cost of the data space. This suggests the focus of SDS, and SDN for that matter, should be on containerization rather than virtualization.

Since the preferred method of using containerized, or hypervisor-virtualized, storage and network data services is likely to be a stream model where data is processed through a sequence of such services under the control of configuration files or metadata, having a standard API that facilitates the stream processing sequence makes sense. With SDS/SDN, life can be more complex, with some services being called dynamically in other servers. Automated setup and teardown of the VPNs required to link these servers will need to be fitted into the toolsets for administering the datacenter.

WILL THE PRIVATE DATACENTER SURVIVE?

One thread that has run through this chapter is the pressure the cloud is placing on technology directions, on pricing, and on security of data. If the mega-CSPs all deliver a very robust and secure operation with the lowest cost hardware and scale leverage of software and personnel, how, in the end, will private datacenters and clouds justify their existence [73].

With businesses under increasing competitive pressure, most CEOs should be asking the question, "How can I get more IT for less money?" rather than arguing about the fine details of business as usual.

The counter is that larger companies need to think like CSPs [74] if they want to keep any IT in house. The issues of compliance and security that are thrown up as a rationale are becoming weaker as the cloud matures without any signs of major security failures.

To survive, then, the CIO has to move to the cloud model. That's not buying a cloud from HPE or VMware or Oracle. It's sourcing hardware like Google, building datacenters like Google, renting software and paying only for what is used, and maintaining systems like Google.

The hardware issue means buying minimalist servers from the ODMs or other inexpensive volume manufacturers. The Open Compute Project doesn't go far enough to get the best solutions, since the designs tend to be hand-me-downs from one or two CSPs with their own special needs. There will be more choice as the ODMs move into a direct-selling mode.

Containerization works for any COTS solution. There are plenty of vendors who build semi-custom containers with their own or third party gear. Parking containers may be a problem if you only have one or two, but we are seeing container barns operated to provide just this service. Containers come in a variety of sizes too, from 6 foot long to 20 foot or 40 foot intermodal sizes, so rightsizing isn't an issue.

Getting power to your own containers can be an issue if you park them behind the office. You are looking at tens to hundreds of kilowatts. The economics of power and WAN connections might make colocation more attractive.

On the software licensing side, SaaS probably will be the cheapest route overall [75]. Google writes its own search engines, and AWS writes its retail packages, but in both cases the software cost is amortized over literally millions of servers and is moreover very business unique. ERP on the other hand is a common need and renting looks to be the cheapest way to go and that's true of much business software.

The maintenance approach of the large CSP is that unit repair is either done when enough units fail in a container to merit a visit, or it isn't done at all. The logic is that failure rates are so low that it's better to overprovision the configuration somewhat and just use the extra gear to replace failed units.

Units have a 4-year life [76], partly due to the Moore's Law cycle of system performance and partly due to the no-repair philosophy. Mainly, the issue is economic. When operating costs are calculated, including power and support, and amortized against the number of virtual machines in a server, and then residual equipment values are considered, a 4-year life makes sense.

The ratio of staff to gear is different [77] for the CSPs. Instead of one admin per 100 servers, we are looking at 1 admin per 10,000. In storage, instead of 1 per 10 Tb we are looking at 1 admin per 10 PB. That's a direct result of the no-repair approach, coupled with heavy automation and thousands to millions of identical boxes. Google has jobs like firmware updates automated to be push button, for example.

The bottom line is that the in-house datacenter is a threatened species [78]. Fighting back [79] involves throwing tradition out the door and using the same approaches the CSPs employ. Is it possible to win under these circumstances? The future will tell, but don't expect the 30–40 year "long goodbye [80]" that legacy mainframe computing has enjoyed!

REFERENCES

[1] Azure – http://www.azure.microsoft.com/.
[2] Verari – http://www.hpcwire.com/2009/01/22/verari_systems_from_clusters_to_containers/.
[3] Rackable – http://www.infoworld.com/article/2632392/m-a/rackable-systems-becomes-sgi–closes-deal.html.
[4] Chinese ODMs – https://en.wikipedia.org/wiki/Original_design_manufacturer.
[5] ODMs to Enter the US and EU Markets – https://technology.ihs.com/571073/chinese-brands-are-expanding-in-overseas-markets.
[6] Very Bleak Future for Middleman – http://www.theregister.co.uk/2015/08/04/china_and_the_cloud_sinking_teeth_into_server_sales/.
[7] Rackspace Company Website – http://www.rackspace.com/.
[8] Docker – http://www.docker.com/.
[9] Massive Cloud Price War – http://www.businesscloudnews.com/2016/01/18/aws-azure-and-google-intensify-cloud-price-war/.
[10] Open Compute Project – http://www.opencompute.org/.
[11] Solid-State Power Supplies – http://www.vicorpower.com/flatpac.
[12] Ethernet-Connected OSD for Ceph – http://ceph.com/community/50-osd-ceph-cluster/.
[13] Kinetic Ethernet Drive – https://www.openkinetic.org/.
[14] HGST Ethernet Drive – http://www.skylable.com/products/use-cases/hgst/.
[15] OpenStack – http://www.openstack.org/.
[16] Current Project List for OpenStack – www.openstack.org/software/project-navigator/.
[17] Amazon Web Services – https://aws.amazon.com/.
[18] Online Retailing Decimating the High Streets – http://www.telegraph.co.uk/finance/newsbysector/retailandconsumer/11714847/Online-shopping-is-king-high-street-stores-must-adapt-or-die.html.
[19] Azure – http://www.azure.com/.
[20] Google – http://www.cloud.google.com/.
[21] VMware – http://www.vmware.com/.
[22] US Navy Has a Plan – https://thestack.com/cloud/2015/05/18/u-s-navy-abandons-cloud-and-data-centre-plans-in-favour-of-new-strategy/.
[23] Army is Close Behind – www.army.mil/article/169635/reaching_for_the_cloud.
[24] Traditional Datacenters – https://journal.uptimeinstitute.com/a-look-at-data-center-cooling-technologies/.
[25] Google and the Others Aim for Numbers Better Than 1.05 PUE – http://blogs.wsj.com/cio/2015/11/09/intel-cio-building-efficient-data-center-to-rival-google-facebook-efforts/.
[26] Some Wild Cooling Schemes – http://arstechnica.com/information-technology/2016/02/microsofts-new-way-for-cooling-its-datacenters-throw-them-in-the-sea/.
[27] Water From the Bottom of a Deep Lake – http://arstechnica.com/information-technology/2016/02/microsofts-new-way-for-cooling-its-datacenters-throw-them-in-the-sea/.
[28] Outside Air Works Best With Containerized Datacenters – http://www.datacenterknowledge.com/archives/2009/07/15/googles-chiller-less-data-center/.
[29] Zero-Chill Model – http://www.networkcomputing.com/data-centers/evolving-pue-containerized-datacenters/844954697.
[30] M2 SSD Versions Without the External Case – http://www.pcworld.com/article/2977024/storage/m2-ssd-roundup-tiny-drives-deliver-huge-performance.html.

[31] Rotational Vibration in HDDs – www.hgst.com/sites/default/files/resources/WP-RVS-25March.pdf.

[32] The Containerized Datacenter – http://www.cablinginstall.com/articles/print/volume-24/issue-4/departments/infrastructure-insights/containerized-data-center-market-to-reach-us-10b-by-2021.html.

[33] Containerized Datacenters Can Save a Great Deal of Money – http://hweblog.com/containerized-data-center-saves-the-university-30-energy-consumption.

[34] Data Security – http://www.gartner.com/smarterwithgartner/assessing-security-in-the-cloud/.

[35] Public Clouds Are Handling Security Issues Well – http://www.informationweek.com/cloud/infrastructure-as-a-service/why-cloud-security-beats-your-data-center/d/d-id/1321354.

[36] Consistent Choice of Interface – https://blog.architecting.it/2016/02/19/object-storage-standardising-on-the-s3-api/.

[37] S3 API – http://docs.aws.amazon.com/AmazonS3/latest/API/Welcome.html.

[38] Poor WAN Communications – http://www.networkcomputing.com/storage/primary-storage-shifts-cloud/634178622.

[39] Getting Bandwidth to Gigabit ETHERNET Levels – http://www.sfchronicle.com/business/article/SF-explores-blazing-fast-gigabit-Internet-6889799.php.

[40] Velostrata – http://www.velostrata.com/.

[41] Why Can't We Trust Public Cloud Completely? – http://www.crn.com/news/security/300071877/security-experts-the-public-cloud-is-a-safe-place-for-storing-data.htm.

[42] MS Azure, Verizon and NetApp – http://www.netapp.com/us/company/news/press-releases/news-rel-20141028-186087.aspx.

[43] Secure Enough – http://www.druva.com/blog/if-youre-going-to-worry-about-cloud-security-says-gartner-worry-about-the-right-things/.

[44] Intel Company Website – http://www.intel.com/.

[45] AMD Company Website – http://www.amd.com/.

[46] ARM64 Processors – https://en.wikipedia.org/wiki/ARM_architecture.

[47] Microserver Concept and the Traditional Virtual Server – http://searchservervirtualization.techtarget.com/tip/Choosing-the-best-cloud-server-for-your-hybrid-cloud.

[48] Optane – http://www.pcworld.com/article/3056178/storage/intel-claims-storage-supremacy-with-swift-3d-xpoint-optane-drives-1-petabyte-3d-nand.html.

[49] Data Centers Will Shrink – http://www.computerworld.com/article/2550400/data-center/the-incredible-shrinking-data-center.html.

[50] Carbon Nanotubes Support Ultrafast Transistors – http://www.eetimes.com/document.asp?doc_id=1328370.

[51] Graphene – http://wccftech.com/graphene-transistors-427-ghz/.

[52] Room Temperature Superconductors – http://www.eetimes.com/document.asp?doc_id=1329419.

[53] SDN and SDS – http://searchservervirtualization.techtarget.com/tip/How-SDN-and-SDS-are-shaping-future-clouds.

[54] Drives Talk Directly to Ethernet – http://ceph.com/community/500-osd-ceph-cluster/.

[55] Ceph Likely the Preferred OpenStack Solution – http://redhatstorage.redhat.com/2015/10/26/latest-openstack-user-survey-shows-ceph-continues-to-dominate/.

[56] Legacy Problem – http://searchservervirtualization.techtarget.com/opinion/Moving-from-legacy-IT-to-a-private-cloud.

[57] NoE, NVMe Over an Ethernet Fabric – http://www.theregister.co.uk/2016/06/10/tegile_nvme_over_ethernet_is_future/.

[58] Building Object Stores Onto Each Drive – http://ceph.com/community/500-osd-ceph-cluster/.

[59] 2017 Should See the NoE Approach Hitting Mainstream – https://lcccna2016.sched.org/event/7JWK/scalable-storage-with-ethernet-disk-drives-kinetic-on-thellip.

[60] Tape Is Dead!" – http://www.networkcomputing.com/storage/tape-storage-really-dead/1521473970.

[61] The M2 Form-Factor – http://www.samsung.com/uk/consumer/memory-storage/memory-storage/ssd/MZ-V5P512BW.

[62] Data Problem – http://www.cloudtp.com/2015/10/27/12-step-guide-data-governance-cloud-first-world/.

[63] Latencies of WAN Traffic – http://www.techrepublic.com/article/dont-let-data-gravity-get-you-down-use-these-options-to-combat-cloud-latency/.

[64] Public Clouds Are At Least as Secure as In-house Datacenters – http://www.infoworld.com/article/3010006/data-security/sorry-it-the-public-cloud-is-more-secure-than-your-data-center.html.

[65] 256-Bit AES May be Broken – http://yournewswire.com/encryption-security-may-not-be-secure-anymore/.

[66] Google Throws Down the Gauntlet – http://www.bdlive.co.za/world/americas/2016/04/26/google-fiber-drives-down-us-internet-prices.

[67] Governance – http://blogs.gartner.com/andrew_white/2015/10/09/the-gathering-storm-information-governance-in-the-cloud/.

[68] Orphaned Copies of Critical Data – http://www.slideshare.net/DruvaInc/black-hat-2015-attendee-survey-the-challenge-of-data-sprawl.

[69] Governance Service Vendors – http://www.navigant.com/~/media/www/site/downloads/financial services/2016/fs_vendorsourcingandgovernanceservices_br_0116nocrops.pdf.

[70] Docker – https://www.docker.com/.

[71] Security Has Been an Issue – http://searchservervirtualization.techtarget.com/tip/Linux-container-security-is-on-the-evolutionary-fast-track.

[72] Storage, Too, Is Impacted by Containers – http://www.networkcomputing.com/storage/shrinking-storage-farm/1037538141.

[73] Will Private Datacenters and Clouds Justify Their Existence? – http://www.itbusinessedge.com/blogs/infrastructure/the-enterprise-data-center-can-it-last-in-the-cloud.html.

[74] Larger Companies Need to Think Like CSPs – http://www.nextplatform.com/2015/09/17/the-cloud-rains-down-on-enterprises/.

[75] SaaS Probably Will be the Cheapest Route Overall – http://www.zdnet.com/article/at-cloud-tipping-point-how-saas-is-becoming-the-status-quo/.

[76] 4 Year Life – http://www.tracetm.com/blog/it-asset-lifecycle-management-answers-when-is-it-time-to-replace-your-data-center/.

[77] Ratio of Staff to Gear Is Different – http://www.networkcomputing.com/careers/hello-automation-goodbye-it-jobs/1317550508.

[78] The In-house Datacenter Is a Threatened Species – http://www.forbes.com/sites/tomgillis/2015/09/02/cost-wars-data-center-vs-public-cloud/#3cb410a33e39.

[79] Fighting Back – http://www.networkcomputing.com/data-centers/enterprise-data-center-not-dead-yet/2010534008.

[80] Long Goodbye – http://www.emory.edu/EMORY_REPORT/erarchive/1998/March/ermarch.30/3_30_98FirstPerson.html.

Data Integrity

11

Ensuring that the data written to storage can be recovered over extended periods is a challenge. Storage gear fails at fairly high rates [1] at both the microscopic and macroscopic levels, and occasionally a bad design or a problem in the manufacturing process for drives can lead to failures occurring in whole batches of units in the field. Each of these failure mechanisms needs its own recovery tools.

Microscopic failures can be dealt with quickly. HDD have actual or latent defects in the recording media, while SSD may have a single die or a group of cells that collectively are failure prone. These flaws manifest as corrupted data blocks and all drives have them. In fact, the reason we created SCSI back in the 1980s was to overcome much higher flaw rates in media.

Drives today are "scrubbed" for errors prior to shipment, and bad blocks are aliased to good blocks. Every drive has a bad block table identifying where flaws live. In operation, flaw counts slowly grow, and each flaw is detected by a failure on reading. The mechanism to do this is a type of parity code created across all the data in a block and appended at the end. Early on, there was hope that this could allow flaws up to say 56 bits in length per block to be recovered, but the reality was that recovery couldn't be guaranteed, since the failure might be bigger or multiple error areas might exist in the bad block. These codes are now just used for detection of errors. Most drives today also have a background scanning task built in that looks for errors and marks any unreadable blocks as bad.

Clearly, the industry needed a better solution and by the mid-1980s replication of data was in vogue. This was considered expensive to do, and the industry searched around for better alternatives. A solution came in the form of RAID (redundant array of inexpensive disks [2]) using parity techniques to cut down the size of the protective codes.

In the early 1990s, EMC took RAID to an art-form level, with fast controllers and robust code. They rapidly built a reputation for having a bulletproof solution and most large enterprises became customers. In the process, EMC renamed RAID to mean redundant array of *independent* disks, given that their drive markups were very high and thus not "inexpensive"!

Roll forward to the early 2000s and we see a concept of data integrity at the appliance [3], rather than drive level, entering the market. The realization that data availability, being able to use the data at any time, was as important as data integrity led to some rethinking. RAID controller failures were mitigated by redundant controllers and redundant power supplies, etc., but the cost was high and the solution wasn't bulletproof. As storage farms increased in size, this was becoming a problem.

Replicating data [4] to multiple storage appliances was the alternative proposed. On the surface, this looked like mirroring or RAID 1, with the cost of doubling capacity, but all of that redundancy, plus the protectionism of the vendors had led to expensive dual-ported fibre-channel drives being used in RAID and, while these were being replaced by dual-ported SAS drives, the cost profile wasn't changing much.

The replication approach [5] uses single-port commodity drives at roughly 10% of the price per gigabyte. Moreover, appliances had no redundancy in controllers or switch boards and often just a single nonredundant PSU. The use of COTS motherboards in the head nodes and very inexpensive SAS switch designs made these new appliances very cost effective.

Traditional storage vendors reacted (after a while) by offering their own versions, mainly by acquiring start-up companies with the new products. Needless to say, drives became "Nearline" and proprietary and the markups were still high!

Still, replication offers the advantage that it covers disaster protection by allowing more than two copies, with at least one at a remote datacenter. Using this approach, the cloud storage farms got huge in the late 2000s. The cloud approach of striping data over many appliances also overcame one of RAID's big problems. As drives grew in size, rebuilding them after a drive failure took a longer time, and this was especially an issue with RAID 6 setups. In fact, it looked like a drive failure in a RAID set could be expected occasionally before the rebuild was complete. This is what drove the move from RAID 5 to RAID 6, which could tolerate two drives failing at the same time, but rebuilding looked to become high risk even with RAID 6 as drives passed through the 1 TB mark.

Replication comes at a price and new methods to give appliance-level protection with RAID-level capacity overhead were the focus of a lot of research, culminating in the idea of erasure coding data so that by expanding say 10 blocks to 16 there was protection from up to six drives or appliance failures.

Erasure coding [6] is now mainstream in tandem with replication. Using higher drive counts, it is possible to achieve geographic dispersion of the blocks and provide the same protection as replication. For example, using a 10 + 10 model and dispersing the data over four sites, any two sites could go down and the data are still available. Erasure coding approaches appear to be replacing RAID.

Calculating the erasure code syndromes is time consuming and for SSD is too slow. The result is that we see many appliances that journal write operations to an SSD mirror, then convert the data to erasure codes for writing to the final set of drives. This is not a very satisfactory situation, especially in the cloud where moving drives from failed appliance to be able to read their data is never going to happen.

Real-time erasure code calculation will be a critical storage capability by 2017, as we move to an all-SSD environment.

In the next sections, we'll examine how the protection approach works and what issues arise in a bit more detail.

RAID AND ITS PROBLEMS

David Patterson, Garth A. Gibson, and Randy Katz [7] at the University of California, Berkeley, in 1987 formulated the RAID (Redundant Array of Inexpensive Disks) concept as a way to protect against data loss caused by a drive failure. RAID evolved over time to include mirror copies of data on pairs of drives, as well as more complex schemes involving the generation of parity blocks and the striping of data+parity over a set of drives.

HOW RAID WORKS?

RAID is put together in a variety of configurations, known as RAID "levels" [8] (Fig. 11.1).

RAID Levels

RAID 1, mirroring is the fastest solution, but also uses the most disk capacity, at 2X the original. It is commonly used for journal files. Read operations typically access either copy, effectively doubling read speed, but the downside cost is that write operations take two sets of IOs.

   RAID 5, striping with parity, typically uses six drives in a stripe, balancing parity calculation with capacity overhead due to the parity blocks. The parity block rotates across the drive set, so that updates do not access the same parity drive for each block rewritten.

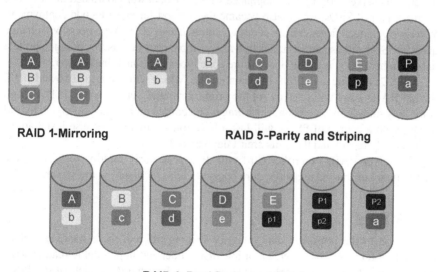

RAID 1-Mirroring   RAID 5-Parity and Striping

RAID 6-Dual Parity and Striping

FIGURE 11.1

Common RAID types.

RAID 6, double-parity, adds a second parity chunk to each stripe, also rotated around the drive set. This provides correction even if a second drive fails. The calculation of parity involves a diagonal process so that a write update involves reading the target block and two parity blocks, removing the old target block data from the parity calculations, generating new parity data from the new block and then writing all three blocks back to disk.

In both RAID 5 and RAID 6, calculating parity is time consuming. RAID controller boards are often used to offload the host, with high-speed Ex-Or capabilities to generate and check parity. Parity generation becomes a real chore with RAID 6 because these engines are not optimized for diagonal parity striping.

A whole bunch of RAID flavors grew out of the basic ideas of RAID 1 and 5. These (RAID 50, RAID 10, etc.) are combinations of both mirroring and parity, together with concatenating drives in series to make larger virtual drives.

RAID 5 was the workhorse of storage for two decades, until increasing drive capacities brought the realization that the probability of a second drive in a RAID volume failing before a bad drive was rebuilt on the spare. RAID 6 was the result, with a second parity calculated diagonally across chunks of data. Even this became an issue as drives reached several terabytes in capacity and so the writing was on the wall for RAID as and approach. This is called the "drive rebuild problem" [9].

Except for SSDs! The alternatives to RAID, such as erasure coding and replication, all had problems. While they overcame the drive rebuild issues, performance took a big hit if SSDs used erasure code protection. Replication also was usually deployed by the creating server writing to an appliance where the data were journaled in a RAID 1 mirrored pair of SSDs, which also became the method for erasure code deployment. When we get much faster erasure code generation late in 2016, the process will change quickly. SSDs will use direct replication across appliances or erasure coding to protect data. Another option is to use new erasure code types [10] that rebuild faster.

As SSDs become ubiquitous in the enterprise, which will occur in 2016 and 2017, the old RAID array will drop out of the primary storage tier altogether [11], though some may find a home as secondary storage for a couple more years. So-called hybrid arrays, with a couple of SSDs, will last a little longer, mainly because installations are relatively recent and the units aren't depreciated.

The server RAID controller card will disappear fairly rapidly, too. These are slower than host bus adapters. Erasure codes will be calculated in the server.

RAID MYTHS

In addition to the improved data integrity striping offered, there was a perceived benefit that IO would be faster if multiple drives operated in parallel to read or write data in a file. This was certainly true in the single-threaded IO models of the 1980s but most storage was rapidly evolving to multithreaded IO, where the parallel IO approach generally slowed performance down by increasing seek latency as a portion of total IO time. This is an important issue, because it frames many of the optimization decisions in later technology.

The thesis was that IOs would be shorter if all the drives in a RAID set transferred in parallel, breaking up a big transfer into a set of smaller transfers, called chunks that were written as a stripe across the set of RAID drives. As drive bit densities increased dramatically, we went from 32 KB per track to 2 MB per track. RAID, and for that matter everyone else including replication, followed the early guidance for chunk sizes and increased very slowly from 8 or 16 KB to only 64 KB, with the result that payload time in a transfer (the amount of time actually reading or writing on the disk) dropped from around 70% to just 5% of the total operation time.

We still struggle with chunk size [12]. In object storage, too big a chunk size means an object is all on one drive and there is no IO parallelism, but if multiple objects are being loaded in parallel using large chunks is probably the fastest way to load them all. With big files it doesn't matter as long as the number of drives used to store a file is large enough to saturate the servers during load. Still, it's a complex issue that depends on use cases and one, moreover, that is neglected by admins because there is little guidance on the process of choosing a chunk size.

Don't be beguiled by the argument that small chunks force IO to be parallel and therefore faster. That was true only with single-threaded IO systems about 25 years ago! Today's drives are hit by large IO queues and that's the level to optimize at. There is a finite number of IOs per cluster of drives and using six of them (say) to get a tiny object while the same six IOs could have gotten six bigger objects is a poor way to optimize.

With SSDs, the chunking problem is very different. Mostly, it doesn't matter as long as the chunk is substantial enough to amortize the IO setup time in booth host and SSD. 64-KB chunks probably achieve that well, though 256 KB might match Windows transfer sizes better.

REPLICATION

Replication is a simple concept [13]. Just make extra copies of the data! It comes loaded with subtleties, however, and it isn't as simple and straightforward as one might assume.

In one sense, replication is the grown-up version of RAID 1 mirroring. A weakness of RAID is that data protection is contained completely with the storage appliance. Efforts to protect against the controller or power supply failing meant proprietary controller hardware and redundant power supplies and other features and essentially doubled the cost of storage. In fact redundancy may have driven users to buy products that were much more than double the price, since the complexity of redundancy limited the vendor base.

Replication is a mirroring scheme where each copy is on a different storage appliance. Now there is no need for any redundancy at the individual appliance basis, and the cost of that appliance can be much lower. COTS drives can be used instead of expensive enterprise class dual-ported drives. The result is a drop in the price of storage that may be as much as 5X overall, depending on whether you buy white boxes or traditional vendors' products.

Replication also works between datacenters and most object stores, following the AWS S3 model, have one copy of data replicated asynchronously to a remote datacenter site. This allows a much easier recovery in zone failures, which are rare events but ones that do happen. Experience during a major AWS outage a few years back was that sites using a remotely backed copy were up and running very quickly, while the sites with just local copies languished for as much as 48 h.

Even though the paradigm calls for cheap drives for storage and not dual-port units, the fact that three replicas mean 3X, the raw storage is an issue with replication approaches. However, for critical workloads that need high availability, having a ready-to-go copy remotely is the ultimate assurance of availability. Some companies even keep four or more replicas active, so that work load can be spread out on a site failure.

The need to create replicas is a performance hit, as we've seen previously. In the ideal world, replicas are created at the host server and distributed directly to the storage nodes. This prevents the need for retransmission. The reality is that this slows down processing jobs, since the work has to wait for the last replica to flag write complete. If this were a remote copy, computing would be slow indeed.

Compromise is needed and the answer is to write the data from the host server out to an ingesting appliance that does all the replication work in background. In one sense, we are cheating since there is a finite window where the only copies of the data are on the ingestor. With the no-repair approach this is a problem—who is going to move the drives to a working server?

We therefore need a better approach. The safest and fastest solution is that the two local copies are written directly by the host server. If these have persistent DRAM, the performance of writes in this situation is very good, since RDMA basically can place the data directly into the memory of the storage nodes.

Still, there is always that extra capacity cost associated with replication and 3X or more bandwidth results from all the copies and the associated communications.

ERASURE CODING

Erasure coding [14] is sort of the RAID 5 of appliance-level integrity. Protection is achieved by mapping K data chunks into N chunks of data + parity. The N chunks are then written out to N storage devices, which often are N different appliances. The algorithm used to create the erasure codes is designed so that reading any set of K drives allows reconstruction of the original data. With typical values of $K=10$ and $N=16$, that means that six drives or appliances can fail before data is lost.

Now, we can remotely protect data, just as with replication, but with a much higher level of assurance. Let's set $K=10$ and $N=20$. That's as much storage used as local replication. If, however, we put 10 copies in the local site and 5 in each of 2 remote sites, any one site can go down and the data is available and still protected against further 5 drives or nodes going down. That needs three copies in the replication model, and we only get total of three node protection. So erasure coding saves space and lowers bandwidth needs.

That looks pretty powerful, but there is a computing cost to generating longer codes and this limits practical use today. The calculation for the example takes too long to be used with any fast SSD. The slowdown would almost bring the SSD back into HDD range and would eat up most of the computing power in the server to boot.

The result is that we typically use an indirect method to protect data with erasure codes. This involves the host server writing to a mirrored SSD journal file in an ingestor storage node. Writes post "complete" very quickly, but as was said in the previous section, no one will move the drives to a working server if the ingestor fails.

The erasure codes for the journaled data are created as an asynchronous background job and the data is either stored on drives in the node or spread out over a set of nodes (Storing data in the same node leaves it vulnerable to node failure, and isn't the best policy, by far).

We'll see the erasure coding speed problem resolved by 2017, making a major change in the way dataflows are processed. The best solution, of creating the erasure codes in the host server and forwarding the resulting N chunks directly to storage nodes will be feasible, and this will make erasure codes the storage approach for all but the most demanding performance use cases. Erasure code technology is still evolving and new code schemes such as regenerating codes and locally repairable [15] codes may help the rebuild problem.

A couple of further comments. Strictly speaking, RAID 5 and RAID 6 are simple forms of erasure coding, but their intent and use is within a single-storage node and the resulting protection guards against too few drive failures [16] as previously said.

There is another way to create erasure codes, aiming to reduce the amount of extra chunks needed even further. Compute power goes up with the number of syndrome chunks needed, so a scheme that uses less extra chunks is attractive. $12+4$ schemes have been described that allow up to four failures but achieve recovery from as few as 5 or 6 drives. The problem is that they cannot guarantee recovery from all failures of four drives, which makes them of limited value. The lower "compute cost" of recovery is not a good offset for potential data loss, and anyway will be moot once accelerated erasure code processing is available.

It is theoretically possible to create coding schemes where $K=200$ and $N=210$, for example. These give very low-overhead levels (just 5% for up to 10 drives failing), but the compute cost scales with set size and the time to code up or recover will be too long for real-time operation. This could be an excellent approach to archiving, however. Archiving, incidentally, is characterizable as a write-once read-occasionally process, with the potential of higher drive failure rates over the long life of the stored element. That sounds like a good match for a slower creation process, but one tolerant of a lot of failures.

DISASTER PROTECTION IN THE CLOUD

The cloud looks like the ultimate data repository. It's cheap, easy to use, and fast enough. There are enough resources that are self-repairing and data can be recovered from anywhere, anytime. Backup and archiving though are a passive type of data protection. They capture what data was, not what it is. There is a value in static, passive protection [17], since a fair number of data problems are caused by human error or deliberate hacking and active data normally has little or no protection against these.

Protecting against human-induced disasters requires a bit of strategy. Suppose that we have a system where the data is never overwritten or deleted. That means more capacity will be needed to store all the versions, but it also means that one can dial back to any point in time and recreate an earlier version of a file or object. This approach is essentially snapshotting of the data system but at a very fine granularity.

In such a system, we'd only be storing the blocks or chunks that are changed, so the impact to total storage capacity is much less than if we rewrite the object with its revisions as a new object. Any system doing this type of perpetual storage has to have a mechanism for tiering out the older chunks that have a newer replacement, so freeing up primary storage for current stuff. We also need to distinguish delete commands as meaning, "Get rid of the object" or "Hide the object from my file systems" and a few other nuances.

We aren't at this point yet, but we are close with some of the latest firmware implementations for appliances and all-flash arrays. Even databases can be treated this way, too.

What to do with the old data? Back *it up and archive it* in one shot! Send the data out to the cloud. It might hit secondary storage for a while, and it may be economical to let it sit there, because low-cost commodity drives and appliances, plus compression and deduplication should make that storage pretty cheap. Inevitably, it will hit the cloud, where there are two or three hierarchies of performance. Using all of these layers is counterproductive, and a read of the small print in the cloud contracts shows that fees for moving data from one service to another can be expensive.

The bottom line is that three tiers are enough. So, does primary storage that just got overwritten or deleted go straight to Nearline or Glacier? Does it go through in-house secondary storage? Do I even need in-house secondary storage and should I use S3's top tier instead?

These are all questions that require a lot of thought today. Pricing changes rapidly. Code is not quite there in the tools available. WAN speeds are abysmal. What works best?

The answer is subject to use cases, but remember that if good replication or backup processes are in place, there will be a replica of the current data at all times in the cloud (or remote datacenter) on some storage. This will be the remote copy in replication, for instance. This means that no additional transfer is required. It's more a housekeeping issue but not a trivial one. This means a tool capable of recovering individual objects as well as volumes or buckets.

Assuming that we have achieved the goal of perpetual data storage, we need to decide if that's really what is needed. Perhaps we need to consider mechanisms to delete files after 7 years, to be compliant. The challenge now is we are really deleting the discarded chunks of objects that meet the time-out criteria—we don't want to discard chunks we still use or ones that are less aged.

All of this is within the scope of today's tools but not yet cohesively structured. That will probably get fixed as we move ahead with better software, especially when SDS really hits its stride. One consideration is the security and integrity of the process for archiving and any final deletions. This has to be bulletproof, not only against equipment failure but also against human error and malice. At a minimum, access to command and control of the archives, as opposed to query and read retrieval, has to be limited to a few trusted individuals and audited as often as possible.

On another plane, when failures occur, an automated recovery process is needed. Normally, this is in the hands of the Cloud Service Provider, but hybrid clouds require local policies and procedures, including recovery from either in-house failures or public-cloud failures up to the failure of a whole site or zone.

Zone failures usually come about from a router problem, though a major natural disaster could cause problems. Google, for example, has sites in Northern California and a big quake could take out those zones. Recovery could imply rebuilding replicas on the one copy left, in someone's cloud. Good practice is to have a circuit breaker on the normal rebuild process in such a situation because the LANs would all saturate with rebuild traffic, and the resulting traffic jams would last many hours. Often in such situations the best practice is to put rebuilding on hold and only create replicas for newly written data.

The bottom line is that the cloud and replication allow a much more robust approach to disaster recovery than we've had in the past. Well implemented, service could be returned to normal in minutes to hours, rather than the days to weeks of the old tape-based approach. That's enough reason in itself to use a cloud approach!

REFERENCES

[1] Storage gear fails at fairly high rates. https://www.backblaze.com/blog/hard-drive-reliability-stats-for-q2-2015/.

[2] Redundant array of inexpensive disks. https://www.howtoforge.com/redundant-array-of-inexpensive-disks-raid-technical-paper.

[3] Data integrity at the appliance. http://www.networkcomputing.com/storage/going-all-ssd-side-effects/732249354.

[4] Replicating data. http://www.zerto.com/blog/dr/dr-101-synchronous-a-synchronous-and-near-synchronous-replication-technologies/.

[5] Replication approach. http://www.snia.org/sites/default/files/SDC15_presentations/datacenter_infra/Shenoy_The_Pros_and_Cons_of_Erasure_v3-rev.pdf.

[6] Erasure coding. http://www.computerweekly.com/feature/Erasure-coding-vs-Raid-for-disk-rebuilds.

[7] D. Patterson, G.A. Gibson, R. Katz. http://www.computerhistory.org/storageengine/u-c-berkeley-paper-catalyses-interest-in-raid/.

[8] RAID "levels". http://www.dell.com/support/article/us/en/04/SLN292050?c=us&l=en&s=bsd&cs=04.

[9] Drive rebuild problem. https://www.servint.net/university/article/even-ssd-longer-enough-ensure-quality-service-hosting/.

[10] New erasure code types. https://storagemojo.com/2013/06/21/facebooks-advanced-erasure-codes/.

[11] RAID array will drop out of the primary storage tier altogether. http://wikibon.org/wiki/v/Is_RAID_Obsolete%3F.

[12] Struggle with chunk size. http://www.computerweekly.com/RAID-chunk-size-the-key-to-RAID-striping-performance.

[13] Replication is a simple concept. http://www.storagenewsletter.com/rubriques/market-reportsresearch/caringo-carpentier/.

[14] Erasure coding. http://www.snia.org/sites/default/files/JasonResch_Erasure_Codes_SDC_2013.pdf.

[15] Regenerating codes and locally repairable. https://storagemojo.com/2013/06/21/facebooks-advanced-erasure-codes/.

[16] Protection guards against too few drive failures. http://www.networkcomputing.com/storage/raid-vs-erasure-coding/1792588127.

[17] Value in static, passive protection. http://www.cioinsight.com/it-strategy/cloud-virtualization/slideshows/ten-ways-to-ensure-disaster-protection-in-the-cloud.

Data Security

12

What is the cost of losing your data? As various instances recently have shown, the cost can run into the millions of dollars, while CEOs and CIOs find the events to be severely career-limiting. With all that hoopla around famous hacks and the pain for the customers whose credit data were compromised, one would think that business would be intensely security-conscious.

Sadly, that isn't the case. A study in 2015 showed that only 30% of the major retailers [1] could have resisted the attacks in 2014. That's a sorry state of affairs, but given the fact that executives get fired over this [2], one would be excused for wondering if IT in these organizations has a death wish.

The problem is bound to get worse. There is huge money to be made from hacking and it is a hard crime to crush. Most hackers don't get caught; they hide behind Tor and other clever cyber-masks and may even have help from government agencies or their former employees.

There are plenty of tools to deploy against hacker. We have firewalls, intrusion detection software, and multipart authentication systems, for example, but the truth is that we have to assume that a hacker will get into our systems at some point, doing damage or stealing data.

The advent of the cloud has thrown the security issue onto the table almost as much as hacking has—"Clearly the cloud is insecure"—hooted the marketeers from 2006 to 2014, but they were trying to sell you systems for in-house use. The truth was much less black and white. In fact, by 2015, Gartner was telling the world that the cloud is as secure as the best in-house operations [3].

Looking at the cloud issue, though, is a good way to figure out how to really solve in-house security problems. We can learn how to deal with BYOD (Bring Your Own Device), POS (Point of Sale), and IoT (Internet of Things) by looking at how the mega-CSPs (Certified Safety Professionals) deliver safe service to millions of co-tenanted users every minute of the day. The cloud is a shining example of how to do things right, and while the average business has resources nowhere near those of AWS or Azure to develop security systems, one shouldn't be so proud as not to emulate their best practices [4].

Even so, there are cloud weaknesses [5]. While cross-tenant interaction is all but ruled out during operations by software design and some features provided in the CPU for this purpose, mistakes do occur, such as being able to read an instance store solid-state drive (SSD) after the tenant has closed an instant. Encryption, which is a powerful tool against the black-hatters, is so poorly deployed that one might weep. Moreover, we are moving a Software-Defined model [6] that makes everything more evanescent and difficult to track.

Network Storage. http://dx.doi.org/10.1016/B978-0-12-803863-5.00012-1

SDS makes the protection of the control plane [7] networks a crucial factor in security. Because most virtual infrastructure is temporary, setup traffic is likely to be very high compared with traditional networks. This traffic also suffers from having highly predictable content. Commands are in standard formats, and are anyway very short, which gives a hacker ideal conditions for breaking in. Once in, the damage extra commands can do is scary. It ranges from deleting volumes or objects, to reverting versions, to reading files or writing fake data.

The next sections discuss these issues in more detail.

LOSING YOUR DATA

It's worth examining in more detail some of the ways data can be lost to a hacker. There's a movie image of the hacker as a geeky 14-year-old with a joystick in one hand and a keyboard under the other. In reality, while the geeky kids do exist, most of them are just nuisances and rarely get into a real system.

The real problems come from the grown-ups who make hacking a serious business [8]. These are people who know a lot about systems and networks, and how operating systems and tools try to protect data. At least a few come from government agencies [9] where they've worked or more likely been a contractor with access to privileged information on hacking techniques and targets. In other words, they are professional, and for want of a better word, are professional thieves.

Assume that these enemies are very smart and very determined. Most, but by no means all, are after financially useful information, such as credit card details, bank accounts or personal profile data that might be embarrassing (been on any dating sites recently???). Once they get these data, they sell it on, usually several times, to people who pull the funds from compromised accounts.

Not all of the data are financial, though. Spies [10] use the same approach to getting data. They are looking for trade secrets or the personal details of government employees, but they also look where they can do damage in the case of hostilities. Infrastructure such as utilities and communications come to mind immediately.

Some of this spying is quasi-overt [11]. The US National Security Administration (NSA) is looking at a huge data flow from cell-phones [12]. They have a mandate to look outside the US and to monitor any communications coming in and out of the US, but they've stretched the rules via Bush's Patriot Act to monitor US traffic too. After all, the technology is sited in communications hubs and doesn't really care where calls are going!

NSA also gets feed of "processed" data from other countries [13], notably the UK. The strict interpretation of the US law allows such data to be used even if it involves purely US citizens in the US. It is also worth noting that metadata is almost as useful as the call or email contents, since it gives pointers to people contacting known terrorist sites or using arcane crypto. NSA is not above feeding novel encryption to unsuspecting terrorist and criminal wannabes. Of course, using that encryption is an instant red flag [14].

There have been rumors that some countries use their top-notch spying services to help commercial operations win deals [15]. In this sense, government snooping is in no way benign, even if the snoopers are "looking at the best interests of the country". This ranges from stealing design docs for fighter planes to bid details for international contracts.

The point of this is that IT is swimming in a sea full of hungry sharks. Protecting your data is crucial. This is true even for smaller companies. You might argue that hackers only go after the big guys, but reality is that many small companies are wide open to exploits. They don't have any real security, don't much care and don't consider there is enough "stuff" in IT to be worth stealing.

This is low-hanging fruit for data thieves. There is a major campaign behind every loudly publicized hack. A good hack on JP Morgan [16] takes months of planning and probing, and may require a few insiders to be bribed.

Misguided efforts at protection are rife too. As I write, the US government has just published a GAO analysis of the $6 Billion "National Cybersecurity Protection System (NCPS)". This piece of incompetent spending has delivered a solution that catches only 29 out of 489 total vulnerabilities [17] in Adobe Flash and other products. That, to put it mildly, is embarrassing [18] and many heads should roll!

The point is that throwing money at the problem doesn't necessarily solve it. We need a good plan and diligent execution to make this work. We also need app vendors to take encryption seriously [19].

So what sort of exploits are we talking about? We are not going to look at the vulnerabilities of servers or operating systems, which would be a book of its own. The scope of the discussion is limited to what can happen to data that are stored or transmitted on the storage networks.

First, a bit of terminology. There are four states of data. Data being processed is the server's province and in the main we'll skip the issues. Data at rest are data in some form of storage, whether in the server, the storage nodes, or a virtual SAN. Data in transit have data in the network, buzzing down copper and fibre lines. Each of these data-states has its own set of risks and appropriate remedies. Finally, data get old and perhaps somewhat irrelevant. It becomes cold data and are moved into some archiving system.

DATA AT REST

Most data have relatively short periods when they are valuable. After a while, data become irrelevant or is superseded, but laws and common-sense require it to be kept. Keeping storage uncluttered by the obsolete is part of a good security system for data at rest. While some things are apparently valueless, they might give hackers insights into current operations. An example might be an old business plan erased from an executive's computer. The data are a bit old, but the gameplan hasn't changed!

Another major source of data sprawl [20] is the natural tendency to keep copies in an organization. I remember in the early days of spreadsheets having a budget template sent to each manager. When we received them back, over 70% had mods in the calculation and parameters section, and every spreadsheet had the same original name! If you look in any file server, you'll see the same sprawl of identical files, mixed with nonidentical files with the same name. Sorting that out is a glorious mess!

HIPAA [21], SOX [22], and other regulations place requirements [23] on keeping a lot of patient or client data. Access has to be tightly controlled and data should be stored encrypted. That has led to plenty of misunderstandings. Who has the encryption keys? AWS and others offer to encrypt data using built in systems on drives. That's a great idea, except, first, the drives support only 32 unique keys [24], in at least one case, and what's more, with plenty of those drives around finding the keys is easy; and second, the keys are in the hands of the CSP and not the data owner and that is a no–no under the laws for financial or medical data.

The third major issue is **protecting access to the data** itself [25]. Why share a network between storage and Internet traffic? People do it all the time. It's a combination of being cheap (one network is cheaper than several), sloppy (not thinking through the issues) and under-informed.

As soon as a network is exposed to the outside world, it is going to be vulnerable to attack. That means the storage servers will be bombarded. That also means traffic on the network might be sniffed. Why not just start with a physical firewall? One might argue that VLANS do this, but remember the SDN issue and that networks exposed to the outside are exposed period!

Anyway, as we have seen in many places in this book, storage network performance is critical to maximizing configuration value. The storage net needs all the bandwidth it can get, and sharing with the Internet will slow it down a lot. Practically, when storage is exposed to the Internet, say in REST services from the cloud, having a gateway device between the storage node and the Internet may be very good practice, making it impossible to directly see the storage cluster.

Let's get back to **the encryption issue** [26]. Data is often stored for extended periods. This means a LOT of data in storage over time, even with the aggressive pruning we just talked about. In a sense, the vulnerability of your data is in direct ratio to its size. The bigger the target, the easier it is to hit. Even more, the chances of a mistake leaving a weak spot in defense goes up with size, and probably more like exponentially than linearly.

The longer data is kept, the more likely it is to become unwatched and relatively unprotected. We used to relegate it to tapes that were never read. As they aged, they were thrown out, often without being erased. A good rule of thumb is that all media must be scrubbed, and/or crushed and incinerated prior to disposal. Drive companies love that since no drive is ever returned after failing. This is really important with clouds, since CSPs don't know what data are on the drives, shouldn't look, and probably have no time to peek anyway.

Any drives removed from platforms should be locked up, tracked, and the whole process regularly audited—likewise with tape or other media. Sending this to the salt mine is a decent way to preserve it, but remember that hard disks develop stiction problems as they sit powered down for years, with issues in motors and positioners as well as between the heads and the disk. Tape develops adherence issues and should be spooled regularly to protect data.

The bigger issue is **current data at rest** [27]. The best protection by far is end-to-end encryption, often called source encryption [28]. This means generating a key in the server that creates the data and encrypting all stored data before it goes onto the LAN. The problem, as we've said before, is that encryption is far too slow today because of hardware constraints in CPUs. The result is a trade-off between security and performance and usually security loses. Getting a good encryption scheme for active data is a high priority for the industry.

Data are sometimes encrypted after arriving in a storage appliance, following compression and/or deduplication. This can be effective in protection against a hack that reaches the storage appliance directly, but is less effective than host-generated security, since the output of the appliance is unencrypted plaintext that could be read by anyone on the LAN into the storage appliance. Good authentication provides some protection against this happening, but once in a hacker has access to everything with storage appliance side encryption.

Drive-based encryption is a temptation, but it appears only in HDDs because of performance issues, although that may change. There are tremendous risks involved [29], since the key selection may be very limited and the encryption class too weak (128-bit keys, for instance). Such drives are worse than useless, since they lull the user into a false sense of security while costing considerably more than standard drives.

We also have to worry about where data are resting. Instance stores [30] and persistent NVDIMM memories are potential trouble spots. A related problem is the security of virtual SAN storage [31]. In all three cases, active data are being kept in the server, so there is no physical barrier between LANs or appliances. If the server talks to the Internet, storage may be exposed.

Here, data are most probably unencrypted at rest. This is because expected data access is of very low latency and ultrahigh bandwidth. In the case of locally used memory, that doesn't matter in operation, but the natural progression of technology is to tie the three types of fast local memory into virtual SANs or similar sharing schemes to allow clustering to take place efficiently.

Each server in the cluster usually has direct Internet connection or connection to a user LAN with many tenants. This makes the shared local data model more vulnerable than the dedicated storage appliance model. If any single server is hacked, it potentially gives access to all of the virtual SAN. Segregating servers in the clusters using VLANs may offer some protection, but the shifting nature of VLANs in these clusters might be an issue that is hard to control.

Instance stores [32] using SSD suffer from pseudoerase problems, where deleting files doesn't actually get rid of the blocks on the device due to overprovisioning. The deleted blocks are moved to the overprovisioned side of the drive and replaced with fresh spare blocks, so when a tenant decommits an instance, there is the possibility that tenant's data still exist on the drive. A new tenant might then be able to read it by executing a command that provides access to all the space on the drive.

There are a couple of ways to deal with this. One is to only allow reading by a tenant of blocks that tenant has written to. Any block that is allocated to the tenant but not yet written to is returned as all-ones or all-zeroes, irrespective of the contents. This protects data from previous tenants. The alternative is to do an explicit erase of the blocks by writing all-zero data. Currently, such overwrite capability is only available to the operating system.

Deleting of hard-drive data also had a leave-behind effect. Delete normally just flags the data as unwanted and doesn't explicitly overwrite the block contents. In either SSD or HDD cases, you will need a solidly tested policy on how to handle this issue in your cluster or private cloud. For public clouds, the methods of protection differ and you should find out how the CSP protects your data and be satisfied it works for your needs.

Don't be fobbed of with hand waving by the CSP. There have been reports of reading another tenant's data [33] on a "deleted" SSD instance. One user saw 20 GB of someone else's files.

DATA IN TRANSIT

There are a number of well-known exploits for data moving around [34] in the networks. Spoofing the traffic by getting data routed to a hacking device or piece of software is a man-in-the-middle attack. With SDI, this is likely easier, since the intruding node could be a hacker's app running in a virtual machine or container.

The solution is again encryption of the data before it leaves the host server. In fact, keeping the data encrypted on the round-trip-out and back-to-storage is by far and away the best plan. With the performance problem as yet unresolved, this may mean only applying round-trip encryption to critical data, but that involves some serious data management and mistakes will happen.

Keeping storage on its own network not only safeguards data at rest. It protects data in transit.

SDI will bring some new challenges. With networks regularly changing and structures lasting for minutes, protecting the "control plane" that sets up switches, etc., becomes a major priority. The same answer comes to mind that applies to the data side. Keep things on their own network. The problem here is that the avowed aim of SDI is to use data services tied in to VMs to achieve control of data and this is 180 degrees from network separation, since the control plane needs access to VMs to do its job. In the end, this is an orchestration task and authentication and security at the orchestration level are still not well thought out for SDI, as opposed to fixed architectures.

COLD DATA

Today, cold data [35] usually means data stored cheaply in the cloud. We covered a lot of this in Chapter 10, but here it's worth touching on the implications of backup a bit more. For many in IT, backup and archiving is a write-once-read-never experience and it's rated pretty lowly. Many consider that replication systems are adequate protection for data, especially if they follow the S3 model with one replica geographically distant.

But wait, replicas are still active data. If I delete a file, all the replicas eventually go away. If it is hacked, all the copies are hacked. Replication does not protect against admin finger trouble or hackers, or software errors in their many forms. Backup, snapshots, and archiving are all necessary to protect data.

Assuming that you've figured out your data lifecycle policies and can demonstrate legal compliance, what does backup and archiving look like? Backup most likely is incremental backup, with the ability to restore to points in time with a self-consistent data set and app modules. Copies still exist on the primary storage, which is an important point, since it obviates a lot of caching requirements for the backed up data.

Archiving goes a step further, insofar as the copies in primary storage are deleted. Both backup and archiving are two-replica storage solutions. These need to be geographically distributed replicas, especially with archive data. This brings up the how and where of storage with the CSP.

Adjacent datacenters offer no geographic dispersion, for example, and tape media brings up the spooling issue, even if it is Glacier's tapes doing the storage. Disk systems raise the question of how long drives are allowed to remain inactive. Governance requires you know the answers!

It's crucial that access to the archives is tightly controlled. First, data in the archives are usually important, almost always a trade secret and, unfortunately, prone to out-of-sight, out-of-mind. That means that illegal access might not be spotted. The best solution is to limit who is allowed access and to periodically change the locks. Detection of high levels of archive extraction are also a flag that something is going on that needs investigation, since outsiders usually don't know where the data they want live and may just dump bulk data to search at their leisure.

Limiting access is critical. Much data loss occurs from insider activity [36]. It's much easier to audit two people every month than the whole firm! Does this apply just to write and deletion commands? Or does it also restrict who can read data in the archives. The latter is more secure of course, since it protects against former employees and disgruntled admins. It all comes down to your company's policies.

It goes without saying that archives and backups are encrypted at source. This may mean decrypting the original stored files and then re-encrypting them with different keys to keep out any departmental types that have gone rogue, or alternatively using superencryption, where a second encryption is applied to all data irrespective of whether it is already encrypted or not.

Snapshots are another way of protecting against the software bug/finger trouble/hacker triumvirate. Snapshots [37] allow files/objects, volumes or images to be rolled back to a point in time. Provided the bug or hack is cleaned up, it's possible to recover back before a virus or whatever hit. Usually, some data is lost but the result is self-consistent and journal files may be adequate to complete missing transactions. Make sure the journal file isn't cleared until a snapshot is taken!

Using Snapshots tends to add a lot of extra stored data. It's useful if your software allows for building a clean copy and relegating the snapshots to archival storage. Remember how snapshots work. When a block is updated, a new block is created and linked into the block chain. This happens each time an update occurs, while appends add blocks and deletes remove them. The old block is kept, and the file or object structure for the previous version still points to it as the correct block for that version.

It's thus possible to rebuild any version of the file, but the process can get quite slow if there are a lot of changes. There's no need to burden the system with all of this, nor take up extra capacity in primary memory. Done properly, this demotion process can be a background job.

PROTECTING CLOUD DATA

Much of what has been discussed about data protection applies equally to the cloud. The one problem for a tenant is that physical infrastructure is invisible to tenants in most cases, though a deliberate hack to a virtual machine in a hypervisor might find a way into the rest of the cloud. CSPs work very hard to prevent this and, other than a case of data not erased on an instance store SSD, they seem to succeed.

Because the infrastructure is so virtual, physical protection concepts like separate storage LANs are at the mercy of the CSP rather than in the tenant's control. The same would be true if the CSP created virtual SAN structures to take advantage of persistent NVDIMM and instance drives.

Connectivity of all these pieces is under the control of the orchestration system, which should interpret the scripted requests for configuration changes in VLANs and prevent anomalies from messing up the system or the data. Good authentication is the key here and operations need to be encrypted, with source verification on all the messages passed to and from the control plane.

The challenge for the tenant is to decide who can alter the configurations. There will be huge pressure for central IT to delegate that capability to the departmental level and, in truth, that's where it belongs. This will only work if the scripts are produced using some template system with policy constraints [38] built in. The central team creates these with a view to making them foolproof. This, incidentally, applies to any datacenter where real or virtual SDN is used. If the scripts need to be formatted to OpenStack or AWS or whatever, there should be an appropriate script manager [39] or two to do the job, and likely a library of the most frequently used scripts.

The scripting process should use strong authentication to protect against abuse and all transactions should be logged and regularly audited.

We've already addressed encryption and the issues with instance drives in the previous section. Replica management and keeping the data stored or accessible to the cloud at a minimum is possibly low on most IT departments worry list, however. I remember seeing many file servers with redundant copies of files sprinkled everywhere and old directories of obsolete data drifting around.

Cloud storage is cheap and unlimited, so the old habits from file server days are likely to continue into the cloud. That means many pools of data lying around for no useful reason all of which are unmonitored and exposed to hacking. Having a global deduplication process that runs in the background will get rid of some of this, but proper lifecycle management tools enforcing policies on data are necessary to win the battle. Much of the data will come from departmental computing, so they will need policy control for their own data, within the policy guidelines set by central IT.

SOFTWARE-AS-A-SERVICE (SAAS)

The cloud approach has a unique problem in dealing with SaaS software and storage. Today, the trend is for SaaS vendors to use public clouds for their services, which makes sense since the workload tends to be diurnally variable and the cloud provides a cheap computing solution that's in line with renting software out. Indeed, some SaaS vendors offer pay as you go [40] rental agreements rather than fixed monthly subscription fees.

This raises a tough problem. Where is the data? Who controls it? The answer to the first is "in the cloud", but what service are we talking about and does it have geodiversity in storage? Don't assume that the vendor has their act together [41] on this issue. Protection costs money and there are budget versions of all the storage schemes that offer significantly less protection to the data.

Control of the data is another issue. Check if it is encrypted, and whether that's host-based or drive-based. Then the awkward question is who owns the keys. The SaaS vendor needs them to access your data, so they need a way to get them, which most likely means they keep them continuously since SaaS will tend to be a 24/7 environment from the users perspective even if evenings and weekends get little activity. Legal requirements constrain flexibility in this area, but SaaS vendors can access the data as your agent, provided they follow tight guidelines and allow regular governance audits.

It's important to get this right, since SaaS looks set to be the end-point of a lot of software evolutions. Backup, snapshot, and archiving should also be at a high standard and easily audited.

To complicate things, we are facing an era of the SaaS mashup [42], where more-than-one vendor gets to play on the data. This will bring together disparate companies that may share a common data pool or who my copy the data from a previous vendor in the chain. This adds the complication of losing synch between versions if any vendor has a failure plus the issue of keeping the data secure with such a broad exposure.

This won't just happen in noncritical operations. An example that's real is a video-editing hosting operation with a variety of specialized video-editing and effects companies under one roof. They all benefit from having the huge files that make up a movie in one place and can speed up editing by as much as 50% or more. Now this is really valuable IP we are talking about. What if it were Star Wars—$3 Billion dollars? But the gains in productivity and collaborative synergy may complete the job much better, faster and cheaper, offsetting the risks to data security. I bet the producers of the movie vet the operations very thoroughly before using them!

Security techniques in the clouds, both public and private are continuing to evolve. There is a penalty for not having fast, cheap encryption that potentially exposes everyone right now. This isn't a cloud problem. It's more a hardware vendor issue and as I've said elsewhere, one that should be addressed within a year or so.

HYBRID CLOUDS AND DATA GOVERNANCE

Hybrid clouds complicate the security and governance issue both because there are multiple entities to deal with, each with their own rules and agendas and because these entities, or rather their data flows, have to interact efficiently. It seems likely that the hybrid cloud concept [43] won't stop at one private cloud and one public cloud. Rather, several of each may be involved and the mix may change slowly over time. SaaS vendors, with their changing vendor base, may add to the stress on the IT governance system.

The security issue is mostly covered in the previous section but recognizing that all of the issues are now multiplied by the set of cloud vendors means that rules need to be structured for each service, while a system to keep them coherent and to create a single governance strategy [44] and architecture is needed. This implies maintaining different script libraries for each cloud, for example, but there is also the deeper need to understand how the CSPs and SaaS vendors manage their governance processes [45] and to qualify them fit for use.

One of the challenges faced with hybrid as opposed to single site clouds is the transition of governance as data moves between cloud entities. It's no good having a full data-lifetime management schema in your private cloud if the data are moving into or out of a cloud with little control.

One might argue that the lifecycle management issue is addressed by tools that sit in the cloud. This is true, but the tools have to be rigorously applied. Here are a couple of instances that could easily occur. A departmental marketer creating a video for a new product jobs out editing to a third party residing in a cloud. The marketer transfers a bunch of files to the cloud. All this is done ad hoc and with typical avoidance of the governance rules. Another scenario—the sales department likes a SaaS CRM package and signs up. They do this without asking IT, since it is just a service. Key customer data reside in the cloud without any governance.

Many departmental types don't see the value of the governance system, while having the budget flexibility to buy as they want. This is part of the shadow IT nightmare [46] that plagues many companies. Mobile-use just makes the problem even more difficult.

Fixing all the problems of shadow IT and mobile abuse would merit a book all of its own, but some comments from a data storage perspective may help address the issues. In many ways, governance is an ease-of use issue. Make a complex procedure oriented system for governance and no one but IT will use it. Being dictatorial will cause hackles to rise and with department and divisional heads holding much of the power in a corporation that will not go well.

THE MODERN GOVERNANCE APPROACH

A governance system has to be all but invisible. Build company data repositories in all the useful clouds. Some suggestions:

Make it easy to add or remove objects to these clouds, all the while making the data subject to controls.

Publish lists of precertified SaaS vendors. This focuses buying decisions, especially if there is a company negotiated discount.

Encrypt data exiting the company; only vendors with the keys can see the data, and if central IT holds those! This means end-runs are more difficult.
Audit monthly, which means some automation.
Decide if some data may never be copied and shipped out of the in-house operation and automate its protection.
Be very responsive to requests for help or innovation.

Central IT needs to operate with a service mentality. The organization is aiming to add value to the data process, but if IT is seen as a nay-saying gate-keeper the customers at the departmental level will take the line of least resistance and do their own thing in the cloud. That's what caused shadow IT to appear in the first place!

ENCRYPTION

Encryption is a really old way to keep secrets. Julius Caesar used it [47], but it was old then. We've come a long way since stick cyphers, though. Today's schemes are very robust and designed to make brute-force cracking tough to do.

Passwords or cypher keys can be surprisingly short. Eight-character is 256 bits, for instance, but most passwords fail on common guessable words (of which password, a frequent default, is the most common). Encryption goes beyond that and usually creates a string of random 8-bit characters.

Current cyphering technology uses the cypher key to initiate a sequence of mathematical processes using complicated binary arithmetic. This prevents the impact of repetitive keys from weakening the encryption. These approaches are a balance of performance and security level.

Governments certify the reliability of cyphers, while academics get their jollies from attempting to crack them. As computers get more powerful, and as renting a cloud space drops in price, the amount of horsepower these legal hacking exercises can deploy increases. As a result, weaker versions of encryption become insecure over time. An example is the much-used AES encryption [48], which is now no longer recommended with 128-bit keys.

IMPORTANT ENCRYPTION SCHEMES

A good rule of thumb is that the longer the key, the better the encryption. There is a very clever private key/public key encryption scheme, often called RSA [49], which uses the product of two very large prime numbers to generate part of a key system. With a bit more manipulation, a public key is generated that can be sent out to anyone. The recipient can encrypt data using the public key, with the only way to decrypt it being a different private key.

RSA is considered way too difficult to break with today's computers. Unfortunately, even with acceleration, encryption is slow because of the key size and math complexity, so we use RSA to just pass the AES code between pairs when setting up a secure socket, rather than for all data transmissions.

The AES code superseded the Data Encryption Standard (DES) algorithm [50] a few years ago. Mathematically and computationally, it is much simpler than RSA, but its level of protection is also reduced. Even so, with a 256-bit key, the US Government supports its use for Top-Secret files. AES is used for media streaming to prevent movie piracy, as well as in the Secure Sockets Layer (SSL) security approach common on LANs and the Internet.

There are rumors swirling that national agencies can break these codes [51]. It's probably true, at least with small key AES, but it takes a lot of horsepower, so the agency isn't likely to be looking at your video of your pet dog real soon! Of course, it does matter if you are a defense contractor. New cyphers are being tested, but the process is long-winded, due to the need to look for trapdoors and other vulnerabilities. AES 256 itself will probably be superseded before 2020, though.

The encryption schemes are currently deployed mainly in a SSL [52], which replaces the standard LAN Socket. To connect two nodes for secure communication, SSL uses RSA to set up an AES session key that is then used for all traffic between the nodes. Since SSL decrypts the data on receipt, this method doesn't protect the data at rest. That would require a storage node to re-encrypt, which means that node has key ownership which we have seen to be problematic, especially in the cloud.

COMMAND AND STATUS MESSAGES

There's another serious weakness of the SSL approach when used with storage. Standard encryption is good for long data packets, but a significant amount of short messages are created for commands and statuses. Worse, the format of these commands is very predictable, with many characters within a small range of choices. This amounts to knowing part of the plaintext of a message and could be used to dramatically shorten a brute force attack.

To make matters worse, unless the underlying communication system has a way of identifying the sequence of messages, a hacker could insert a message identical to a previous one, probably tagged as a write, and corrupt that same section of the stored data.

Protecting against this type of exploit is not trivial. Adding pad characters to the messages helps, especially if the pad length before and after the payload is variable (using a predictable pattern for this isn't a good idea; all zeros makes hacking easier!). Adding a command sequence number is a good idea, and also adds the value of keeping the system synced and detecting lost messages.

Putting a random seed of say 8 or 16 characters at the start of a short message also confuses attacks based on known formats, since the payload never encodes the same way. This on its own would not avoid the repeated message exploit above, so a sequence number would also be needed for safety.

Secure sessions can exist for a long time, due to the cost of creating a new one via RSA. More frequent AES key changes would make sense, however, since they could use the original RSA key, which is still in session. This would make cracking of the command key unlikely before a key is changed.

Since the recommended approach is to encrypt data end to end, it would be a good idea to use different keys to encrypt the data from the commands and to do so before submitting the data to the socket. Ideally, there would be a way of preventing the socket layer from encrypting that encrypted data again, but today's standard software packages don't do this. That's one of the issues we should get an industry consensus to correct.

STANDARD FILE FORMATS

It is a sad fact that many file types have large sections of identically formatted data. One of the best examples is the Word Document format. Have you ever wondered why a 1 character file takes up 13 KB on disk? There are data on fonts and formatting and so on. This rarely changes between documents. Companies use Word's default fonts on almost all documents, for instance. Anyone knowing this can use it to help brute force a hack.

A good solution to this is to compress the file before ending it to encryption. A really good compression package will dedupe all the standard blocks in a word doc, leaving just a couple of d-words as placeholders. Not only does this protect the data better, it cuts down on transmission time and storage.

All of these comments apply on any LAN connection, whether it is Ethernet, Ethernet with RDMA or InfiniBand. Any traffic going across a WAN connection most assuredly needs protection. Being exposed to the Internet makes that data and command stream extra vulnerable.

Many other file types have this tendency to boilerplate. A CAD file may include objects from the shape libraries and such, which are likely also at the receiving end. It's worth that compression pass!

KEY MANAGEMENT

Keeping-Keys safe is going to be a serious challenge, especially with hybrid clouds using SaaS solutions. Key management [53] has to be automated. It must work in such a way that a malcontent anywhere in the system is unable to read the keys or copy and open the key depository file.

Any key management system must be extendable to any cloud and any SaaS vendor. Importing files into a different format or typing keys in by hand just are not acceptable ways of doing business. As this process evolves, expect standards for the key manager API, or a de facto standard from an industry leader.

Watch out for key-management offered by the CSPs. If they can also directly access the keys those keys are exposed and the system will fail compliance tests. This is true of encrypting drives.

Some keys may have a long life, consistent with the life of the data, but session keys should be kept short-lived and Information Rights Management (IRM) authentication certificates need to be very carefully managed. Specifically, the set of IRM certs out in the cloud needs to be held closely and pruned quickly when a use is terminated. If, for example, they are in an (encrypted) file and the job goes away from a location, all copies of the file should be destroyed and if necessary replaced with a new file for current work. This could be an issue, for the natural tendency is to keep the IRM file with the image, which will exist for a very long time in most cases. That isn't good practice.

INFORMATION RIGHTS MANAGEMENT

On a higher level, we need something like an IRM [54] tool for our own data. In reality, there isn't much difference between me loading a movie and me loading a corporate file. They both need protection from abuse, be it illegal copies, illicit sharing or even accidentally get lost.

Those rights might exclude copying or exclude sending to another server or client, etc. This could work with mobiles, too. This ultimately would give us encrypted data with full rights management, removing us from the present focus on hardware, operating systems and networks for data protection. Let the data protect itself!

This may become critical as we expand data flow levels with the IoT and whatever follows that. Our current system of policing objects as they move by is going to struggle with sheer volume. IRM reduces the vulnerability window considerably, while providing a hardened single point of entry and exit for data from any system, whether storage, server or mobile.

Rights management could control more than just copying and forwarding. It's metadata concerning the lifecycle of the data itself. By extension, adding information about ownership (which allows decryption for older data, as well as current strong authentication), useful life, disposal at end of lie, and even permitted users are all additions to the basic process that could open up data flows while enhancing security.

Combining IRM and encryption essentially creates a two-factor authentication scheme. Anyone accessing an individual data object now has to have both IRM permission and the encryption key, which can't be changed for the original object. Extra and lost copies no longer matter. The data are protecting themselves.

IRM, at this level, is still in its infancy. The strongest pressure for it has come from the movie industry, very keen to stream online but plagued by illegal copying, pushing DRM (Digital Rights Management). Generalizing DRM to the broader scale is a novel concept. Getting the tools in place will be a challenge for the key operating systems developers, Microsoft and the Linux teams.

As has been said here several times, encryption needs a good hardware accelerator to become ubiquitous. The IRM protection could be embedded there or alternatively sit in a Trusted Platform Module [55], which might be a more general solution.

Can we make IRM/encryption completely secure? That's an ongoing discussion. The risk is making it secure enough for most cases. Even if this is done, it might get used for data that really needs more security or that will get the attentions of nation-state hacking. This battle between the black hats and the white knights doesn't look likely to end soon!

Unfortunately, the term DRM gets every hacker wannabee excited. The sense that someone might limit the God-given right to freely copy any movie to Facebook seems pervasive, which may suggest the approach generally works really well. We need to move past that debate to get over-the-top streaming out of the sidelines, and then potentially we'll see its extension to corporate files, perhaps in 2017.

REFERENCES

[1] Only 30 percent of the major retailers ready. http://www.fierceretail.com/story/retailers-far-behind-tech-firms-it-security-spending/2015-03-11.

[2] Executives get fired over this. http://www.informationweek.com/government/cybersecurity/14-security-fails-that-cost-executives-their-jobs/d/d-id/1321279.

[3] Cloud is as secure as the best in-house operations. https://www.gartner.com/doc/3134527/clouds-secure-using-securely.

[4] Emulate their best practices. http://www.questsys.com/files/Cloud-Computing-Best-Practices.pdf.

[5] Cloud weaknesses. http://www.infoworld.com/article/3041078/security/the-dirty-dozen-12-cloud-security-threats.html.

[6] Software-defined model. http://www.networkcomputing.com/cloud-infrastructure/bumpy-road-software-defined-infrastructure/1297643120.

[7] Protection of the control plane. http://www.vanillaplus.com/2015/08/10/10555-the-security-challenges-posed-by-sdns-centralised-control-plane-and-roots-of-trust-rot-and-how-attacks-can-be-prevented-and-addressed/.

[8] Make hacking a serious business. http://fortune.com/2015/10/02/heres-whos-been-hacked-in-the-past-two-years/.

[9] At least a few come from government agencies. https://www.washingtonpost.com/news/the-switch/wp/2015/10/24/how-the-government-tries-to-recruit-hackers-on-their-own-turf/.

[10] Spies. http://www.express.co.uk/news/uk/610024/Edward-Snowden-UK-Government-hack-smartphones.

[11] Spying is quasi-overt. http://motherboard.vice.com/read/here-are-all-the-sketchy-government-agencies-buying-hacking-teams-spy-tech.

[12] Huge data flow from cell-phones. http://www.reuters.com/article/us-usa-nsa-termination-idUSKBN0TG27120151127.

[13] Data from other countries. https://techcrunch.com/2015/08/03/uncovering-echelon-the-top-secret-nsa-program-that-has-been-watching-you-your-entire-life/.

[14] Instant red flag. http://www.theregister.co.uk/2016/01/27/nsa_loves_it_when_you_use_pgp/.

[15] Help commercial operations win deals. http://www.wsj.com/articles/u-s-plans-to-use-spy-law-to-battle-corporate-espionage-1437688169.

[16] Hack on JP Morgan. http://fortune.com/2014/10/02/jpmorgan-chase-disclosed-cyber-breach/.

[17] Solution catches 29 out of 489 total vulnerabilities. http://searchsecurity.techtarget.com/news/4500272454/Costly-government-cybersecurity-system-needs-major-changes.

[18] Embarrassing. http://www.cnbc.com/2016/02/01/federal-government-confirms-that-it-still-sucks-at-cyber-security.html.

[19] Need app vendors to take encryption seriously. https://www.skyhighnetworks.com/cloud-security-blog/only-9-4-of-cloud-providers-are-encrypting-data-at-rest/.

[20] Data sprawl. http://www.slideshare.net/DruvaInc/black-hat-2015-attendee-survey-the-challenge-of-data-sprawl.

[21] HIPAA. http://www.hhs.gov/hipaa/for-professionals/privacy/.

[22] SOX. http://www.soxlaw.com/.

[23] Place requirements. https://www.sans.org/reading-room/whitepapers/analyst/regulations-standards-encryption-applies-34675.

[24] Drives only support 32 unique keys. http://www.theregister.co.uk/2015/10/20/western_digital_bad_hard_drive_encryption/.

[25] Protecting access to the data itself. https://digitalguardian.com/blog/enterprise-data-security-breaches-experts-how-companies-can-protect-themselves-big-data.

[26] The encryption issue. http://www.findmysoft.com/news/Mozilla-Explains-Why-Encryption-Matters-Using-Thought-Provoking-Videos/.

[27] CURRENT data at rest. https://www.owasp.org/index.php/Cryptographic_Storage_Cheat_Sheet.

[28] Source encryption. https://www.veeam.com/backup-files-encryption.html.

[29] There are tremendous risks involved. http://arstechnica.com/security/2015/10/western-digital-self-encrypting-hard-drives-riddled-with-security-flaws/.

[30] Instance stores. https://discuss.aerospike.com/t/do-data-persist-on-instance-store-when-rebooting-an-instance-on-amazon-ec2/1283.

[31] Virtual SAN storage. http://www.infostor.com/index/articles/display/138898/articles/infostor/volume-6/issue-3/features/data-security-in-the-virtual-san.html.

[32] Instance stores. http://docs.aws.amazon.com/AWSEC2/latest/UserGuide/InstanceStorage.html.

[33] Reading another tenant's data. http://searchservervirtualization.techtarget.com/opinion/Are-we-witnessing-the-death-of-local-instance-storage.

[34] Exploits for data moving around. http://blog.rackspace.com/keep-data-private-encrypt-at-rest-in-transit-and-in-use/.

[35] Cold data. https://www.emc.com/corporate/glossary/cold-data-storage.htm.

[36] Insider activity. http://www.itbusinessedge.com/blogs/data-security/insider-threats-responsible-for-surprising-amount-of-data-loss.html.

[37] Snapshots. http://searchstorage.techtarget.com/definition/storage-snapshot.

[38] Policy constraints. http://www.nuagenetworks.net/blog/sdn-policy-architecture-sneddon/.

[39] Script manager. https://www.sdxcentral.com/sdn/definitions/sdn-controllers/.

[40] SaaS pay as you go. https://www.linkedin.com/pulse/20140512065424-7018284-both-pay-as-you-go-and-subscription-pricing-for-saas.

[41] Don't assume that the vendor has their act together. http://www.slideshare.net/huynh_victor/2015-data-integrity-conference-managing-changes-made-to-cloud-systems-53180152/.

[42] SaaS mashup. http://cloudsecurity.org/blog/2008/04/21/security-in-the-cloud-introducing-cloud-mashups.html.

[43] Hybrid cloud concept. http://www.zdnet.com/article/hybrid-cloud-what-it-is-why-it-matters/.

[44] Single governance strategy. http://www.cloudtp.com/2015/10/27/12-step-guide-data-governance-cloud-first-world/.

[45] Manage their governance processes. https://d0.awsstatic.com/whitepapers/compliance/Automating_Governance_on_AWS.pdf.

[46] Shadow IT nightmare. http://www.cio.com/article/2968281/cio-role/cios-vastly-underestimate-extent-of-shadow-it.html.

[47] Julius Caesar used it. http://www.counton.org/explorer/codebreaking/caesar-cipher.php.

[48] AES encryption. https://www.cryptopp.com/wiki/Advanced_Encryption_Standard.

[49] RSA encryption. https://cryptopp.com/wiki/RSA_Cryptography.

[50] DES algorithm. https://hacked.com/wiki/Data_Encryption_Standard.

[51] National agencies can break these codes. http://www.zdnet.com/article/has-the-nsa-broken-ssl-tls-aes/.

[52] Secure Sockets Layer. http://blog.hubspot.com/marketing/what-is-ssl#sm.00000vqu1k2 5tkdd1xg4h4uufj7sx.

[53] Key management. http://nvlpubs.nist.gov/nistpubs/SpecialPublications/NIST.SP.800-57pt1r4.pdf.

[54] Information Rights Management. http://searchcontentmanagement.techtarget.com/definition/information-rights-management-IRM.

[55] Trusted Platform Module. http://www.trustedcomputinggroup.org/trusted-platform-module-tpm-summary/https://en.wikipedia.org/wiki/Trusted_Computing.

On the Horizon

13

In this chapter, we are going to take a deeper look at the impact of emerging technologies that have the potential to enter the market mainstream within a year and disrupt the way we store data and configure systems. All of these technologies have been mentioned elsewhere in the book, as they impinge on existing storage approaches and offer improvement for the future, but here the focus is on what they do to change storage [1].

Bringing these five technologies together highlights the radical nature of the changes that loom in front of us. In the end, servers will look very different. They'll probably be smaller physically, but much more powerful, which, combined with drive capacity increases and compression, means that the datacenter will shrink. We'll buy less gear, and with the unleashing of buyers from traditional vendors, the revenue for the hardware segment will continue to drop.

Clearly, there are other technologies that will factor strongly in IT's future. Some, the cloud and SDS, for example, we've covered earlier in their own chapters. Containers also fall into that list. SaaS via the cloud is still emerging into the industry and is on the brink of mainstream adoption. Neither of the last two are directly storage technologies.

The following five sections discuss radical change in storage.

1. Solid-State Replaces Spinning Rust
2. NVDIMMs: Changing The Balance of Storage
3. The Hybrid Memory Cube
4. VSANs
5. Internet of Things

The first marks a turning point in how we think about storage and a major inflexion point in the bandwidth needed in the storage network. The next three change the relationship between the CPU and data storage, making for a more tightly bound solution in servers that demands new approaches. Finally, the Internet of Things (IoT) will, at some point, generate volumes of data far exceeding what we do today.

SOLID-STATE REPLACES SPINNING RUST

By now, we all can recite the wondrous benefits of SSD compared with spinning disks. They are much faster, lower power, more reliable and very quiet! OK; so why isn't everyone using them?

The answer [2] lies in an old game played by enterprise vendors, who typically mark up the drives by huge factors. In the game of SSD, these vendors have chosen

Network Storage. http://dx.doi.org/10.1016/B978-0-12-803863-5.00013-3

to charge for the performance, and the markups are amazing. EMC sells an 800-GB $300-SSD at a list price of $14,000, while the hard-drive equivalent, which actually *costs more*, sells for around $1800.

This has more to do with: (1) charging what the market will bear and (2) accepting that many arrays are so slow that 4×SSD will saturate their performance, than it has to do with real-world pricing.

But imagine a world where SSD are priced at $300 for that 800 GB and are serial AT attachment (SATA), not SAS. These drives don't have squirrely proprietary firmware that is required for an array to recognize them. They are designed to fit into object stores and block-IO appliances where the bandwidth matches the SSD more closely, so a set of 10 drives in an appliance makes sense. Now we can build arrays using commodity appliances, open-source software such as Ceph or OpenStack, and drives bought inexpensively from distributors, and know that they will work well all of the time.

Under the covers, this is what hyper-converged systems do, with a software package managing resource orchestration. With software becoming unbundled and open-source, this type of compact server/storage appliance should commoditize in price quickly.

At the start of 2016—that's where we are—SSD are cheaper than enterprise hard drives and much better value for money, and the buyers are beginning to believe that. They've done their sand-box tests, tried pilot operations and found them good!

So what will happen over 2016? First, the technology of 3D NAND flash [3] will continue to improve rapidly in 2016 and on into 2017. Prices for SSD will therefore continue to drop, while capacity will increase. Intel projected capacity parity by 2017, but we are already there. A 16-TB SSD has been announced, while spinning rust is stuck at 10TB due to the laws of physics, and will be for the next 2 years.

(An aside: there was talk in 2015 of resurrecting the 5.25-inch diameter form factor to allow a 40-TB HDD to be made, but realizing that it would still do only 100 IOPS made it very-near useless.)

Second, the realization that SSDs have reached price parity with enterprise hard drives, at least in the open market, takes away the last protection such HDDs enjoyed. This should result in the rapid demise of the enterprise-class HDD, replaced in the main by commodity SSDs.

This will have the knock-on effect of moving sales of storage units from traditional high-markup vendors to commodity vendors from China [4], just as has happened with the CSPs. The market-share shift that results will still leave the traditional vendors in the leading revenue positions for a while longer, simply because they see around three times the revenue per unit, but the unit count will swing rapidly to favor the original design manufacturers (ODMs) and in 3 or 4 years will have migrated the leader charts in revenue, too. It's already starting to happen, with enterprise hard drive sales falling across the board as of the end of 2015.

The drive vendors will be hurting as a result of the loss of the enterprise business to more commodity-priced SATA SSD. The Non-Volatile Memory express (NVMe) over Fabrics (NoF) approach will begin to be seriously entertained in 2017, but this is an ultrafast solution that will be initially priced high and so limited to a few market niches until the NVMe approach moves down market.

But there's more! 4-bit NAND cells are looking feasible [5], and would be more than adequate for write-once-read-occasionally applications like archiving and backup. That's the currently huge market for bulk SATA HDD as a secondary storage. The SSDs have advantages that they can be made more compact than HDD, simply by removing the case and this coupled with capacity per 2.5-inch drive of 20 TB or perhaps much more, low power needs and the ability to drop to a few milliwatts in standby means that from 2017-on, the SATA hard disk drive (HDD) secondary storage market will be under siege.

Another hit technology for flash is the 3D negative-AND (NAND) approach. This allows cells to be stacked vertically in chains of 32 or 64 cells, which instantly expands per die capacity by a major factor. Vendors are taking advantage of this to use larger NAND cells, which increases write endurance by big factors. As a result, C 3D NAND is as good as or better than multilevel cell (MLC) single-layer devices.

3D NAND is already bringing us 3.2 TB SSDs in a gum-stick [6] sized package. The impact of this on the mobile PC market is to make HDD obsolete, since much smaller, lighter and faster [7] PCs can be built with these tiny TLC NAND SSDs. Small PC modules [8] that fit in the back of LCD monitors are replacing desktop units as the new "hot" PC thing. The combination effect of tiny drives, SSD with large capacity and the low prices of 3D TLC NAND likely will deal a death blow to the desktop HDD market in the 2017 timeframe.

Overall, the drop in prices of the combination of 3D NAND and TLC/QLC bring will put enormous pressure on the HDD in servers, too. Intel has predicted price parity in 2017 between SSD and HDD, and even if delayed a few months, this will trigger an inflexion in HDD sales and increase the speed of the downward spiral.

NVMe over PCIe will usurp the SAS interface for high-end drives in the 2017 timeframe. Performance is much better, and the pacing item is NVMe support in the CPU chipsets, which will hide under the umbrella of SATA-Express. This dual interface allows NVMe and SATA drives to be plugged into the same drive bays in servers and appliances.

NoF will take this a step further, allowing drives to connect to the server and to each other, etc., via Remote Direct Memory Access (RDMA) Ethernet. This will be slower than a PCIe link, but will allow much longer connections between servers and drives, making the drives essentially remote storage appliances. An alternative view is that the data services are subsumed into the virtual server pool, so allowing data transfers directly from the storage device to the requesting server, which is the fastest storage solution around.

One direction the industry might take is to migrate completely to NoF for drives. We would see massive networks of storage nodes each consisting of a single drive, which would maximize throughput and give us scalability and flexibility that would be much better than anything we currently have. The major risk here is that drive vendors attempt to make NVMe an "enterprise" feature much as SAS was used to create a high-priced tier. Whether that happens or not may depend on the Googles of this world, who can individually exercise the negotiating clout of the aggregated server vendors or storage vendors.

NAND flash may not rule the roost forever. Intel and Micron are announcing their X-Point memory, which appears to be a Phase-Change Memory (PCM). They claim it to be 10 times the speed or more compared with flash, and to be more compact, more durable, and lower power. There's more of that under "NAND-Killers" in Chapter 14.

THE IMPACT ON APPLIANCE DESIGN

Radical performance changes like those we see with SSD have a ripple effect in to the appliances that house them. The traditional Fibre-Channel (FO) RAID array approach can't handle more than a handful of SSD, so we've seen the so-called "hybrid" arrays that have some SSDs and the rest of the slots filled with HDDs. These boxes have high-markup SSD, which makes them an expensive way of adding massive IOPS to a cluster.

The failure of the RAID array to cope with SSD has created two new lines of product. On the one hand, we have All-Flash Arrays, with 10s to 100s of terabytes of raw capacity, background compression to eke out even more space, and RDMA interfaces. On the other side, small object or universal storage appliances (sometimes called converged systems) are handling the balancing of performance by holding just 10 or 12 SSD, while still having fast interfaces.

Which will win is up for grabs right now. The All-Flash Array is currently winning [9] all hands down, but this is mainly because the early units plugged into standard FO SANs. If the RDMA units were reported separately by IDC, we'd probably see less enthusiasm and growth. In the end, the FC approach has hit a performance ceiling and so the real competition is between the NVMe/RDMA units of both the all-flash type and the small SSD appliances.

The FC special interest group (SIG) is pushing for RDMA over FC, but reality is that this is a radical change for FC, involving all new gear and the opportunity to move to established Ethernet RDMA is a very attractive alternative.

The migration to NVMe/RDMA in the AFA space [10] in 2016 will likely trigger a consolidation of the All-Flash Array market, with the weaker players falling off or being bought out.

The SSD appliances have the advantage of price from using mainstream drives and COTS engines as controllers. This fits better with the SDI model of the new data-center and opens up commodity sourcing for the hardware. Linked with open-source or unbundled software stacks from a number of vendors, this will open up a low-cost storage option with very high performance and much more flexibility than the All-Flash proprietary solutions can deliver.

The move to appliance-level data integrity/availability [11], rather than the single-box RAID approach, combined with a real-time compression technology that can keep up with SSD will allow prosumer Serial ATA (SATA) solid-state drive (SSD) to be used even in high Input/Output Operations Per Second (IOPS) environments, as opposed to expensive NVMe drives. Prosumer drive usage would be enhanced even further with real-time erasure coding, since the combination of compression with the distribution and parallel access to drives would result in a large multiplier to effective throughput rates.

NVMe, however, could move to be the preferred storage interface, especially with a seamless integration with NVMe over Fabrics. This could lead us to a model of direct drive connection in storage appliances, further reducing latency and allowing massive parallelism in large object accesses. Most likely, ultrafast NVMe/PCIe drives will remain as a near-in solution for the lowest latency applications.

The impact of 3D NAND is that the highest capacity SSDs are already in 2.5-inch form-factors. With drives shrinking further in size, it is just a matter of time before M2 size drives with NVMe are available. PCIe drives would also benefit from the same packaging approach, allowing them to be mounted directly to the motherboard without the current cabling mess that SATA drives require.

COLLATERAL CONSIDERATIONS

The impact of all this superfast storage is profound. Servers literally will run better. Thus, server sales will be lower than if they had HDD. Indirectly, this puts pressure on networks to run faster to keep up with traffic. This has already driven the move to early release of 25-GbE technology, while making RDMA an attractive solution especially for storage.

Companies making HDDs will need to adjust to the new world order. WD appears to be doing a good job of this, using their war chest to buy SanDisk [12], one of the premier SSD manufacturers. It isn't clear if this will prevent an overall revenue shrink [13] for the company, since SSD drives will be generally larger capacity drives and so fewer will be sold.

Seagate has bet more heavily on box side of the business [14], especially with its Xyratex acquisition and lately with Dot Hill, and is much weaker in the SSD arena. With the limited set of viable choices for potential acquisitions they now have, Seagate will struggle to acquire a major SSD player and is at risk of being left behind [15] in the fight for survival in the drive business that is now beginning.

Toshiba, the third HDD maker, is indicating an exit from the HDD business [16] to allow concentration on its flash products, while it is noteworthy that the slide in unit volumes (including enterprise drives) across the whole HDD industry already appears to be well underway as of the start of 2016.

The Intel/Micron X-Point memory could upset even WD in this situation. X-Point looks to have fabulous specifications and will be a hot item. If the dynamic duo can keep up with X-Point demand, the revenue from storage drives will shift materially in their favor.

The projected speed of X-Point will impact the contest between virtual SANS and classical storage boxes. Most likely, the virtual SAN model will be favored by the need to close couple the drives to the host; especially if Intel invents special interfaces for the drives, as rumors have it; we may see NVMe over OmniPath connections to the drives, for example.

In the appliance space, the traditional vendors were slow to respond to SSD availability and even today are considerably more expensive than whitebox appliances and apply massive markups to their drives. This has made them vulnerable to a pack of startups. Still, 2016 is likely to be a shakeout year for the storage industry and so some of those startups face absorption into other companies or extinction.

On the other hand, the ODMs are going from strength to strength, and it is in fact from this direction that the traditional storage vendors can expect the most competition. Erosion of market share is moving along, with the ODMs growing unit share at as much as three times their rate of revenue growth, which is to be expected. But, they are growing, while the rest of the vendors see market shares eroding away.

The migration to these so-called whiteboxes is a reaction to the slow rollout of SSD by the majors and the clear gouging in prices. This opened the door for alternatives, especially in software stacks for storage, and like Pandora's Box, there is no stopping the macroscopic shift in the market that this implies.

In the longer haul, the traditional market leaders in storage will see their share diminished significantly. This is the root of the DellEMC merger [17], for example, and other consolidations are likely in 2016 and 2017. To survive, they will need to become software and services centric, but they are in a horserace with SDI, which will reduce the need for the support and code that they offer.

The advent of SSD is triggering profound changes in the IT industry. This is still an unfolding sage, as we'll see in the next section, on nonvolatile dual in-line memory module (NVDIMM) and X-Point memory.

NVDIMMS: CHANGING THE BALANCE OF STORAGE

In 2014, the advent of in-memory databases boosted performance by a widely attested factor of 100+ times. That huge gain made databases more than interesting, again. Every database from Oracle to SAP to Hadoop made the quantum leap quickly. The result meant either more throughput or less servers, depending on your need.

All this effective acceleration led to some imbalances in the system, however. The first issue was getting input to the database. Network loads effectively increased by a big factor, perhaps not by 100 times but certainly a large multiplier, while the demand for write IOPS expanded, too (In-memory operation eased the need for lookup operations, but writes still go through the lock procedures we know and hate.).

Clearly, better networks are needed, which is where RDMA comes into its own. The storage issue is, however, more complex. Common sense and good practice call for multiple copies of the data to be accessible at all times to the server pool, so that a single point of failure doesn't bring the system to its knees. With normal networked storage, this is a disaster for in-memory operation, since the latency for the two write operations will be way too long.

Even RDMA doesn't resolve this, though it helps a lot, as we'll shortly see. To really get IO to the level of performance needed for in-memory operation, we need a close-in storage. A year ago, this meant PCIe flash cards or PCIe/NVMe SSDs, both of which are very fast, possibly operating into the millions of IOPS range.

The problem with this solution is that the stored data are still in the original server, and if it fails, there is no second copy in another appliance to carry on operations. A manual transfer of the SSD or flash card would be needed, which is a pain in any datacenter, and a royal problem in a CSP shop.

Even with the PCIe interface, the flash card or SSD solution fails to satisfy IOPS demand. Latency is still a problem. While 20–100 µs is doable for a low IO rate, at load, things stretch out into the milliseconds. To attack that problem, we need an interface that is even closer in.

Enter the NVDIMM. The idea of putting flash on a DIMM is very intriguing. If we are already on the hook for not having easy transportability, why not go all in and put flash on DIMMS. The result is a much lower latency than via PCIe.

There are two approaches to NVDIMMS. One (NVDIMM-F [18]) is simply to have DIMMS full of flash chips. With this approach, data is transferred to the DIMM as a block using a simplified storage stack. Writes go directly to a dynamic random access memory (DRAM) journal buffer, so they are very fast. When enough blocks are in the write journal, the buffered data are written into a superblock of flash. Protection against power fail is provided by supercaps that allow the journaled data to be saved to a special flash location. This type of NVDIMM is mounted to the operating system to look like a block-storage device.

The other type of NVDIMM-N [19] matches DRAM and flash sizes on the DIMM. Data are read or written as though normal DRAM, while the flash sits idle. On a power down or failure, the DRAM is dumped into the flash and then recalled when power comes back. That means all operations are at DRAM speed.

The operating system, compilers, and link-editors all need to acknowledge the existence of the persistent space. From some pioneering work I did in this area, I can say that the easiest solution is to build a persistent RAMDisk structure that also can be mounted to the OS. Using a RAMDisk can be done without playing with compilers or link-editors.

The RAMDisk approach is very fast, even compared to the other class of NVDIMM. However, it misses on many of the powerful opportunities this class of NV memory can bring to the table. If the compilers and link-editors are extended just a little, mainly by adding a *"Persistent Memory"* class and setting it up properly, atomic read and write memory-register operations are possible, changing just a single byte [20] if necessary.

This hybrid approach is blindingly fast compared with RAMDisk or block-IO approaches. It means that a few words being changed in a database are persisted in one or two DRAM cycles. That's nanosecond latency instead of 10s or 100s of microseconds, or longer! That becomes a game changer, and it's just some software changes and a lot of testing away.

For those of you who put on face-paint and grass skirts and code at 3 am, it isn't quite this simple, of course. Data have to be identified in some way so that on recovery from a fail the apps point to the right stuff. Also, if serious use of persistent memory hits mainstream, we'll need the equivalent of bit-error recovery and mirror operations, which means that the machine-fault logic on the system has to change. There are already precedents for this, with soft recovery from memory errors on the Itanium, for example.

These are tractable problems. What this means is that we are heading down a path where persistent memory could be byte addressable and extremely fast, on one hand or bulk block-IO could be low latency.

Both approaches are game-changer class events in storage. With software approaches that are already tested with caching systems, we are going to have servers with a couple of terabytes (or more) of real DRAM and 10 or more terabytes of flash memory to extend the effective DRAM capacity no end. If real time compression is possible, we'll have the equivalent of 30 TB servers!

Things don't stop here, though. Intel and Micron announced that they have jointly developed 3D X-Point Memory. The betting is that this is a PCM-type memory, though it could be a ReRAM-type of product. No matter, early information "leaks" put it at around 200–300 ns access time, which means it displaces flash in the block type NVDIMM, although the hybrid type doesn't get much benefit from X-Point.

Intel is mum about whether the design supports byte operations as an NVDIMM. There is an X-Point version that uses NVMe, although Intel hasn't used the magic words PCIe in context with that. In fact, there is a hint that OmniPath may be the chosen interface for the drive, which would be faster and also extend to longer distances.

3D X-Point is aiming to hit the mainstream at the end of 2016. By that point, there will be most, if not all, of the software extensions need for all of the options above, so server design will be exciting for a while. To add to the fun, a concept called Hybrid Memory Cube (HMC) looks to be hitting its stride about the same time. We'll look at that in the next section.

In all this excitement, we may have neglected a pressing issue. That good-practice rule of keeping data copies in multiple appliances hasn't gone away. We still have to figure a way to protect data and keep it available.

The simplest way to do this is to copy out the persistent memory to either another NVDIMM or SSD in a different appliance or to a free-standing storage appliance. Today's interface of choice is RDMA over Ethernet, though Intel is talking up OmniPath for this as an alternative (OmniPath will run at 100 Gbps with RDMA).

One question is whether this still constitutes a bottleneck; if it does, that means data will be in a single point of failure situation for a short while, maybe a few microseconds. This may be acceptable if there are ways to recover even that small a loss.

Another alternative is to connect the NVDIMM directly to an RDMA line and provide it enough standby power to flush the journal to a second appliance when a failure occurs. This might also be the efficient way to share data between appliances in normal operation, since data do not have to go through the server DRAM and PCIe busses to be transmitted out.

As I write, NVDIMM continues to evolve. By the time you read this, it might be something else again! But, whatever happens, the cat is out of the bag and servers and storage will be changed a lot!

THE HYBRID MEMORY CUBE

The HMC idea [21] is that, by packing the CPU and DRAM on a silicon substrate as a module, the speed of the DRAM interface goes way up, while power goes way down since the distance between devices is so small that driver transistors are no longer needed.

The combination of capacity and performance makes the HMC approach look like a winner across a broad spectrum of products, ranging from servers to smartphones. In the latter, it looks like packaging the CPU in the same stack as the DRAM is feasible. Moreover, the work on NVDIMM will likely lead to nonvolatile storage planes in the HMC model, too. A typical module of HMC might thus consist of a couple of terabytes of DRAM and several more terabytes of flash or X-Point memory.

Performance-wise, we are looking at transfer rates beginning at 360 GBps and reaching 1 TBps in the 2018 timeframe, if not earlier. HMC is CPU-agnostic, so expect support out of x64, ARM and GPU solutions.

As is common in our industry, there are already proprietary flavors of HMC in the market. AMD is planning High-Bandwidth Memory [22] (HBM) with NVidia, Intel has a version of HMC [23] that will be delivered on Knight's Landing, the top end of their XEON family with 72 cores onboard. Samsung has Wide-IO [24]. All involve 3D-die stacking.

HMC's impact on system design will be substantial. Servers will shrink in size even though becoming much more powerful. The removal of all those driver transistors means more compute-cores can be incorporated, serviced by the faster memory. This means much more IOs are needed to keep the HMC system busy, especially if one considers the need to write to multiple locations.

The combination of bandwidth, capacity, and nonvolatility beg for an RDMA solution to interconnect clustered servers. The faster memory allows plenty of extra bandwidth for sharing. First generation products will access this RDMA through PCIe, but it looks likely that this will be a bottleneck and as memory sharing ideas mature, we might see some form of direct transfer to LAN connections. Alternatively, an extension of a bus such as OmniPath to be a cluster interconnect could be used to remove the PCIe latencies.

HMC implies that servers will become much smaller physically. Local disk storage may well migrate away from the traditional 3.5-in format to use M2 or 2.5-In SSD. The traditional disk caddy will disappear as well. I suspect the sweet-spot server will be a single or dual module unit that is 1/4U wide and 1U high.

The HMC approach will of course impact storage appliances even if these don't follow the SDS model and end up virtualized in the server pool. The computer element will shrink and get much faster, while the larger memory opens up new opportunities for caching data both on reads and writes.

It will be 2017 before hitting its stride, but HMC is a real revolution in the server world. Memory has been a bottleneck in systems for years, with L1, L2, and even L3 caches being the result. Getting into the terabytes per second range will change system behavior and capabilities a great deal, completing the trifecta of CPU improvement, SSD storage, and now DRAM boosting that has eluded us for years.

VIRTUAL SANS

The virtual SAN is available today [25], but still hasn't achieved mainstream status. The concept is that instead of free-standing storage appliances, storage is provided by sharing the drives in a server cluster via RDMA.

It's a plausible idea. On the pro-side, it provides local instance storage on the server hosting the drive and sharing over RDMA is fast. With 12-drive servers and 10-TB drives, a cluster of 10 servers could deliver 1.2 petabytes of raw capacity, expandable by compression to around 6 petabytes.

On the con-side, it adds the storage network bandwidth [26] to the server load, which given the shortage in bandwidth we already see could be a bad thing. Another major con is that virtual SANs usually are conflated with hyper-converged systems sales. This is nice for the vendor, since it locks you in to the vendor, who gets storage revenue on top of server revenue.

Software-only virtual SANs are available that can be hosted on any COTS platform. This opens up some architectural flexibility, including having some bulk storage or universal storage systems on the storage network. There are even virtual filers available.

The software approach forms part of the SDS effort in reality. Hostable in containers, there is most, if not all, of the makings of data-service abstraction and flexible scaling that mark an SDS approach. Expanding the concept of virtual SANs to a more holistic SDS virtual storage and we have a way to reduce storage costs and increase agility tremendously.

In this SDS world, drives would sit in servers or appliances that look much like servers. The data services that demarcate block, file, and object will sit in container instances and be flexibly scalable. The difference would be the use of some portion of the server-storage space as a way to speed up local accesses. This would require a sense of affinity within the orchestration system distributing tasks to servers, so that the data for a task are localized inside that server, but the net result would be a crackingly fast system compared with a pure SDS approach where data are distributed randomly.

This issue of affinity becomes more important when the storage devices are on the DRAM bus, as with 3D X-Point memory. Here the speed disparity between a local access to the X-Point and a remote access is very high, by perhaps 500 times. This would hinder X-Point being a byte-accessed memory, for instance. Lack of affinity would also increase LAN traffic tremendously. This makes the affinity approach very interesting for system tuners.

This world view of virtual SANs blending in to SDS and encompassing all storage in a cluster opens up configurations to include dedicated bulk storage and object-storage appliances. These will either use a COTS engine as a controller or offer drives with a native Ethernet interface.

Somewhere in this transition to SDS, we may see that block-IO finally disappears, as a result of its scalability limitations. Following that thought, the conclusion is that virtual block-IO SANs are a stepping stone to virtual storage. The question is whether the effort to create virtual SANs will impede going to SDS, and how short the transition period will be.

Whether virtual SANs gain a significant market share or not is still an open question. The vendor lock issue looms large, and much of the gear available is very expensive, often being positioned as a cheap server with expensive proprietary drives.

So, in conclusion, virtual SANs are a step in the direction of SDS, but hyperconverged versions fall short in the openness area. The evolution to SDS may be relatively short term. The ideal endpoint of this technology area is that we see SDS-compliant storage services that can support either the in-server storage model or the storage appliance model, or a hybrid of both of these, built on top of COTS-based inexpensive hardware.

INTERNET OF THINGS

The IoT is IT's latest urban myth. By 2015, the hypesters had convinced the pundits that we would be knee deep in sensors within 5 years, all generating streams of data that needed real-time processing. Daily data flows into the range of many Exabytes were discussed.

Sadly, reality met budgets [27] and technology had to deliver. IoT looks to be running late. It will get to stupendous levels at some point, but the realities of a damaged Chinese economy and the ripple effect into other economies including the EU and most of Asia has slowed deployment.

Delay is probably good. There were many signs of the haste that messed up the internet for instance, with security problems that were almost laughable [28], since they'd be seen before, but were painful in their implications.

Examples were heart monitors that had no encryption on communications, and pacemakers that could be hacked by a 16-year-old. The auto industry got called out for shipping auto control systems that an easy hack could use [29] to stop engines on a freeway. The list went on.

A lack of standards and a desire to be first to market drove this shoddy engineering. Sensors may be much cheaper than computers, but their sheer ubiquity should point to the need for tight security, never mind the fact that some hacks could kill.

There seems also to be a fallacy in thinking of the data flow that IoT will generate. Most people seem to dream of all that data coming into datacenters to be crunched. That isn't going to happen! Most of the data will be crunched on the edge [30] of the network. There isn't any need to send repeat images of an office at night if the scene doesn't change, so that particular data will get compressed and only a tiny fraction of "same-as-last-time" messages will be sent.

Cheap computers will do the data reduction work, so the amount of data to be stored will end up as much less than the pundits considered probable. Analyzing compressed flows like this is just as easy as taking the raw data, but it should be much faster than raw, simply because the amount of data being transferred into the analytics clusters will be reduced by orders of magnitude.

IoT has also gotten tied up with the privacy debate. We've all seen crime shows where the good guys get video footage from a local business that shows the bad guys in the street or whatever. Britain uses cameras to record license plates passing by, allowing footage to be recovered on suspected criminals—PBS has a British cop doing it almost every week, in fiction!

But where does the greater good stop and privacy take over. That's a huge, unfinished debate. Government agencies want access to everything, but the recent history of Nazis in Germany, KGB in Russia, and of Tiananmen Square all show that the good guys aren't always the winners. Having the KGB meet IoT would be a nightmare of immense dimension, for examples.

The effect of this debate is to delay the storage of data. The NSA has had to stop listening to US cell-phone calls, at least in theory, so recording content has become less valuable. That means less storage is needed. This is, in fact, an IoT issue, since the phone is a sensor that shows a host of activities from movement to purchases and communication.

RETAIL AND IOT

The retail industry is happy to bombard us with apps that offer little value to us, but turn on GPS, cameras, sensors and local Bluetooths, and near-field transmissions and such to find out all sorts of interesting titbits about what we do. They need to analyze that data in near real-time, since often its value goes away in minutes.

Right now, the retail sector appears to be the main driver [31] for big data analytics, with bricks and mortar retailing in a death struggle with Internet selling. In both cases, sensor data is being extracted from every retail interaction. Where you stand in a store is detected from cameras or cell phones. Hovering on an ad on a webpage is noted.

This is getting rapidly more sophisticated. Where you are looking, even what you are saying, may be used to build a selling profile. At the current rate, when you grab a can of sardines at the supermarket, a disembodied voice will likely say "Jim! Buy another can and we'll give you 25 cents off" or some such come-along. All this analysis strains analytics. The need for in-memory databases stems from this fascination with IoT minutia.

The data created by this gathering process are fondly believed to be "unstructured". That isn't usually true, but the format is very variable, so a database may contain a mix of very disparate data segments. We have software, such as Hadoop, capable of dealing with this type of data.

Storing the data is best done in object storage systems. The bandwidth needed to feed the analytics servers comes from parallel access to data across many appliances (so much for the Virtual SAN model). Current file systems such as Hadoop are server-centric, in the sense that the server parses the structure to identify which blocks are required.

Future systems may be much more data-centric. These approaches use key-data structures on the storage appliances which allow data to be presorted and deliver to servers in the cluster with the proper affinity. All the records with keys starting with letter A go to server number 1, etc. Of course, the real implementation may be much smarter.

At the limit, the optimum storage for Big Data might be Ethernet drives storing data as key/data pairs, like Seagate's Kinetic [32]. This would give direct access to the data without intervening controllers. However, really fast access into a cloud of Ethernet drives probably means that an indexing service will be needed, likely in the form of in-memory databases running on virtual instances. This is pure speculation, since we have nothing like it yet, though interfacing Kinetic drives has occurred within the Ceph project.

THE OTHER BIG DATA

Another form of Big Data exists. This is the result of large-scale scientific experiments such as CERN or the Square-Kilometer Array (SKA) [33], which will generate more data than the Internet in 2020. The data pattern here is a large number of continuous data streams or very large files.

These are best handled by object stores, with files being distributed over many nodes for parallel performance. The issue is achieving massive scaling out of the number of nodes so that the amount of bandwidth is achievable, with headroom for future innovations in detectors, etc.

An alternative is to use a scaled-out file system such as Gluster to manage the data. In either case, careful naming conventions and a cataloging scheme will be needed to keep the data straight.

There are real challenges storing and networking this sort of data. We are talking petabytes per day levels for the SKA. Compounding these issues is location. Short-list SKA sites are currently in Botswana and the Australian outback, while most of the researchers are in Europe, Asia or America. The data itself are relatively incompressible, which means that ways to edge-process the raw streams at the observatory site are needed. Even with this, there'll be a lot of new fiber cable laid!

Edge computing is a must here, but what should be stored. It's not a trivial question and the IT stakes are huge.

REFERENCES

[1] What they do to change storage. http://www.networkcomputing.com/storage/storage-market-out-old-new/355694318.
[2] The answer. http://www.computerworld.com/article/2939438/data-storage-solutions/the-rise-of-ssds-over-hard-drives-debunked.html.
[3] 3D NAND flash. http://seekingalpha.com/article/3942376-micron-intel-3d-nand-post-2016.
[4] Commodity vendors from China. http://www.forbes.com/sites/greatspeculations/2015/07/13/odm-storage-vendors-gain-share-from-giants-emc-hp-ibm-netapp-lose-market-presence/#3bd66cde173e.
[5] 4-bit NAND cells are looking feasible. http://www.digitaltrends.com/computing/toshiba-ups-its-storage-game-with-reveal-of-4-bit-mlc-memory/.
[6] 3.2 TB SSDs in a gum-stick. http://www.providecoalition.com/samsung-ssd-saves-5gb-video-in-3-seconds/.
[7] Much smaller, lighter and faster. http://gizmodo.com/this-130-windows-pc-on-a-stick-might-be-the-best-yet-1728258745.
[8] Small PC modules. http://www.computerworld.com/article/2941759/computer-hardware/why-pc-on-a-stick-is-a-really-bad-idea.html.
[9] All-Flash Array is currently winning. https://flashdba.com/2015/10/14/all-flash-arrays-ssd-based-versus-ground-up-design/.

[10] NVMe/RDMA in the AFA space. https://www.mangstor.com/page/nx-series-flash-storage-arrays.

[11] Appliance-level data integrity/availability. http://www.networkcomputing.com/storage/going-all-ssd-side-effects/732249354.

[12] WDC to buy SanDisk. http://www.fool.com/investing/general/2015/10/28/did-western-digital-corp-overpay-for-sandisk-corpo.aspx.

[13] Prevent an overall revenue shrink. http://www.bloomberg.com/gadfly/articles/2016-02-23/western-digital-still-needs-sandisk-deal.

[14] Seagate focus on box side of the business. http://blogs.barrons.com/techtraderdaily/2015/10/19/seagate-benchmark-asks-if-acquisitions-have-run-into-trouble/.

[15] Seagate at risk of being left behind. http://www.tomsitpro.com/articles/micron-seagate-storage-ssd-cloud,1-3243.html.

[16] Toshiba indicates possible exit from the HDD business. http://www.storagenewsletter.com/rubriques/mas/toshiba-could-stop-or-sell-hdd-business/.

[17] Dell-EMC merger. http://www.itbusinessedge.com/blogs/unfiltered-opinion/dellemc-merger-why-people-dont-get-this-is-different.html.

[18] NVDIMM-F. http://www.tomsitpro.com/articles/samsung-netlist-3d-xpoint-nvdimm,1-3048.html.

[19] NVDIMM-N. https://www.micron.com/products/dram-modules/nvdimm#/.

[20] Changing just a single byte. http://searchservervirtualization.techtarget.com/tip/NVDIMM-and-RDMA-offer-significant-virtualization-advantages.

[21] HMC idea. http://www.hybridmemorycube.org/.

[22] High-Bandwidth Memory. http://www.amd.com/en-us/innovations/software-technologies/hbm.

[23] Version of HMC. http://wccftech.com/intel-knights-landing-detailed-16-gb-highband-width-ondie-memory-384-gb-ddr4-system-memory-support-8-billion-transistors/.

[24] Wide-IO. http://www.samsung.com/us/business/oem-solutions/pdfs/Web_DAC2012_TSV_demo-ah.pdf.

[25] The virtual SAN is available today. https://www.datacore.com/products/datacore-hyper-converged-virtual-san.

[26] Storage network bandwidth. https://storageswiss.com/2014/03/31/the-problems-with-server-side-storage-like-vsan/.

[27] Reality met budgets. http://www.computerworld.com/article/2925956/internet-of-things/overcoming-the-massive-friction-slowing-the-internet-of-things.html.

[28] Security problems that were almost laughable. http://www.economist.com/news/leaders/21606829-hooking-up-gadgets-web-promises-huge-benefits-security-must-not-be.

[29] Auto control systems that an easy hack could use. http://www.wired.com/2015/12/2015-the-year-the-internet-of-things-got-hacked/.

[30] Crunching on the edge. http://www.govtech.com/transportation/Is-Edge-Computing-Key-to-the-Internet-of-Things.html.

[31] Retail sector appears to be the main driver. http://www.comqi.com/internet-things-reinventing-retail/.

[32] Seagate's Kinetic. http://www.seagate.com/tech-insights/kinetic-vision-how-seagate-new-developer-tools-meets-the-needs-of-cloud-storage-platforms-master-ti/.

[33] Square-Kilometer Array (SKA). http://www.computerworld.com.au/article/392735/ska_telescope_generate_more_data_than_entire_internet_2020/.

Just Over the Horizon 14

The previous chapter looked at some key technologies that are in early production or just about to become so. These technologies all will enter the mainstream by the end of 2017 or earlier and each will change storage networking in a major way.

The technologies in this chapter are very much still in the R&D lab. Each of them is getting a lot of attention and many dollars are being spent to bring them to production. Each one offers a step forward in IT, while at least one, graphene, could create a major revolution in its own right.

In toto, these ideas, and ones still yet to surface, promise a vibrant and rapidly evolving future for storage. Despite the decline of the traditional disk-based vendors, the opportunities for creative startup companies to open up a place in the sun will increase dramatically, while the user base will profit from much more computing at lower costs.

NAND KILLERS

This is a convenient name for a set of technologies all aiming to beat NAND flash in price and/or performance terms. They've been in development for a few years, which demonstrates the complexity of the technical tasks involved. Each technology has required breakthroughs in physics and material science, which have come piecemeal over the last half decade or so.

Once the pure science was done, implementation of the designs found basic flaws in each approach, just as the write life problem bedeviled flash memory. Issues with stability or yield or performance sent the technology back to the labs a good few times.

Today, we have a good deal of promise, but still no solid reality. Small spintronics devices are being manufactured, and even used in solid-state drives (SSDs) as a fast persistent buffer for incoming data, with the aim to remove the supercapacitors used for backup power. For the other technologies, the "Product-next-year" refrain has grown a bit tedious, but a successful outcome could change dynamic random access memory (DRAM) structures and SSDs significantly.

Most of the technologies are attempting to get closer to DRAM speed as their primary goal. DRAM is a power hog, even in the HMC incarnation, and a way to persist DRAM and, using non-volatile memory as a DRAM extension, saving cost and power is seen as worthy of the investments being made.

Network Storage. http://dx.doi.org/10.1016/B978-0-12-803863-5.00014-5

We've already looked at one of the challengers to NAND in the previous chapter 3D X-Point memory [1] (being renamed Optane) looks like a strong contender and both Intel and Micron are very bullish about business opportunities. It was in early sampling to large customers as this was written at the start of 2016 and Micron expects it to be in system products by the year end. After that, the gloves come off between Intel Micron (who is a major NAND flash provider) and the rest of the industry.

Between them, 3D X-Point and NAND could take the wind out of the sails for other solid-state memory technologies, at least for a while. NAND, especially in the 3D NAND flavor, is a powerful incumbent in the solid-state memory market and there is a barrier to displacing it. Recent work looks to increase write wear life by a large factor, making QLC 4-bit NAND a viable storage for colder, less volatile data, so obviating the need for hard drives in the cold storage tier. Add a successful 3D X-Point and the barrier for other entries to the game could well be too high.

The argument could become one of investing millions to get a flash replacement that is say 2× the performance versus working flash or X-Point processes to get the same result. We've already seen a process change to use 3D stacking raise the barrier for X-Point considerably; for example, 100 nS X-Point and 3D NAND with huge capacity might shrink the opportunity for anything else to the point that the ROI doesn't fly.

Still, at this stage in the game, there are far too many questions unanswered. We don't even have specs for X-Point yet, and I suspect the two partners cooking it up couldn't give final specs either… It's still a work in progress!

For all the technologies, a strong 3D stacking strategy will be essential. This is an underlying process technology that could make computer central processing units (CPUs), graphics processing units (GPUs), and various memory types all part of a single hardware management console (HMC)-like module stack, on the macro-stacking level.

At the same time, each die of persistent memory will need 3D layering to achieve very high densities of storage cells. We are currently seeing production devices with 32 layers and 48 or even 64 layers are promised. From a cost perspective, this could cut the per-bit cost in half or better, with infinitely better yield costs for the larger node cells this allows.

Superfast, tightly coupled memories bring software challenges. Handling tiering at high speed without dragging down system-performance requires new code. We are already seeing a promising open-source solution called Alluxio [2], which not only tiers from a non-volatile dual in-line memory module (NVDIMM) through multiple layers out to slower networked storage but does so by abstracting the underlying storage type. In other words, Alluxio is a storage virtualizer that truly creates a lake, if not ocean, of storage.

PHASE-CHANGE MEMORY

Phase-change memory (PCM) [3] uses the unusual behavior of a class of materials called chalcogenide glasses. The product derives from the technology pioneered by the late Stan Ovshinsky [4] beginning in the 1960s. Difficulties in production kept the product out of the mainstream for storage of data, although it found uses in lightning arrestors and other devices.

NAND flash runs into scaling problems as devices get very small, since the technology relies on trapped charge and very small cells trap only a few electrons, making them difficult to write reliably and prone to data loss through leakage. As a result, PCM resurfaced as a potential alternative, taking advantage of massive improvements in material science and process control that had occurred over the previous three decades.

Chalcogenide is used in rewritable DVDs and CDs giving a substantial boost to understanding its properties and behavior at the phase boundary. The storage mechanism switches the material from crystalline to amorphous state or vice versa. This changes both the electrical properties (resistance), which is used in PCM, and optical properties used in DVDs.

This process is a nanoscale mechanical change. Heating the glass to a high temperature and then cooling it induces an amorphous high-resistance state. Then, heating it above its crystallization point creates a low-resistance crystal state. All of this is done on tiny cells. Switching times have been coming down, with Samsung claiming to have as low as 5 ns. Likely, the cycle time will be higher, perhaps in the 50-ns range, in the early commercial parts.

With the potentially very small size of a cell and the fast switching speed, PCM is an attractive alternative to flash. There is no need to block-erase PCM memory, which can slow writing with NAND flash by as much as 50%. Each bit can be directly written. At 5 ns, the speed would be enough to match DRAM [5] directly, although this is a technology projection rather than a reality today. Coupled with being able to write individual bytes, this speed could give us a direct alternative to DRAM, but that looks to be in the future list right now.

PCM has its own set of lifetime challenges. The resistance of the amorphous state can increase slowly, making multi-bit cell design very difficult. High local currents are needed for driving the thermal phase changes and these pose design problems for the driving transistors, which can lead to limitations in the operating range for the memory device.

All of this is still a work in progress in the lab. As of the time of writing, it is likely that Intel's X-Point memory will turn out to be PCM [6], as both Intel and Micron have invested strongly in this area of technology for years. There are other interested parties. In 2014, Western Digital demonstrated prototype parts that, while slower than DRAM by almost two orders of magnitude, are still way faster than NAND. Samsung and Micron also have shown prototypes over the last few years, but it's an indication of the difficulties in the technology that nothing hit the market before 2016.

RESISTIVE RAM

Resistive RAM (ReRAM) [7] comes in a number of forms. HPE has been a leader, at least in the hype stakes, for some years. HPEs product concept [8], the memristor, is described by them as a ReRAM solution, but the scope of the technologies used in ReRAM alternatives has led to some debate on the use of the term. Another leader, Crossbar [9], demonstrated a prototype 1-TB chip in 2013, but this still is not in production as of January 2016.

This debate, though, highlights the problems in productizing the ReRAM idea. It's got the same sort of materials and processes problem that PCM has, although the range of materials under investigation in the lab in the ReRAM case is much larger.

ReRAMs, as a class, work by applying a high voltage across a dielectric barrier, sufficient to create paths through the barrier that lower its resistance. If this can persist for a long time without power, and also be reversed, we have the makings of a memory device.

The attraction of the ReRAM approach is that switching is faster than PCM, in the 10-ns range and the cell structure can be much smaller than either PCM or NAND flash. Essentially, storage is arranged at the intersections of conductor traces on the die that cross at right angles on either side of a thin dielectric layer. This makes the data byte-addressable, which means a whole different spectrum of use cases open up as a true persistent DRAM.

The crossbar structure lends itself to replication in 3D, so very-high capacity chips are a possibility. However, a "sneak-path" current problem plagues most approaches, interfering with reliable reading of data. Inability to suppress this has delayed productization for a couple of years now. Fixes for the problem either involve balancing the low-resistance channel with a high-resistance channel, so keeping the overall resistance high and allowing larger arrays of crossbars to be built, or it involves a complex combination of read, reset, and set operations simultaneously.

Even if PCM moves forward, ReRAM offers possibilities for even higher density, speed and lowered power, so research will continue.

SPINTRONICS MRAM

The idea of setting and detecting the quantum spin states of a bunch of electrons seems pure Sci-Fi. However, spin physics allowed the invention of the *giant magnetoresistance* approach to magnetic recording heads that led to 10-TB hard drives.

In late 2013, Everspin [10] delivered a 4-Mb die using magnetoresistive RAM (MRAM) as an approach. Further development is needed to make this design scalable, involving techniques such as thermally assisted switching or spin-transfer torque (STT).

STT aligns the spin of the electrons in a current by passing them through a fixed, thick magnetic layer before passing them to a thin, "free" layer. Angular momentum from the current can be transferred to this layer causing it to flip. Everspin used this approach to create a 64-Mb memory module.

It's obvious that spintronics has a long way to go [11] to reach the densities of NAND, PCM, and ReRAM, so this is the NAND killer with the longest time before reaching a commercial maturity. By the time it reaches market, it will face steep competition from entrenched technologies and must find a clear advantage in cost, speed, or power to win over them.

In summary, PCM looks to be the likely contender for the next bout in the ring with flash. Having vanquished HDD and looking to surpass HDD revenues in 2016, flash is now being accepted well. This may lead the normally conservative storage industry to stick with flash, but I suspect the doors are now open to much more risk-taking by the buyers and thus more innovation in solutions. One thing is certain, the next few years are going to be interesting!

GRAPHENE

Graphene is a material that has been talked of for years, but the ability to make testable amounts eluded scientists until the turn of the century. In 2004, Geim and Novoselov of Manchester University [12] managed to characterize it, winning a Nobel Prize in 2010 in the process.

Graphene is a two-dimensional lattice of carbon atoms, a flat sheet of atoms arranged in a regular array. It is now relatively easy to produce and many scientists are hard at work trying to figure how to take advantage of its low resistance and other unusual properties. Graphene has very high thermal conductivity and can act much like a waveguide with little to no scattering of electrons running in the edges of the sheet, for example. It is also incredibly strong. Because it is a flat sheet, it is also very light in weight.

Applications of this wonder-material cover a broad spectrum [13] from improving batteries [14] to acting as a filter. One use is in printer inks. However, it is the use of graphene in the IT world that interests us. IBM Labs announced that they had fabricated the world's smallest transistor [15] using graphene back in 2008. This was one-atom thick and 10 across and could switch at GHz speeds.

Transistors running at 100 GHz [16] have since been demonstrated and just 3 years later, in 2013, 25-GHz transistors were built on plastic sheets that could be folded. Graphene science is truly in its infancy. It has the ability to impact adjacent magnetic materials, so don't be surprised if graphene and spintronics intersect at some point.

What could be much more exciting is the application to 3D stacking [17] and even interconnection of devices. This could lead to very high core count computers with very small and efficient transistors that don't generate a lot of heat individually. The amount of heat generated is generated can be removed easily using graphene's excellent thermal characteristics.

In a decade, that could mean today's computer systems would be shrunk to the size of a single CPU, with all the DRAM and solid-state memory on board and perhaps as many as 1000 cores. With everything virtualized, it would be possible to ignore failed cores, etc., ensuring a decent yield from a multilevel die creation process.

It goes without saying that this would really change the profile of IT. No more need for datacenters (assuming the cloud hasn't already swallowed up IT). The whole company's computing could be done in a box on someone's desk!

Interconnecting all of this could be fun. We are going to need terabyte bandwidths. With the need to keep power low at the server box, this could lead to graphene-based photonics interconnect [18],... using light created by transistors or similar electronics. Similar to the efforts to get LEDS working off silicon substrates to create a photonics interconnect, we might see sheets of graphene that glow as needed.

There are related technologies that are also creating a lot of interest in the scientific community. Carbon nanotubes [19] are effectively graphene sheets that have curled up into hollow tubes with sidewalls just an atom thick and with length to diameter ratios in the 100s of millions to one range. Work on creating transistors with these and on 3D stacking and self-stacking properties may yield all sorts of wonders, but like graphene, it's early days.

Nanotubes in the electronics space suffer from a lack of fabrication methods. Laying down devices, connecting them together and so on are all daunting issues, especially when on realizes that basic properties of tubes like length and diameter are hard to control today.

Graphene is going to take at least five and possibly more than 10 years to impact mainstream IT, but when it does we will have yet another major revolution in IT.

FURTHER OUT

The march of technology is inexorable and new ideas surface from university and industry research labs all the time. Some look like science fiction. A recent announcement from the University of Southampton in the United Kingdom is a 5D optical storage system [20] perhaps capable of reaching a petabyte in a few square inches, all while being able to withstand 1000°C temperatures and last for millions of years. I think I first saw that in the movie "2001-A Space Odyssey"!

Time will tell if it is a viable product, but it really does make the point that we aren't even close to the end of invention in storage.

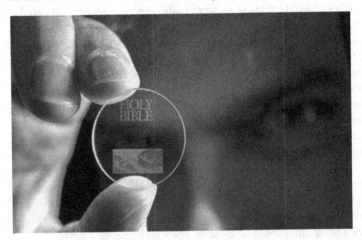

REFERENCES

[1] 3D X-Point memory. http://thememoryguy.com/intel-to-use-micron-hybrid-memory-cube/.
[2] Alluxio SIG Website. http://www.alluxio.org/.
[3] Phase-change memory. https://en.wikipedia.org/wiki/Phase-change_memory.

[4] Stan Ovshinsky. https://www.aip.org/commentary/profile-american-innovation.

[5] Fast enough to match DRAM. http://www.zdnet.com/article/micron-says-new-memory-will-break-performance-bottleneck/.

[6] Intel's X-Point memory will turn out to be PCM. http://www.newelectronics.co.uk/electronics-blogs/have-intel-and-micron-updated-phase-change-memory/88291/.

[7] Resistive RAM (ReRAM). https://en.wikipedia.org/wiki/Resistive_random-access_memory.

[8] HPE's product concept. http://www.computerworld.com/article/2990809/data-storage-solutions/hp-sandisk-partner-to-bring-storage-class-memory-to-market.html.

[9] Crossbar Company Website. http://www.crossbar-inc.com/.

[10] Everspin Company Website. https://www.everspin.com/news/everspin-releases-highest-density-mram-products-create-fastest-and-most-reliable-non-volatile.

[11] Spintronics has a long way to go. http://eandt.theiet.org/magazine/2015/10/spintronics.cfm.

[12] Geim and Novoselov of Manchester University. http://www.graphene.manchester.ac.uk/explore/what-can-graphene-do/.

[13] Graphene Applications' Broad Spectrum. https://cosmosmagazine.com/technology/five-new-uses-miracle-material-graphene.

[14] Graphene improving batteries. http://www.autoblog.com/2016/03/23/graphene-batteries-wave-of-the-future-or-snake-oil/.

[15] World's smallest transistor. http://www.theverge.com/2015/4/29/8515281/tmd-graphene-materials-science-ultrathin-electronics.

[16] Transistors running at 100GHz. http://nextbigfuture.com/2015/07/pathway-to-terahertz-graphene.html.

[17] 3D stacking. http://www.livescience.com/52207-faster-3d-computer-chip.html.

[18] Graphene-based photonics interconnect. http://www.optics.org/news/7/4/8.

[19] Carbon nanotubes. http://www.nanocomptech.com/what-are-carbon-nanotubes.

[20] 5D optical storage system. http://www.southampton.ac.uk/news/2016/02/5d-data-storage-update.page.

Conclusion

We have looked at a period of enormous changes looming in computer storage. The results can only be described as a revolution. Technologies are migrating rapidly from 50-year-old spinning disks to all solid-state solutions that are much faster and robust, whereas on the software side, we are entering a period of virtualized data services that are no longer pinned to the underlying hardware.

Connectivity is rapidly moving to Ethernet and away from Fibre-Channel. Scale-out storage more and more means object storage, but in the end the concept of universal storage boxes that handle all protocols will be the winning approach. NVMe will replace both SAS and SATA, simply because it is a faster protocol that uses much less host compute power.

The server will also change a good deal. Persistent memory on the DRAM bus will bring a new dimension to in-memory operation. While this won't be application-transparent, the benefits of a rewrite to use the new storage could be massive speed-up for programs, especially in-memory databases.

Prices for storage will fall dramatically as COTS boxes from the ODMs hit the market and, with all the changes in pricing and margin structures that this implies, the old, traditional vendor base will be drastically reshaped. Many companies will merge or fall by the wayside.

New companies, especially in software, will appear and add to the pace of revitalization. Under the umbrella of "Software-Defined Storage," these companies will offer a software Lego that allows configurations of storage data services to be provisioned on demand. The subsequent agility will improve performance and lower costs in storage, while reducing the need for manual management of the storage pool.

Some of these data services involve compressing the capacity required to store data by relatively large factors. Combined with the capacities we are already seeing for solid-state storage, the size of a given storage farm should shrink considerably. This will offset expected growth in "Big Data" and, for many datacenters, will result in net shrinkage in size.

Networking remains a bottleneck in storage. Most of the innovation aimed at correcting this is coming in the Ethernet area, which as a result is rising to transcend Fibre-Channel as the interconnect of choice for storage. Speeds of 25/100 GbE will be the standard by 2018, with RDMA getting a big boost as a low-cost way of moving data rapidly with low CPU overhead. If Intel includes iWARP in its chipsets, this will become the mainstream storage solution well within the decade, using NVMe over Fabrics as a storage protocol.

Overarching all of this is the impact of cloud computing. Purchasing gear with just a 20% markup has allowed the cloud to be the economic solution for a great deal of IT. There is no room for the 3× to 20× markups of the "mainframe" school of computing, which is why EMC, NetApp, Dell, and HPE are shut out of supplying the major cloud providers.

Growth in the cloud has radically reduced the growth outside the cloud. Revenue-centric reports such as IDC and Gartner produce do not reflect this properly, since the revenue per unit for the cloud will be much smaller than for the traditional sale to an end-user. As the cloud outpaces the in-house systems in growth, we can expect shrinkage in the total revenue in the hardware side of the industry. More importantly, the cloud margin structure will put downward pricing pressure on all vendors. This is the root of the Dell-EMC merger and massive layoffs at NetApp and IBM.

With the advent of containers software, as opposed to hypervisor-based virtualization, the cost curve for cloud providers will further accelerate its downward spiral. In the end, this spells doom for in-house computing in the SMB space—it will be much cheaper to just go into the cloud. In parallel, SaaS vendors will see accelerated growth to service the needs of the SMB in the cloud, further sheltering the users from IT complexity.

SMB migration will add to the pressure on traditional vendors, while the ODMs who service the cloud are expanding into the mainstream end-user markets. Aiming to capture the enterprise space, the ODMs will enjoy the benefit of having very large production volumes, high quality, and the interchangeability of COTS all working with low prices to attack the market.

Longer-term forces may challenge ODM supremacy. Modules that contain most of the values of a server or storage engine by combining CPU and DRAM/persistent memory may onshore both component production and conjure-to-order, leading to a second-generation ODM process with different economic dynamics and strategic implications.

I hope that this book has awakened a new interest in storage and its implications. It's a complex area and changing at a pace that often is hard to grasp. My aim was to cover a big picture strategic view of where we are going and what the options are. I hope I succeeded.

All crystal balls have haziness to their predictions. A new technology could derail the flow I've described, for instance, though not for a few years. One thing is certain, we live in interesting times!

A Brief History of Storage Networking

Prior to 1981, storage and systems were connected via point-to-point links at relatively low speeds. Storage sharing was effectively nonexistent.

October 1981	Shugart Associates and NCR, Wichita, agreed to merge their respective SASI and BYSE interface efforts and present them to ANSI for standardization
February 1982	ANSI agreed to accept the interface as a new standard under the name SCSI, for small computer systems interface, suggested by Control Data's Gene Milligan
April 1982	NCR delivered the first SCSI ASICs. The first working chip is now in the Smithsonian
May 1982	Adaptec proposed an open-collector version of SCSI aimed at the direct-connected storage market
March 1983	Novell introduces Shareware, the first network OS, at NCC, while NCR, on the next booth, introduces Modus, the first dedicated file-server. Shareware later is renamed as Netware
1983	3.5-inch drive form-factor patented and delivered by Rodime
April 1984	NCR halts Modus program to focus on UNIX Tower systems
1984	NFS developed by Sun Microsystems
June 1988	Dave Patterson, Garth Gibson and Randy Katz at UC Berkeley publish "A Case for Redundant Arrays of Inexpensive Disks". There was prior art on the various RAID methods, but this was the first coherent look at the approach
1988	Fiber Channel first conceived at NCR, Wichita by Randy Meals (who led the Modus team) and the author. Meals moved to head up HP's FC efforts that led to the first FC chip
1988	PrairieTek introduces 2.5-inch drive form-factor
1990	EMC (founded 1979) expands into computer data storage and release their first Symmetrix RAID array
1990	Microsoft merges SMB and LAN Manager, (later in 1996) attempting to rename it CIFS
1992	QLogic founded
1994	ANSI finally approves FC standard
1995	Brocade founded
1997	Brocade announce Silkworm, the first FC switch
1997	SNIA founded
1998	iSCSI pioneered by IBM and Cisco
March 2000	iSCSI proposed as ANSI standard
2001	Mellanox ships InfiniBand—RDMA arrives
2002	Chelsio takes RDMA to Ethernet
January 2003	SATA Rel. 1.0 released

2004	SAS introduced as a replacement for SCSI and competitor to SATA
2006	Caringo releases COTS-based object storage software
2009	FCoE standard published
2006	Ceph conceived by Sage Weil at UC Santa Cruz
2007	First useful SSD drives reach market (early failed products go back to 1989)
2007	Fusion-IO announces PCIe flash card
2010	First All-Flash arrays reach market
2011	NVMe specification released
2011	First NVDIMMs announced
2011	Red Hat acquires Gluster
2012	Ceph reaches market
2014	Red Hat purchases InkTank, the drivers of the Ceph project
2014	3D flash programs announced by major chip vendors
2015	10-TB hard drives using helium or shingled recoding delivered
2015	16-TB SSD announced by Samsung, passing HDD for the first time in capacity
2015	EMC and Dell announce merger
2015	Intel/Micron announce 3D X-Point memory, for delivery in 2016
2016	Seagate announces 10 Gigabyte per second SSD
2016	Alluxio, a software-only universal protocol translator, announced

Glossary

3D NAND		Stacking of flash cells vertically on a die and/or stacking die within a chip, aiming to increase density and lower cost of production
AAT	Average access time	On a spinning disk drive, the total time for all possible seeks, divided by the number of seeks
AF	All-Flash array	Cabinet holding a set of hard drives using proprietary flash cards for high performance
API	Application program interface	Common method for software module–module communication
ASIC	Application-specific integrated circuit	1980's term for a computer chip
CIFS	Common internet file system	Old version of SMB (qv)
FC	Fiber channel	Copper or fiber-based interconnect for storage units and their hosts
FCoE	Fiber channel over Ethernet	An FC protocol using Ethernet to make connections
GbE	Gigabit Ethernet	Used as a suffix to the speed factor, e.g., 100 GbE
Gbps	Gigabits per second	Speed modifier for raw data rate
Gigabaud		Speed modifier for net information rate
HDD	Hard disk drive	Any drive that spins rigid disks
HBA	Host bus adapter	A plug-in card for a server that creates a storage connection other than Ethernet or InfiniBand
HPC	High-performance computing	Performance-oriented and typically massively parallel computing
IB	InfiniBand	Connection scheme supporting RDMA
IOPS	Inputs/Outputs per second	Measure of number of independent IO operations that a device or software supports
iSCSI	Internet SCSI	SCSI over Ethernet protocol
JBOD	Just a box of disks	A set of drives in a cabinet, usually with a switch connecting them to the outside world
LAN	Local-area network	Ethernet, IB or Wi-Fi connected network of devices
MBPS	Mega-bytes per second	Millions of bytes per second
MTBF	Mean time between failures	Estimate of frequency of equipment failures, not always accurate

Continued

257

—Cont'd

MTTR	Mean time to repair	Average time to fix a problem, excluding waiting and travel
NAND	Flash type	Refers to gat system in flash chips
NFS	Network file system	Very common industry-standard way to share file data
NIC	Network interface card	PC or server card connecting a LAN link
NVDIMM	Non-volatile dual inline memory Module	A Jedec-standard memory card for a computer system
NVMe	Non-volatile memory-express	Protocol for fast drive connection
PCIe	Peripheral component interface express	Standard adapter card interface in COTS servers and systems
PCM	Phase-change memory	A type of non-volatile memory, faster than flash
RAID	Redundant array of inexpensive disks	A way to build data integrity and performance
RDBMS	Relational Database Management System	A structured database software package
ReRAM	Resistive RAM	A class of non-volatile memories
RTT	Round trip time	The time to complete an operation across a network and obtain a response
SAN	Storage area network	Block-IO based shareable storage network
SAS	Serial-attached SCSI	One way to attach disk drives to hosts, usually "enterprise" drives
SATA	Serial-ATA	Another way to attach drives to hosts, usually commodity drives
SCSI	Small computer standard interface	The first storage network protocol
SMB	Server message block	A Microsoft-developed file-sharing protocol using Ethernet
SSD	Solid-state drive	Typically a flash-based drive, though early units used DRAM
USB	Universal system bus	Network for connecting low-speed peripherals to systems
ViPR		EMC storage protocol translator/router
VM	Virtual machine	An instance in a hypervisor or containers that can hold software and data, and be independent of the underlying platform
VNX		AN EMC RAID array
vSAN	VMware virtual SAN	VMWare's version of a virtual SAN
WAN	Wide area network	A long-haul network linking facilities together
Wi-Fi	Wireless fidelity	Common wireless network that allows connection to LANs and the Internet

Atomic writes/reads	Memory operations that complete while precluding other operations on the same data
Big Data	Hyped-up term for very large amounts of unstructured stored data
Big Data analytics	Analytics applied (often with parallel computing) to Big Data
Block storage	Data moved and stored as fixed length blocks with no file structure at the protocol level
Bulk storage	Little-used cold data usually stored on large capacity drives
Ceph	Open-source universal storage software based on object storage
Compression	Process to remove duplicated data chunks from objects, saving drive capacity
Containers	Alternative virtualization system to hypervisors, where one copy of OS image services many containers, saving space
Converged system	Hyped term implying storage appliances and servers using the same type of hardware
Copperhead	Open-source version of ViPR (qv)
Data availability	Concept of making data always available to using servers, even if hardware or systems fail
Data integrity	Concept of not delivering a bad block of data even when hardware or systems fail
Deduplication	Removal of duplicate files/objects in a storage system, sometimes erroneously used for compression
Encryption	Using a reversible algorithm to make data unreadable to anyone but owners
Enterprise hard drives	Term used by vendors for expensive semi-proprietary hard drives, usually with SAS interface
Erasure codes	Coding schemes used to protect data from loss by appending blocks calculated across the original data
File-sharing	Allowing multiple users to access the same data, either individually or simultaneously
Global file system	A file system capable of holding very large numbers of files
Hyper-converged system	Hype term for converged systems
Hypervisor	Software package that hosts virtual machines
Kinetic	A key-/data-based protocol for Ethernet drives promulgated by Seagate
Lossless	Applied to connections between systems or switches, referring to error-free connections. Also applied to compression schemes that can decompress back to the original data
Metadata	Additional data that define an object in storage
Mirrored data	Two copies of all data are stored, usually on the same storage array or server. This is often referred to as RAID 1 (see below)

Continued

Multi-tenant	In a virtualized server, having multiple tenants or users sharing the memory space and compute power
Object storage	A storage system that treats data as objects each of which is a peer of all the other objects, so allowing vast scales of storage
Open-Source	Code written by a community of interested parties, communally owned and freely available
Parity	A simple data integrity system where a set of data block are exclusive-or'd together to create an additional parity block for failure protection (see also RAID 5 below)
RAID 1	Data integrity system where a mirror copy of data is kept on different drives, allowing continued operations if one drive fails
RAID 5	Data integrity system based on generating parity blocks
RAID array	A storage appliance using RAID technology to protect data
Scale-out	The concept of very large, and inherently unlimited, storage capacity
Software-defined infrastructure	Separation of data services from data handling throughout infrastructure, essentially virtualizing the underlying storage, network, and server platforms in a datacenter
Storage appliance	A box containing storage, named to differentiate it from a traditional RAID array. Usually much more intelligence than an array
Tiering	By tiering the data in a system (usually with automated software) older data can be stored on cheaper slower drives and compression, etc. applied in background
Virtual machine	A distinct segment of a virtualized server designed to provide a share of server performance and resources to a hosted application. Implicitly, virtual machines are isolated from each other for security

Index

Printed in the United States
By Bookmasters